Joyce and Dante: The Shaping Imagination

DANTE ALIGHIERI

LA DIVINA COMMEDIA

CON L'INTRODUZIONE E IL COMMENTO

DI

EUGENIO CAMERINI

CASA EDITRICE SONZOGNO - MILANO
VIA PASQUIROLO, 14

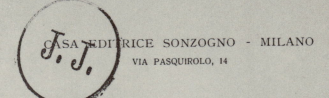

1. Joyce's copy of *The Divine Comedy*.

Joyce and Dante

The Shaping Imagination

By Mary T. Reynolds

Princeton University Press, Princeton, N.J.

for
L.G.R.
Mountaineer and poet,
and
"libero, dritto e sano."

Contents

Illustrations

Preface

WHEN this book came to my door asking to be written, I knew that I was not the person to do it. Judgment is reserved on that initial reaction. I began the project without illusion, sensible above all of the ironic view my authors would have taken of such a trespass. In the fifty years since *Ulysses* first appeared, wiser minds than mine had perceived affinities and had warily skirted the problems of defining them. Some critical assessment now seemed overdue. No voice spoke from the cloud, yet at some point, paraphrasing Molly Bloom, "I thought well as well me as another."

I incurred many debts along the way and acknowledge these with gratitude, including the contribution of my students, through whom I came to a new appreciation of my own teachers. The friendship and assistance of knowledgeable librarians has been indispensable, and I am especially grateful to Marjorie Wynne and Donald Gallup at Yale, and to the staff of the Beinecke Library; the late George Harris Healey at Cornell; Patrick Henchy and Alf MacLochlainn, successively Directors of the National Library in Dublin; Karl Gay at Buffalo; and Dr. Wilma Swearingen, at Marquette. At Princeton University Press I am greatly indebted to the kindly support of my editor, Marjorie Sherwood, and to the competent and intelligent work of Joanna Ajdukiewicz.

With all students of Joyce I am indebted in every dimension to Richard Ellmann's work, which has given a broad and firm basis to Joyce scholarship and set the direction for studies of Joyce's relationship to Dante and other authors. To me as to so many others he has also given professional support, friendship, and penetrating criticism. Professor Thomas G. Bergin shared with me his "long study and great love" of Dante, and allowed me two delightful years of auditing his seminar on the *Divine Comedy*. My debt to him as a great teacher and friend is incalculable, not least for his expressions of mistrust of Joyce and of me, with the mordant wit for which he is famous, through many discussions that sharpened my argument.

The book could not have come into being without the magnanimous response of friends at Yale and elsewhere who gave me expert and sensitive advice. Early versions were read by Professor Freeman

Twaddell, who introduced me to Joyce and gave me my first copy of *Ulysses*, and by Professor Cleanth Brooks, who first encouraged me to write about Joyce and showed me his place in modern literature. Martin Price, Stephen Barney, and Thomas M. Greene gave invaluable counsel. John V. Kelleher and Adaline Glasheen shared with me their great knowledge of *Finnegans Wake*, and Peter Rudnytsky gave me the benefit of his work on Freud. Father Robert Boyle, S.J., patiently argued me through doctrinal intricacies, forestalling embarrassing errors. Rachel Jacoff has my gratitude for help in shortening the manuscript and for her substantial contributions in the development and tightening of my critical argument. I am under special obligation to A. Walton Litz for his detailed and constructive reading, with numerous suggestions which were all gratefully used. Particular thanks go to Jackson Cope, Paul Fry, and Lowry Nelson for a full review; and again to Richard Ellmann, whose insights and comment on successive revisions improved both structure and statement. I am indebted to the busy people who set aside their own work to help me; errors and infelicities are my own.

I have been sustained at all times and in innumerable ways by my family's thoughtful affection, constancy, and never-failing help.

Berkeley College, Yale
"Ivy Day," October 6, 1979

M.T.R.

Acknowledgments

SELECTED passages from the *Commentary* of Charles Singleton, and from his translation of the text of *Dante Alighieri, The Divine Comedy*, 6 vols., Princeton University Press. Copyright 1970, 1973, 1975 by Princeton University Press. Reprinted by permission of Princeton University Press.

Selected passages from Dante Alighieri: *The Divine Comedy*, translated by Thomas G. Bergin, 3 vols. Copyright 1969 by Grossman Publishers, New York. Reprinted by permission of Grossman Publishers.

Selected passages from La Vita Nuova *of Dante Alighieri*, translated by Mark Musa, Rutgers University Press, New Brunswick. Copyright 1957, 1968 by Rutgers, the State University. Reprinted by permission.

James Joyce, *Collected Poems*, Viking Press, 1937. "Tilly" and "A Memory of the Players at Midnight." Copyright The Society of Authors, London, as Executors of the James Joyce Estate. Reprinted by permission of the Executors of the Joyce Estate.

The Critical Writings of James Joyce, ed. Ellsworth Mason and Richard Ellmann, Viking Press, 1959, 1964. Copyright 1959 the Executors of the James Joyce Estate. Selected short quotations reprinted by permission of the Executors of the Joyce Estate.

James Joyce, *Dubliners*, Viking Press, 1969. Copyright 1967 by The Society of Authors as Executors of the James Joyce Estate. Selected short quotations published by permission of the Executors of the Joyce Estate.

James Joyce, *Exiles*, Viking Press, 1951. Copyright 1951 by The Society of Authors as Executors of the James Joyce Estate. Selected short quotations published by permission of the Executors of the Joyce Estate.

James Joyce, *A Portrait of the Artist as a Young Man*, the definitive text corrected from the Dublin holograph by Chester G. Anderson and edited by Richard Ellmann, Viking Press, 1964. Copyright by The Society of Authors of London as Executors of the James Joyce Estate. Selected short quotations published by permission of the Executors of the Joyce Estate.

James Joyce, *Ulysses*, Random House, 1934, 1946. Copyright 1961 by The Society of Authors as Executors of the Joyce Estate. Selected short quotations published by permission.

James Joyce, *Finnegans Wake*, Viking Press, 1939; London Faber & Faber, 1939. Copyright by The Society of Authors as Executors of the James Joyce Estate. Selected short quotations published by permission.

James Joyce, *Stephen Hero*, ed. John J. Slocum and Herbert Cahoon. New York, New York, New Directions Press, 1944, 1963. Copyright New Directions Press and Southern Illinois University Press (Carbondale), and The Society of Authors, London, as Executors of the James Joyce Estate. Selected short quotations published by permission.

James Joyce, *Giacomo Joyce*, ed. Richard Ellmann, Viking Press, 1968. Copyright 1968 by Richard Ellmann and The Society of Authors as Executors of the James Joyce Estate. Selected short quotations published by permission.

The James Joyce Archive: A Facsimile of Manuscripts, Typescripts and Proofs, general editor Michael Groden, Garland Publishing, Inc., New York, 1978, 1979. Copyright 1978, 1979 by Garland Publishing, Inc., and The Society of Authors, London, as Executors of the James Joyce Estate. Selected short quotations and reproduction of twelve pages, reprinted by permission.

James Joyce, Ulysses: *A Fascimile of the Manuscript*, ed. Clive Driver, 3 vols., Octagon Books, Farrar, Straus & Giroux, New York, in association with the Philip H. and A. S. W. Rosenbach Foundation, Philadelphia, 1975. Copyright by the Philip H. and A. S. W. Rosenbach Foundation, 1975; copyright by Lucia and George Joyce, 1962. Two pages reproduced by permission of the Philip H. and A. S. W. Rosenbach Foundation, Philadelphia, and by The Society of Authors, London, Executors of the James Joyce Estate.

Letters of James Joyce, Vols. I and II, ed. Richard Ellmann, Viking Press, 1966. Copyright Vol. II, 1957, by Richard Ellmann and The Society of Authors as Executors of the James Joyce Estate. Six short quotations published by permission.

James Joyce, *Selected Letters of James Joyce*, ed. Richard Ellmann, Viking Press, 1975. Copyright 1975 by Richard Ellmann and The Society of Authors as Executors of the James Joyce Estate. Twelve lines quoted by permission.

James Joyce in Padua, ed. Louis Berrone, Random House, New York, 1977. Copyright 1977 by Louis Berrone and The Society of Authors as Trustees of the James Joyce Estate. Thirteen lines quoted by permission.

Richard Ellmann, *James Joyce*, Oxford University Press, 1959. Copyright 1959 by Richard Ellmann. Six short quotations published by permission of Richard Ellmann.

The Complete Dublin Diary of Stanislaus Joyce, ed. George Harris Healey, Cornell University Press, 1971. Copyright 1971 by Cornell University. Two sentences quoted by permission of Cornell University.

The Workshop of Daedalus, ed. Robert Scholes and Richard M. Kain, Northwestern University Press, Evanston, 1965. Copyright 1965 by Northwestern University Press and The Society of Authors as Executors of the James Joyce Estate. Selected passages and one quotation of eight lines, reprinted by permission.

Samuel Beckett et al., *Our Exagmination round his Factification for Incamination of Work in Progress*, New Directions Press, 1939 and 1972. Copyright 1929 by Sylvia Beach. One quotation of seven lines reprinted by permission.

Portraits of the Artist in Exile: Recollections of James Joyce by Europeans, ed. Willard Potts, University of Washington Press, Seattle, 1979. Copyright 1979 by the University of Washington Press. Six brief quotations reprinted by permission.

Constantine Curran, *James Joyce Remembered*, Oxford University Press, 1968. Copyright 1968 by Oxford University Press. Two sentences quoted by permission.

Francesco de Sanctis, *History of Italian Literature*, trans. Joan Redfern, Harcourt Brace and World, and Barnes and Noble (reprint), 1931, 1959. Copyright 1931 and 1959 by Harcourt Brace and World. Eight lines quoted by permission.

James Joyce's Ulysses, ed. Clive Hart and David Hayman, University of California Press, 1974. Copyright 1974 by the Regents of the University of California. Six lines quoted by permission.

W. B. Stanford, *The Ulysses Theme*, Oxford, Basil Blackwell, 1954. Four short passages quoted by permission.

Aldo Palazzeschi, *Via Della Cento Stelle*, Mondadori, 1972. "Apprezzamenti Celesti," quoted by permission of the translator.

Bernard Stambler, *Dante's Other World*, New York University Press, 1957. Copyright 1957 by New York University Press. Ten lines quoted by permission.

Parts of this book have appeared in *Italian Literature, Roots and Branches*, ed. Giose Rimanelli and Kenneth John Atchity, Yale University Press, 1976; copyright 1976 by Yale University. Sections from two chapters have appeared in the *James Joyce Quarterly*, copyright the University of Tulsa, and a portion of one chapter has appeared in the *Journal of Modern Literature*, Temple University, Philadelphia. These passages are reprinted by permission.

Editions and Abbreviations

PAGE references to the works of Joyce and Dante are incorporated in the text, enclosed in parentheses. Editions used and abbreviations are as follows. For Joyce:

CP	Joyce, James. *Collected Poems*. New York: Viking Press, 1957.
CW	Joyce, James. *The Critical Writings of James Joyce*, ed. Ellsworth Mason and Richard Ellmann. New York: Viking Press, 1959.
D	Joyce, James. *Dubliners*, ed. Robert Scholes in consultation with Richard Ellmann. New York: Viking Press, 1967.
E	Joyce, James. *Exiles*. New York: New Directions, New Classics Series, n.d.
FW	Joyce, James. *Finnegans Wake*. New York: Viking Press, 1939, 1947.
GJ	Joyce, James. *Giacomo Joyce*, ed. Richard Ellmann. New York: Viking Press, 1968.
P	Joyce, James. *A Portrait of the Artist as a Young Man*. The definitive text corrected from the Dublin Holograph by Chester G. Anderson and edited by Richard Ellmann. New York: Viking Press, 1966.
SH	Joyce, James. *Stephen Hero*, ed. John J. Slocum and Herbert Cahoon. New York: New Directions, 1944, 1963.
U	Joyce, James. *Ulysses*. New York: Random House, Modern Library, 1934, 1946.
Letters, I	Joyce, James. *Letters of James Joyce*. Vol. I, ed. Stuart Gilbert. New York: Viking Press, 1957.
Letters, II, III	Joyce, James. *Letters of James Joyce*. Vols. II and III, ed. Richard Ellmann. New York: Viking Press, 1966.
Selected Letters	Joyce, James. *Selected Letters*, ed. Richard Ellmann. New York: Viking Press, 1975.
Archive	*The James Joyce Archive*, general editor Michael Groden; associate editors, Hans Walter Ga-

	bler, David Hayman, A. Walton Litz, and Danis Rose. Drafts, Typescripts and Proofs, 63 vols. New York: Garland Publishing Co., 1978, 1979.
Ros. MS	*James Joyce: Ulysses*. A Facsimile of the Manuscript. With a critical introduction by Harry Levin and a bibliographical preface by Clive Driver. New York: Octagon Books, 1975. 2 vols.
	James Joyce: Ulysses. The Manuscript and First Printings Compared. Annotated by Clive Driver. New York: Octagon Books, 1975.
RE: *JJ*	Ellmann, Richard. *James Joyce*. Oxford Univ. Press, 1959.

For Dante, editions used and abbreviations are as follows:

DC	Petrocchi Giorgio. *La Commedia secondo l'antica vulgata*; vol. II, *Inferno*; vol. III, *Purgatorio*; vol. IV, *Paradiso*. Milan: Arnoldo Mondadori Editore, 1966, 1975.
VN	La Vita Nuova *of Dante Alighieri*, translated by Mark Musa. New Brunswick: Rutgers Univ. Press, 1957. Midland Book ed., Bloomington: Indiana Univ. Press, 1962; new ed. and trans. 1973.
Toynbee	*Dante Dictionary. A Dictionary of Proper Names and Notable Matters in the Works of Dante*, ed. Paget Toynbee, revised by Charles S. Singleton. Oxford: Clarendon Press, 1968.

For translations in prose used in the text, and for all translations in the Appendix:

	Dante Alighieri. *The Divine Comedy*, translated, with a commentary, by Charles S. Singleton. 6 vols. *Inferno*: I, Italian Text and Translation; II, *Commentary*. *Purgatorio*: I, Italian Text and Translation; II, *Commentary*. *Paradiso*: I, Italian Text and Translation; II, *Commentary*. Princeton Univ. Press, 1970, 1973, 1975.

For translations in verse used in the text:

> Dante Alighieri. *The Divine Comedy*, translated by
> Thomas G. Bergin. 3 vols. New York: Gross-
> man Publishers, 1969.

Joyce's edition was: Dante Alighieri, *La Divina Commedia*: con l'introduzione e il commento di Eugenio Camerini. Milan: Sonzogno, n.d.
His copy of the *Vita Nuova* was *La Vita Nova di Dante Alighieri*. Illus-
trata dei quadri di D. G. Rossetti. Prima edizione Prerafaellistica, con
due studi di Antonio Agresti, decorazioni e fregi del Prof. R. Carlucci,
curata da Marcus de Rubris. Turin: S.T.E.N., 1911.

Joyce and Dante: The Shaping Imagination

Introduction

SOME writers labor to disconnect themselves from their predecessors, others seek out a tradition to which they can comfortably conform. Joyce did neither. His estimate of his own genius would not have allowed subservience to a defined tradition, yet few writers have written with such an educated critical awareness. At an early stage he marked out a small number of his predecessors for lifetime engagement, attaching their work to his.

But this was a peculiarly loose attachment, which encroached while maintaining its distance. For *Ulysses*, Joyce announced that Homer was his model and Shakespeare his illustration, the one by his title, the other by a crucial theory of *Hamlet* advanced by a principal character. Yet along with these, Joyce also had a covert relation to another writer, whose place in the book was intimated only by quotation. This third presence was Dante. It is easy enough to find traces of Dante in Joyce's work; the difficulty comes when one tries to fit them into a pattern. I propose to show that Joyce achieved a reasoned critical view of Dante's art, which he embodied in his fiction and did not otherwise express. In all Joyce's work Dante is a massive presence, judged, evaluated, and measured in every dimension. Joyce was probably engaged with Dante more broadly and deeply than he was with any other author except Shakespeare and Homer. To read Joyce by this theory is to discover, among other things, a poetics of Dante.

Joyce's imagination was saturated with Dante, as poet rather than as Catholic. Joyce read Dante secularly, and used his reading comprehensively and deliberately. At times the central characters are positioned in Dantesque terms; again, they may embody Dante's attitudes and the point of view of his poem, sometimes seriously and sometimes jocularly. In *Ulysses*, for example, Joyce alludes to Bloom as a figure just slightly older than Dante at the beginning of the Divine Comedy: "It was now for more than the middle span of our allotted years that he had passed through the thousand vicissitudes of existence . . ." (*U* 400:41; *Inf.* 1:1). And again Joyce says, "at the critical turning point of human existence he desired to amend many social conditions, the product of inequality and avarice and international animosity" (*U* 681:16). These parallels are deliberately inexact and comic, yet they are not pointless.

Like Dante, Joyce gives the artist a central position in his fiction: Stephen Dedalus the poet, Richard Rowan the novelist, Shem the Penman. Even Bloom has "a touch of the artist," and "there's a great poet" in Earwicker. Stephen knows the *Divine Comedy* and quotes it; Richard Rowan too seems to echo some of Dante's lines. Mr Bloom could not possibly have known the *Divine Comedy*; it is Stephen Dedalus who has read and appreciated Dante, and Stephen is presented as a figure of the poet-pilgrim in exile: "Now I eat his salt bread" (*U* 21:40; *Par.* 17:58). But Bloom is also described in terms that identify Dante's pilgrim.

Moreover, Joyce's work contains mimetic elements and complex transformations of Dante. What are we to infer from these—some of them lying on the surface, but most of them buried? Clearly, there is no simple answer to this question. Joyce made use of Dante in a great variety of ways. The simplest are easily discernible as verbal clues, direct quotations, and allusions. The more subtle uses are much harder to detect. Often what Joyce is *not* doing is easier to identify than to fix his purposes. Though the compression of Dante attracts him, he is not imitating Dante's style directly, any more than Dante, in the *Commedia*, could be said to be imitating Virgil's. The roots of relationship lie much deeper. Joyce is also not engaging in gratuitous parody; when he allows his characters to allude jocularly to Dante, he does so for a purpose related to the specific fictional occasion. Joyce's own transformations, like the comments on Dante he made to friends, often have elements of burlesque and frequently of irony, but they never imply a reductive view of the poem, its purposes, or its author. Nor was he embroidering his fiction with Dantean allusions to flatter the reader or to display erudition.

The problem, then, is to describe an influence that is elusive yet pervasive, and I have taken a dual approach to this problem in order to ask the right questions of the text. To begin with, Joyce's allusions to Dante are complexly intermingled with other material: in an opening chapter I hope to convey a sense of their great variety and range. This will be combined with an account of the stages of development in his reading of Dante.

The rest of the book divides along two paths, both traversing Joyce's texts but in different ways. First, in a central section of three chapters, the interrelations of theme, style and narrative will be explored. Herein, I believe, we find the best evidence of Joyce's penetration to the poetic heart of Dante's work. His protean transformations can be understood only in terms of an abiding interest in the *poetic* unity of the Divine Comedy, in the sources of its imaginative power.

Each of the three chapters in this section conveys its own pattern of connections between particular areas of Joyce's fiction and Dante's poem. The first of these deals with paternal figures and shows their importance in the design of Dante's poem and of Joyce's fictions. The schematic use of the Telemachus-Odysseus relationship is familiar. Dante's quite different use of the Ulysses figure directs attention to the likenesses and differences of other pairs of fathers and sons, of which there are a great many in the poem. Joyce also presents a number of such pairs. Ulysses, the central figure in the Odyssey, is in the *Commedia* barely granted a single canto—yet he is actively present in the *Inferno, Purgatorio*, and *Paradiso* (*Inf.* 26; *Purg.* 19:22; *Par.* 27:82). In *Inferno* 26, Ulysses is a powerful image of pride, a supreme illustration of the way Dante uses such a single figure. Joyce admired this technique of Dante's and sought to reproduce it. The use made of Hamlet, the archetypal son, as part of the character of Stephen Dedalus is not a minor touch; yet Joyce maneuvers his Hamlet-Stephen toward an ambiguous identification with all artists, not least in their awareness of holding a place in a chain of spiritual begetters and begotten. Hamlet and Dante together make Joyce's *Ulysses*, among other things, an account of poetic continuity. The fatal pride of Dante's Ulysses becomes an element in the configuration.

Dante's fathers and sons come straight out of the experience that brought about the writing of his poem: his banishment and exile under sentence of death. They are images of social order and disorder, and of the place of the poet in a fallen and yet redeemable world. Dante's own family is conspicuously absent from the *Divine Comedy*, but Dante's sense of family is just as conspicuously present. "Paternity," says Joyce's Stephen Dedalus, "may be a legal fiction," and again, "a father is a necessary evil" (*U* 204:30-31; 205:7). In the account that follows these epigrams Stephen refers to Shakespeare in Dante's words, "nel mezzo del cammin di nostra vita," and to the writing of *Hamlet* in terms that could as well describe the writing of the *Divine Comedy*. I hope to disentangle some of these intricately woven effects by comparing two patterns of paternal imagery: first, the consanguineous father or ancestor, and second, the surrogate father, shown as priest, teacher, or ruler. Within this setting we find in contrast to each other both the affirmative and the negative images of each as they appear in Joyce's work and in Dante's.

Dante confers on Virgil the privilege of spiritual fatherhood, and

Joyce implicitly allows Dante this role in relation to himself. In Joyce's youth his friends called him "the Dante of Dublin," and when he came to write *Ulysses* he expressed more than once a sense of being at the same phase as the poet of the *Divine Comedy*. In a letter of 1918 (when he was in fact 36) he wrote:

> "I am old—and feel even older than I am. Perhaps I have lived too long. I am 35. It is the age at which Shakespeare conceived his dolorous passion for the 'dark lady.' It is the age at which Dante entered the night of his being." (*Letters* II: 433)

And to his friend Georges Borach, he said: "I want to be candid: at twelve I liked the mysticism in Ulysses. When I was writing *Dubliners*, I first wished to choose the title *Ulysses in Dublin*, but gave up the idea. In Rome, when I had finished about half of the *Portrait*, I realized that the Odyssey had to be the sequel . . . now, *in mezzo del cammin*, I find the subject of Odysseus the most human in world literature" (RE:*JJ* 430). Joyce took from his own life the complex intermingling of life and art that he allows Stephen Dedalus to describe as a form of paternity. His use of Homer, Shakespeare, and Dante is thus more passionate and personal than the professional decision to select and reproduce archetypal characters. As Ellmann has said, "By force of individual passion we body ourselves forth in human and artistic offspring. The interbreeding is constant."[1]

The second of the core chapters will deal with another aspect of the *Divine Comedy*, the theme of love, and its counterpart in Joyce's *Ulysses*. In contrast to the great number of stories (some very brief) about fathers and sons, Dante has presented only one pair of lovers as such: Francesca and Paolo, the tragic lovers of *Inferno* 5. Joyce seems to have felt a particular attachment to this canto, for his writings contain more allusions to it, through direct and paraphrased quotations, than to any other single part of the *Divine Comedy*. As with paternal imagery, the theme of love between man and woman is a central design in Dante that was echoed by Joyce. Both themes are used, moreover, with a similar ambiguity. The *Divine Comedy*, on the testimony of the final lines of the *Vita Nuova*, is a poem written for the glorification of Beatrice, the *gentil donna* who was the abiding source of Dante's poetic inspiration. But it is, of course, much more. Paternal images provide the matrix, love provides the binding force, of the fictional three-layered world of the *Commedia*. The stylistic focus of this chapter will be the allusive variation of sound effects in Dante's poetry, and the reproduction of some of these in the prose with which Joyce developed his version of Dante's theme of love as the force that moves the world.

The final substantive chapter will deal with another centripetal theme, the representation of the imagination in action. It will focus on lustration patterns, small discrete mechanisms of representation that use metaphorically the ritual aspect of myth. Joyce's use of lustration imagery suggests that he made a close study of Dante's references to the operation of his own poetic genius. But in Joyce's hands, that pattern goes beyond the level of metaphor and becomes an instrument of myth-making, in part through a conscious literariness. Once again he artfully exploits what Frye has called "the doubleness of literature."[2]

T. S. Eliot saw that Joyce had taken a new turn with myth-making, and in a famous statement he said that Joyce had discovered unexpected capacities in literary allusion. Joyce's use of the Homeric myths, Eliot said, was "manipulating a continuous parallel between contemporaneity and antiquity . . . as a way of controlling, of ordering, of giving a shape and a significance. . . ."[3] The sentence ended somewhat less than objectively, but it remains unmatched as a statement of the ability of literary allusion to fill an imagined world with resonant echoes. Joyce wrote out of a disciplined and highly endowed consciousness, out of a totality of thought and feeling that was the product of widely eclectic reading that had, moreover, been felt and ordered by an exceptional intellect fully aware of its powers. The more deeply we excavate the record of Joyce's reading, the more reluctant we become to make final statements about how it entered his own art.

We can, however, see the *process as process*: as restoration of the hidden side of literary history, revelation of what Foucault has called the "positive unconscious of knowledge, a level that eludes the consciousness . . . and yet is part of discourse; the influences that affected it, the implicit philosophies that were subjacent to it, the unformulated thematics, the unseen obstacles."[4] In observing Joyce's imitation of Dante's lustration patterns we discover something of this critical approach, and become aware that Joyce has created in his own fiction a commentary on the sources and the historical dimension of style. He sees the totality of rhetorical artifice, the manner in which something is said, as an aspect of continuity. Like a chromosome in mutation, the rhetorical unit migrates across great gulfs of time and cultural change.

Toward the end of this book, I shall try to make explicit some of the assessments that appear in the central section. The last two chapters will display the progressively more important impact of Dante on Joyce's art consecutively, first reviewing his early works, then his major fictions, *A Portrait*, *Ulysses*, and *Finnegans Wake*. In an appendix, the allusions to Dante in all Joyce's works are listed as page references, with indications of the earliest surviving manuscript in which each occurs.

The design of the book thus functions as a structural hypothesis, and conclusions are allowed to emerge from each of the sections as well as in the final general summary. Indeed, the study does not claim to deal fully or finally with all the critical problems raised by Joyce's use of Dante. I think it is sufficiently ambitious to demonstrate his deep and permanent interest in Dante, and to display in a critical perspective the dimensions of that interest. At some point their imaginations meet in agreement, and at other points there is a great gulf between their attitudes, aesthetics, beliefs, and views of life and the world. I have tried to show the most important areas of agreement and disagreement, in the process sometimes setting forth Joyce's artistic aims and methods by the new illumination of his Dantesque allusions. I believe and have sought to demonstrate that Dante was in some sense Joyce's chosen precursor and lifetime model, first in the triad with Shakespeare and Homer. But I am mindful that Dante alone is not the key to Joyce, and I doubt very much that one single explanation can be found that will completely satisfy our critical interest in Joyce's use of Dante.

My own attention to theme, style, and form represents an effort to move beyond the merely inferential and implicit, in order to show that Joyce's relation to Dante was not merely appreciative but purposeful. Idea and technique, studied as the author's thought-form configuration, provide the key, as Jackson Cope says, to "the ideational center" of Joyce's work.[5] The pattern of study was affected also by two specific concerns. In the first place, the influence of Dante on Joyce has been obscured, to some extent, by the manifest presence of so *much* architectural artifice in both Dante and Joyce. The natural thing to do, and what has in fact been done, is to search for a counterpart to the tripartite structure of Dante's hell, purgatory, and heaven. But this has led to a somewhat crude equation of hell with sin, purgatory with repentance, and heaven with bliss. Dante's poem deserves more sensitive inspection and weighing than this, and I believe Joyce did so reflect and deliberate. His interest in the characters Dante created and in the episodes in which they are found is therefore the prime basis for comparison. Dante's art takes on a fresh perspective as an instrument in Joyce's work.

A closely related matter concerns the expectations aroused by studies of Joyce's use of Shakespeare and Homer. Diligent searches have been made for similar correspondences and comparable parallels with Dante's *Commedia*. We remember that some of Dante's characters came indirectly from Homer (Dante did not know Homer at all), and that others are found in Shakespeare as well as in Dante. Ulysses himself is an example. The multivalence of Joyce's writing is patent, and it is obvious that Joyce exploited the reappearance of Homeric characters. It seems to be the rule for Joyce's figures that the more roles or role-playing the better; Joyce gives his characters auras that will evoke both Shakespeare and Dante, as well as Homer, and often other authors as well. He likes to set a recognizable allusion or even quotation from Shakespeare alongside one from the *Divine Comedy*. The significant connections, as Hugh Kenner said of Joyce and Homer, are not to be found in parallels of incident but rather in the more protean evocation of situational parallels.[6]

The Dantean elements in Joyce's work do not, indeed, operate in the same way as the observable elements from Shakespeare and Homer. Joyce does not take a single coherent frame from the *Divine Comedy* to be some sort of heaven-hell-purgatory structure. If there is to be a demonstrable connection of Joyce's work with Dante's poem, these conceptions and this structure are too important in the *Divine Comedy* to be used loosely or to be dealt with in terms other than those Dante has given them. An essential element is the spiritual progress of the Pilgrim toward justification: the poem is the record of a conversion, and to ignore this would reduce the connection with Dante to something at best indirect, at worst vague and unresolved.

Joyce has taken Dante's pattern and epistemology to reproduce in Dublin a spiritual journey, in conscious emulation of Dante's similar use of Virgil, whose *Aeneid* in turn adapted Homer. Dante's syncretism successfully met the challenge of providing a pagan guide for a Christian poet, an achievement closely observed by Joyce. I suggest that his transformation of Dante's journey required a comparable boldness. He demonstrates simultaneously the continuing presence of Dante's world in the Dublin of 1904, and the vast gulf between these worlds—a reading of Dante that is continuously informed by a sense of otherness arising from Joyce's awareness of the relativity of modern man's view of his universe. Stephen Daedalus (in *Stephen Hero*: subsequently the spelling became Dedalus) argues that the distinction between "the feudal spirit" (a phrase he associates with Dante), and the spirit of modern man is not merely "a phrase of the men of letters." His author embodied these distinctions in his fictions, humanely and with wit, and the spiritual journey in *Ulysses* thus becomes Joyce's comedy.

When we concentrate on narrower matters of character and incident, it becomes clear that Joyce's use of Dante was not altogether different from his use of Homer and Shakespeare. In all three, the root of the similarity is existential, with a core of psychic reality that Joyce observed and reproduced for his own purposes. Thus Joyce makes a new and original connection between the surface level of Dante's poem and its allegorical dimension.

My observations are not merely a bow drawn at a venture. In Joyce's library in Trieste, while he was finishing *A Portrait*, writing *Exiles*, and beginning *Ulysses*, there were, in addition to Homer, Shakespeare and Dante, two copies of a little book by Francis Bacon, *The Wisdom of the Ancients*. It is a compendium of reflections on the Greek myths, taken, as the epigraph says, as "invention's storehouse." The stories of Proteus, Daedalus, Scylla, the Lestrygonians, Cyclops, and the Sirens are treated as fictions, "poetical fables," from which Bacon drew the inner meaning. Joyce wrote his name in one of the two copies, and marked a passage in Bacon's account of the Sirens, whose music is described as "violent enticing mischief," which the reflective and religious man avoids by appropriate means.[7]

> The first means to shun these inordinate pleasures is, to withstand and resist them in their beginnings, and seriously to shun all occasions that are offered to debauch and entice the mind, which is signified in that stopping of the ears; and that remedy is properly used by the meaner and baser sort of people, as it were Ulysses' followers or mariners. Whereas more heroic and noble spirits may boldly converse even in the midst of these seducing pleasures, if with a resolved constancy they stand upon their guard and fortify their minds; and so take greater contentment in the trial and experience of this their approved virtue, learning rather thoroughly to understand the follies and vanities of those pleasures by contemplation, than by submission . . .

The quality of Bloom as a Homeric character derives at least as much from this gloss as from the overt resemblances of the Sirens episode of *Ulysses* to Homer's twelfth book. The Baconian recognition of allegory identifies also one of the root-causes of Joyce's interest in Dante, whose sirens (in *Purgatorio* 19 and 31) bear little resemblance to Homer's.

Joyce's Dante, however, was not the Dante of his day, who had become something of an establishment figure. On one side were Joyce's Jesuit teachers: the Church had long since adopted the *Divine Comedy* as its own instrument in defense of a narrow orthodoxy. On the other side were the serious students of the *Divine Comedy* in England (in Dublin there was no counterpart of the Oxford Dante Society), where the work of Moore and Toynbee had brought explication a long way. Joyce's opinions about the *Divine Comedy*, shaped by his broad reading in European literature and his natural independence of mind, were thoroughly distrusted by the Jesuit authorities. The level of academic training in Dante was not very high in Dublin when Joyce was a student. But these negative factors worked to his advantage. His ambition to use Dante in a creative work developed very early in his college years, and this must have given a marked intensity of purpose and a broader critical focus to his independent study of the *Divine Comedy*.

Joyce, then, like other writers, attached his work to a tradition, but with a more comprehensive notion of that tradition and a larger intention. In each of his major works there is a structure of literary allusion and imitation that is consciously built and wide-ranging. Homer, Shakespeare, and Dante are the dominant triad in *Ulysses*. Their presence together, since Joyce's work is focused entirely on Ireland, suggests that Joyce was sensitive not only to literary norms but to cultural patterns, and that he was interested not only in the currents of European literary history but in the historical tradition of his country. Catholic configurations of thought had dominated European life for more than a millennium, and Roman Catholic institutions were a central force in Joyce's Dublin because they had been so through all of Christian Irish history; these influences had to be taken into account if Ireland was to be presented in the comprehensive way that Joyce undertook. Dante had represented the whole of Catholicism as no one had done before or since, and in doing so had expressed as one total view the great scholastic structure of thought and the European world in which it had developed. The association of Dante, whom Joyce called "the first poet of the Europeans," with a fictional account of life in Ireland at the beginning of the twentieth century seems incongruous. It is a radical displacement, and to some readers may seem even bizarre. But it is not really out of keeping if we take literally (as I believe we must) Joyce's expressed ambition to bring Ireland into the mainstream of European literature. One has to conceive of Joyce's mind as being saturated with Dante, and as looking both consciously and unconsciously for Dantean effects. Joyce's preferred focus of interest was not the Ireland of the pre-Christian sagas, nor the contemporary peasant Ireland of Yeats and Synge and the Irish literary movement. He proposed nothing less than to make Dublin, as Dante made Florence, the center and projection of a universal drama.

ᔕᔐ Chapter One
The Presence of Dante in Joyce's Fiction

THE patterns of Joyce's interest in Dante form a larger design, which developed over a long span of years. A dominant element from the beginning was his desire, shared with other writers in the English language, to absorb the great poem into a later age, a different language, an alien culture. Joyce might have translated Dante (as Chaucer translated Petrarch, and as Byron translated Dante's Francesca episode). But he chose instead to assimilate Dante's poetic effects in his own fictions.

As we read his books we see the questions Joyce asked of Dante's text. These range from minute questions of word choice and placement to the manner of Dante's creation of the structures and sequences by which he shaped imaginatively a particular experience of life in a particular time and space. Joyce scrutinized closely Dante's combination of poetic structures in a sublime whole. Dante's rhetorical management of complexity was Joyce's most pervading interest. His approach is epitomized in Pound's remark: "The best critic is the next fellow to do the job."[1]

As a reading of the *Divine Comedy*, such a preoccupation with the literary rather than the theological aspects of the poem, such an interest in craftsmanship rather than in doctrine, followed a critical tradition of long standing. The tradition began with the *Commentary* of Benvenuto da Imola, only some fifty years after Dante's death, and it has furnished matter for argument and controversy down to the present day.[2] Whatever we may think of its merits or defects, this critical stance, which argues that the *Comedy* can be understood through a primarily literary interpretation, is an inclusive critical position that has been validated by time, and it is the approach that governed Joyce's perception of Dante.

An account of Joyce's study of the *Divine Comedy*, so far as we can reconstruct it, will help in understanding the Dantean allusions in his work. As a preliminary, it is useful to examine a small sample of those allusions. As Joyce's art developed and matured, his imitations of Dante submerged into the fabric of his fiction. This process was less a matter of deliberate concealment (although this factor is not absent) than of Joyce's making more and more fully his own the artistic devices and maneuvers he found in Dante's poetry. It was a matter of indifference to him whether the borrowings were detected and traced to their originals. On the other hand he did not conceal the *presence* of Dante in his work; to the contrary, his overt allusions to Dante, Shakespeare, Goethe, Ibsen and others are a proud acknowledgment of kinship. In this they resemble Dante's acknowledgment of his debt to Virgil.

*

Joyce's imitation of Dante is, of course, too protean to be pinned down in neat categories. It is possible, however, to identify five kinds of imitation, which he often used together: first, the echo of Dante's cadences, a more or less faithful translation from Italian into English; second, the reproduction of Dante's visual imagery; third, the appropriation of Dante's characters; fourth, an adaptation of Dante's analogies in such a way that distinctive components of simile or metaphor reappear in a new setting; and fifth, the creation of a narrative pattern modeled on one of Dante's situations or narrative sequences.

Even a small sample of Joyce's allusions to Dante suggests the presence of an important design: Joyce's recognition of literary allegory in the *Divine Comedy* and his mimetic attachment of Dante's literary allegory to his own fiction. The elements of literary allegory are most prominent in *A Portrait of the Artist* and in *Ulysses*, but the design is an important feature, and a Dantean element, throughout Joyce's work.

An important element of Joyce's originality in his critical observation of Dante was the recognition of broadly metaphorical patterns in the *Divine Comedy*. Metaphor has become a focus of interest in Dante criticism only in recent years. The older view implicit in T. S. Eliot's comment that "Dante makes us see what he sees" has been recognized to be unduly restrictive, so that a larger critical interest now probes the *Comedy* for images in which the visual element is relatively weak and the design seems rather to be focused on "making us feel what Dante feels."[3] It was in this larger figural mode that Joyce found his strategic instrument for creation of a complex poetic unity.

Let us observe first the simple form of allusion that is recognizable because the cadences of the original are present. Joyce puts this statement in the Ithaca episode of *Ulysses*:

> He thought that he thought that he was a jew whereas he knew that he knew that he knew that he was not . . .

The sentence is an unmistakable echo of the lines given by Dante to Pier della Vigne in *Inferno* 13:25, "Cred'io che' ei credette ch'io credesse . . ." ("I believe that he believed that I believed . . ."). Allusions of this kind, for which Karl Vossler coined the happy term "quotations in solution," are a feature particularly of *Finnegans Wake*.[4] In that book they are by no means confined to Dante, but range widely over all kinds of written material, perhaps most notably Irish poetry and song.

Joyce, when he echoes Dante, shows an awareness of Dante's context. The allusive construction is delicately and subtly connected with Dante's text in some way that at the very least indicates Joyce's recognition of *why Dante wrote the line as he did*. In *Inferno* 13 the "conceit" of this line represents the artificial, flowery style of the speaker, Pier, a contemporary poet of the Sicilian school at the court of Frederick II.[5] Joyce's reconstruction indicates awareness of Dante's taste for parody and imitation. Joyce's line thus becomes a parody of a parody, and also, like Dante's, a comment on fashions in literary style. Since a poet and his poetry are involved at both levels, Joyce's allusion also becomes an oblique comment on the literary act.

A second sample pattern finds Joyce reproducing one of Dante's visual images. In the closing paragraph of the Cyclops episode of *Ulysses*, Leopold Bloom takes form suddenly as Elijah, ascending to Heaven in a chariot of fire drawn by horses of fire:[6]

> When, lo, there came about them all a great brightness and they beheld the chariot wherein He stood ascend to heaven. And they beheld Him in the chariot, clothed upon in the glory of the brightness, having raiment as of the sun, fair as the moon and terrible that for awe they durst not look upon him. And there came a voice out of heaven, calling: Elijah! Elijah! And he answered with a main cry: Abba! Adonai! And they beheld Him even Him, ben Bloom Elijah, amid clouds of angels ascend to the glory of the brightness at an angle of forty-five degrees over Donohoes in Little Green Street like a shot off a shovel. (*U* 339:14-23)

Here Joyce has in mind the famous simile in *Inferno* 26, the canto of Ulysses. There Dante is reminded of Elijah's fiery ascent because he is watching the flames, each one holding an evil counsellor.

And as he who was avenged by the bears saw Elijah's chariot at its departure, when the horses rose erect to heaven—for he could not so follow it with his eyes as to see aught save the flame alone, like a little cloud ascending: so each flame moves along the gullet of the ditch . . . (*Inf.* 26:34-40, trans. Singleton)

While Dante is building on the Old Testament, II *Kings* 2:11, he puts much emphasis upon the fiery nature of the ascent, and his flames reappear (with due modification) in Joyce's "glory of the brightness," and "raiment as of the sun." Dante's "little cloud" also reverberates slightly in Joyce's "clouds of angels," which is notably not in the Biblical reference. (Joyce named one of his short stories "A Little Cloud," and gave the name of Nuvoletta, the Italian word in Dante's passage, to one of the characters in *Finnegans Wake*.)

Richard Lansing has demonstrated that elements of the simile at this point in the *Divine Comedy* mimic the epic action of the poem as a whole.[7] Dante emphasizes the spectator who watched the ascent of the chariot, and this reflects Dante's own situation as a pilgrim-spectator in *Inferno* 26. His role as watcher, seeking to learn the meaning of the scene—the valley filled with flames—suggests by extension the role of the pilgrim in the *Commedia*. But that spectator, the Dante who watches, is the poet and author of the Comedy. The reader who receives this small bit of knowledge observes that Dante is externalizing an aspect of the imagination that created the text we are reading.

Bloom's comic ascent identifies him passingly with the sternest of the Hebrew prophets, champion of freedom and purity of life, who not only ascended to heaven in a fiery chariot but was able to call down from heaven consuming fires to destroy his detractors. Dante's simile is given in the voice of the traveler as watcher. The spectators of Bloom's apotheosis are the Dublin bystanders, and the voice is that of an anonymous narrator. As a comic miracle this unforgettable little vignette sets Bloom/Elijah in a relation to the hostile crowd he has escaped. The reader smiles but is reminded, however jocosely, that Elijah triumphed over his enemies. Unquestionably this element of triumph was important to Dante in selecting the simile, for Dante—as we learn much later in the poem—has a stern political message through which he will win an ultimate victory over the enemies who exiled him, though not until his journey has given him a full Christian perspective. Now, in the comparison of the two metaphorical constructions, and especially in Joyce's placement of Dante's simile at the close of the chapter, the reader becomes aware that the mind of the author is reflected indirectly, as Dante's is more directly reflected, in this double vision. It is the mind of a writer who wished, he said, to stir the conscience of Ireland by becoming the poet of his race.[8]

In the chapters that follow we will move from the single line parody, and the brief, single-paragraph simile dominated by a visual image, to Joyce's larger mimetic constructions. Joyce did occasionally pick out from the *Divine Comedy* a single telling piece of detail that could be used for a fleeting identification of one of Dante's characters. More commonly, however, he reconstructs the portrait by a broad selection of compositional features that distinctively identify Dante's personage. The form and placement of the Elijah simile in Joyce's Cyclops chapter momentarily reinforces the Ulyssean identity of Leopold Bloom at the same time that he is comically seen as a Biblical prophet, because the reader is reminded of the hero of *Inferno* 26, Ulysses in Dante's rather than Homer's version. It was to introduce him that Dante created the Elijah simile, with its companion simile of fireflies watched—the spectator again—by the peasant above Fiesole. Such complications and ambiguities are purposeful. Joyce told Beckett, in discussing the use of Dante, "The danger lies in the neatness of identifications."[9]

*

Joyce's interest in Dante has been undervalued, if it has not been unnoticed. Many areas coincide. Both Joyce and Dante deal with man in the most fundamental terms and over the largest range of behavior. Both intend to set forth the universal in the particular. Both show a marked pride in their epistemology. Both writers make use of the artist in the work as one of the characters, and describe the artist with autobiographical detail. Moreover, both are concerned with man as creative artist ("There's a touch of the artist about old Bloom"). This is a mode of writing, and an aspect of the work, that Thomas Bergin in writing about Dante has described as literary allegory, that is, an allegory about the literary act.

The unity of Dante's poem demands the reader's involvement, at least temporarily, with scholastic theology. This was not a problem for Joyce, who had a thoroughly Catholic as well as a poetic knowledge of Dante. The poetry of the *Paradiso* may indeed be more accessible to a mind that has very early been conditioned to the intricate patterns of Catholic apologetics and doctrine. Joyce would not have regarded the theological aspects of the *Commedia* as an impediment, as T. S. Eliot (despite his express recognition of the sublimity of the *Paradiso*) apparently did, nor would he have wanted to separate Dante's lyric passages from his theology, as Croce insisted.[10] Rather, Joyce saw the intellectual structure of scholasticism as one of the monuments of civilization, a noble product of the human mind—beautiful not merely in its intricacy and subtlety but also as an embodiment of an elevated moral and ethical conception of life.[11]

Moreover, the poetic imagination in Joyce's view would be shaped by the same imperative that produces those higher qualities of the mind that have led to all the great visions and visionary systems. Joyce, like Renan, would have distinguished between the supernatural, which is meaningless or of no account in human affairs, and the ideal, which, whether in poetry or philosophical speculation or mysticism, has always implied a noble effort of the mind to pass beyond the limits of its knowledge.

Joyce was aware that in Britain Dante was highly esteemed but seldom carefully read. In the Wandering Rocks section of *Ulysses*, Stephen Dedalus is the subject of discussion between his enemy, Buck Mulligan, and the English visitor, Haines. In Mulligan's disparaging remarks a contrast appears between his view of Dante and Stephen's.

> They drove his wits astray, he said, with visions of hell. He will never capture the Attic note. The note of Swinburne, of all poets, the white death and the ruddy birth. That is his tragedy. He can never be a poet. The joy of creation. (*U* 245:25)

Buck Mulligan, self-proclaimed Hellenist, really knows nothing about Dante; Swinburne is his model for the poets of Ireland. "Visions of hell" are not considered by him to be the stuff of poetry; the sense of the passage is that Stephen, because of his ingrained Catholicism, is incapable of following the lead of Yeats, Russell, and the group of Dublin intellectuals who wish to Celticize Homer—to graft onto native Irish themes the "Attic note" of classical Greece. Neopaganism and paganism both exclude the kind of introspective and spiritual quest that Dante provides.

> Eternal punishment, Haines said, nodding curtly. I see. I tackled him this morning on belief. There was something on his mind, I saw. . . . He can find no trace of hell in ancient Irish myth. The moral idea seems lacking, the sense of destiny, of retribution. (*U* 245)

But Stephen, unsuspected by the Dublin cult, is following Dante's lead—the example of the poet who, with skills comparable only to Shakespeare's, made use in an original fashion of classical themes and models. Mulligan's scornful answer is equivocally met by Haines:

> —Ten years, he [Mulligan] said, chewing and laughing. He's going to write something in ten years.

—Seems a long way off, Haines said, thoughtfully. Still, I shouldn't wonder if he did after all. (*U* 245-246)

So Joyce announced the inception of *Ulysses*, a Dublin *Commedia*. Dante could hardly have handled the event more precisely or violently.

Joyce, who was by training as thoroughly Catholic as Dante, rejected the authority of the Church in the form in which he found it in his day. Dante, bitterly critical and hostile to a corrupt Papacy, still accepted and exalted the Church as an institution divinely created and inspired. Joyce had lost his faith and was unable to accept the Church's claim to supernatural inspiration: his predicament here resembled that of Renan. In respect to his loss of faith it is impossible to find Joyce in the same position spiritually as Dante.

No more complex question can be asked, in estimating Joyce's view of Dante's poem, than what effect the tensions that arose from Joyce's loss of faith had on his imagination and his art. If Joyce needed to mark out his distance from Dante, he also needed and accepted the sense of identity that came with their shared inheritance. Joyce was an unbeliever who saw his Church with "the spirit of an acute, sympathetic alien" (*SH* 73). He said, moreover, "To get the right perspective on me, you really should allude to me as a Jesuit." Judging the Irish Church by its own standards and in its own terms, his indictment of worldliness and simony takes a position that much resembles Dante's. He never formally apostatized, and when asked whether he had left the Church he replied, "That's for the Church to say."[12]

Another element in the pattern of Joyce's critical interest in the *Divine Comedy* is his perception of Dante as a critic of society. Joyce took seriously Shelley's dictum that poets are "the unacknowledged legislators of mankind," and architects of social change. Like Vico, Joyce recognized the importance of Dante's role as "first of Italian historians," the allegories of the *Divine Comedy* being "very like the reflections that a reader of history ought to make for himself, leading him to profit by the examples of others."[13]

Joyce undoubtedly sought to be "the poet of my race," as Dante had been; to be the first writer who would "present Ireland to the world." He shared many of Dante's attitudes, including a preference for social order rather than disorder and a distrust of the temporal power of the Church. In Joyce's Ireland the issue of anticlericalism, long since dead in England and France, was still as alive as in Dante's time. There was a special attraction for Joyce in Dante's indictment of clerical corruption and his images of simony.

One of Joyce's special grievances was the papal tolerance of the

English domination of Ireland. The English Catholics were led by a cardinal while the appointment of an Irish cardinal was long delayed despite the fact that Catholics made up more than ninety percent of the population of Ireland. Joyce referred to the Pope as "the real sovereign of Ireland," quite correctly perceiving that the Irish Catholic population had no voice in Rome. Joyce suspected, moreover, that the Catholic hierarchy in England was secretly opposed to Irish independence, because the creation of an independent Irish parliament would diminish the political power and influence of English Catholics under the British parliament. In Joyce's day, when Ireland was governed by the Parliament at Westminster, the presence in that House of eighty or more Catholic members from Ireland gave a degree of support and even representation to the English Catholics which they could not have had if Ireland had been independent.[14]

In Rome, where Joyce worked as a bank clerk for several months in 1906, he and his family lived in extreme poverty. In a period of extraordinary stress, he berated the Dominicans for their wealth. "An order like this couldn't support their immense church with rent etc. on the obolos of the religious but parsimonious Italian. And the same, I expect, in France. They must have vast landed estates under various names, and invested moneys. This is one reason why they oppose the quite unheretical theory of socialism because they know that one of its items is expropriation" (*Letters* II: 165-166). He made similar comments about the Irish clergy. In Trieste, he wrote three newspaper articles about Irish Home Rule, and commented that the Irish people continued to increase their contribution to Peter's Pence (the special papal tribute collected from all Irish congregations on the Sunday within the Octave of SS. Peter and Paul) in spite of increasing poverty. He described the steady depopulation of Ireland, through "the uninterrupted emigration to the U.S. or Europe of Irishmen for whom the economic and intellectual conditions of their native land are unbearable. And almost as if to set in relief this depopulation there is a long parade of churches, cathedrals, convents, monasteries, and seminaries to tend to the spiritual needs of those who have been unable to find courage or money enough to undertake the voyage. . . . Ireland is serving both God and Mammon, letting herself be milked by England and yet increasing Peter's Pence" (*CW* 190).

These criticisms constituted a theme that was driven home in each of Joyce's books. Joyce attacked the Church's temporal power as Dante did, by mocking its worldliness and suggesting simoniacal practices. These themes begin very early, in *Stephen Hero*, and continue in the *Dubliners* stories.

In his critical approach to Dante, Joyce departed radically from standard nineteenth-century attitudes. His reading of the *Divine Comedy* over a period of years from 1900 to 1915, when he lived briefly in Paris and later in Rome and Trieste, coincided with his exposure to late nineteenth-century French literary movements and to early twentieth-century Dante criticism in Italy. Joyce had taken his degree in Romance languages in October 1902, and his reading in European literature had gone far beyond the prescribed course of study. He was already prepared to receive and interpret European views of the *Divine Comedy*.

Joyce began the study of Italian in secondary school when he was twelve or thirteen. His best subjects over a five year period at school and University were consistently French, Latin and arithmetic, with Italian and English alternating in fourth or fifth place. (Euclid, algebra, trigonometry and science were at the bottom of the list) (RE:*JJ* 768 n. 65). French was his second language; Italian became the "house language" after his children were born in Trieste. The Latin-French-Italian combination, however, influenced his reading at a formative stage.

He has left us the record of his first serious interest in Dante in the autobiographical novel *Stephen Hero*, which Joyce described as the first draft of *A Portrait of the Artist*. The surviving chapters cover only the period of the protagonist's studies at University College, but they do this with great precision of detail and with many established biographical connections. "The second year of Stephen's University life opened early in October. . . . He chose Italian as his optional subject, partly from a desire to read Dante seriously, and partly to escape the crush of French and German lectures. No one else in the college studied Italian and every second morning he came to the college at ten o'clock and went up to Father Artifoni's bedroom. . . . The Italian lessons often extended beyond the hour and much less grammar and literature was discussed than philosophy. The teacher . . . was inclined to be lenient towards the audacities of his pupil, which, he supposed, must have been the outcome of too fervid Irishism. He was unable to associate *audacity of thought* with any temper but that of the irredentist" (*SH* 169-170; italics mine).

Stephen's aesthetic theories are represented, in the early novel, as having been argued out with the North Italian Jesuit who was his Italian teacher. Fiction here coincides with historical event. Joyce did have as his instructor in Italian literature an Italian Jesuit, Father Charles Ghezzi. Only one other student, Eugene Sheehy, elected this course, so the tuition was virtually private. The freedom of Joyce's discussions with Father Ghezzi is reproduced in *Stephen Hero* but not in *A Portrait*. Richard Ellmann's biography reports that Sheehy sat silent through many impassioned conversations. "Except for Ibsen and Dante," says Judge Sheehy in his autobiography, "the only other author whom he [Joyce] favored was James Clarence Mangan" (RE:*JJ* 60-61).

Corroboration in a broader perspective comes from the memoirs of another college friend, the president of the college literary society, C. P. Curran. "He was working for a modern literature degree in Italian, French and English, but his reading was a good deal off the course. I suspect there were few young men in these islands at that date so equally interested in Guido Cavalcanti and the Scandinavians, in Dante and Arthur Rimbaud."[15]

Joyce took four Intermediate examinations in Italian while he was a student at Belvedere, and probably three more at University College.[16] (The record does not show whether he wrote the Italian or the French paper.) The questions set for the 1897 Intermediate examination included nothing on the *Divine Comedy*. The students were required to translate from the Italian passages from Machiavelli, Vincenzo Monti (1754-1828; his *Caio Gracco*), and from a selection of colloquial phrases. The rest of the examination dealt with grammar.

The matriculation examination, taken at the end of the first year of college, was a much more advanced and complicated paper. Required readings for the 1902 matriculation requirement in Italian (Joyce's matriculation examination was written in 1899) included, for a passing grade, Dante's *Purgatorio*; other readings were Antonio Fogazzaro (1842-1911; poet, playwright and novelist), Vincenzo Monti, and Lorenzo Mascheroni (minor poet; 1750-1800). The history of Italian language and literature was to be covered, and a piece of English would be translated into Italian. For an honors grade the students were required to be prepared with Tasso's *Gerusalemme Liberata*, Alessandro Manzoni's (1785-1873) *Conte di Carmagnola* and *La Vita Italiana nel Trecento*, and a selection of thirteenth-century prose, *Crestomazia di Prosa del Trecento*. They could offer a translation of passages from any other Italian author, and an essay in Italian, and would be required to translate a second piece of English into Italian. Works on the history of the Italian language (Demattio), and the history of Italian literature from the death of Boccaccio to the end of the 19th century were also on the course.

For this examination there were three papers, one containing three questions on the *Divine Comedy*, such as: "Discuss Bembo's statement on Purgatory: 'È forse in tutto la più bella parte della *Divina Commedia*, o quella almeno dove meglio si dimostra la più bella parte dell' anima di Dante.' " (Pietro Bembo, 1470-1547, prepared the text of the first Aldine edition of the *Divine Comedy* in 1502.) A second was a translation of the first 21 lines of *Purgatorio* 31.

The record suggests strongly that Joyce's discovery of the *Divine Comedy* began with the matriculation examination, and that this led to his decision in the second year to embark on a "serious reading" of Dante. Joyce's brother, Stanislaus, said of his last examination in Italian, before graduation from University College, "It is more than possible that he was examined in Italian, the language of Dante, whom he already considered an artist superior to Shakespeare." Ellmann says that the examiners passed him after some disagreement (RE:*JJ* 61).

In *Stephen Hero* Joyce presented his Jesuit teachers at the University as totally uncomprehending of his own spiritual development and of Dante's place in it. Thus he produces a satirical dialogue between the Jesuit who acted as spiritual director of the college debating society and the defiant young artist.

> [Stephen begins]—Even admitting the corruption you speak of I see nothing unlawful in an examination of corruption.
> —Yes, it may be lawful—for the scientist, for the reformer.
> —Why not for the poet too? Dante surely examines and upbraids society.
> —Ah yes, said the President explanitorily [*sic*],—with a moral purpose in view: Dante was a great poet.
> —Ibsen is also a great poet.
> —You cannot compare Dante and Ibsen.
> —I am not doing so.
> —Dante, the lofty upholder of beauty, the greatest of Italian poets, and Ibsen, the writer above and beyond all others, Ibsen and Zola, who seek to degrade their art, who pander to a corrupt taste . . .
> —But you are comparing them!
> —No, you cannot compare them. One has a high moral aim—he ennobles the human race: the other degrades it.
> —I mean [said Stephen] that Ibsen's account of modern society is as genuinely ironical as Newman's account of English Protestant morality and belief. (*SH* 92:1-28)

It is of course quite possible that this is a faithful transcription.

There is a great deal of narrative material in *Stephen Hero* that enlightens the reader about this young poet's views of Dante and the *Divine Comedy*. How much of it represents the mature James Joyce is problematic, but it probably represents the youthful Joyce. Some of this narrative material is direct and immediate, as in the lines cited above;

some of it takes the form of quotation and allusion to the *Divine Comedy*; and some of it presents Stephen as having a view of Dante (as of other writers) that is inexplicable to his teachers. By implication Stephen's view is superior—it is an interpretation of Dante, that is, which would be as iconoclastic at that time as would Joyce's anticipation of neo-scholastic, neo-Thomist aesthetics. As Father Noon points out, "The Louvain revival of Thomism was in the offing but had not yet come to pass; Etienne Gilson and Jacques Maritain, like so many other capable twentieth-century Aquinian scholars, had their work cut out for them, but the work still remained to be done." Father Noon also remarks on the presence in *Stephen Hero* of indications that Stephen, wherever he found them, did quote passages from Aquinas in support of his ideas: "Father Butt is represented in rather broad caricature . . . but when he remarks of Stephen's 'Thomistic' essay, read before the Literary Society in this early version of *A Portrait*, that 'it was a new sensation for him to hear Thomas Aquinas quoted as an authority on esthetic philosophy,' there is much to be said for Father Butt's reserve." And Father Noon concludes that the presence of Aquinas and scholasticism is important primarily for the characterization of the artist-figures in Joyce's fiction; that is, Joyce was using Aquinas as fictional material, and the fictional patterns might or might not carry indications of Joyce's own thought.[17]

Aquinas and Scholasticism continue into *A Portrait* in recognizable form. But the study of Dante by the hero of the earlier book is almost completely suppressed. In that earlier version Joyce also made one substantial conversion, cleverly hidden, of a canto of the *Divine Comedy*, an imitation that will be discussed in Chapter Two below. His Chapter XVIII is clearly modeled on *Inferno* 15, the canto of Brunetto Latini. It is by this kind of direct imitation of Dante that stages in Joyce's critical reading of the *Divine Comedy* can be identified. The use of Brunetto is a crude effort, not in its application of Dante's devices but in its *interpretation* of the canto. In *Ulysses*, as will be demonstrated in a later chapter, Joyce refined his view and his fictional use of it. Between the two, he must have studied the *Divine Comedy* carefully and reached a mature conception of Dante's art.

*

The five years from 1897 to 1905, then, are the first period of Joyce's interest in Dante. Besides the autobiographical connections of the novel, Joyce left a trail of allusions to Dante and the *Divine Comedy* in essays he wrote in this period.

The most important of these is a paper on the Irish poet, James

Clarence Mangan, that he read to the Literary and Historical Society on February 1, 1902. The peroration of this essay makes it clear that he regarded himself as akin to Blake and Dante. "The philosophic mind inclines always to an elaborate life—the life of Goethe or of Leonardo da Vinci; but the life of the poet is intense—the life of Blake or of Dante—taking into its centre the life that surrounds it and flinging it abroad again amid planetary music." But another allusion makes it equally clear that Joyce's impulse is revisionist, and that his concerns are secular. In a statement of his critical theory, he describes the classical temper in contrast to the romantic, using an allusion to a phrase from *Purgatorio* 31, "le presenti cose," "these present things." The classical temper, he says, is "a method which bends upon these present things and so works upon them and fashions them that the quick intelligence may go beyond them to their meaning which is still unuttered" (*Purg.* 31:34; *CW* 74, 79, 81-82). The essay contains additional allusions to Dante. But the words borrowed from the *Purgatorio* are used in a sense that is just the reverse of Dante's. When Beatrice reproaches Dante in *Purgatorio* 31 for forgetting her memory, his sorrowful reply is really a statement that the mundane things of this world, "le presenti cose," obscure our vision of the true goals of life. Joyce picked up the little phrase as he would a banner. In this essay he announces his belief that our goals are here on earth and that the artist reaches higher truth through a preoccupation with the everyday and the domestic, and he suggests a secular use of Dante's figurative mode.

This is the paper to which, in *Stephen Hero*, Joyce gave the title and identity of an earlier paper, "Drama and Life," written at the age of eighteen in his second year at University College. He deliberately confused the two; the earlier essay has no suggestion of Dante. By the time he wrote the second paper, Joyce had begun his "serious reading" of Dante and had begun to think of himself as a European, and he conflates the two essays to make a fictional account of a process that carried over several years.

In 1903, the year after Joyce's graduation from college, he made a little money writing book reviews, and in two of these he made passing reference to Dante's poetry (*CW* 89, 110). In the third, a review of Ibsen's play *Catilina*, Joyce made a more significant statement—a comment on Ibsen that linked him artistically with Dante, and implied that they were the sources of his own modernism. Returning to the line from *Purgatorio* 31, "le presenti cose," Joyce says that Ibsen "has united with his strong, ample, imaginative faculty a preoccupation with the things present to him." Then he adds, "But meanwhile a young generation which has cast away belief and thrown precision after it, for which Balzac is a great intellect and every sampler who chooses to wander amid his own shapeless hells and heavens a Dante without the unfortunate prejudices of Dante, will be troubled by this preoccupation, and out of very conscience will denounce a method so calm, so ironical" (*CW* 101).

By this time Joyce was in open conflict with the writers of the Irish Literary Theatre, most of them Protestants or defected Catholics, and had expressed his scorn for the Irish movement. Dante's realms are, beyond all else, precisely shaped and crafted; the ironically termed "unfortunate prejudices" of Dante suggest the comments later given to Buck Mulligan and Haines, in *Ulysses*, about "visions of hell." When Joyce left Dublin for the Continent in October, 1904, he left behind him an angry verse broadside to be distributed to various members of the Dublin literary establishment, whom he satirized individually and as a group. He called this broadside "The Holy Office," and in it he repeated his Dantean allusion to the "unprejudiced" Protestant literati, this time in rhyme, as a last barbed thrust at the cenacle.

> For every true-born mysticist
> A Dante is, unprejudiced,
> Who safe at ingle-nook, by proxy,
> Hazards extremes of heterodoxy
> Like him who finds a joy at table
> Pondering the uncomfortable.
> Ruling one's life by commonsense
> How can one fail to be intense?   (*CW* 150)

The writing of *Stephen Hero* had begun before Joyce left Dublin, and was a direct result of Joyce's conflict with the clique led by Yeats, George Russell, and William Magee. Joyce had written an essay, "A Portrait of the Artist," for their new magazine, *Dana*. The essay contains the basic theme of the final book and, in embryo, some of its structure as well: it was rejected by the editors in January, 1904. Joyce thereupon decided to turn it into a novel. We know from the diary of his brother that eleven chapters had been written by the end of March, and Stanislaus Joyce wrote on March 29: "It is a lying autobiography and a raking satire. He is putting nearly all his acquaintances in it, and the Catholic Church comes in for a bad quarter of an hour."[18] Joyce's letters from Pola and Trieste show him continuing to write the novel; the surviving fragment covers only chapters 15 through 25. The first stage of Joyce's reading of Dante thus ends sometime in mid-1905, when he finished writing the 914 pages of *Stephen Hero*.

A second stage in the development of Joyce's knowledge of Dante is the short period between 1904 and 1907, marked by the decision to make a complete revision of *Stephen Hero* into *A Portrait of the Artist as a Young Man* and by the writing of the *Dubliners* stories. When he left Dublin he had written ten chapters of his autobiographical novel; in Pola and Trieste in the next two years he wrote the next eight chapters; in 1907, convalescing from an attack of rheumatic fever, he decided to make a radical revision of the book (RE:*JJ* 197, 274).

During these three years he also wrote most of the stories of *Dubliners*. Three had been published in Dublin before 1905 but were heavily revised, and the last story, "The Dead," was completed in September 1907. Jackson Cope has noted the significance of the revisions. In the new version of the first story, Joyce set down as the opening words of his book, "There was no hope," the words placed by Dante over the gate of Hell in *Inferno* 3, and closed the last story with snow, reproducing the final image of a frozen world with which Dante closes the *Inferno* in Canto 34.[19]

In 1907 Joyce also wrote three articles on Ireland for the Trieste paper, *Il Piccolo della Sera*, and gave three public lectures at the Università Popolare in Trieste, all written in Italian. These six essays gave Joyce an opportunity to set down more or less systematically his thoughts about his country. They are the record of a shift in viewpoint that began in mid-1907, was fully apparent by the end of September, 1907, and was later extended in four additional articles on Ireland published in 1910 and 1912. The essays and lectures of 1907 register accurately the recurrent frustrations of nationalist aspirations in the history of Protestant England's colonial domination over Catholic Ireland: these matters are set in the framework of a more general display of significant elements of Irish literature, history and culture. The sympathetic tone of the essays stands in marked contrast to the preoccupations of the young man represented in *Stephen Hero*.

When Joyce first came to Trieste his command of spoken Italian was competent but stiff and archaic. "I learned my Italian from Dante and Dino," he told his closest friend in Trieste, Alessandro Francini (RE:*JJ* 193). By an exchange of lessons with Francini, who teased Joyce about his lack of colloquial diction, Joyce rapidly acquired a full command of the language. This must have changed his modes of thought as well. Certainly he read widely in Italian in this period, and came to know the people about whom Dante had written as he could not have known them before—the result of not just living in Italy, as

Henry James had done, but of living intimately with the Italians. He shared the Francini household for some years, and always lived in Trieste as a native rather than a tourist, or temporary resident. Francini has recorded, in a lecture he gave in Trieste in 1922, one of Joyce's remarks about Dante in this period:[20] "Italian literature begins with Dante and finishes with Dante. That's more than a little. In Dante dwells the whole spirit of the Renaissance" (RE:*JJ* 226).

Joyce was in Rome for six months at the end of 1906, working in a bank. The hours were long and the work more confining than his employment in Trieste, where he taught English at a Berlitz School. He returned to Trieste on March 7, 1907, and resumed his teaching. Two of his articles and his three lectures were written in the spring of 1907.

The six-month sojourn in Rome was a fiasco: Joyce discovered that he could not hold the kind of job he was able to get and still do the serious writing he intended to do. The unpleasantness of this period may have become a factor in Joyce's marked dislike of Rome, a revulsion which was unquestionably worsened by his sense of the city as the center of Catholicism. His reactions to Rome express an unremitting hostility to the temporal power of the Church. While he was there, the Jesuits elected a new general; Joyce wrote to his brother that he had gone up to their headquarters to find out the decision of the "black lice," as he had learned to call them in Italy. He took his small son to St. Peter's, and wrote to Stanislaus that the child had begun to shout immediately "when the lazy whores of priests began to chant" (*Letters* II:152). From Rome he wrote, "For my part I believe that to establish the church in full power again in Europe would mean a renewal of the Inquisition" (*Letters* II:148). Joyce's thoroughly unromantic view of Italy, the Italians, and Rome, which was consolidated in these years, must have contributed to his modern rendering of Dante's anticlericalism.

In the first of his lectures, given April 27, 1907, with the title, "Ireland, Island of Saints and Sages," Joyce reminds the Italians that Dante met a Celt in the *Inferno*.

It would be easy to make a list of the Irishmen who carried the torch of knowledge from country to country as pilgrims and hermits, as scholars and wisemen. Their traces are still seen today in abandoned altars, in traditions and legends where even the name of the hero is scarcely recognizable, or in poetic allusions, such as the passage in Dante's *Inferno* where his mentor points to one of the Celtic magicians tormented by infernal pains and says: "Quell' altro, che ne' fianchi è così poco,/Michele Scotto fu, che veramente/de le magiche frode seppe 'l gioco." ("That other one so meagre in the flanks/was Michael Scott, who really knew/the tricks of false magic.") (*Inf*. 20:115-117; *CW* 154, trans. editors)

In the second lecture, on the Irish poet James Clarence Mangan, Joyce made a graceful allusion to the Paradiso, saying: ". . . The world in which Mangan wishes his lady to dwell is different from the marble temple built by Buonarotti, and from the peaceful oriflamme of the Florentine theologian" (*CW* 183). The third lecture, which was on the Irish Literary Renaissance, has not survived.

Joyce's essays and lectures are on the level of popular rather than scholarly writing, but they are informed and thoughtful. *Ulysses* was to represent a more complete view. There is a consistency in Joyce's preoccupation with Irish political problems, and to the extent that his essays and lectures represent an unfinished excursion down the road toward practical policy they are a reminder of similar preoccupations and a similar consistency in Dante's political interests with the unfinished *De Monarchia* reappearing in the *Divine Comedy*.

Finally, the renewed interest in D'Annunzio that Joyce manifested during this period suggests that D'Annunzio's use of Dante and his glorification of Rome were moving Joyce toward a fresh appraisal of the *Divine Comedy*. In 1901 D'Annunzio had written *Francesca da Rimini* as a version of Dante's great love story, composed in a manner imitative of Dante and giving a new and original treatment to the historical details. Joyce first read the play in Arthur Symon's translation in 1902, in Paris (*Letters* II:19). This play became the standard and unequaled model for historical plays in Italy; performed again and again, it was a subject of active discussion in Italy and in Trieste while Joyce was there. D'Annunzio's first novel, *Il Piacere* (*The Child of Pleasure*), had been purchased by Joyce when he was eighteen. Rome is more vividly realized in *Il Piacere* than is Venice in D'Annunzio's later novel, *Il Fuoco*, and it is hard to think of a novel in which a city has been more fully and lovingly represented. Its effect on Joyce may be implicit in a letter to his publisher, Grant Richards, in October, 1905:

> I do not think that any writer has yet presented Dublin to the world. It has been a capital of Europe for thousands of years, it is supposed to be the second city of the British Empire and it is nearly three times as big as Venice. Moreover, on account of many circumstances which I cannot detail here, the expression Dubliner seems to me to bear some meaning and I doubt whether the same can be said for such words as "Londoner" and "Parisian," both of which have been used by writers as titles. (*Letters* II:122)

Joyce in this year had been reading D'Annunzio with sufficient care to consider writing a serious article about him. He saw and read D'Annunzio's plays, and was exposed to a constant stream of articles about him in the press.[21] Joyce did not need to go to D'Annunzio for the idea of imitating Dante, but it may well have clarified his ideas.

For Joyce's knowledge of Dante this was a period of consolidation, like the winding-up of a spring. Following the return from Rome, and the writing of the first articles and lectures, he was incapacitated for several months with rheumatic fever (during this period his second child was born, in the pauper's ward of the Trieste hospital), and the enforced bedrest this disease required must have been a factor in the major alterations he made in his literary plans. On September 6 he dictated the ending of "The Dead" to Stanislaus; on September 8 Stanislaus noted in his diary (unpublished) that his brother planned to revise *Stephen Hero* completely; and another entry on November 10 announced the conception of *Ulysses* (RE:*JJ* 274; 780 n. 54).

These years might be described as the period in which Joyce became as truly exiled as Dante, whose excoriation of Florence is accompanied by the description, "del bello ovile ov' io dormi' agnello," "Fair sheepfold where slept I as a lamb" (*Par.* 25:5).

*

The third period marks the development of Joyce's mature knowledge of the *Divine Comedy*. It must have begun soon after that extraordinary year of 1907, and it continued through the rest of Joyce's stay in Trieste and his residence in Zurich, until 1919-1920, when he moved to Paris and finished writing *Ulysses*. Several events mark off this period: the purchase of a copy of the *Vita Nuova* and a copy of the *Divine Comedy*, apparently specifically for renewed reading and close study; the writing, in Trieste between 1914 (possibly earlier) and 1915, of *A Portrait of the Artist as a Young Man*, and the play *Exiles* (both these works contain a sub-text of concealed allusions to sections of Dante's poetry); and, finally, the writing of the greater part of *Ulysses*.

Joyce bought a copy of the *Vita Nuova* in Trieste, and used it in completing *A Portrait of the Artist as a Young Man*. The "acted-out" allusion which he had tried with a heavier and less practiced hand in *Stephen Hero*, Joyce now maneuvered into a more subtle and ingenious arrangement of detail. The allusion in the diary entry with which the book ends, and the brief situational parallel to the *Vita Nuova* at the end of the first section of Chapter Five of *A Portrait*, were surely composed with reference to Dante's text. The date of composition of Chapter Five thus identifies significantly a stage in Joyce's mature

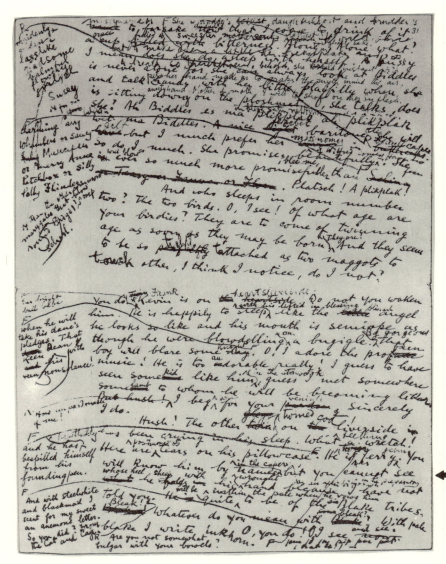

2. In this manuscript draft of *Finnegans Wake*, Chap. III.iv, we see a Dantean allusion come into Joyce's mind as he writes of the sleeping twins. In his first version the line is: "You cannot see what he holds in his hand because I have not told you." He crosses out "what" and "in" and changes "folds" to "holds." Finally he adds "whose heel," and "sheepfolds." The ultimate substitution of "with" for "in" was changed back in a later draft that has not survived, when he also added, "O, foetal sleep!" The published version is: "You cannot see whose heel he sheepfolds in his wrought hand because I have not told you. O, foetal sleep!" (*FW* 563:9). The Dantean original is, "Fair sheepfold, where slept I as a lamb" (del bello ovile ov'io dormi' angnello, *Par.* 25:5), a reminiscence of Florence, Dante's birthplace.

grasp of Dante's work. This final chapter was written contemporaneously with the serialization of the early chapters.[22]

At some time in this period Joyce bought a little paperback copy of
the *Divine Comedy*, an edition with full notes and commentary by
Eugenio Camerini, published by E. Sonzogno (Milan) as a title in the
Camerini series of inexpensive editions of the classics. The book is in-
tact, but worn and fragile; Joyce's stamp, "J. J.," is on the flyleaf. Since
there is no record of the seller it is impossible to fix the exact date of
Joyce's purchase. It is probably an undated reprinting of the 1904
edition.[23]

Why this particular edition was bought by Joyce in preference to
others is problematic. Camerini's literary reputation as "scrittore" was
respectable, though not distinguished. He is on Paget Toynbee's list
of modern commentators (continued into the Singleton revision) in
the *Dante Dictionary*, and is cited in several places in W. W. Vernon's
encyclopedic commentary. Dante scholars, however, would have
ranked the Camerini edition below that of Scartazzini and of several
other editors as well. Other pocket size and paperback editions were
available while Joyce was living in Italy.

A copy of the edition Joyce owned, in an 1891 printing, is in the
National Library in Dublin, but it was received in 1926 as part of a
large bequest of 2,000 volumes of French, Italian, and Spanish works,
a scholarly library. The interesting fact is that it was specially bound
for school use, in a series of French, Italian and Spanish classics, im-
ported and in effect re-published by David Nutt, a firm that also published extensively in the field of Irish studies and Irish myth. It is
quite possible that this edition had been known and even perhaps
used by Joyce as a student, and that he made the Trieste purchase for
this reason.[24]

What does seem certain is that Joyce bought this book for the sake
of the notes and to have at hand the means of exact reference to
Dante's text. It was part of his working library at the time he wrote
Ulysses, and he left it in Trieste when he moved to Paris. The development of his mature knowledge of the *Divine Comedy* probably
never ended, but it must have begun with the purchase of this copy.

From the pre-Zurich years of this third period, one critical comment on Dante survives in an essay on the Renaissance which Joyce
wrote in Padua in April, 1912. This forms part of an examination
paper written in an attempt to qualify for a teaching position in Italy,
and thus it is an extemporaneous effort. It indicates a developing
critical position.[25]

A great modern artist wishing to put the sentiment of love to music reproduces, as far as his art permits, each pulsation, each trembling, the lightest shivering, the lightest sigh; the harmonies intertwine and oppose each other secretly: one loves even as one grows more cruel, suffers when and as much as one enjoys, hate and doubt flash in the lovers' eyes, their bodies become one single flesh. Place *Tristan and Isolde* next to the *Inferno* and you will notice how the poet's hate follows its path from abyss to abyss in the wake of an idea that intensifies; and the more intensely the poet consumes himself in the fire of the idea of hate, the more violent becomes the art with which the artist communicates his passion. One is the art of circumstance, the other is ideational. [L'una è un'arte di circostanze, l'altra è ideativa.] (trans. Louis Berrone)

At the time of Joyce's residence in Italy, discussions of the *Divine Comedy* by Italian critics had begun seriously to distinguish between the doctrinal and epic dimensions of the poem, between the didactic and descriptive, and between the discursive and emotional elements. Italian criticism thus fathered a new view of Dante which ultimately focused on assent to the *Divine Comedy* as a whole rather than to selected parts or features.[26] As Luigi Sturzo puts it, this was "an assent based on human empathy and poetical catharsis."[27] Subsequently this reevaluation was importantly challenged. Controversy on the importance of doctrine in the aesthetic assessment of the poem continues today.[28]

Joyce did not need to make a systematic study of Dante criticism to be aware of these intellectual currents, which were, of course, part of a general movement of thought, in France and Germany as well as Italy, that had begun with Vico's powerful aesthetic interpretation of Dante. Joyce's first knowledge of Vico came, either in his college years or soon after, through Michelet.[29] Joyce was always aware of contemporary currents of opinion, and in Italy he read the Italian reviews as well as those from Paris and London. It seems clear that a major current of interpretation, which reinforced his own natural tendency to seek out the intentions of Dante as poet, reached Joyce through Continental studies of the *Divine Comedy*. We have no direct evidence for this, but we do have a good deal of knowledge of his reading habits.[30] Joyce's reading, like his art, is marked by an intense regard for the poetics of the work of art. The same preoccupation, differently presented, is visible in each of his books. From *Dubliners* to *Finnegans Wake*, the manner of making is central, and it was central to Joyce's interest in Dante.

AT THE center of Joyce's and Dante's work, narrative and style come together and are mutually reinforced by conceptions embodied in the construction of dominant images. In the three chapters that follow, three such configurations will be presented in which clear reference to the *Divine Comedy* is found in Joyce's fictions.

Joyce's recovery of Dante resembled Dante's recovery of Virgil in being a combination of devoted attachment and radical difference. Out of all the antique world Dante chose Virgil for comprehensive reincarnation in his fictional journey. He thus entered fully into the genius of ancient art. So also with Joyce, who set out to clothe his own new ideas with the formal qualities of Dante's poetry, in a massive effort of what Coleridge called the "shaping imagination."

Such a revisiting of the literary past became a reflection of older patterns of the soul's descent, like the journey of Orpheus into the underworld to recover Eurydice. It is a perilous return, for the past encumbers even while it enriches and invigorates. Dante was compared to Orpheus by Benvenuto da Imola, author of the earliest commentary on the *Divine Comedy*. In Benvenuto's Christianizing allegory Orpheus is the man of greatest wisdom and eloquence, and his journey is an effort to recover his soul, poetically embodied as Eurydice, his beloved. Benvenuto saw in Dante a Christian singer who resisted successfully the fatal backward look that had trapped Orpheus. Revelation armed Dante with insight denied to the pagans. His peril was the loss of salvation and the reality with which he has drawn the antique pantheon is vivid testimony to the depth of his attachment to the pagan world. Joyce, though not so threatened, does show a similarly powerful conflict between two opposing forces that claimed his mind and imagination. Joyce's secular imagination had its origins rooted as firmly as Dante's in Catholicism.

In his re-shaping of Dante's characters and patterns to fit the Ireland of his day, the clash of antagonistic principles is often apparent. Yet Joyce also presses forward from that recapture of Dante's poetry in which, like Orpheus, he recovered a lost vitality—what John B. Friedman calls the "best voice of the intellect"—and in which the imaginative intellect is reunited with passion as Orpheus with Eurydice.[1] His imitations resisted the backward look. He put Dante's characters and scenes into modern attire and into constructions as novel as Dante's transformations of Virgil. His inventions, particularly in the distortions of some of Dante's paternal figures, indicate the modernist quality of Joyce's reading of Dante. In spite of his denials, Joyce's later work reflects the basic Freudian concept of inevitable ambivalence toward father figures.[2]

Dante uses the idea of fatherhood poetically as a central principle of order. Paternal imagery begins in the *Inferno* and continues through the three divisions of the *Commedia*. By its use Dante expresses the condition of people under civil government as brothers under the rule of their sire. Ultimately the vision extends to the family of Man, as brothers under the rule of God the Father. Within this pattern Dante explores the mystery of generation, the inheritance of intelligence and talent. The negative image also is sharply and subtly drawn; not only the benevolent ruler but the tyrant is shown. The simoniac priest and corrupt pope are an aspect of the configuration, as are also the teacher and the poet who misuse their trust.

Joyce did not need any literary prototype (and there were many from whom he could have chosen) to make the association of family with social order. It is a relation of thought that Joyce, like anyone else, could have made from his own experience and his knowledge of the human heart. But Joyce did read Dante, and did transfer to his own fiction some of Dante's patterns. It is appropriate to remark, as James Atherton has said, the tightly organized and unusually controlled character of Joyce's allusive art, which makes sheer coincidence relatively unlikely as an explanation for the presence of an allusion.[3] His indebtedness to the *Comedy* seems most marked in the consistent association of the poet with the paternal image, in one way or another. Art, for Joyce, is fatherhood. Dante similarly allows Virgil to describe art as in some sense the grandchild of God (*Inf.* 11:105).

This chapter will be concerned principally with *Ulysses*, in which the theme of fatherhood serves to identify Leopold Bloom as Homer's hero and Stephen Dedalus as in some sense Telemachus. This theme, in combination with the structure of a journey through a succession of perils, is undoubtedly the most powerful device that Joyce could have used to link his novel with the *Odyssey*. But Joyce's preference for a richly allusive mode of writing, demonstrated in earlier books, was now reinforced by his exploration of the literary tradition. Stanislaus Joyce told W. B. Stanford that his brother had made a comparative study of writers on Ulysses: "Virgil, Ovid, Dante, Shakespeare, Racine, Fénelon, Tennyson, Stephen Phillips, D'Annunzio, and Gerhardt Hauptmann, as well as Samuel Butler's *The Authoress of the Odyssey* and Bérard's *Les Phéniciens et l'Odysée*, and the translations by Butler and Cowper."[4] The *Odyssey* offered a solid basis for Joyce's own intricate weaving of literary cognates. Shakespeare's Hamlet and Dante's two travelers were additional beguiling archetypes for subtle manipulation of the paternal relationship.

Paternal feelings were not, perhaps, the most marked among the characteristics of the first Ulysses. In Homer's story it is the wanderer's aging wife, rather than his son, and his attachment to the general idea of home, that account for his persistence against all odds and dangers. Leopold Bloom fulfills this pattern, but takes on other roles as well. In the terms of Joyce's novel, Bloom cannot be a father to Stephen Dedalus in the Ulyssean sense but he can play the Dantesque fatherly role of Virgil as Stephen's protector and guide.[5] Bloom can also search out his own spiritual inheritance, in the process meeting a remote and unfamiliar ancestor, as does Dante.

*

Benevolent Fathers: Dante's Virgil and Joyce's Mr Bloom

In the Eumaeus chapter of *Ulysses*, Stephen Dedalus and Mr Bloom walk together toward Eccles Street, in the manner of Dante and Virgil.

> As they walked, they at times stopped and walked again, continuing their tête à tête . . . about sirens, enemies of man's reason, mingled with a number of topics of the same category, usurpers, historical cases of the kind . . . (*U* 649:25-29)

Their actual association is brief, only 92 pages, or one-eighth of the book, and the Virgilian aspect is overlaid on a context that also gives Bloom the role of Dante as he journeys across Dublin. Bloom's paternal metamorphosis begins part way through the Oxen of the Sun chapter (*U* 406:3), and continues until Stephen leaves Bloom's house (*U* 688-689), part way through the Ithaca chapter.

The brevity of Bloom's actual conversation with Stephen is Virgilian, for it points to the fact that Virgil accompanies Dante only part of the way. Virgil himself makes us aware that he knows this, with the re-echoing, "So far as I can go with thee."

Only once does Dante address Virgil by name, at their first meeting in the Dark Wood: "Are you, then, Virgil?" Bloom calls Dedalus by his first name, "Stephen," only on one occasion, at the close of the Circe episode as he tries to wake the young man. Stephen stirs and groans, and murmurs the lines of Yeats:

> Who . . . drive . . . Fergus now.
> And pierce . . . wood's woven shade?

Bloom, recognizing a reference to poetry though he does not know whose, completes the reference to Dante's recognition scene with "In the shady wood." There are other echoes as well. Stephen's fragmentary "black panther vampire" continues the allusive pattern, reflecting Dante's plea for help against "the beast that turned me back." Joyce's authorial inclusion of "A barking dog in the distance" suggests Virgil's statement that the vicious beast who, vampire-like, "after feeding is hungrier than before," will be routed by the mysterious Hound who is yet to come and who will be born "between feltro and feltro" (*Inf.* 1:79; 88-90; 99; 101-105 / *U* 592:16-17; 21-22; 24; 593:1-2; 5).

The final leave-taking of Bloom and Stephen in the Ithaca chapter of *Ulysses* seems to be a reconstruction of a section of *Purgatorio* 30. Here, Virgil silently disappears between one thought and the next. There follows the ringing triple repetition of Virgil's name, combined with the superlative form of the affectionate adjective, "dolcissimo." "Caro," a word frequently applied to Virgil, is never used by Dante in the superlative and only at their parting is the combination, "dolce padre," developed with such poignant music.[6]

> Ma Virgilio n'avea lasciati scemi
>   di sé, Virgilio dolcissimo patre,
>   Virgilio a cui per mia salute die'mi.

Dante calls him "father" in his own language, *"Patre."*

> But Virgil had left us bereft of him,
>   Virgil, tender loving father mine,
>   Virgil, to whom I gave me for my weal.
>   (*Purg.* 30:49-51, trans. Bergin)

The echoing effect of the thrice-uttered name, as Edward Moore noted in an early study of Dante's use of Virgil, is a close reproduction of Virgil's poetic account of Orpheus. Dante has put Virgil's name in exactly the same position that Virgil placed Eurydice's in each line. The poignancy of that last farewell is expressed in a threefold cry:

> . . . Eurydicen vox ipsa et frigida lingua,
> a miseram Eurydicen! anima fugiente vocabat,
> Eurydicen toto referebant flumine ripae.   (*Georg.* IV.525-527)

> The bare voice and death-cold tongue, with fleeting breath, called Eurydice—ah, hapless Eurydice! "Eurydice!" the banks re-echoed, all adown the stream. (trans. Singleton, *Purg.* II.741)

The Singleton commentary points out that the reiteration of Virgil's name, five times in nine lines, is connected with the dramatic (and unique) naming of Dante by Beatrice. Unquestionably the personal identification marks the moment of Dante's individualization in a journey that is allegorically the journey of Everyman. It is a Christian and a sacramental naming, Dante's personal confession.

But the accumulated echoes of Virgil's poetic fatherhood here give another context as well to the scene of farewell or parting. As Dante is named by Beatrice, Dante names Virgil and quotes his poetry. When Dante turns to Virgil to tell him that he recognizes Beatrice, Virgil's own line is used: "Agnosco veteris vestigia flammae" (*Aen.* VI.23) becomes "conosco i segni de l'antica fiamma," "I know the tokens of the ancient flame" (*Purg.* 30:48, Singleton trans.). Still more remarkable is Dante's use of Virgil's line, untranslated, from the parting of Aeneas and Anchises at the close of *Aeneid* VI. Dante adds one word, "Oh," and brings to life the cry of Anchises in an actual scattering of flowers around and over the chariot of Beatrice: "*Manibus, oh, date lilia plenis!*" The naming of Dante in such an enclosing design announces the recovered voice of a Christian Orpheus. Dante's "mistranslations" of Virgil are purposeful. Before Petrarch or Spenser or Milton, Dante faced down what Harold Bloom has called "the anguish of attempting to reconcile poetry and religion."[7] Both confrontation and outcome were closely scrutinized by Joyce.

In the Ithaca chapter of *Ulysses*, Joyce reverses Dante's pattern, for it is Stephen who leaves Bloom. Dante sometimes makes such reversals of Virgil, and it is clear that Joyce has deliberately constructed a parallel to the farewell scene in *Purgatorio* 30. Joyce was a Latinist—he had made his own study of Virgil as well as of Dante. His copy of the *Divine Comedy* carried notes to the *Aeneid* VI allusions described above, and while Joyce was at University College the National Library in Dublin had accessioned the Oxford edition of Dante to which Moore had made such a large contribution. It is possible that Joyce saw Moore's account of Dante's use of classical themes and authors, but he did not really need to go beyond his own reading. We have, in fact, a contemporary account of Joyce's comparison of Dante's poetic devices with Virgil's that indicates his absorption in *Aeneid* VI.[8] This is described in the next chapter (see page 83).

Stephen goes out of the story as completely as Virgil leaves Dante in *Purgatorio* 30. Dante records his own feelings at Virgil's departure, but Joyce records only Bloom's sense of loss.

> Alone, what did Bloom feel? The cold of interstellar space, thousands of degrees below freezing point or the absolute zero of Fahrenheit, Centigrade or Reaumur: the incipient intimations of proximate dawn. (*U* 689:14-16)

Where, after all, is Virgil at the moment of parting from Dante? On the naturalistic level of the narrative Virgil may be said to be in "interstellar space," above the earth (though attached to it) and below the heavens. He does not go back the way he came. He must leave the Mountaintop and return to Limbo by some magical route, perhaps the route of the Heavenly Messenger of *Inferno* 9:81, and he is certainly alone. Joyce's antiphonal prose takes account of all this, and also records the emotional response to the leavetaking. Joyce has also reproduced something of the musical quality of Dante's terzina, which repeats in the rhyme words and also internally the principal vowels in Virgil's name: Virgilio, Virgilio/dolcissimo, Virgilio . . . perdeo. In Joyce's two sentences the "o" is reduplicated like an echo lost in infinity: alone, Bloom, cold, below, or, zero, Reaumur.

In the course of their association, Stephen and Bloom are placed in a Dantean model by events, topics, and descriptive comment. The narrative voice describes Bloom's Virgilian role in a phrase from the *Aeneid*: "The other, who was acting as his [Stephen's] *fidus Achates*." Bloom knows no Latin and a misquotation from the *Aeneid* is put into indirect discourse as Stephen's thought: "haud ignarus malorum miseris succurrere disco etcetera, as the Latin poet remarks" (*U* 601:34). Bloom moves around to get on Stephen's right, the narrator commenting, "a habit of his, the right side being, in classical idiom, his tender Achilles" (*U* 642:31).

Their conversation has a number of echoes of the *Divine Comedy*. A showpiece is Bloom's and Stephen's encounter with the redbearded sailor, whose tale of a shipwreck in the southern hemisphere is unmistakably parallel to Dante's account of Ulysses's last voyage in *Inferno* 26.[9] Virgil and Dante in the *Inferno* keep always (with two exceptions that point to the design) to the left; Bloom and Stephen "made tracks to the left" (*U* 597:27).[10] They stop to look at a heap of barren cobblestones, possibly a reminiscence of the shattered rockfall seen by Virgil and Dante in *Inferno* 12 and explained as a result of the earthquake at the time of Christ's crucifixion (*Inf.* 12:34-39; *U* 599:39-42).

Joyce would have recognized Virgil's earlier trip through hell as one of Dante's inventions, designed, as Mark Musa comments, to emphasize Virgil's competence as a guide.[11] Bloom also is a non-Christian guide, and something of Dante's syncretism may be present as well in Joyce's selection of details. The paragraph describing the stonepile is gratuitously given an atmosphere of fire and gloom, and Stephen begins to "remember that this had happened, or had been mentioned as having happened, before" (*U* 600:1-2), these words referring to the opening phrase of the paragraph, "Discussing these and kindred topics."

In Eumaeus also Bloom and Stephen talk about the soul. In the *Divine Comedy* it is Statius who explains to Dante the generation of the soul. Stephen's stages are fundamentally the same as the stages in the development of the embryo as set forth by Statius, although described in different terms and in less detail.[12] Mr Bloom, in the maundering diction of the chapter, seems to agree with the argument, "though the mystical finesse involved was a bit out of his sublunary depth" (*U* 618:10-11), as Virgil in *Purgatorio* 25 is still below the heaven of the Moon and can go no farther than the Earthly Paradise. Their conversation at this point is an echo of Stephen's earlier exposition of the origin of the soul, which Bloom heard at the maternity hospital in the Oxen of the Sun chapter. Stephen also alludes to Virgil; Dante's Virgil is out of his depth in the discussion with Statius, for he can go only so far as the light of natural reason will carry him, while Statius, having been converted to Christianity in Dante's poetic fiction, has the advantage of Divine Revelation as well.[13]

Stephen, in the maternity hospital, spoke of the generation of the embryo from semen, as Statius does in *Purgatorio* 25. Statius, whose argument comes via Scholasticism from Aristotle's *De Anima*, tells Dante that Averroës, "a wiser one than thou" ("che più savio di te," *Purg.* 25:63), had the wrong idea; Stephen also attributes a wrong idea, though a different one, to Averroës.

The discourse of Statius, Virgil, and Dante, who are together through five cantos of the *Purgatorio* (Cantos 21 to 25), has been called Dante's most notable portrayal of poetic fatherhood and sonship. Joyce appropriated the substance of the discussion of Statius to support a like effect in the association of Bloom and Stephen. More generally, Joyce has created a mimetic verbal context, partly made up of visual images and partly of rhetorical and substantive connections, that recalls the association of Virgil and Dante in the *Inferno* and *Purgatorio*. He establishes *a paternal quality* in Bloom that makes him a Virgilian guide and protector for Stephen Dedalus.

The figure of Virgil as a paternal image is developed throughout the *Inferno* and the first 27 cantos of the *Purgatorio* by a combination of rhetorical cues with incident and conversational exchange. From their initial meeting in *Inferno* 1, Dante's attitude is consistently respectful; he speaks to Virgil as one does to a teacher and exemplar. Only when encouraged to do so, and even then sparingly, does Dante call Virgil "father." It is Virgil who, by speaking paternally and many times calling him "son," "figliuol," sets the verbal pattern. In Joyce's novel it is Bloom (unsought by Stephen) whose paternal actions set the pattern.

In the *Divine Comedy*, Dante's frugal applications of the word "padre" suggest its importance, particularly in the presence of a very large amount of paternal imagery spread throughout the *Divine Comedy*. The word is used 17 times in the *Inferno*, 20 in the *Purgatorio*, and 29 in the *Paradiso*. Dante applies the word to Guido Guinizelli, addressed as poetic father in *Purgatorio* 26; and he uses it in direct address to his own ancestor Cacciaguida, to Apollo, to St. Peter, and to St. Bernard.

Dante never addresses Virgil as "father" in the *Inferno*, and describes him thus only once. This is in Canto 8, where use of the word emphasizes and makes more real Dante's fear of the demons who are barring them from the gates of Dis. In Purgatory, the word suggests a growing self confidence; Dante addresses Virgil directly as "father" eight times, and he speaks more freely both to Virgil and in general. In Canto 4, as an exhausted Dante says that he can go no farther, it is "O dolce padre" and elsewhere it is the simpler "Padre," or "dolce padre mio," or "dolce padre caro" (*Purg.* 13:34; 15:25; 17:82; 23:13). It is not merely the use of the noun that sets the tone of their exchanges, but the addition of the tender "dolce" or "caro." Nine of the eleven occurrences of the word have this form, and in direct address the adjective is only once omitted. Dante's use of "figlio," of course, reinforces the image. With many additional locutions, the associations of "padre" are given to Virgil and other fathers as well, to represent the paternal bond.

Virgil is primarily the teacher and exemplar. He is directly Dante's teacher, as Dante makes clear in *Inferno* 1, but on the journey he becomes something more. He shows himself to be a knowledgeable guide, a powerful protector, and above all an exemplar. These are precisely the qualities that Bloom exhibits as he successfully guides Stephen out of the Circe episode. His Virgilian role is an indication that Bloom possesses qualities of inner strength that are developed and made apparent as the novel progresses. Joyce told Frank Budgen, "As the day wears on Bloom should overshadow them all," and referred to him as "a battery that is being recharged."

Virgil is a model of behavior for Dante, as well as a poetic figure whose *Aeneid* was, Dante says, his norm of artistic style. The term "padre," as applied to Virgil, seems to have been reserved by Dante to mark the stages in progress toward self-awareness as it develops in his association with Virgil. Dante develops a context, a constellation of attitudes and actions, that are "paternal" because they are the habitual actions of the natural father with a small helpless child. Virgil becomes a father figure because he acts like a natural father and also, of course, because Dante accepts his guidance. Stephen's acceptance of Bloom's guidance to Number Seven Eccles Street is Joyce's parallel, understated but adequate for the production of a significant echo.

At the beginning of the poem, Dante is fearful and indecisive, the figure of a personality in acute emotional crisis. The evocation of a paternal relationship comes in a dramatic context that is marked by Dante's display of fear. This happens five times, beginning dramatically in the second canto of the poem, when Dante's "fainting courage," "di mia virtute stanca," is restored by Virgil's vigorous admonition to be bold and free.

> Why then this hesitation and this pause?
>> and whence this shameful shrinking in your heart?
>> and why should courage now abandon you?
> Three ladies blessed in the court above
>> have care for you, and what I have set forth
>> is all a pledge and promise of your weal.
>
> Dunque: che è? perché, perché restai?
>> perché tanta viltà nel core allette?
>> perché ardire e franchezza non hai,
> poscia che tai tre donne benedette
>> curan di te ne la corte del cielo,
>> e'l mio parlar tanto ben ti promette?
>
> *(Inf.* 2:121-126, trans. Bergin)

Aeneas, father of Sylvius, and the meeting of Aeneas with Anchises, appear in Canto 2 as additional paternal images. Dante's fear returns again at the entrance to the city of Dis, when the Furies appear on the

walls and Virgil has to summon the Heavenly Messenger to get the
pilgrims through; when the Monster Geryon comes to transport the
travelers down to the Malebolge; when they are menaced by Malacoda's savage band of demons; and when the giant Antaeus bends down
to pick up the two little figures and lift them to the next level. The
rare times when Virgil carries Dante, "Come suo figlio, non come
compagno" (*Inf.* 23:49-51), are dramatically connected with Dante's
fear.

Often, however, the tone of Virgil's remarks to Dante is hortatory
or even chiding. Virgil exhorts him to courage, though not harshly,
and occasionally reproves his behavior. When Dante is lingering Virgil urges him to quicken his pace; when Dante asks too many questions Virgil suggests that this is an unconscious attempt to hold off
from a frightening descent into a dark chasm; when he is depressed at
the sad plight of a sinner, Virgil makes him acknowledge the right-
ness of Divine Justice; when Dante is fearful Virgil bids him be coura-
geous, "forte et ardito."

The appearance of the Virgilian Bloom begins at a specific moment
in the chapter called Oxen of the Sun, when Bloom first looks at Stephen with a paternal vision. Invited to sit down with the roistering
medical students, Bloom sits at the head of the table and thinks of his
own dead son and of Stephen, "his friend's son." Bloom wishes that
he might have a son like Stephen, "of such gentle courage (for all ac-
counted him of real parts)." Bloom is also sad to see Stephen wasting
his talent: "for that he lived riotously with those wastrels" (*U* 384:25-
30).

As these reflections continue, there follows a passage of dreamlike
visionary prose, a release from earthly connections, that invokes
"parallax" to invite an alteration in the angle of vision, and "metem-
psychosis" to suggest the reappearance of an individual soul in a
different human form, a new embodiment. This passage (*U* 407:36-
40) concludes with "currents of cold interstellar wind." This phrase
will come again as part of the description of the Virgilian Bloom when
the two have parted. It seems a rhetorical connection deliberately an-
nouncing the arrival of Virgil to guide a Dantesque Stephen.

Stephen Dedalus says, "There can be no reconciliation without a
sundering." The *Divine Comedy* brings Dante on stage when he is already in the full tide of dissociation: "so bitter was it that death is
scarcely more" (*Inf.* 1:7). The first appearance of the Dantesque
Stephen occurs at the end of the book's first chapter, with his remark,
"Now I eat his salt bread," and it is marked again, and more strongly,
by Stephen's silent thought of the opening line of the *Divine Comedy* in

the Library chapter. In *Ulysses*, Stephen as an artist shows greater potential than he had in *A Portrait of the Artist*, but he is also more menaced. Joyce's construction reminds us that the physical and material dangers Dante faced in his exile were less than the peril of shattered selfhood. When Stephen is described as "battling against hopelessness" (*U* 204:30), his predicament resembles Dante's in the Dark Wood, the "selva oscura," and "selva selvaggia" of *Inferno* 1. For this reason, Joyce puts the opening line of Dante's poem as a direct quotation, into Stephen's exposition of Shakespeare's *Hamlet* (*U* 204:33). It is also the reason, in the terms of the novel, why his effort to persuade his elders to accept his ideas about *Hamlet* must fail. Bloom and Stephen have not yet met. Before the arrival of the Virgilian Bloom, Joyce puts Stephen into the role of Dante *as he might have been before the appearance of Virgil* at line 63 of *Inferno* 1.

Joyce also gives Stephen a theory of artistic creation as a form of fatherhood. "To a son he speaks, the son of his soul, the prince, young Hamlet, and to the son of his body, Hamnet Shakespeare, who has died in Stratford that his namesake may live forever" (*U* 186). The presence of the artist in Dante's poem becomes part of the design of the Virgilian Bloom. Assigned by his author to this role, Bloom will follow and watch over Stephen in the pattern of Virgil responding to the call of Beatrice. The writing of Joyce's book thus becomes by analogy an act of filiation. The leavetaking of Stephen and Bloom also holds an analogous design, for it identifies a finality as marked as that which separates Joyce's age from Dante's. The impossibility of Orpheus's keeping Eurydice is a model for Bloom's inability to keep Stephen, as it was for Dante's inevitable parting from Virgil.

Joyce's Virgilian Bloom indicates how completely he had abandoned the nineteenth-century Romantic view of Dante which, in Joyce's youth, dominated English opinion of the poem. (As we shall see, Joyce's treatment of Brunetto is further evidence of a modern rather than Romantic reading of the canto.) Virgil and Beatrice were romantic figures to such nineteenth-century critics as John Addington Symonds; he describes them as flawed. His account of the Beatrice of *Purgatorio* 30, indeed, employs the same vocabulary that Joyce gives to Stephen Dedalus for the oblique comment on Dante in Stephen's diary at the end of *A Portrait of the Artist*. Symonds writes: "In the *Vita Nuova* she interests as a beautiful maiden, the 'youngest of the angels.' . . . But when she begins the sermon against Dante's sins (worthy of some Lady Ida before she felt the power of love), or when she is explaining the spots on the moon and smiling in sublime contempt of Dante's mortal grossness, our interest is considerably refrigerated."[14] This attitude, which should not be attributed to Joyce himself, seems to be echoed in Stephen's phrase, "the spiritual-heroic refrigerating apparatus invented and patented in all countries by Dante Alighieri" (*P* 252).

Symonds also fails to see Dante's affection for Virgil as a successful poetic element. "Dante dismisses Virgil with a facile tear," he writes, indignant that the poet has left "the good, the trusty Virgil eternally condemned to Limbo." The mixture of symbolism with reality Symonds saw as a flaw in the poetry and he found "both Virgil and Beatrice frigid as persons." His book was enormously popular and may very well have been seen by Joyce.

*

Fraudulent Fathers: Dante's Brunetto; Joyce's Wells,
Artifoni, Father Conmee

As Virgil is Dante's paramount image of the father figure, Brunetto Latini is the image equivocally drawn, a failed or fraudulent father whom Dante knew in the world and meets in *Inferno* 15. Joyce focused his mimetic reproduction of *Inferno* 15 on the central element of Brunetto's condemnation. Romantic criticism, taking a different line, concentrated wholly on Dante's expressed affection for Brunetto and the dismay with which that affection is expressed in the poem. This indicated a degree of confusion between the central matter of the canto and the dramatic detail of its presentation.

All of the *Inferno* is a tragic drama, but the only character in the poem who can be called a truly tragic figure is Virgil, the virtuous soul eternally excluded from Paradise through an accident of birth. Characters like Francesca, Ulysses, and Brunetto, as Joyce recognized, are not simply allegorical figures, but neither are they fully tragic figures, for their eternal state is represented most truly and completely as an embodiment of deliberate moral choice—the wrong choice. As Thomas M. Greene has shown, we see in these characters a "peculiar ontology," a selfconsciousness resulting from the perspective acquired through the dramatically dominant fact of death, from the soul's new "retrospective vision" and the divine judgment upon the former living self.[15] Such a conception of the *Inferno* is obviously present in Joyce's imitations—there are two of them—of Brunetto's canto. In *Stephen Hero* it is quite clear that Joyce read the *Comedy* from the perspective of a full understanding of Dante's moral scheme. He brought to his reading the perspective of his scholastic training, a rooted mediaeval pattern of thought that he shared with Dante. Joyce's selfconscious awareness of their common heritage accounts in part for the marked contrast between two Dantesque passages in *Stephen Hero*: the artistically immature blending of a mock hell and a mock heaven in the fantasied imitation of Dante by Stephen Daedalus in Chapter 22, and the achieved imitation, carefully wrought, of Brunetto's canto by the young Joyce in Chapter 18 (*SH* 158:25-159:11; *SH* 69-75).

In *Stephen Hero*, Joyce announced an intention: to imitate Dante's criticism of society. Arguing with the Jesuit rector of his college, Stephen Daedalus insists that it is in the tradition of the Catholic Church to examine corruption. "Why not for the poet too? Dante surely examines and upbraids society" (*SH* 92:05). This direct reference to Dante's censure of the simoniac clergy, along with the ensuing comments, constitute one of the five extended allusions to the *Divine Comedy* that reflect, in this fragment of a long manuscript, Joyce's early and concentrated, but immature, reading of Dante.[16]

In *Stephen Hero*, Stephen Daedalus makes a direct connection, never again made by Joyce inside or outside his fiction, between fraud in the mediaeval Church and the pious fraud of his Jesuit teachers and classmates. Stephen, as a student, is angry about the puritanical censorship with which the Jesuits control their young men. A clerical adviser is actively present at all the extracurricular meetings in the college. When Shakespeare is read in class the professor skips the bawdy songs. Stephen despises what he calls "the ugly artificiality of the lives over which Father Healy was comfortably presiding" (*SH* 28-29, 158:31). In Stephen's private thoughts he quotes Dante:

> He went on repeating to himself a line from Dante for no other reason except that it contained the angry dissyllable "frode." Surely, he thought, I have as much right to use the word [*i.e., frode,* trans. fraud] as ever Dante had. The spirits of Moynihan and O'Neill and Glynn seemed to him worthy of some blowing about round the verges of a hell which would be a caricature of Dante's. The spirits of the patriotic and religious enthusiasts seemed to him fit to inhabit the fraudulent circles where hidden in hives of immaculate ice they might work their bodies to the due pitch of frenzy. The spirits of the tame sodalists, unsullied and undeserving, he would petrify amid a ring of Jesuits in the circle of foolish and grotesque virginities and ascend above them and their baffled icons to where his Emma, with no detail of her earthly form or vesture abated, invoked him from a Mohammadan [*sic*] paradise. (*SH* 158-159)

Here, Stephen is thinking of *Inferno* 11 (lines 22-24), where Virgil explains to Dante that the circles of hell correspond to the seriousness of the sins punished. Virgil says, "because fraud is an evil peculiar to man, it more displeases God, and therefore the fraudulent are the lower, and more painfully punished."

This is a clear enough allusion to the *Divine Comedy*. But Joyce also makes Chapter 18 of this unfinished novel a silent imitation of *Inferno* 15. It is not Stephen Daedalus but Joyce who writes this chapter; and the object of Joyce's irony is not the little society of the College, but a larger target. The fraudulent aspect of the Irish clergy, as Joyce saw the matter, is set forth in a mimetic reproduction of one of Dante's paternal images, Brunetto Latini.

Here, in the positing of a Dantean sub-text, is the first clear-cut distinction between Stephen and his author. It is a dramatization, in which the absence of explicit mention of Dante is noteworthy especially because there are so many overt references elsewhere in the book. Joyce goes to the poetic center of the canto: to recognize what he has done it is necessary to identify the compositional patterns and the poetic maneuvers that make *Inferno* 15 what it is. The parallel is established in three principal elements, of which the first is an ambiguous portrait of a spiritual father; the second, a recognition scene, in which the protagonist meets an old acquaintance greatly changed; and third, a sequence of parallel details of naturalistic construction— the time of day, the scene and its characters, a pattern of continual movement with clear symbolic overtones, the content of the protagonists' conversation, and the distinctive ending of the episode.

Dante puts into hell his old teacher, Brunetto Latini, who is described with marked affection and sympathy as a spiritual father. "For in my memory warmly lingers on, / To move me still, your dear and kindly mien / Paternal, when in life you patiently / Taught me how men may cast beyond their time / The shadow of their labors; while I live / Your lessons shall my tongue commemorate" (*Inf.* 15:82-87, trans. Bergin). Elsewhere in the *Inferno* Dante sometimes displays an evident sympathy and even identification with the people he meets, but he makes no overt statement matching the warmth of this one. The situation is equivocal in many ways. But there is no ambiguity at all in the portrait of Brunetto as a fully individualized paternal figure, even though condemned for eternity, to whom Dante has the deep attachment of a spiritual son.

For his spiritual father Joyce chose, instead of a teacher, a parish priest. The equivalent of Brunetto is Wells, a young man who is preparing for the priesthood, by which he will become a spiritual father.

The Catholic priest is traditionally addressed by this title, and in Joyce's Ireland with its legacy of oppressive poverty the rural parish priest was historically a benign and fatherly figure. But in Joyce's chapter, Wells sees the priesthood as his best road to an easy life. He is thus marked as a simoniac, a fraudulent father. "Stephen felt indignant that anyone should expect him to entrust spiritual difficulties to such a confessor" (*SH* 73:30). This comment is clearly a reference to Wells's approaching ordination, and specifically to the sacrament of penance (the rite of Confession) in which the penitent begins by addressing the priest with the words, "Bless me, father, for I have sinned."

Wells is a student at Clonliffe Seminary: this reminds us that all the characters in *Inferno* 15 are tonsured clerics. Stephen had known Wells at Clongowes Wood School. In *A Portrait of the Artist* he appears as the school bully, the boy who pushed six-year-old Stephen into the ditch. His conversation shows that he has not changed. As a priest he will be a blustering tyrant, and it is this quality combined with fraudulence that rouses Stephen's indignation. Joyce, as Ellmann comments, made a complicated chain of association that linked schoolboy bullying with homosexuality (*Letters* II: 199 n. 3). Undoubtedly something of this pattern is responsible for his impulse to put Wells into Dante's canto of the sodomites. His skill in creating the parody, however, reveals as well a larger understanding of Dante's Brunetto. Joyce suggests the original relationship only in potential and sets it in an entirely new environment, yet he preserves the moral focus of falseness to a spiritual trusteeship.

Stephen's encounter with Wells, and their mutual recognition, is composed in the terms that Dante uses. Dante says that he "was recognized by one who took me by the skirt and said, 'What a wonder!' " Stephen, in the narrator's words, is "very much surprised" when he feels his arm seized from behind (*SH* 70; *Inf.* 15:23-24). Both texts convey the same sensation of shock and unreality that accompanies unexpected recognition of an old acquaintance greatly changed. Stephen "stared for a few moments, trying to recall the face," while Dante says, "when he [Brunetto] stretched out his arm to me, fixing my eyes on his burned face so that the scorching of his visage hindered not my mind from recognition" (*SH* 70; *Inf.* 15:25-28). In both cases it is the change in face that is emphasized. Stephen "saw a tall young man with many eruptions on his face," and finally says that he would not have known Wells, he has so much changed.

Brunetto appeals to Dante to walk with him, saying, "O my son! if it does not displease thee, let Brunetto Latini turn back with thee a little." Stephen, on the contrary, is distressed by Wells's interruption, for Stephen has gone walking to think through a problem. But when Wells says, "See me down a bit of the way, will you?" Stephen replies, "Certainly." Then the two young men, in the manner of Dante and Brunetto, walk on together (*SH* 71; *Inf.* 15:40-43).

Joyce recognized and used the ambiguities of Dante's canto. Why does Dante put Brunetto in hell? He cites no evidence, and historically there is none, that Brunetto was guilty of the sin that condemns him to this circle, which is the fiery desert of the sodomites. The ambiguity concerns identification of the sin of Brunetto and the other personages—all of them scholars, clerics, notable men of letters—whom he identifies for Virgil and Dante. As Richard Kay notes, Dante registers shocked surprise at finding his admired mentor in this circle of hell. But if Dante the pilgrim and friend of Brunetto did know of Brunetto's guilt then the note of surprise is uncalled for; while if Dante the poet and author of the canto did not know of this circumstance, then he has unjustly libeled the man whom he professes to admire.[17]

Brunetto, although not false to Dante, is represented as having betrayed the spiritual trusteeship of a teacher. Joyce reproduces this effect by making Wells a clearly fraudulent father-figure, far more so than Brunetto. The character of Wells was presumably established in the early chapters of *Stephen Hero* which were lost or destroyed, using approximately the same particulars that Joyce later put into the Clongowes episodes of *A Portrait of the Artist*. In Chapter 18 the older Wells is described as loudmouthed and "blatant," a vulgarian. Joyce of course is suggesting that Wells is representative of the Irish seminarians, with an irony that extends also to what Stephen calls the "repressive enforcement of a creed." Through Stephen's reaction to Wells, Joyce is able to suggest that the Irish Church has deprived its candidates for the priesthood of the capacity for moral leadership, in the wasting away of free will. This is the key to Joyce's use of the Brunetto parallel.

Joyce's chapter and Dante's Canto 15 both begin with a pattern of continuous movement. But perambulation is more than just a mechanism for bringing together the two principal figures. Dante describes another and a more hellish kind of change of place. The unremittent movement of the Brunetto episode portrays the souls as walking fast without ever stopping because they are on a fiery desert, moving along under a rain of flakes of fire. It is explained that any who stop for one instant are condemned thereby to lie a hundred years immobilized, unable even to fan themselves under the fiery rain.[18] This restless, meaningless change of place is reproduced in Joyce's chapter, where all the seminarians are in constant motion, walking about the grounds in small groups. Another kind of resemblance of the seminarians to the sinners of *Inferno* 15 is indicated in the way that the seminarians hold up their soutanes (the long black tunic, or cassock, worn by Catholic priests), "as women do with their skirts." Joyce repeats the sense of this phrase more explicitly in a later chapter of *Stephen Hero*, when one of the priests is described as gathering up his soutane "with a slow hermaphroditic gesture" (*SH* 72:28; 75:13; 98:15; *P* 154-155; *P* 199:19). The implication is that the seminarians have given up their manhood in giving up their moral freedom.

Brunetto is imprisoned eternally in a fixed repetitive pattern, with naturalistic details that mark Joyce's imitation by their reproduction in *Stephen Hero*. The time in both works is evening, which in *Inferno* 15 is an impression of gathering darkness. Dante's hell is smoky and dusky. This effect is reinforced by the poet's imagery when he compares the spirits' sidelong glances at Virgil and himself with the glances of men in the evening under a new moon—they look from one to another and squint in the half-light, "as an aged tailor does at the eye of his needle" (*Inf.* 15:19-21). The fiery rain is matched by actual rain in Joyce's chapter, where murkiness is suggested by phrases, too often repeated to be merely casual, such as "uncertain light," "rather dark," and "faint daylight" (*SH* 72, 73; *Inf.* 15:2-3; 18-21).

Minor descriptive effects reinforce the likeness to Dante's canto. The reiterated "little band of students," and "vagrant bands of students" suggests Dante's "troop of spirits who were coming alongside the bank" (*SH* 72, 73, 74; *Inf.* 15:16). To this is added the detail of a side-alley where students are playing handball "against the concrete wall." This concrete alley, which serves no purpose in the chapter, recalls the "hard margins" of the opening lines of *Inferno* 15, which Dante describes as resembling the walls that Italian towns have built to hold back a river or the sea. Joyce's concrete wall of the alley imitates Dante's stony banks as the latter are themselves said to resemble the dykes of the Paduans and the Flemings (*SH* 72:25; *Inf.* 15:11-12). The accumulation of suggestive detail, though individually trivial, announces the presence of correspondences between Joyce's chapter and Dante's canto.

The sense of compulsion and restricted freedom thus becomes a Joycean image of hell through the suggestion of spiritual confinement. Some of this comes from the physical description of the seminary as an "ecclesiastical barracks," and again the prison-like effect of "a big square block of masonry looming . . . through the faint daylight." But Joyce's real indictment is principally contained in the portrayal, through the conversation of Wells and Stephen, of the "iron hand," as the chapter calls it, of the Church's discipline over its members' minds. Joyce makes the content of their conversation follow the design in Dante's canto. It recalls the past the protagonists have shared, and it also markedly emphasizes the difference in their futures.

Dante and Brunetto have a long colloquy, in which Brunetto first indicates that "in the fair life" above he had recognized Dante's talent and that if he had not been cut off by death, "dato t'avrei a l'opera conforto," "I would have brought you comfort in your toil" (*Inf.* 15:60). Brunetto prophetically reveals that his former pupil will be sought by both warring factions of Florence and will receive great honors but he will also be envied and maligned for his good deeds. Dante listens and responds, all the while walking (he is above Brunetto) in an attitude of respect, his head bent "com' uom che reverente vada," "like a man walking in reverence"[19] (*Inf.* 15:45).

The content of the colloquy of the reunited protagonists is similar in both episodes. Wells begins, "Well, and what have you been doing with yourself?" while Brunetto asks Dante, "What chance, or destiny, brings thee, ere thy last day, down here?" (*SH* 71; *Inf.* 15:46-47). Brunetto speaks admiringly of Dante's work and says that if he follows his star he cannot fail to reach a glorious haven. Wells says that he has heard that Stephen is going in for literature and prophesies fame for him—"When you're a great writer yourself—as the author of a second *Trilby* or something of that sort," a sharply ironic echo of Brunetto's prophetic remarks about Dante's future (*SH* 72; *Inf.* 15:55-60). Brunetto has no future, while Dante does have, and this component of the Dantesque portrayal is reflected in *Stephen Hero* by Wells' references to the discipline and intellectual limitations of the seminarians' life (*SH* 72:2, 7-8, 10; *Inf.* 15:41-42). Wells, again like Brunetto, is aware of his loss of freedom. He is even vaguely resentful, but he has a careerist view of the matter and looks forward to a comfortable living.

Finally, the distinctive ending of Dante's canto is preserved by Joyce. Brunetto says, "I would say more, but my going and my speech must not be longer," and then he runs off literally at top speed. "Then he turned back and seemed like one of those who run for the green cloth at Verona through the open fields; and of them, seemed he who wins, not he who loses" (*Inf.* 15:121-124). In Joyce's reconstruction a similar sense of compulsion and confinement is established by shutting the gates of the great wall around the seminary grounds so that Stephen must exit through a little side door. Here, Wells "looked out for a second or two almost enviously," and then said: "I must run. Goodbye." That last envious look outward reproduces the effect on the reader that comes from Dante's account of Brunetto's last look at the world, when he asks Dante to commend his book, *Il Tesoro* "in which I still live" (*Inf.* 15:119-120; *SH* 75:8-11), and the extended analogy of Wells to Brunetto Latini culminates in a reference to running. In the last lines of the chapter, the last view of Wells, the seminarian "tucked up his soutane high and ran awkwardly up the drive . . . he looked a strange, almost criminal fugitive in the dreary dusk. Stephen's eyes followed the running figure for a moment: and as he passed through the door into the lamplit street he smiled at his own impulse of pity." The ending of Dante's canto has been reproduced in the running figure and in the characterization, "a strange almost criminal fugitive." The reader of *Inferno* 15 also sees Dante in that closing scene, speaking as pilgrim and as author, watching and appraising, and Joyce's parallel becomes complete with Stephen's following gaze and impulse of pity.

*

In *Ulysses*, two father-figures are associated with Brunetto Latini. One is John Eglinton, editor of a Dublin journal; the other is Almidano Artifoni, Stephen's singing teacher. They appear in different chapters and the first reference to Brunetto is by name with a quotation from his book, the *Tresor*. Addressed directly, he is brought back to life in twentieth century Dublin. The second reference is another concealed imitation of *Inferno* 15. Both the historical and the fictional Brunetto are summoned to a new existence in Joyce's novel.

The first mention of Brunetto is in the Library chapter (Scylla and Charybdis), where Stephen is talking to three elders of the Dublin literary establishment. John Eglinton, the editor, has callously announced a forthcoming volume of work by the young poets of Dublin: Stephen is left out. It is in Stephen's private thoughts that John Eglinton is associated with the chief personage of *Inferno* 15, and silently Stephen also has the related thought, "Love that dare not speak its name" (*U* 199:42). Stephen thinks of the editor as a basilisk, using terms borrowed from Brunetto's book, following out the touching request to Dante in *Inferno* 15 that the *Tresor*, "in which I still live," not be forgotten. Stephen recalls Brunetto's line in Italian, "E quando vede l'uomo l'atosca," actually a paraphrase that supplies him with a cruel description of the obtuse editor, "miscreant eyes glinting stern under wrinkled brows," and he says to himself, "Messer Brunetto, I thank thee for the word" (*U* 192:11).[20] Brunetto is recalled from *Inferno* 15 by quotation and by name; Stephen, like Glendower, can call spirits from the vasty deep.

Once again Joyce is paying off old scores. He obviously realized that Wells was too weak a figure to match Dante's Brunetto. The real life model for John Eglinton was a stronger enemy figure. He is in *Ulysses* under his own status and established pseudonym, the editor of *Dana* who rejected James Joyce's very first version of *A Portrait of the Artist*—an essay with that title written in 1904.

The model for the concealed Brunetto figure in *Ulysses* was also a stronger and more believable father image. Joyce's real life Italian teacher becomes Stephen's singing teacher, Almidano Artifoni, in the Wandering Rocks chapter. Stephen meets this man very briefly, on the street in front of Trinity College, not far from the Library. Artifoni's name and occupation make it plausible to have the conversation in Italian—not such a simple matter in a novel about Dublin. Italian is carefully used in *Ulysses*, and except for this episode Stephen speaks Italian only in connection with the *Divine Comedy*. Moreover, *only* Stephen Dedalus is allowed to quote the *Divine Comedy* in the original.

Artifoni is a fully sympathetic figure, like Brunetto, recalling the lines from Canto 15, "When in the world, hour by hour, you taught me how man makes himself eternal." This aspect of the character comes from the real life model. Joyce's Italian teacher at University College was a young Jesuit from Bergamo, Father Charles Ghezzi, with whom Joyce undertook his first serious reading of Dante. Ghezzi is in Joyce's other novels, with the same physical characteristics but with the name or the role changed: in all cases he is a re-creation from life.

In *Ulysses*, Artifoni is a precursor of Leopold Bloom: these are the only two personages in the book who have a sympathetic understanding of Stephen's predicament. Here again Artifoni resembles Brunetto, who is a precursor of a strong and quite unequivocal father figure, Cacciaguida. As a structural element in Joyce's novel, the Artifoni episode shows Joyce's perception of the strategic placement by Dante of his two most important fathers, Brunetto and Cacciaguida, at the structural center of the *Inferno* and the *Paradiso* respectively, both making prophetic comments about Dante's future.

Observe how Joyce ties this little episode to the Eglinton episode in the preceding chapter by the use of "eyes." Stephen has told Artifoni something related to the events in the Library chapter—not what happened, but his reaction to the rejection. This sets up a contrast: the negative father image in John Eglinton, the affirmative image in Artifoni.

The scene opens with Artifoni's exclamation of sympathy: "Ma!" After a few words of conversation, he says again, "Ma, sul serio, eh?" and then the narrator says: "His heavy hand took Stephen's firmly. Human eyes. They gazed curiously an instant" (*U* 225). Artifoni's eyes are "human" eyes, in contrast to John Eglinton's "basilisk" eyes. There is also another echo of the *Divine Comedy*. In the Library chapter the narrator's voice describes Stephen as "battling against hopelessness," at the moment when, trying to get a hearing from the Dublin literary establishment, a direct quotation from the *Divine Comedy* comes into his mind. This is the only time he says one aloud, and it is the first line of the *Inferno*, "nel mezzo del cammin di nostra vita," recalling the moment of Dante's despair to match Stephen's battle against hopelessness.

The rest of the episode reproduces the naturalistic detail of *Inferno* 15. The conversation is ambiguous. Artifoni reminds Stephen that he has a fine voice, a talent that should not be sacrificed, an echo of Brunetto's statement that Dante's talents should command good fortune in his future life despite his enemies (*U* 225:24-25; *Inf*. 15:55-57; 70). Brunetto's advice, "Let the beasts of Fiesole make litter of themselves" ["Faccian le bestie fiesolane strame / di lor medesme . . ." (*Inf*. 15:73-74)], is echoed in Artifoni's comment that in his youth he too felt that the world was beastly: "Eppoi mi sono convinto che il monde è una bestia" (*Inf*. 15:73-74; *U* 225:15-20). The Italian word "bestia" ties these passages together. The brief episode ends exactly as *Inferno* 15 ends, and also the 18th chapter of *Stephen Hero*: Artifoni is running, "In vain he trotted, signalling [to a tram] in vain" (*U* 225-226), as Brunetto runs off in *Inferno* 15, and as Wells runs up the driveway of the seminary. Artifoni is the last person seen in the chapter, as an ironic and mockingly obscene gesture to the Lord Lieutenant's parade: "the salute of Almidano Artifoni's sturdy trousers swallowed by a closing door" (*U* 251:18-19).

*

Joyce initially wanted to associate Dante's *Inferno* 15 with an attack on the worldly materialism of the Irish clergy, but by the time he came to write *Ulysses*, his perception of the canto's contrasts led him toward a more detached view and a different compositional decision. He apparently concluded that his anticlerical polemic would be stronger if it were not directly given the associations of *Inferno* 15. He kept a strong and attractive clerical personality as his target, however, and kept the association with the *Divine Comedy* by showing this false spiritual father in a telling reference to another canto, *Inferno* 10. The chosen target is Father Conmee, whose story has pride of place as the open-ing episode of the Wandering Rocks chapter.[21]

Joyce's account of the simoniac Irish clergy in the eighteenth chap-ter of *Stephen Hero* represents them as false to their spiritual trustee-ship. It is an indictment of the failure of the seminaries, preparing young men for the priesthood, to inculcate spiritual values. Wells, the young man at the center of the chapter, is a careerist, a materialist, a pragmatist; Joyce is suggesting that young Irishmen were encouraged to seek the priesthood for the status and power it offered. There is a good deal of historical reality behind this. For two hundred years and more, under the penal laws, the seminary was indeed the only pro-fessional education available to Irish boys. William Carleton's stories of the hedge schools, and especially his story of Denis O'Shaughnessy going to Maynooth Seminary, are a vivid portrayal of the long road the Irish Catholic population had to travel to reach the level of an es-tablished middle class.[22]

By Joyce's day, this long association of the clergy with the move-ment upward from helotism had created a solid institutional basis for the Irish Church—large and devoted parish congregations, a disci-plined hierarchy, schools, seminaries, and the Catholic branches of the Royal University, including University College in Dublin (Joyce's College), which was taken over by the Jesuits in 1883. The Jesuits of Joyce's day saw their functions, at least in part, as the education and social training of a Catholic elite that would be prepared to exercise power on equal terms with the Protestant Anglo-Irish ruling caste, and to take the reins when Irish independence was achieved.[23]

Although this posture had a rational basis, with Joyce it was also a temperamental matter. Joyce's attitude is reminiscent, perhaps, of Dante's absolute exclusion from the *Divine Comedy* of any approval, any suggestion that positive values might result from the rise in Flor-ence of the bourgeoisie—the merchants and traders who were mak-ing the city prosperous and powerful, but whom Dante despised. Joyce, to the extent that specific political ideas can be found in his writings, can fairly be described as opposing altogether the enlarge-ment of temporal power in the Church. In this he resembles Dante. In a notebook Joyce kept in 1905, in Pola, while he was preparing to write the book that became *A Portrait*, his jottings included the isolated phrases, "Spiritual and temporal power," "Priests and police in Ire-land."[24] Both Dante and Joyce no doubt took a one-sided view of the politics of their time and their city. This strengthened the poetry, whatever one may think of the accuracy of their estimate of historical events. Joyce's charge that the Irish Church was more interested in worldly than in spiritual matters, and even that the clergy were prepared to use their spiritual authority for the temporal goals of power, was an adequate parallel to Dante's indictment of the clerics of his day, an indictment that extended all the way up to the Papacy.[25]

Joyce, by the time he came to write *Ulysses*, was ready for a more subtle portrait of the clerical figure as fraudulent spiritual father. This is the role he assigned to Father Conmee in Wandering Rocks. In the choice of this real life model—a cultivated, gifted, and amiable man—Joyce also took account of the rising currents of liberal humanism, knowing as he did that the Church's strength has always been in its adaptability to change, but he attacked the pragmatic humanism that showed itself willing to exchange spiritual values for political power and social snobbery.

Between the "first draft" and the final version of *A Portrait*, and between his early books and *Ulysses*, Joyce's imitation of Dante became not only more subtle in its literary aspects but more pointed in social criticism and more humane in viewpoint. As his transformations of the *Divine Comedy* submerged into his fiction, Joyce continued to make open references to Dante, but all traces of overt didacticism vanished. By the time Joyce wrote *Ulysses*, his borrowings, although more numerous, were also better concealed. In particular, Joyce redrew and elaborated his portrait of the fraudulent spiritual father and pulled together all the threads of his indictment of the Irish Church.

In the Wandering Rocks chapter of *Ulysses* Joyce gives a full portrayal of the false father as a worldly and influential priest, a construction allusively though briefly connected with the *Divine Comedy*. The priest is Father Conmee. The Dantesque allusion is not found in Wandering Rocks but much later in the book, in the Circe episode, and it is a precise visual recall of *Inferno* 10:32-33, presented as a hallucination of Stephen's.

Father Conmee and Father Dolan rise from coffin-like structures as the two fathers of *Inferno* 10, Farinata and Cavalcante, rise up from the fiery tombs of the Epicureans. Father Dolan is a comic figure: "Twice loudly a pandybat cracks, the coffin of the pianola flies open, the bald little round jack-in-the-box head of Father Dolan springs up." Father Conmee, on the other hand, "Mild, rectorial, reproving . . . rises from the pianola coffin," very much as the shade of Farinata rises up and with a similar dignity. Father Dolan's plight has nothing to do with Cavalcante but comes from Joyce's opposition to corporal punishment for children. For the fictional Father Conmee there are much more complicated reasons behind the use of Dante's image, for Joyce took Conmee out of his teaching role to make him a figure of unfaithful stewardship.

Dante's two fathers are Cavalcante, father of Dante's friend Guido, and Farinata, the Ghibelline Captain whose forces expelled Dante's ancestors from Florence. Farinata was later condemned as a heretic (the Epicurean heresy), and very likely unjustly condemned by his political enemies. Dante nevertheless selects that official condemnation, out of all the matter of Farinata's earthly life, as the basis for putting him in hell. He is also the father-in-law of Dante's best friend, the poet Guido, whose own father is in the adjoining tomb. The Cavalcanti family were Guelphs: the marriage of Farinata's daughter was an event in the brief policy of armistice between the warring factions, when matrimonial alliances were encouraged in an attempt to bring peace to Florence.

Hearing Dante's voice, Cavalcante rises to his knees in the fiery tomb that imprisons him; "piangendo," weeping, he asks why his son is not with Dante, as he was in the upper world. Dante's reply uses the past tense: in tones of heightened anguish, Cavalcante rises "subito," instantly erect, and cries, "What are you saying? lives he no longer?" ("non viv' elli ancora?") "do his eyes no longer see the sweet light?" ("non fiere li occhi suoi lo dolce lume?") (*Inf.* 10:68-69). Farinata, however, stands erect and challenges Dante so coldly that his pride "seems to hold even hell in disdain."

The encounter with these two fathers forms a continuous and discrete episode, which was given a classic analysis by Auerbach.[26] Cavalcante interrupts Dante's reply to Farinata; when Cavalcante falls back into his tomb, Farinata continues his sentence without taking notice of the interruption; and when Farinata has finished, Dante asks him to tell Cavalcante that his son Guido is indeed still alive (thus still capable of being saved).

Joyce's attention to the artistry of the little drama is suggested by an entry in his Trieste Notebook.[27] Under the heading, "cavalcanti (Guido)," Joyce wrote, "His father . . . asks Dante where he is (Inf. cant. X) Dante hesitates before he replies." The rest of the entry suggests that Joyce followed up his reading with a little investigation into the life of Guido, for there follows a brief note on Boccaccio's story. Joyce allows Stephen to recall these details in the Proteus chapter of *Ulysses*, as a silent comparison between Guido's retort to the baiting of his friends, and Stephen's reactions earlier that morning under the attack of the "usurpers" Mulligan and Haines. "The couriers who mocked Guido in Or san Michele were in their own house," Stephen thinks. Mulligan, as one of a brood of mockers, a gay betrayer of Irish Catholicism, is a figure of the Establishment, the Irish ruling class, while Haines is a representative—harmless, to be sure—of the English oppressors; both are interested in Stephen for what they can get out of him. "In their own house" is an intimation of the Martello Tower, for which Stephen has paid the rent, but it carries a larger sense of Catholic Ireland as Stephen's house. The young poet now thinks of himself in Dante's words, "Now I eat his salt bread," as an exile (*Par.* 17:58-59). The reference to Guido in Proteus thus connects Stephen Dedalus indirectly with Dante's *Inferno* 10, and in Circe the connection is made directly with *Inferno* 10 and with Father Conmee. What warrant has Joyce for this apparent placement of Father Conmee in hell?

In Wandering Rocks, Father Conmee's itinerary across Dublin is matched by the itinerary of the Viceregal cavalcade.[28] Though their paths seem to cross, because of the complexities of the text, in fact they do not; but each is "saluted" (a term used 17 times) by a carefully selected group of Dubliners, who in theory are showing respectful homage and receiving in return a courteous recognition in feudal fashion. With these reminders of old ceremonials, Joyce comments ironically on the contemporary condition of the institutions of secular and ecclesiastical power in Dublin.

But the opening section of the chapter has another dimension that can only be called a spiritual structure, for the progress of Father Conmee and the people he meets form a running commentary on his personal exercise of the priestly office. The little narrative takes its shape from the Divine Office, the seven canonical "Hours" that every priest is required to recite every day, some lines from which are quoted as the section ends. In doing this, Joyce follows Dante's use of the Office of Complin in another episode, in which the negative image of the father surrogate is shown. In the beautiful valley of *Purgatorio* 8, Virgil and Dante hear the hymn, *Te lucis ante*, which is invariably sung at Complin, the Office recited at sunset. The souls of *Purgatorio* 8, the negligent rulers (who were thus not truly fathers to the people they ruled) are still able to expiate their sins. But Father Conmee will be shown in his last appearance in the book in one of the striking images of the *Inferno*, symbolically condemned.

The Dantesque elements of Joyce's version begin with the narrative aspect, for the story is told by an impersonal voice and by Father Conmee himself through his private thoughts. Like so many of Dante's fictions, it deals with matters the truth of which can be known only to the individual and his Creator. The choice of a strong individual with appealing personal qualities to represent a spiritual father false to his trust goes to the heart of Dante's construction in *Inferno* 15. A lesser figure than Conmee would not be a believable symbol of the authority of the Irish Church. The moral dimensions of Joyce's episode even go some way beyond Dante's *Inferno* 15; for Brunetto's sin no evidence is given, but Joyce's Conmee stands condemned by his own standards and in his own thoughts.

Father Conmee is walking through the northern part of Dublin: "He smiled and nodded and smiled and walked." Motion in the *Commedia* in general is an indication of moral state; the condition of the damned is an absence of motion, which becomes more marked as the pilgrim goes deeper into the realm of evil. Twice, however, the pattern of punishment is one of unremittent motion: in *Inferno* 5, the souls are ceaselessly whirled on the whirlwind of unchecked carnal desire; in *Inferno* 15, the canto of the sodomites, the souls must run unceasingly under a rain of fire. These are the two cantos in which Dante has placed his most ambiguous portraits, Francesca and Brunetto.[29] In Father Conmee's episode the reiterated emphasis on movement may reflect Joyce's observation of Dante's pattern in *Inferno* 15.

Near the end of his walk Father Conmee begins to read his breviary; it is late in the day, and he is reading the "Little Hours," which includes the Psalm "Beati immaculati." The act of walking becomes a reflection of the Divine Office as, in the Psalm, it is a symbol of man's passage through life.[30] The theme of "Beati immaculati" is the path, the way, the Latin "via": "Blessed are the undefiled in the way, who walk in the law of the Lord." ("Beati immaculati in via, qui ambulant in lege Domini.") As Father Conmee proceeds along his walk, it becomes clear that he is not one of those who "walk in the way of the Lord." It is the breviary that convicts him.

In Joyce's time every religious, whether conventual or one of the secular clergy, recited the Divine Office every day, from his breviary. "Father Conmee took his rededged breviary out. An ivory bookmark told him the page." This exercise amounts to a daily dramatic recital (if the Office is not chanted communally, it is supposed to be read half-aloud) that keeps before the mind of the religious the best poetry in the Catholic liturgy as well as the Church's continuity of tradition in moral theology. It is a compendium of psalms (so arranged that in the course of a week all the psalms are recited), hymns, canticles, hagiographic fragments, biblical texts, homilies and prayers, much of which reflects the historical development of the Catholic liturgy. Reading the breviary is not unlike a continuous re-reading of Dante's poetry, and indeed this comparison has often been made. But it was emphatically not a literary exercise. Recitation of the Divine Office was obligatory on all ministers of the Church in major Orders. Every candidate for the priesthood, particularly in the Irish seminaries, received instruction in the history and moral significance of the bre-viary.[31]

Father Conmee would be reminded of his priestly charge every day of his life, as he read the first psalm with which the daily Office invari-ably opens: "Beatus vir qui non abiit in consilio impiorum; et in via peccatorum non stetit; et in cathedra pestilentiae non sedit." ("Blessed is the man that walketh not in the counsel of the ungodly, nor stand-eth in the way of sinners, nor sitteth in the seat of the scornful.") The triple negative is a special charge on the man called to the sacred office of the priesthood, for at his ordination this man receives the unique power to dispense the treasure of Divine grace.

The meaning of this admonition is avoidance of the habits of worldliness, and the triple negative is followed by a triple exhortation to seek the higher spiritual aspirations. Thus the devout ecclesiastic in Holy Orders is required to remind himself daily that he must not busy himself with purely temporal concerns, secular friendships and diversions; that he must not consort with those who lack piety; that he must not by example make a mockery of virtue that will scandalize the weak and corrupt the young.

Father Conmee's progress across Dublin, his encounters and salu-tations, have been carefully selected and placed to show him in vio-lation of this crucial admonition. He is a figure of the career priest, shown at a moment when his efforts have brought him power in the political affairs of city and state, recognition and influence in his Or-der, and comfort amounting to luxury in his personal life. The posi-tion he holds is strategic; he is Father Superior ("The Superior, the Very Reverend John Conmee, S.J.") of the presbytery (that is, the res-idence of a group of priests), of the Jesuit house in upper Gardiner Street, attached to the parish Church of St. Francis Xavier. His power is announced by his introduction under this formal title.

On this 16th of June he is going to Artane, a region in north-east Dublin, where there is an industrial school for boys; his objective is an interview seeking a place in the school for young Patrick Aloysius Dignam, whose father's funeral took place that morning. Thus Father Conmee is emphatically seen as a father figure, assisting an orphan in the traditional role of his church as father of the fatherless. But the priest's private thoughts reveal more complex motivation, foremost in which as a crucial element is the extension of his personal political in-fluence. Martin Cunningham has asked Conmee to secure this place for the Dignam boy, as a personal favor; the good Jesuit will "oblige him" if he can. "Good practical catholic: useful at mission time" (*U* 216:6-7). Both lay Catholics and clergy are a part of his apparatus of power. Father Conmee's concern for "mission time," for example, indicates his grasp of a complex phenomenon: the way the clergy secure the church's secular power (and incidentally the individual cleric's route to promotion in the hierarchy) by building up their congregations for practical as well as for spiritual reasons. Conmee has made an alliance, which is in effect political, with Martin Cunningham, who is a minor functionary at "The Castle," the seat of British Government. Martin Cunningham is a good "practical" Catholic who will see that his friends turn up to swell the congregation at the three-day "mission" service at which special collections are taken up for the causes sponsored by the bishops and the Pope. Conmee, like any other sensible parish priest, will seek out the most popular preacher he can find for the mission. The one he chooses, Father Bernard Vaughan, is described in Wandering Rocks as a mission preacher of "very great success." Father Conmee dislikes his colleague's cockney voice and his vulgarising of the New Testament, but the crowds love Vaughan's preaching.

The larger political objective, establishment of a Catholic ruling elite in Ireland, is quietly indicated by the author's demonstration that Father Conmee meets and converses on equal social terms with the wife of David Sheehy M.P., whose sons are at Belvedere, the Jesuit school in Dublin. The two talk about Conmee's vacation plans, and he is cordially invited to call on the Sheehys.

Some of this is harmless vanity; his action that afternoon is clearly charitable; where is the harm, the evil? Here is found Joyce's imitation of Dante's *Inferno*. In Francesca, Farinata, Ulysses, Brunetto and lesser figures, Dante shows that evil is a complicated matter, not easily recognized, often attractive, and even mingled with good. But Dante's characters in the *Inferno* do not stand each of them alone; they form a pattern. Similarly Father Conmee has a place in a larger pattern, most carefully worked out in *Ulysses* but present in all Joyce's works, which condemns as simoniacal the Irish clerics' use of the instruments of Divine Grace for worldly ends—whether their own personal ends, or some larger institutional purpose. This was Dante's viewpoint also, and it received a far more powerful expression by attachment in a fictional context to a real historical figure. Joyce reduces the Dantean pattern in *Ulysses* to a least common denominator, dealing with ward politicians rather than with the thrones and empires of Dante's day.

The cadences of Father Conmee's episode are the rhythms and intonations of the psalter. Sentences are short, and are joined in units of two or three so that an antiphonal effect is produced.

> Near Aldborough house Father Conmee thought of that spend-
> thrift nobelman. And now it was an office or something.
>
> Father Conmee smelled incense on his right hand as he walked.
> Saint Joseph's church, Portland row. For aged and virtuous females.
> Father Conmee raised his hat to the Blessed Sacrament. Virtuous:
> but occasionally they were also bad-tempered. (*U* 218:6-12)

Two quotations from Psalm 118 are made to form part of Conmee's
reading. One is verse 160, the other verse 161. Psalm 118 is very long,
and is thus divided among the four parts of the "Little Hours," prime,
terce, sext and none. It moves in sections of five or six verses, each
with a letter of the Hebrew alphabet; verse 160 is the last verse of
"Res," and verse 161 is the first verse of "Sin." Joyce puns on this letter, making the last event on Father Conmee's walk the sight of a
"flushed young man" and a young woman emerging from a hedge.
Father Conmee "blessed both gravely," making the description correspond to verse 158 of the Psalm: "I beheld the transgressors and was
grieved; because they kept not thy word." ("Vide praevaericantes, et
tabescebam; quia eloquia tua non custodierunt.") The last verse of the
psalm is also echoed: "I have gone astray like a lost sheep" (*Tau*: v.
176) in the sight of the "muttoning clouds over Rathcoffey." "The sky
showed him a flock of small white clouds going slowly down the wind.
Moutonner, the French said, a homely and just word" (*U* 220-221).

The combination of soliloquy with antiphonal cadences gives this
episode a style quite different from the other episodes in Wandering
Rocks. Joyce laid out a walk for Father Conmee that would make a
dramatic scene out of the admonitions of Psalm 118, by the author's
selection of Dublin citizens to be met and greeted by Conmee. This
urbane and worldly Jesuit is the bad shepherd of *Purgatorio* 16, "il
pastor," who knows and professes the letter of the law of God—
Conmee reading his breviary—but who disregards the welfare of his
flock, his spiritual charges. Joyce has made his construction an extended image of Dante's faithless shepherd; later, he echoes Dante's
enigmatic phrase in *Finnegans Wake*, "Who wants to cheat the choker's
got to learn to chew the cud" (*FW* 278:03).

> Laws there are, but who puts his hand to them? None, because the
> shepherd that leads may chew the cud but has not the hoofs di-
> vided. Wherefore the people, who see their guide snatch only at
> that good whereof they are greedy, feed upon that, and seek no
> further.

Le leggi son, ma chi pon mano ad esse?
   Nullo, però che 'l pastor che procede,
   rugumar può, ma non ha l'unghie fesse;
per che la gente, che sua guida vede
   pur a quel ben fedire ond' ella è ghiotta,
   di quel si pasce, e più oltre non chiede.
(*Purg*. 16:97-102, trans. Singleton)

Father Conmee traffics with the mammon of iniquity, which is the sense of the prohibition in Psalm 1, "Beatus Vir," the psalm which opens the musical chant of the Divine Office. The man who accepts the call to the sacred office of priesthood is thereby canonized by the Holy Ghost. Such a man must not become the "secular," the man "qui abiit in consilio impiorum," one of those who run about consorting with worldlings: "that class of restless clerics who are rarely at home, and yet whose wanderings abroad are not after the lost or straying sheep of the flock, but after secular diversions and friendships; for such is the meaning of *impiorum*."

Joyce's text combines the actions of Psalm 1 with the words of Psalm 118, the first line of which is "Beati immaculati in via: qui ambulant in lege Domini" (Blessed are the undefiled in the Way: who walk in the law of the Lord"). The words *via* and *ambulant* are a concealed source of the motif that makes Conmee the focus of the Wandering Rocks chapter. As he walks across the city, he is recognizably the spiritual power of Dublin.

But in Joyce's ironic application of *via* and *ambulant*, Father Conmee encounters Dubliners whose occupation is significantly connected with the problem of poverty, and he shows only a bland reaction.

One is the pawnbroker, Mrs. M'Guinness, who bows to him from across the street. Father Conmee's mind makes an adjustment of focus, reflecting the contrast, as he sees it, between her low occupation and her aristocratic appearance. He meets three schoolboys from Belvedere, the sons of a pawnbroker, a bookmaker, and a raffish young journalist.[32] Though these boys may have been at Belvedere on scholarships, as Joyce himself was, it is far more likely that two of them, at least, are there because their fathers have become rich by squeezing pennies from those who have little money to spare. The third boy, as Ellmann discovered, is placed here anachronistically, with a name that attaches him to Ignatius Gallaher, Joyce's portrait of the successful but morally callous journalist. Combined with the praise of Mrs. M'Guinness's "queenly mien," Joyce's construction is meant to suggest the Jesuits' extreme practicality where money and power are concerned.

The role of the church in relation to the unfortunate is presented through the thoughts of this humane Jesuit. The Irish peasant's lot in life becomes the subject of a paragraph that carries the antiphonal cadence and also some of the sense of verse 75: "I know O Lord that thy judgments are right and that thou in faithfulness hast afflicted me." Conmee goes along Charleville Mall and sees a turf-barge moored under the trees. "It was idyllic: and Father Conmee reflected on the providence of the Creator who had made turf to be in bogs where men might dig it out and bring it to town and hamlet to make fires in the houses of poor people."

He meets a beggar who asks for alms, a one-legged sailor. Father Conmee has with him only a silver crown—five shillings, about a dollar in 1904. But he intends to walk, not ride, to Artane; why does he not give this relatively small amount to the beggar? We learn some paragraphs later in the chapter that five shillings is the amount that Leopold Bloom contributes to the fund for the Dignam children. Almsgiving by Christian and Jew is contrasted, and Conmee's act of charity toward the Dignam boy is put into a truer perspective. The priest does not ignore the beggar: "he blessed him in the sun." Pauperism, another traditional concern of his church, is in his mind, "but not for long." The pauperized Dignam family, the one-legged beggar, and the other evidences of Catholic poverty in Dublin are less important to Father Conmee than the "mission." It is more important for him to collect large sums for "the millions of black and brown and yellow souls . . . to whom the faith had not (D.V.) been brought" (*U* 219-220).

So the silver crown that Conmee has in his purse remains there. The reason why the Jesuit does not give his five shillings to the one-legged sailor is revealed. He has saved it for a short tram ride, from Newcomen bridge to the Howth road stop. The brief ride costs only one penny, we learn as Conmee puts the change back into his purse, but "He disliked to traverse on foot the dingy way past Mud Island" (*U* 219:4). Here is Joyce's ironic translation of the first line of Psalm 118, "Beati immaculati in via." Father Conmee himself lives free from cares and worry: this is learned from his immaculate mode of dress, his silk hat, "plump kid gloves," and smooth watch in an interior pocket. His vow of poverty is not burdensome. For his vacation, he tells Mrs. Sheehy, "he would go to Buxton probably for the waters." These indications of Conmee's refined, sensuous enjoyment of life may be a deliberate dramatization of the ordinary dictionary meaning of "epicurean," the heresy that Dante chose to associate with the two fathers of *Inferno* 10.

In his self-image Father Conmee is an aristocrat and he identifies with aristocratic society. His education is combined with an easy worldliness of manner and intellect; Lady Maxwell comes to see him at the presbytery. He has written a little book, *Old Times in the Barony*, about Jesuit houses that historically were the homes of noble families. In fantasy he sees himself in "Gay Malahide," home of Lord Talbot, as Don John Conmee (the Spanish honorific presumably because of the Spanish origin of the Jesuits), "humane and honoured there. He bore in mind secrets confessed and he smiled at smiling noble faces in a beeswaxed drawingroom, ceiled with full fruit clusters. And the hands of a bride and of a bridegroom, noble to noble, were impalmed by Don John Conmee" (*U* 220:33-35). He looks like a romantic, sentimentally attached to the medieval past, but this is only the secret of his charm. Joyce has made him a very practical figure, a portrait that goes a long way toward explaining the Jesuits' success in creating a Catholic Irish elite to displace the Protestant monopoly of power.

There is hostility in the Conmee portrait, genuine and deep, but it is not hostility toward the real life Jesuit for whom Joyce had a great and lasting affection. Joyce's anger is institutional and judgmental, and his decision for the Conmee portrait was a compliment, a guarantee of immortality. He appropriated a personality that would command attention to carry one of his most cherished arguments, and placed the resulting portrait at the very center of his novel. Dante had similarly answered the demands of his poem when he put into hell his beloved old teacher Brunetto, the great savior of Florence, Farinata, and others drawn from life.

If Joyce had really believed there was a hell, he would probably never have written the Conmee episode as he did. But he did believe in the existence of evil, for the depiction of which the old notion of hell is still useful, as it was in Dante's time. Like Dante (and practically every other Christian writer), Joyce insists that man's will is free, that it can be exercised for good or evil, and that the state of the world's affairs will vary with the quality of moral leadership in the world at one time or another. His themes, as social criticism, bear out his statement that, "with me, the thought is always simple." But he also said that his "means" were "quadrivial." Dante's poet-traveler was able to have his poetic mission ratified at the highest levels of Paradise, but only after his sense of purpose had been refined and strengthened. Poetic fatherhood was Dante's metaphor. Joyce constructed his own literary allegory, with analogous theme and purpose but in a different intellectual climate. This was the writer who, in arguing for the publication of a book (*Dubliners*) that opens with Dante's words for the gate of hell, had said, "I want to write a chapter of the moral history of my country" (*Letters* II 135; 5 May 1906).

When Dante wrote of Virgil, to paraphrase Dorothy Sayers, he taught Joyce how to write of Bloom and Father Conmee. The reader who has followed me this far will see that we are dealing with a fictional design in which a markedly specific literal base—with detail often taken directly from real life, often involving local and private reference—is given multiple symbolic extension. In Joyce's treatment of fatherhood, and specifically in his Virgilian Bloom, conceptual imagery is extended into literary allegory by thematic development. The true subject is the fostering of the intellectual imagination in the production of art at a particular time and place—Ireland at the turn of the century. Such an allegorical narrative, describing his subject under the guise of another which is suggestively similar, is Joyce's characteristic mode and is most plainly discernible in *A Portrait of the Artist* and *Ulysses*. In the case of the latter work, Joyce actually invited a Dantean reading—fourfold or even more—by the *schema* (his word) that he constructed and gave to a few friends: Stuart Gilbert, Sylvia Beach, Carlo Linati. The *Schema* was Joyce's equivalent of Dante's *Letter to Can Grande*, a document in which Joyce indicated the complicated patterning of his work, specified some but not all of its connections and extensions, and invited multiple interpretations of the characters and incidents in the book. Joyce's construction of such a *schema* is evidence of a formal principle which attaches his work to Dante's.

It is the business of this study, in this chapter and the two that follow, to discover both the traces and the dimensions of that attachment. Obviously this is not simply a matter of selecting parallel passages for explication, although a degree of parallelism is necessarily involved. As the preceding sections of this chapter have shown, theme, style, and form are intermingled; each contributes some essential part of a design which is intricately woven into the fabric of the book as a whole. We are looking beyond thematic equivalence to identify those of the author's compositional decisions that transform theme into structure. Joyce's portrait of Father Conmee is a subtle treatment of a Dantean theme, simony. But some of the force of his portrayal comes also from our observed reminiscence of a specific element of structure. Dante censures the simoniac Pope Boniface

VIII, his arch-enemy, in widely separated passages of the *Divine Comedy*, first at *Inferno* 19:52-57 and then definitively at *Paradiso* 30:146-48. Each time the condemnation is made in a passage of the poem that is notable for its quality of subtle indirection. Joyce puts more than three hundred pages between Conmee in the Wandering Rocks chapter and Conmee as he emerges from a Dantesque fiery coffin in the Circe episode. It is the author, Joyce, who draws the portrait of Conmee walking and reading; thus we are made aware of the theme, and we sense intuitively its personal importance to Joyce. It is the apprentice poet, Stephen Dedalus, whose hallucination completes the Dantean pattern. From a general insight that Dante is a presence behind Joyce's writing, we move to a reading of Joyce's work which, in going beyond the literal sense of the text, becomes a Dantean reading—"polysemous," as Dante called the method in his *Letter to Can Grande*. In Joyce's complex treatment of fatherhood, the connection of his work with Dante's becomes relatively overt. As Northrop Frye has said, themes as well as plots "have their elements of discovery."

*

*Ancestral Fathers: Dante's Cacciaguida
and Joyce's Virag*

> Speaking of Cacciaguida now
> We must thank Dante
> for relaying
> a truth improbable, incredible,
> at first downright dismaying.
> For his account reveals the sorry fact is
> that in those lofty realms
> slander is an honorable practice.
> Paradise fifteen
> displays the art in action
> and indicates the scope of its attraction.
> Think what a revelation such as this
> can mean
> to us poor anxious insects,
> full of fears,
> crawling on this old crumbling shell!
> Why, we have been in Heaven all these years,
> thinking it was Hell!
> (Aldo Palazzeschi, trans. Bergin)[33]

Joyce, like Dante, uses pride of family lineage to reinforce the authority of the artist's critical examination of society—his city, his country, his church. Dante's portrait of the natural father is presented in a single episode and focused on one individual, Cacciaguida, who is authentically Dante's ancestor but so remote and unverifiable that he is truly a fiction. Joyce's representation differs markedly from Dante's in many respects, but with discernible echoes of the original. His portrayal is in the modern tradition indicated by Aldo Palazzeschi's poem, a composite graphic rendering of the incongruities of Dante's episode.

In Canto 15 of the *Paradiso* Dante meets one of his own ancestors, much as Aeneas encounters his father, Anchises, after death in the sixth book of Virgil's *Aeneid*. Dante's ancestor is Cacciaguida, grandfather of Dante's grandfather, an old Crusader knighted by the Emperor. The encounter is of great importance and is given three entire cantos and parts of two others. Elsewhere Dante has praised nobility of character and deplored misplaced pride of birth. Now, his own pride of family becomes an important element in a crucial episode of the *Comedy*.[34]

Only two other characters in the poem, Virgil and Beatrice, have as much space as does Cacciaguida. Virgil's parting words of encouragement match Cacciaguida's prophecy. By the authority of both the great poet and the great and saintly warrior, Dante's mission is validated for all time. These two personages, seen as two aspects of paternal benevolence, reinforce each other by their differences as well as their similarities. One is the natural or blood-related ancestor, the other the spiritual father. It is a model or paradigm that Joyce refers to as the consubstantial father and the unsubstantial father.

Cacciaguida is above all a man of action, a man of simple tastes and solid basic values. In speech also he is simple and direct. His fierce attachment to what he sees as virtuous and right is a form of stubbornness, and his disdainful scorn of new men and new ways is a form of prejudice. So be it: he is massively self-assured. All these qualities we infer from the substance and tone of his conversation with Dante, and they form part of a pattern begun by another father-figure, Virgil.

It is understandable and artistically right that the paternal figure will be first of all a source of moral authority as commanding as the poet can make him. It is also a sound insight that his personal qualities should match, or be linked to, the personality of his descendant. They confront the world together, facing down Dante's enemies. No less important are Cacciaguida's expressions of pride and love. Three times over Cacciaguida alludes to Dante's journey through the three realms, expressing great satisfaction that a member of his family has been thus signally honored. Dante's attitude is above all respectful to this sturdy patriarch, whom he addresses with the formal *Voi*, but Cacciaguida also inspires faith and trustfulness: Dante is able to ask him for information and advice. The prophetic account of Dante's banishment that follows is the real business of the episode. The prophecy, which is brief, carries most of Cacciaguida's direct political comment, and it is preceded by a leisurely diatribe against the forces of social change in Florence and in Italy.

In Old Florence of Cacciaguida's day, families "abode in peace, sober and chaste," under the rule of the Old Romans. Mothers brought up their children to emulate the brave and civic-minded Trojans and Romans of fabulous history. If these high examples could be followed, all the good objectives of man in society could be attained.

The old city of Florence, "within her walls," was middle-size and no more than moderately wealthy. The root of present troubles, Cacciaguida says, is new men and new money.[35] As Aldo Palazzeschi's poem suggests, Cacciaguida names names freely and slanderously. Citizens have ceased to care for the welfare of their city: they squabble for money and power, in contests for which there can be no victory, because the whole community loses its peacefulness. The message seems deceptively simple, but in fact it is as broad as the whole *Divine Comedy*. The good of the City, that is to say the political order generally, depends on the continued production of good citizens and stable families.

Through his prophetic insight Cacciaguida puts Dante's exile into perspective. Envy and ill-will are to be the fruit of his efforts in the political life of Florence and he will be banished; however, in the end those who have exiled Dante will be bloodied in their turn. And those who have been sent into exile with Dante will turn to fighting among themselves. Cacciaguida warns that Dante's best course will be "to make a party of himself alone." Unsparingly he adds the full account of poverty, humiliation and bitterness which must be endured. The loser, Dante is told, is always the one to be blamed. But the old ancestor, addressing him as "Figlio," "Son," encourages him with the reminder that destiny will bring enduring renown which will continue far beyond the time that Dante's enemies have paid the penalty for their actions.[36]

Gathering courage from the paternal firmness of tone, Dante says that foresight will now forearm him so that, "if the dearest place [that is, Florence, his birthplace] be lost to me," nevertheless by going forward with his poetry he will see to it that he does not lose all. These words bring from his ancestor emboldening reassurance. Dante is told that he must speak out with the full truth, no matter how bitter it may be, in his poetry. Indeed, it is Heaven's purpose he is fulfilling. He was taken through the after-world and shown the future so that he might carry a great message in his poem.[37] Here we see the counterpart of the qualities of pride and scorn that Joyce gives to Stephen Dedalus: Stephen's sense of mission and commitment to an artistic vocation is quite as strong as Dante's.

Joyce abstracted from Dante's story of Cacciaguida some of the specific features that make it a powerful statement of the paternal bond. To understand these, it must be noted precisely which elements of encouragement are uniquely supplied by Dante's ancestor. Why did Cacciaguida have to be a blood relation and a soldier? First of all, the struggle had to be translated from outer to inner: this soldier predicts a victory which is not a soldier's but a poet's, and this ancestor's exhortation to Dante is not to take up arms but to speak the truth in poetry. Next, the bond is a mixture of pride and affection. Dante is told, at a time when he knows his fortunes are waning, that he will yet bring honor to his house and his family. This effect, so much stronger than the reversed situation that the poet might have chosen, in which Dante would express a sense of pride in his connection with the old warrior, is produced in the first lines of the episode. Before Dante knows the spirit's identity, the Latin words of address, "O sanguis meus," establish the importance of the blood relationship. In the appearance of a soldier ancestor, whose foreknowledge sees Dante's poetic triumph, the Farinata episode is completed: reason and poetry will win a victory that was denied to force.

A second effect, connected with the first, is that of a long time-span. Cacciaguida is an extremely remote ancestor, yet the warrior greets the poet with a cry of ardent love, "de l'ardente affetto," and an expression of family pride for deeds of Dante's that are still far in the future, the subject of foreknowledge and prophecy. Still another effect is the implication that poetry can and will be raised to the level of importance that is attached to high statecraft. If Dante speaks out clearly and forcefully about the evils of his day, his poetic achievement will be the equivalent of the victories of his Crusader ancestor. Finally, only a personage of established authority could reinforce Dante's courage, so Cacciaguida, though a disembodied spirit in Paradise, is represented as a very human figure, whose matter-of-fact tones convey the quality of pain, sorrow, and especially hostility that Dante must face.

*

Dante's visual effects are translated, in the Circe episode, from Cacciaguida to a figure that is perhaps Joyce's most wildly imaginative creation. The visual image of a remote and unknown ancestor who tenders advice in an incorporeal setting appears in *Ulysses* as Bloom's grandfather, Lipoti (Leopold) Virag, who is (among other things) a caricature of a warrior, momentarily a primitive African. He is one of Bloom's hallucinations in the brothel in Nighttown.

In constructing a pastiche of Dante's Cacciaguida episode, Joyce conflates incidents that are widely separated in the *Divine Comedy*. To the basic narrative of the three cantos of the *Paradiso* in which Dante meets his ancestor, Joyce adds descriptive details from two cantos of the *Inferno*, the highly coloured episode of the Malebranche. The result, in Virag, is a grotesque parody of a grandfather. Joyce clearly did not have a romantic view of the Crusades and was unsympathetic to the martial element in Dante's choice of his sainted ancestor. In the conversations with Virag, moreover, Joyce borrows for Bloom still another of Dante's most gruesome images, as we shall see. The effect is comic lunacy but, unlike Stephen's hallucinations in the Circe episode, this one carries no tones of anguish.

The manner of Virag's materialization mimics the descent of Cacciaguida when he comes from the Cross of Mars to speak to Dante. The heaven of Mars is all light and motion, a vast cross composed of two sparkling bands of souls who glow with ardor as they did in life when they were knights of the Cross. Now they shine and glitter and swiftly interchange their places in a corruscating effect. From this cross of light a star descends with great rapidity, meteor-like, and Dante is addressed "with the tenderness of Anchises' shade appearing to his son" ("Sì pia l'ombra d'Anchise si porse") (*Par*. 15:25).

When Bloom's ancestor (whom he never knew) appears, he is introduced by his Hungarian name and a descriptive term of Joyce's manufacture: "Lipoti Virag, Basilicogrammate." He "chutes rapidly down the chimney flue," a visual effect suggesting both the coal and the flame of Dante's terzina, "sì come carbon che fiamma rende" (*Par*. 14:52), and also the somewhat incongruous rapidity of Cacciaguida's descent, "a piè di quella croce corse un astro," "down to the cross's foot there darted a star." The likeness of fire and rapid downward movement continues with Dante's "per la lista radial trascorse / che parve foco dietro ad alabastro," an effect of the star running along a downward diagonal line, "like fire burning behind alabaster" (*Par*. 15:20; 23-24). Joyce's apparition, like Cacciaguida, is a warrior captain: "a birdchief, bluestreaked and feathered in war panoply with his assegai" (*U* 539:03), a description that echoes Dante's use of the word "pennuti," "feathered," in his first words to Cacciaguida (*Par.* 15:81). Dante's Cacciaguida, of course, has no physical characteristics but is, like all the souls in the *Paradiso*, a featureless point of light.

Virag's episode, which occupies six pages of text, is complete in itself and is also united with episodes preceding and following.[38] The narrative development of the chapter has brought together Bloom and Stephen in this room, which the prostitutes call the "musicroom" because it contains a pianola (*U* 491:29). This is the first time they have been together. Although they are acquainted, they do not speak to each other. Each has a series of hallucinations, triggered by some word, some object, some remark, that moves his mind out of reality and into perception of things not actually present. Immediately after Virag's appearance, Stephen momentarily sees himself as the Prodigal Son, and Bloom for an instant recalls his own father. For a moment, that is, Stephen becomes a Jewish, Biblical son, saying, "Filling my belly with husks of swine" (*U* 506:37; 506:15; 406:22).

Bloom's momentary recollection of his father's house is contained in the "Jacob's pipe" which he imagines himself carrying. This is a verbal echo of the brief vignette with which, much earlier in the book, Joyce presents Mr Bloom "as in a retrospective arrangement, a mirror within a mirror," as he was at Stephen's present age, working at his first job as "a fullfledged traveller for the family firm," who "brought home at duskfall many a commission to the head of the firm seated *with Jacob's pipe* [italics mine] in the paternal ingle . . ." (*U* 506:15-16; 406:6-7; 21-22).

Although Bloom's hallucination includes his father's Jacob's pipe, Bloom at this point in the Circe chapter imagines himself as "Henry Flower," a troubadour. It is usually possible, in this chapter of hallucinations, to find the event or verbal connection that triggers the hallucination and in this case it seems to be Bloom's reaction to finding himself in a "musicroom" with two young women, an impulse of gallantry. "Grave Bloom regards Zoe's neck. Henry gallant turns . . . to the piano" (*U* 506:25-26). But the brief incarnation of Henry Flower ends with an evocation of Dante's Bertran de Born, the troubadour of *Inferno* 28. In Dante's canto, the troubadour scene, which is surely the original of Joyce's, has an air of comic frightfulness.[39] Dante says that he saw the trunk marching along, holding the severed head ("il capo tronco") by the hair so that it swung like a lantern: the head looked at Dante saying "Ah me!" The sin of Bertran de Born, as he tells Dante, was that "I made the father and the son enemies to each other" ("Io feci il padre e 'l figlio in sé ribelli" [*Inf.* 28:118-126; 136; *U* 506:15-28; *U* 511:20-22; 30-33]). "Henry Flower" holds on his breast a severed head (female); Virag then unscrews his own head and holds it under his arm.

It seems that no statement voiced by any character in the chapter is directly responsible for the apparition of Bloom's grandfather, but the proximate event is certainly the sight of young Stephen. Bloom has been hurrying through the Dublin streets looking for the drunken young man, and now the apparition of Virag and the thought of Bloom's own father seem to be the consequence of protective (paternal) feelings. At the same time, Bloom is apprehensive in these threatening surroundings, which the chapter's rhetoric identifies as the infernal regions of hellish fire. (For example, after an exchange of lascivious remarks with a prostitute, "blue fluid again flows over her flesh" [*U* 500:22].) Bloom's deep sense of guilt and worry about his own responsibility for his domestic crisis is the source of the advice (repellent comment on sexual problems) he gets from his grandfather.

Virag is a Jewish ancestor, and carries a roll of parchment that he calls a book. Presumably this is the scroll of the Torah, but when Virag says, "For all these knotty points see the seventeenth book," he is identifying one of Cacciaguida's cantos, *Paradiso* 17. Cacciaguida's remark to Dante, to the effect that he has satisfied the "hunger drawn from the reading of the mighty volume wherein neither white nor black ever changeth," may be echoed in Virag's references to his "book," as he "taps his parchmentroll" (*Par.* 15:50-52; *U* 503:24).

Dante's definition of contingency is expressed in the request to his ancestor to explain the prophecies that have been made about Dante's future. Dante says that Cacciaguida can do this because he stands at a point so high uplifted that "contingent things, before they come into existence, are visible to you as you gaze from above upon that point which is the present for all times." The sense of this passage is reproduced by Bloom: "I wanted then to have now concluded . . . But tomorrow is a new day will be. Past was is today. What now is will then tomorrow as now was be past yester" (*Par.* 17:17; *U* 504: 6-8).

Cacciaguida's Latin address to Dante very markedly echoes another meeting of father and son—the reunion of Anchises and Aeneas in the underworld, in Virgil's sixth book of the *Aeneid*. Virag is also given some Latin: "*Argumentum ad feminam*, as we said in old Rome and ancient Greece in the consulship of Diplodocus and Ichthyosaurus." Besides the parallel in his reference to old Rome, Virag's word, "consulship," is a reminder of Virgil's passage, where Anchises' prediction that Aeneas will be the "father" of Rome is expressed in words that Dante uses to link Cacciaguida with Julius Caesar: "O sanguis meus" (*U* 502-503; *Par.* 15:28).

Verbal echoes and linguistic parallels, as well as the presence of Dante's themes and subject matter, establish the Virag episode as a construction derived from Dante's. The Cacciaguida episode is particularly noted for a certain rhetorical variety and a crudeness of discourse which Joyce has reproduced, skirting travesty to do so. Some of the incongruities of the original are distinctly inappropriate to a saint in Paradise—one who stands, moreover, in a position nearer to the Divine Throne than St. Thomas Aquinas and St. Francis. The roughness of the old Crusader's conversation stems, of course, from his being a blunt, plain-spoken soldier. The harsh rawness occasionally present in Dante's episode is less pervasive than the same quality in Joyce's chapter, but this is partly a matter of the setting, a comparison of the hellish environment of Bloom with the paradisiacal setting of Dante and Cacciaguida. In both, it is obviously intended to emphasize the unreality of the scene.

When Joyce's imagination collected all the incongruous elements of the Cacciaguida story and made them fantastic, the intended design made Virag a far more equivocal personage than Cacciaguida. Virag is a repulsive figure who changes form several times, and whose remarks are distasteful. But he is indeed an aspect of Bloom's mind, although one with which he is in fact unacquainted—just as the waking Bloom is unacquainted with both his actual grandfather and the Id in his subconscious. The visual images weirdly reinforce the psychic construction: this reminds us that Dante also imagined his ancestor, whose qualities are an aspect of Dante's own mind.[40]

Virag assumes, one after another, a variety of grotesque forms. Joyce has moved one of Dante's saints to the brothel where Bloom finds Stephen, and in such a place the apparition of a grandfather is unlikely to be benevolent. Joyce's warrant for such an exaggerated impulse of transformation may be traceable partly to an apothegm in *Inferno* 22, where the frightened poet says, "Well, in church with saints, and with drunks in the tavern." When the hallucinations of Mr Bloom call up the image of his 19th century Hungarian grandfather, the caricature of an ancestor is taken from Dante's Cacciaguida, but the bizarre metamorphoses have the grisly aspect of Dante's devils.

Anyone in search of a devil could find no better model than Dante's, particularly that band called the Malebranche who pursue Virgil and Dante in three cantos. Visually, Malacoda and his retinue are present in the Virag episode. Joyce's transformation has brought in also, more briefly, the Centaur, Chiron, from *Inferno* 12, and Bertran de Born from *Inferno* 28.

Dante's Malebranche are distinguished not only by their extreme coarseness of expression, but by their lively pursuit of the sinners, by a variety of bestial references, and especially by a series of vivid images deriving from the central devil-image of a great black-winged lightfooted creature armed with a pitchfork. This visual effect is specifically reproduced by Joyce's description of Virag. "Head askew Virag arches his back, with hunched wingshoulders," as does the devil in *Inferno* 21, "his shoulders sharp and high" ("l'omero suo ch'era aguto e superbo" *U* 505:30-31; *Inf*. 21:30-35). Virag has a gargoyle aspect that conveys a universalized sense of evil: "he leans out on tortured forepaws, elbows bent rigid, side eye agonizing, yelps over the mute world" (*U* 509:16-17). The arched back carries an additional Dantean reference, for the dolphin is described in Canto 22 as arching his back to warn the sailors of impending shipwreck, that is, of death (*Inf*. 22:19-21). Virag sticks out his tongue, his hand on his fork: this is the gesture with which Libicocco, Cagnazzo, furious Rubicante, and the rest of the band salute their leader, Malacoda; as they turn, "each of them pressed his tongue between the teeth toward their Captain" (*U* 510:16; *Inf*. 21:136-139). The line that follows, "ed egli avea del cul fatto trombetta" ("and he [Malacoda] of his rump had made a trumpet"), is one of the lines of the *Commedia* which is directly quoted in *Ulysses*. It is a silent thought of Stephen's, in the Library chapter, and the passage is tied to the Virag episode rhetorically. Stephen thinks of it when he sees John Eglinton, "bearded amid darkgreener shadow, an ollav, holyeyed" (*U* 182:32), and the reader remembers this later in the invocation to the Celtic seagod, Mananaan MacLir, with which the Virag episode comically begins: "In the cone of the searchlight behind the coalscuttle, ollave, holyeyed, the bearded figure of Mananaan MacLir broods, chin on knees. He rises slowly. A cold seawind blows from his druid mantle." This fantastic apparition exclaims, "Dark, hidden father!" (*U* 499:13-15, 26).

Stephen and Bloom are linked with Dante by Joyce's double use of the closing line of *Inferno* 21 in still another chapter. The direct quotation is acted out by Mr Bloom, whose flatulence is expressed as a musical direction, "pianissimo" and "triple forte," ending the Sirens chapter (*U* 286:16, 18, 23; *Inf*. 21:139).

Dante develops the horror of the devilish bird figure by a series of similes. The birds of the Malebranche episode are sparrowhawks and falcons; they have talons, the pitchfork is an extension of their claws, they swoop and move swiftly as birds of prey (*Inf*. 21:49-53; 85-87; 100-101; *Inf*. 22:130-131; 139-140; 148-149). All this devilish essence is contained in Dante's phrase, *malvagio uccello*, which exactly describes one manifestation of Virag (*Inf*. 22:96). Like the Malebranche, he is an evil bird. He has a yellow parrotbeak (*U* 504:14); the beaklike image is also seen in his mouth, "projected in hard wrinkles," and his "nose hardhumped" (*U* 505:20; 503:14). He "claws the letters," he "cranes his scraggy neck," he "sloughs his skins, his plumage moulting" (*U* 505:3; 509:12; 511:10). He cackles, and "gabbles nasally" (*U* 505:9; 504:14, 34). Like Dante's two travelers, Bloom is seeing "Nightbird, nightsun, nighttown" (*U* 504:27). Here, as also in "Dark, hidden father!" the episode foreshadows *Finnegans Wake*, where the dreaming consciousness merges with Dante's poem in "the lingerous longerous book of the dark" (*FW* 251:24).

Joyce's use of the image probably traces to the occurrence of "uccello" in both episodes of the *Divine Comedy*. In *Paradiso* 17, Cacciaguida predicts that Dante's first refuge after his banishment will be the hostelry of the great Lombard, Bartolomeo della Scala, whose stairs "carry the holy bird" ("che 'n su scala porta il santo uccello") (*Inf*. 22:96; *Par*. 17:72).

Dante's devils have a quality of beastliness in action that is expressively rendered by unpleasant similes. The sinners raise their faces in the boiling pitch like frogs in a ditch, they are fearful like the mouse with great malevolent cats, they flee like the leveret pursued by dogs (*Inf*. 22:25-26, 33; *Inf*. 23:4-6; *Inf*. 22:58; 21:67-69; 23:16-18). One of Dante's grotesque demons has the tusks of a hog protruding from his jaws (*Inf*. 22:56). Joyce's Virag has "weasel teeth," "speaks in a pig's whisper," chases his tail, wriggles, and worries his butt; he mews and yelps, and "raises his mooncalf nozzle and howls" (*U* 501:31; 504:10; 505:35; 509:17; 509:12). The Centaur, Chiron, casually takes an arrow to fit to his great bowstring, but first uses the shaft to part his beard; Virag, in the same gesture, "closes his jaws by an upward push of his parchment roll" (*Inf*. 12:77; *U* 511:12). Joyce's verbal maneuvers have transformed these Dantean images more comprehensively than parody; it is the spirit of the *Inferno* and the visual aspect of the Malebranche rendered without the context. Thus Virag is not simply a caricature of Cacciaguida. His grotesquerie is all his own and operates within the dimensions of a larger expressive pattern that Joyce found in *both* the *Inferno* and the *Paradiso*.

The Virag episode, as a Dantesque construction, is an elaborate exploration of consciousness. Its placement in the structure of the Circe chapter indicates or marks the point at which Bloom's hallucinations begin to deal with the deeply buried levels of his subconscious mind. Of all the hallucinatory sequences, Virag's is the least "intelligible," the most obscure, the farthest from normality, the farthest from experiential reality. Part of this results from the dizzying metamorphoses of Bloom's grandfather; part, from the language of discourse.[41] In the latter respect it perhaps extends Dante's statement that Cacciaguida said some things unintelligible to Dante's understanding.

Joyce's effects here are poetic rather than intellectual, impressionistic rather than logical or sequential. Both his choice of Cacciaguida and his decision to render the episode in demonic rather than paradisiacal terms show Joyce's interest in Dante's use of paradoxical tensions, expressed in vivid imagery, to render states of consciousness.

* *

The Dantesque theme of paternity discussed in this chapter is embodied by Joyce in a variety of dialectical relations contrasting maturity with immaturity. His central concern is with the importance of an organic quality of maturity in the successful artist. The same idea is expressed in Virgil's statement to Dante that, through his journey, his will has become free, upright, and whole, "Wherefore I crown and mitre you over yourself." The duplication of Virgil's stewardship in the association of Leopold Bloom and Stephen Dedalus is filled with compassionate irony: to look for a naturalistic correspondence with the original would be to defeat Joyce's complex artistic purpose.

The complicated sequence of Joyce's use of the canto of Brunetto Latini is also concerned with moral maturity, this time as the artist's perception of an aspect of social organization. The portrait of Father Conmee is a satiric construction that, however, points to the importance of moral authority in society. Joyce forms an intricate connection between two planes of irony, both drawn from *Inferno* 10 but separately presented in different chapters: on one plane is the condemnation of Father Conmee as an epicurean, and on the other, Stephen Dedalus's image of Father Conmee rising, like Dante's heretics, from the tomb. By this interweaving, an important dimension of the Irish artist's world is set forth and judged. Stephen Dedalus possesses a very strong sense of the force of religion. His author powerfully shows the reader the effect of religious belief in the life of an imaginative individual, and the interaction of Stephen's understanding of the complexities of religious experience with his unqualified rejection of its institutional aspects. The presence of the Dantean parallel thus subtly calls attention to the author's voice in the book: not as narrator, not as persona, but as a vivid presence, revealed by this imaginative structure, and incidentally revealing also a similar presence of Dante in the *Divine Comedy*. Here in *Ulysses*, as S. L. Goldberg has aptly said, the voice of the character "seems to chime in unison with the author's."[42]

The depiction of Virag as an analogue of Dante's ancestor Cacciaguida is once more a treatment of the paternal theme of maturity and self-knowledge as it relates to artistic potential. For Bloom is, in many brief glimpses throughout the book, an artist of sorts; and here in the Circe hallucinations the reader sees Bloom's unbridled imagination. The dizzying metamorphoses in this section of the chapter reveal, in fact, a quality of imagination—breadth, vividness, immediacy—equalled nowhere else in the book except in the representation of Stephen Dedalus's consciousness. In the Virag episode we have, of all things, Dante's own images in the mind of the half-literate advertising canvasser, Leopold Bloom. Can we say that it is a selection of those qualities of Dante's imagination that might fit such a mind? We are given the undisputed coarseness and incongruity of Cacciaguida as well as his forthrightness—but in Bloomian terms, and thoroughly disguised by the application of that firm ancestral tone to the distasteful sexual preoccupations and oddities of the grandson. Then we behold the imaginative humor of the devil-images, and some of the striking infernal vignettes, in a stupefying succession. All these images are clearly Dante's, yet equally clearly they are transformed in the ambiance of Bloom's mind. In the terms of the book the reader thereby acquires a new awareness of what Bloom's imagination is like when all restraints are removed.

The mimetic transformations of Dante's fathers are a modern secularized reading, and therein a reminder of Joyce's distance from Dante. To some extent they are also his expression of that distance. Yet his undoubted sense of "otherness" is not the explanation, at least not solely or centrally, of the exuberant quality of Joyce's misreading, especially when it shades into travesty and broadly comic effects. At such times Joyce is working in the flamboyant tradition of Irish comic satire, consciously displayed in *Ulysses* and *Finnegans Wake*. Vivian Mercier describes, with many examples, the *Irishness* of Joyce's parodic and allusive styles of writing.[43] Caricature and burlesque have medieval as well as Irish precedents, and both are strongly reflected in Joyce's imagination.

In terms of the book as a whole, however, the Dantean theme is neither belittled nor is it used as a *general* disparagement of modern life. To the contrary: Joyce's vision is comparable to Dante's in affirming the desirability of moral certainty and spiritual excellence, and Dante's firm grasp on the present reality of this world in turn anticipates Joyce's. Joyce takes exception to Dante's fondness for the martial strain in his ancestry, and he discountenances the militant religion of the Crusades. However, as Paul deMan suggests, the demystification of the past opens out the prospect of a new and more firmly rooted appreciation of its true worth, of that wherein it deserves our approval for excellence.[44] While the details of Dante's pattern of paternal nurture become the material for ironic and even comic transformation, the pattern as a whole, in its shape and purpose, links Joyce's chapters as the prophecies of Brunetto and Cacciaguida link Dante's cantiche. Joyce in *Stephen Hero* allowed Stephen Dedalus to have the opinion that "no one served the generation into which he was born so well as he who offered it the gift of certitude, either in his art or his life" (*SH* 76:14). This view, which was deemed too mature for the young Stephen in the final version of *A Portrait*, comes back into *Ulysses* as the author's voice.

ะๅ *Chapter Three*
The Theme of Love: Dante's Francesca
and Joyce's "Sirens"

"SHALL I wear a white rose," says Molly Bloom at the close of *Ulysses*, and a few lines farther on, "or shall I wear a red yes." Thus Joyce makes a last connection of his book with Dante's poem, an echo of the "candida rosa" ("pure white rose"), in the first line of *Paradiso* 31. He added the white rose to the typescript of the Penelope episode in July 1921, only a few months before the book's publication, and the red rose even later, at an advanced stage of reading galley proofs. But these were not casual addenda, nor merely an afterthought. The two roses, with their wide range of symbolic reference, are the final element in a complex construction, and they register the presence in Joyce's text of his own secularized version of the *Divine Comedy*'s central theme, the power of love.

A reader's first understanding of the poetic unity of the *Comedy* is likely to come from observation of this theme. Human love and divine love have been complexly interwoven. Dante's Beatrice is the center of a great mysterious imaging of human love in which heart and intellect are integral—both essential. In the poem's opening canto Dante sets in motion a great range and variety of reverberating echoes that resound musically throughout the *Comedy* until the final line of the *Paradiso* evokes the divinest of all conceptions, "the love that moves the Sun and the other stars," "l'amor che move il sole e l'altre stelle." Molly Bloom is not the Dantean Beatrice of the *Paradiso*; instinctively Molly chooses the red rose of earthly love. But the rose is notably the flower of the Virgin Mary, "Mystical Rose" of the litany. Molly Bloom's birthday is September 8, the Church's date for the Nativity of Mary.[1] The key to Joyce's pattern, insofar as it may involve a meditation on Dante's treatment of the theme of love, seems to be an ironic mistrust of the mystical view of love. At the same time his admiration

rivers and lakes and flowers all sorts of shapes and smells and
colours springing up even out of the ditches primroses and violets
nature it is as for them saying there's no God I wouldn't give a
snap of my two fingers for all their learning why don't they go and
create something I often asked him atheists or whatever they call
themselves go and wash the cobbles off themselves first then they go
howling for the priest and they dying and why why because they're
afraid ah yes I know them well who was the first person in the
universe before there was anybody that made it all who ah that they don't
know neither do I so there you are they might as well try to stop
the sun from rising the sun shines for you he said the day we were
lying among the rhododendrons on Howth head in the grey tweed suit and his straw hat the day I got him to
propose to me yes and it was leapyear like now yes sixteen years ago
my God after that long kiss I near lost my breath yes he said I was
a flower of the mountain yes so we are flowers all a woman's body
yes that was one true thing he said in his life and the sun shines

for you today yes that was why I liked him because I saw he
understood or felt what a woman is and I knew I could always get
round him and I gave him all the pleasure I could leading him on till
he asked me to say yes and I wouldn't answer first only looked out
over the sea and the sky I was thinking of so many things he didn't
know of Mulvey and Mr Stanhope and Hester and father and old captain
Groves and the fields in the and cactuses Alameda gardens and Gibraltar as a girl where I was a
flower of the mountain and how he kissed me under the Moorish wall and when I put the red rose in my hair like the Andalusian
and I thought well as well him as another and then I asked him with
my eyes to ask again and then he asked me would I to say yes my
mountain flower and first I put my arms around him and drew him
girls used shall I wear a white rose

3. Joyce's final connection of his book with Dante's poem is Molly Bloom's thought, "Shall I wear a white rose," an echo of the "pure white rose" that opens Canto 31 of the *Paradiso*. He added this to the typescript of "Penelope" at a very late stage of composition. His first version links the red rose and

all who ah that they dont know neither do I so there you are they might as
well try to stop the sun from rising the sun shines for you he said the day we
were lying among the rhododendrons on Howth head in the grey tweed suit
and his straw hat the day I got him to propose to me yes first I gave him the
bit of seedcake out of my mouth and it was leapyear like now yes sixteen
years ago my God after that long kiss I near lost my breath yes he said I was a
flower of the mountain yes so we are flowers all a womans body yes that was
one true thing he said in his life and the sun shines for you today yes that was
why I liked him because I saw he understood or felt what a woman is and
I knew I could always get round him and I gave him all the pleasure I could
leading him on till he asked me to say yes and I wouldnt answer first only
looked out over the sea and the sky I was thinking of so many things he
didnt know of Mulvey and Mr Stanhope and Hester and father and old captain
Groves and the sailors playing all birds fly and I say stoop and washing up
dishes they called it on the pier and the sentry in front of the governors
with the thing round his white helmet poor devil half roasted and the Spanish
girls laughing in their shawls and their tall combs and the auctions in the
morning the Greeks and the jews and the Arabs and the devil knows who
else from all the ends of Europe and Duke street and the fowl market all
clucking and the poor donkeys slipping half asleep and the vague fellows in
the cloaks asleep in the shade on the steps and the big wheels of the carts of
the brills and those handsome Moors all in white and turbans like kings asking
you to sit down in their bit of a shop and Ronda with the old windows two
glancing eyes a lattice hid and O that awful deepdown torrent O and the sea
the sea crimson sometimes like fire and the glorious sunsets and the figtrees in
the Alameda gardens and all the queer little streets and pink and blue and
yellow houses and the rosegardens and the jessamine and cactuses and Gibraltar
as a girl where I was a flower of the mountain yes when I put the rose in my
hair like Andalusian girls used shall I wear a white rose and how he kissed
me under the Moorish wall and I thought well as well him as another and
then I asked him with my eyes to ask again and then he asked me would I to
say yes my mountain flower and first I put my arms around him and drew
him down to me so he could feel my breasts all perfume yes and his heart was
going like mad and I said yes I will yes.

Trieste-Zurich-Paris,
1914-1921.

white rose. In page proof, he moved the white rose to a point two pages earlier, and gave Molly her decision, "or shall I wear a red one yes" by changing
the color of the rose in the final lines of the book.

for Dante's artistry is evident; an admiration revealed in the intricacy with which Joyce himself treats the theme, and the final mystery with which—in the voice of Molly Bloom—he surrounds it.

Joyce's pervasive irony has made his readers wary of claiming for him an affirmative treatment of love anywhere in his fiction. Yet the Sirens chapter of *Ulysses* is clearly one place, and not the only place in Joyce's work, where the theme of love is pervasive, significant, and treated with seriousness as well as with irony. The writing of this chapter, moreover, made such exceptional demands on Joyce's verbal skills that he seems here to be measuring himself against Dante, as he more openly measured himself against Shakespeare at other places. Music, in the schema for *Ulysses*, was specified as the "art" of the Sirens episode. Like Dante, Joyce has manipulated language to produce effects more commonly associated with music—and poetry—than with prose. He does this at many points in *Ulysses*, and in other books as well; here, he calls attention to it. In this chapter we will examine Joyce's verbal techniques as a deliberate reflection of his interest in the rhythmical movement and musical phrasing of Dante's poem. "The poet, for Dante, is a musician with words; his special effect on them is a *legame musaico*. Poets are defined as those who make harmony with words, *armonizantes verba*."[2]

The musical effects that Joyce first developed in writing the Sirens chapter were used more extensively in *Finnegans Wake*. Joyce was especially pleased with the musical quality of the eighth chapter, Anna Livia Plurabelle, of which he said to Ettore Settanni, "Have you ever stopped by a river? Could you give musical values and precise notes to the flowing sound that fills your ears and lulls you to sleep?" His musical use of rhythmic prose in *Ulysses* was the subject of discussions with Jacques Mercanton, to whom he explained the importance of "the rhythm of the text" as a necessary support for descriptive writing. He told Mercanton that this kind of transposition from sight to sound was the very essence of art, as he saw the matter: "After all, the interior monologue in *Ulysses* is just that."[3]

I propose to demonstrate, by a review of syntactical and structural patterns, the presence of Dante in two important rhetorical modes of Joyce's text. In the first section of this comparison the rhythms of Joyce's Sirens chapter (which he saw as a fugue in some sense of this musical term) will be compared with Dante's use of rhythm and rhyme in that most notable portrayal of human love, the Francesca story of two lovers murdered by a jealous husband, in *Inferno* 5. Here, I believe, the tenor of discourse will show a similar use of tone and vocabulary by Dante and by Joyce to create verbal progressions that convey multiple meanings. In the second section I will present an array of structural patterns, with special attention to the construction of an extended metaphor—literature in *Inferno* 5 and music in Joyce's Sirens chapter.

*

In the Francesca episode Dante accomplishes a formidable compression of intellectual and emotional material. Joyce's interest in these rhetorical effects was reported by one of his contemporaries, Oliver St. John Gogarty.

> Joyce had a nose like a rhinoceros for literature. From his appreciations and quotations I learned much . . . Virgil's "procumbit humi bos" he would compare to Dante's "Cade [*sic*] como corpo morte [*sic*] cade." He tried not unsuccessfully *to form his style on the precision and tersity of Dante*.[4] (Italics mine.)

Gogarty's imperfect knowledge of Italian suggests that his reporting of the incident may also be less than reliable. But, due allowance being made, Gogarty has here reproduced with the ring of authenticity one of Joyce's critical observations.

Joyce habitually memorized whatever appealed to him strongly in poetry or prose, a practice which has left in the record of his life and works many lines from *Inferno* 5—more in fact than from any other single area of Dante's writings. Joyce's use of these and other quotations reveals a highly individual reading of Dante. Joyce's critical insights, expressed in the early years of the twentieth century, anticipate the postwar modernist innovators both in modern poetry and in Dante criticism; he is more avant-garde than, for example, are Eliot or Pound.

Richard Ellmann's biography reports that Joyce kept on his desk (in Trieste, in 1914) a picture, cut from an exposition catalogue, showing the sculptured figure of an old woman, naked and ugly, under which Joyce had placed two lines from *Inferno* 5:

> Elena vedi, per cui tanto reo
> Tempo si volse . . .
>
> Helen, mark, for whom so long a term
> of wasteful war was waged.   (*Inf.* 5:64-65, trans. Bergin)

Joyce's pupil, Oscar Schwarz (possibly thinking of the third act of *Faust* II), was distressed at this assault on the traditional image of the beautiful woman and asked, "Why Helen?"

For answer Joyce made a rapid calculation of the number of years Helen lived with Menelaus before she met Paris, of the time she spent at Troy, and of the time she had been back in Sparta when Telemachus met her; he then calculated the age she must have been when Dante saw her in the *Inferno*.

Schwarz, moved by mingled anger and scorn, charged his teacher with having "killed Helen"; at which, Ellmann reports, "Joyce laughed and repeated several times, as though approvingly, "Killed Helen!" (RE:*JJ*, 392).

There are many reports suggesting Joyce's deep absorption in the poetry of *Inferno* 5. He wrote in a 1902 college essay, "Those whom the flames of too-fierce love have wasted on earth become after death pale phantoms among the winds of desire," a paraphrase of lines 31-49 of *Inferno* 5 that foreshadows Joyce's later use of Dante's lines (*CW* 81). In *Finnegans Wake*, his last and densest work, a marginal note says "Undante umoroso," at a passage which recalls Francesca's response when Dante, the pilgrim, asks her how, "al tempo de'dolci sospiri" ("in the time of sweet sighs"), love first made the fateful couple aware of their "dubiosi desiri," their equivocal desires. Francesca says,

> . . . Nessun maggior dolore,
>   che ricordarsi del tempo felice
>   ne la miseria; e ciò sa 'l tuo dottore.

> . . . There is no greater woe
>   Than happiness recalled in misery,
>   And that your learned doctor well should know.
>
>   (*Inf.* 5:121-123)

Joyce renders the spirit of this passage and gives the final line verbatim:

> Is a game over? The game goes on. . . . The beggar the maid the bigger the mauler. And the greater the patrarc the griefer the pinch. And that's what your doctor knows. O love it is the commonknounest thing how it pashes the plutous and the paupe. (*FW* 269)

Dante's line, "Love, that quickly captures the gentle heart," appears in *Finnegans Wake* in a more ambiguous context.

> . . . As though he, a notoriety, a foist edition, were a wrigular writher neonovene babe!—well diarmuee and granyou and Vae Vinctis, if that is what lamoor that of gentle breast rathe is intaken

> seems circling out yondest (it's life that's all chokered by that batch
> of grim rushers) heaven help his hindmost . . . (*FW* 292)

The "grim rushers" in this passage come from the Second Circle of
Dante's hell, where the souls of the lustful are whirled forever on the
wind, "circling out yondest." There is no doubt about the origin of
"lamoor that of gentle breast rathe" in Dante's line, "Amor, ch' al cor
gentil ratto s'apprende" ("Love, that quickly captures the gentle
heart"), with a nice decision for the Old English word "rathe,"
"quickly," as the equivalent of Dante's "ratto." In *Finnegans Wake* such
translations are a principal mode of allusion. Joyce renders the last
line of the canto as, "let drop as a doombody drops" ["fell as a dead
body falls," "E caddi come corpo morto cade" (*FW* 292:1; *Inf.* 5:100;
FW 289:15; *Inf.* 5:142)].

Joyce paraphrased and quoted the *Divine Comedy* in letters to Ezra
Pound, one of the more formidable Dantisti, who had been an early
supporter. In a letter of 1938 Joyce told Pound, "I don't think I ever
worked so hard even at *Ulysses*," and added a line from the Francesca
episode, "Galeotto è il libro e chi lo scrive" ("Galeotto [i.e., a pander] is
the book and he who writes it."), altered to the present tense (*Letters*
III: 415).

Such allusions and quotations can safely be taken as evidence of
knowledgeable attachment to the canto, and they supply pertinent insights into the workings of Joyce's mind. In these respects they illuminate another cluster of direct quotations from the *Divine Comedy* that
provide more compelling evidence of Joyce's special interest in *Inferno*
5. His most substantial direct reference to Dante's poem occurs in
Ulysses, in the Aeolus chapter, which is set in a newspaper office. Here,
in an unspoken monologue passage, Stephen Dedalus's interest in
Dante is shown to be an interest in his craftsmanship, and it is Canto
5, its rhymes and cadences, that becomes the starting point for a mental review by the young poet of Dante's art. In a silent review of
Dante's choice of rhyme-words, Stephen surveys critically the subtle
artifice that ties the long poem together.

Three chapters of the novel focus the reader's attention on the
mind of Stephen Dedalus, each dealing with the young man's potential as a creative artist. Each of these chapters gives a direct view of
Stephen's *thoughts*; each contains a direct quotation from Dante
(among a great deal of other literary and philosophical material) in
the original Italian, demonstrating—if nothing else—Stephen's close
reading and easy recall of the *Divine Comedy*. In the first chapter (Proteus), Stephen thinks of Aristotle, who is identified by Dante's line,

"Maestro di color che sanno," "Master of all them that know" (*U* 38:8; *Inf*. 4:131). This direct quotation from the *Commedia* appears in the earliest draft of the chapter, the 18-page notebook in which Joyce first wrote the episode in the fall of 1917 during a brief visit to Locarno. In the early draft Stephen immediately adds, "Yes; he was bald and a multimillionaire," a line that was slightly modified but retained in final publication.

In the second chapter, Aeolus, the reader sees Stephen's capsule review of Dante's rhymes. In the third, Scylla and Charybdis, a third direct quotation makes the reader more explicitly aware of Stephen's admiration for Dante through a complex association of *Inferno* 5 and Hamlet. It becomes apparent that the young man is deeply immersed in the *Divine Comedy*.

Stephen Dedalus has a new and eccentric view of *Hamlet*, which he proposes (in "Scylla") to some members of the Dublin literary establishment gathered in the National Library. As Stephen does this, the text gives both his spoken words and his unspoken thoughts. Into the latter there comes a silent thought of Dante, a quotation.[5] Stephen is the only character in Joyce's novel who is presented as being capable of such juxtaposition—the only individual in that group of literati who is able to quote extensively, perhaps even capable of understanding, *both* Dante and Shakespeare. It is therefore noteworthy that Joyce has selected for association in such a context the Hamlet love-triangle and the Francesca story.

The reader has been prepared for this by the long passage from the *Divine Comedy* quoted by Stephen—again silently—in the Aeolus chapter. Here, while he waits for an interview with the newspaper editor, Stephen listens to the windy conversation of his elders; to escape his depressing surroundings, he thinks of love, of literature, and particularly of Dante's skill as a poet. The text of the chapter is divided up by headlines (taken together these form a kind of commentary; the voice is unidentifiable), and the headline of what may be called the "Dante section" is "RHYMES AND REASONS."[6] As he looks at the editor's twitching mouth Stephen wonders, "Would anyone wish that mouth for her kiss? How do you know? Why did you write it then?"—a reference to rhymes he has jotted down, "mouth to her mouth's kiss," earlier that morning in the Proteus chapter. Stephen recalls these commonplace rhymes, then a fragment of Dante's poetry:

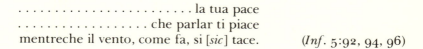

. . . . la tua pace
. . . . che parlar ti piace
mentreche il vento, come fa, si [*sic*] tace.   (*Inf*. 5:92, 94, 96)

These are among Francesca's opening lines. But the terzina, thus placed, seems at first reading to have no direct connection with the theme of love; rather, these lines deal with wind, the great wind of hell which sweeps the carnal sinners through Canto 5, and which is briefly lulled so that Dante can hear Francesca's story:

> . . . . thy peace
> . . . . if thee to speak it please,
> while the wind, as now, for us doth cease.

Aeolus, the newspaper office in Joyce's chapter, is Homer's Cave of the Winds. Dante's lines cut through the windbags. Stephen's mental retreat into Dante's poem has momentarily stilled for him the winds of editorial bombast.

But now Stephen shows himself to be a discriminating reader of the *Divine Comedy*, a poet himself and one who understands Dante's craftsmanship. Apparently Stephen knows the poem, or much of it, by heart; as he reflects on Dante's skill in rhyming, and especially on the "reasons" for Dante's choice of rhyme-words, the young man is able to draw examples from widely separated sections of the *Comedy*. (Dante, in *Inferno* 1, similarly makes the point that he had memorized Virgil's poem.) Rhymes, says Stephen to himself, are "two men dressed the same, looking the same, two by two"; and one man, "he," saw them "three by three"—a tidy specification of Dante's terza rima.

Stephen summons to mind what he knows of Dante's use of color-words as rhyme words. Francesca's triple rhyme becomes a visual image of approaching girls: "He saw them three by three." This moves his mind to Canto 29 of the *Purgatorio*, where Dante first has the vision of seven ladies approaching at the wheel of the gryphon's magic chariot. Three of them are brightly clad, Stephen remembers, "in green, in rose . . . in russet entwining." He knows that the other four are in purple ("in porpora vestite," *Purg.* 29:131), and the associative force of each thought sets off a new impulse: "*per l'aer perso*, in mauve, in purple," he thinks. *Perse*, a kind of murky purple, is the color of the air in Francesca's region of Hell; and it is also the color of the streamlet which trickles into the marshes of Styx and the color of one of the three great stone steps at Purgatory's gate. But only in Canto 5 of the *Inferno* is "perso" used as a rhyme word. Here Dante makes it a sombre image set in contrast, by the other rhymes in its terzina, with omnipotent Goodness, the power of "il Re de l'Universo," whom—if she were able—the gentle Francesca would ask to grant Dante "la tua pace" because he feels compassion for her sad fate, her "mal perverso."[7]

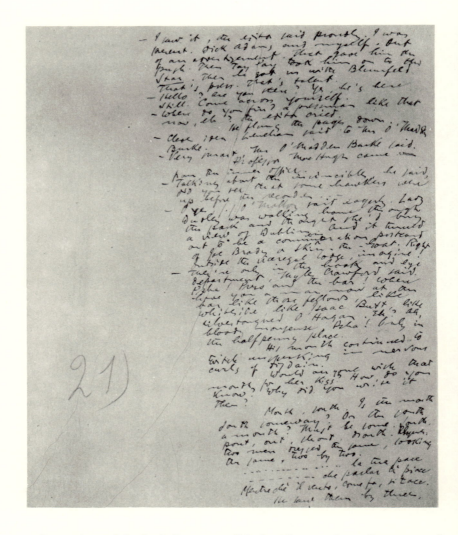

4. Joyce planned the basic Dante parallels for *Ulysses* at the earliest stages of composition. The first manuscript draft of the Aeolus chapter that has survived shows Stephen silently repeating Dante's rhymes. The paragraph is already substantially complete (*U* 137).

approaching girls, in green, in rose, in
gold, entwining, per l'aer perso, in mauve,
in purple, quella pacifica oriafiamma,
in gold of oriflamme, di rimirar fé
più ardenti. But I, old men, penitent,
leadenfooted; mouth south; tomb womb.
— Speak up for yourself, Mr O'Madden Burke
said.

J.J. O'Molloy, smiling palely, took
up the gage. My dear Myles, he said, flinging his
cigarette aside, you told tell a tale
twisted the wrong. I see you. Why not?
bringing Harry Grattan and Flood and
Demosthenes and Edmund Burke? Ignatius
Gallaher we all know and his boss
Harmsworth of the farthing press and
his american cousin of the gutter sheet
not to mention Paddy Kelly's Budget,
Pue's Occurrences and our watchful
friend the Skibbereen Eagle. Why bring
in a master of forensic eloquence like
Whiteside? Sufficient for the day is the
newspaper thereof.
— Grattan and Flood wrote for this very
paper, the editor cried in his face.
Irish volunteers. Where are you now?
Established 1763. Dr Lucas. Who have you
now like John Philpot Curran? Psha.
— Well, J.J. O'Molloy said, Bushe K.C.,
for example.
— Bushe? the editor said. Well, yes:
Bushe, yes. He has a strain of it in his
blood. Kendal Bushe or I mean
Seymour Bushe.
— He would have been on the bench
long ago, the professor said, only ...
J.J. O'Molloy turned to Stephen
and said quietly and slowly:
— One of the most polished periods I
think I ever listened to in my life
fell from the lips of Seymour Bushe.
It was in that case of fratricide, the
Childs murder case. Bushe defended him.

And in the porches of mine ear did pour.

By the way how did he find that out?
He died in his sleep. Or the other story,
beast with two backs?
— What was that? the professor asked.

He spoke on the law of evidence, J.J.
O'Molloy said, of Roman justice as
contrasted with the earlier Mosaic
code, and he spoke of Michelangelo in
the Vatican.
— Ha.

If the reader recalls, as Stephen seems to be doing, the "Reasons" for Dante's use of rhyme words, Dante's color choices in the canto of the dancing ladies extend these associations still further. Red is one of their colors, and the third of the stone slabs at Purgatory's gate is a flaming blood-red. But the word that Stephen renders as "green" is not the simple "verde" which Dante uses 21 times and three times as rhyme word. It is "smeraldo," used only once as a rhyme—in the climactic passage at the close of *Purgatorio* 31 where the eyes of Beatrice are first unveiled to Dante:

> posto t'avem dinanzi a li smeraldi
>   ond' Amor già ti trasse le sue armi.

> We have placed you before the emeralds
>   whence Love ere now has aimed his darts at you.
>
> (Purg. 31:116-117)

In the terzina immediately following there comes a great welling-up of Dante's original love for Beatrice: "a thousand wishes ardent beyond fire." At this point in the poem Dante is escorted by the four ladies in purple, while another three women, singing, urge Beatrice to turn her eyes upon Dante—"al tuo fidele," "thy liegeman." It is the moment when he reaches the highest possible level of human love.

Stephen's last color word is *oriafiamma*, which he sees as gold. Dante uses this as rhyme word at the conclusion of *Paradiso* 31, where, amidst dancing angels, the vision of the Virgin Mary's matchless beauty is revealed:

> così, quella pacifica oriafiamma
>   nel mezzo s'avvivava . . .

> . . . so that great oriflamme
> of peace shone at the center mightily . . .   (*Par.* 31:127-128)

Now Stephen, who presumably has silently recited the whole of this passage—the last sixteen lines of Canto 31—ends his foreshortened overview of the *Divine Comedy* with the last line of Canto 31, expressive of St. Bernard's love for Mary and of Dante's contemplation of Bernard's vision:

> Bernardo, come vide li occhi miei
>   nel caldo suo caler fissi e attenti,
>   li suoi con tanto affetto volse a lei,
> che ' miei di rimirar fé più ardenti.

> Bernardo, seeing that my eyes were fixed
>   upon the shining source of his own warmth,

with such devotion turned his eyes upon her
as to make mine more ardent in their gaze.   (*Par.* 31:139-142)

In only ten lines, Joyce has allowed Stephen to connect three distinct and widely separated examples of the *Comedy's* theme, the role of love in human destiny, and thus to demonstrate how Dante uses language to lock together his poem's three major divisions. Joyce's passage is one of great economy:

RHYMES AND REASONS

Mouth, south. Is the mouth south someway? Or the south a mouth? Must be some. South, pout, out, shout, drouth. Rhymes: two men dressed the same, looking the same, two by two.

. . . . la tua pace
. . . . che parlar ti piace
mentreche il vento, come fa, si tace.

He saw them three by three, approaching girls, in green, in rose, in russet, entwining, *per l'aer perso* in mauve, in purple, *quella pacifica oriafiamma*, in gold of oriflamme, *di rimirar fé più ardenti*. But 1 old men, penitent, leadenfooted, underdarkneath the night: mouth south: tomb womb. (*U* 136-137)

Stephen's interest in Canto 5 is rhetorical but not narrowly so, and his regard for Dante goes to the root of his use of language. "Mouth, south. Is the mouth south someway? . . . Must be some."—the missing words being, in effect, "*reason*, which makes all the difference in the choice of each word the poet selects." To the extent that the fictional Stephen Dedalus resembles in some characteristics the young Joyce of 1904, this passage demonstrates what was involved in the mature Joyce's admiration for "the precision and tersity" of Dante.

In the novel, the way has been opened for exploration of Dante's theme; and the reader's ear will be prepared also for linguistic interlocking of the three major sections of *Ulysses*. An important critical observation about Dante has been made, in the Aeolus chapter, in the voice of Stephen Dedalus. Joyce, who composed with a carefulness almost equal to Dante's, is not likely to have made a casual election of *Inferno* 5 for Stephen's demonstration. Of course the Francesca story is so well known that the names of Paolo and Francesca are familiar even to people who have never read a line of the *Divine Comedy*. With Joyce, it is quite otherwise: his borrowings from Dante are not merely the catchwords but are spread throughout the cantiche. When, therefore, he chooses Canto 5 as the focus of a disquisition on poetic expertness and power, there may be good warrant for closer examination of its appearance in other parts of the book.

The evidence of Joyce's interest in *Inferno* 5 appears, then, to have included both the canto's theme and its verbal devices. We can now turn to a direct comparison. But before examining syntactical patterns in the two works something must be said about the general problem of adapting Dante's story (or any other legend or myth) to fit a modern setting and some indication must be given of Joyce's complex strategies both in *Ulysses* generally and in the Sirens chapter.

A major challenge to Joyce in using Dante's poem would have been the difficulty of connecting it with an improbable protagonist. But, to reverse the terms, the integrity of Joyce's design repeatedly demands some kind of enlargement or extension of Mr Bloom to fit the context of Homer, Shakespeare, Goethe and other literary exemplars as well as Dante. The many subtle connections between Bloom, who is uneducated but intellectually curious, and Stephen, who is precociously erudite by any standard, work to this end. Operating with a gentle contrapuntal irony (gentle, for after all Mr Bloom's intellectual limitations are not of his own making), the author nudges them closer to each other. Moreover, Joyce's invocation of another art, music, takes on extra significance because the reader has discovered in the previous chapter (Wandering Rocks) that Stephen Dedalus is a musician as well as a writer. We may expect Joyce to deploy a variety of non-narrative skills.

The Sirens chapter, all else apart, is a demonstration of verbal skill. In this respect it is consistent with the mind of Stephen Dedalus, as the reader observes it in action in the three chapters where he silently quotes Dante. But the Sirens chapter is all Bloom. Stephen does not appear, nor does the chapter contain any direct quotations from Dante. On the other hand, in the Aeolus chapter Mr Bloom does appear; he sees Stephen without speaking to him, and later on in Sirens Mr Bloom recalls the newspaper office (*U* 137:6; 144:14-32; 256:37). A similar crossing of paths occurs in the Scylla and Charybdis episode in the National Library.[8] Both chapters focus on the writer's craft, though differently; and both suggest Bloom's interest in it and Stephen's character as writer. Stephen's relationship to Bloom is of central importance in the novel; yet it is never explicitly described and must be apprehended from the multitude of verbal clues.

In the episode of *Purgatorio* 31 that Stephen silently recalls, a notable exchange of personalities occurs: the abrupt disappearance of Virgil at the moment when Beatrice first appears. The context is Dante's confession of waywardness in love. Weeping, he admits that, as soon as she had died, "le presenti cose / col falso lor piacer volser miei passi," "the things of the moment, with their false allurement, turned aside my steps" (*Purg.* 31:34-35). Beatrice cautions him to learn from his straying: "perché altra volta / udendo le serene sie più forte," "another time / [you] may be made stronger, hearing sirens sing" (*Purg.* 31:44-45). Something of the flavor of the interplay of Dante's three personages pervades the near-meetings, both physical and psychic, of Stephen and Bloom in the two episodes, first in the newspaper office and then in the Library, where each is shown pursuing, so to speak, his chosen vocation; and finally in the Wandering Rocks chapter where each is engaged in book-buying—a literary activity too, and one in which these two alone among the novel's characters engage.

There is another significant connection also between the book-buying scene in the Wandering Rocks chapter and Stephen's silent recall of *Inferno* 5 in Aeolus. This is the episode, described more fully in Chapter One above, in which Stephen is disparaged by his enemy Buck Mulligan but praised, "thoughtfully," by Mulligan's companion, the English visitor Haines. Mulligan believes that Stephen will never fulfill his prediction of writing something in ten years because his talent has been darkened by "visions of hell." Haines, however, thinks that Stephen may do it after all. A third view is the reader's awareness that the "visions of hell" in Stephen's mind are in fact great poetry, Dante's story of Francesca. Joyce's compositional mode seems to add an element of authorial approval by conveying this information as the voice of a character who is in no way friendly to Stephen. The choice of speaker operates with similar effect for Bloom and Stephen. Bloom, praised by the inimical Lenehan, also receives Joyce's indirect approval.

With this background, the Sirens chapter begins to look like a critical turn in Joyce's novel, related to the other parts of *Ulysses* as *Inferno* 5 is related to Dante's *Purgatorio* and *Paradiso*. The *Divine Comedy* would lie far outside the range of reading that realistically would be possible for Mr Bloom. (He has, on the other hand, made a great effort "aided by a glossary," with Shakespeare.) But the theme of the Sirens chapter, like that of the *Divine Comedy*, is human love—its part in man's destiny. And the chapter's narrative form and focus, like the Francesca episode, concerns an adulterous triangle. Stephen, who is never shown to have any awareness of Bloom's predicament, is nevertheless seen by the reader—and by no one else—making a mental linkage between Shakespeare's Hamlet triangle and Dante's Francesca. Stephen Dedalus has a fine critical understanding of

Dante's treatment of this theme, but the young man has not yet known love in his limited experience of life. Mr Bloom, however, has; and in Sirens his unspoken thoughts pass in review what he has learned about love. On the evidence, the Sirens episode in its many resemblances to Dante's *Inferno* 5 seems to be one more of those instances in which Joyce has Mr Bloom "act out" a more pragmatic, Ulyssean version of ideas and attitudes expressed by Stephen Dedalus—ideas which, transformed by Bloomean experiential realities, are often sounder and more defensible than the younger man's intellectualized verbal formulations. That is a measure of Joyce's art.

*

Turning to the function of technical devices, we may see Joyce's fugue, at least in part, as an emulation of Dante's linguistic virtuosity. Joyce had a craftsman's understanding of Dante's invention of the terza rima and his achievement in using it for so long a poem. Dante's rhyme choices usually have an unforced, effortless quality; yet nine times out of ten he uses the rhyme word to emphasize or even to carry his idea. The rhyme word is the important word in the line not only for sound but for sense; not just for the pleasure it gives the ear but for the progress of Dante's argument. Most of the sentences in the *Divine Comedy* coincide with the terzina; some are just three lines long, but sentence length is varied to avoid mechanical rhythm. Since the middle verse of a terzina prepares the ear for the sound of the rhyme word to come in the next terzina, Dante has used his rhymes as a structural device of great force. They lock the parts of his poem as firmly together as the great blocks of some ancient stone wall.

A suggestion, necessarily subjective, of the close "fit" of acoustic and semantic properties is important everywhere in Joyce's prose. In the Sirens chapter this quality is tightly controlled to produce the circular pattern often used in the musical fugue.[9] One of Dante's notable effects in the *Divine Comedy* is the linkage of sound and meaning, and a comparable achievement lies at the heart of Joyce's technical accomplishment in "Sirens." Here, two things can be observed and related to each other. First, there is the choice of words in which phoneme and morpheme are so related as to construct chains of linked sound that can be made to echo in the ear as rhymes do, and that can be made to carry overtones of defined meaning. Second, there is the effort that Joyce made to prune and cut back syntactic structures so that sound values could come to the fore and make a verbal counterpoint.

In the first endeavor Joyce has created a total of seventeen identifiable voices, in the musical sense of the term "voice." In the second, by a skillful manipulation of connectives, he has concatenated long passages made up of several voices. The author's prose moves the reader's eye and ear from one meaning to the next, as a composer modulates from note to note and from chord to chord. The effect is not unlike Dante's use of the terza rima to move his lines through transitions that are both musically and intellectually meaningful.

Joyce had also observed and admired Dante's manipulation of stress and rhythm by rhyme choices. This is apparent in his selection and placement of the three lines quoted by Stephen Dedalus:

. . . . la tua pace

. . . . che parlar vi piace

mentreche 'l vento, come fa, ci tace.

In the novel, only the last of these three verses is quoted in full; thus the reader is made aware of the cumulative rhythm by Stephen's silent recall of the complete phrase rather than just the rhyme word. The manner of recall suggests an interest in Dante's use of the terza rima in the control and ordering of cadence, which is a notable feature of *Inferno* 5. Cadence is a term which can indicate any measured movement of sound, and may be taken here as "intonation," especially as that modulation of tones which produces a sense of movement toward a conclusion. In their context the rhyme words build a cumulative emotional progression (this last word in its musical sense) and the final rhyme, coming at the end of the last of the series of terzine in which we are introduced to Francesca, accomplishes one of Dante's impressive effects. Geoffrey Bickersteth describes it as bringing a long drawn-out melody to a full close.[10]

Joyce (whose own verses are perhaps the least part of his achievement) transferred this metrical effect to prose, using repetitive sound patterns to perform the function of rhyme in placing and interweaving the stresses. While the eye goes on reading for the literal sense of the line, the ear perceives a triple effect, as recurring sound patterns in the opening pages of "Sirens" identify the fugal voice, involve it in a duet with a second identifiable voice, and move the reader's attention musically through a statement.

In the first 56 lines of connected discourse, for example, Joyce introduces the "Subject" —which in the chapter is the Sirens' Song—

and briefly combines it with the "Answer," stated by Mr Bloom.[11] This initial passage opens and closes with a sentence that arranges sounds to establish a tonal center and is thus a verbal equivalent of the tonic in music: "Bronze by gold, Miss Douce's head by Miss Kennedy's head, over the crossblind of the Ormond bar heard the viceregal hoofs go by, ringing steel" (*U* 253). The rhythm is established and carried forward beyond the opening sentence by a succession of aspirates:

> head . . . head . . . heard . . . hoofs . . . her . . . his

The fugal Subject is heard for the first time through the notation of two barmaids, Miss Douce and Miss Kennedy, who work in the Ormond Hotel and are the sirens of the chapter. For their characterization, or musical voice, Joyce develops a pattern of sibilants and alliterative "l" sounds, combined with light vowel sounds and the light, plosive "t."

It is important to distinguish the fugal *subject* from the fugal *voice*: the former is carried by the content of the *words*, the latter by the *sound*. Thus the Sirens' Song as the fugal subject is flirtatious, falsely welcoming, insincerely promising, mendacious; but these qualities cannot be attributed to phonemic combinations. Moreover, the fugal subject, after its first announcement by the two barmaids, is taken up by other characters present in the Ormond bar, each of whom speaks and otherwise is represented by an individualized sound pattern, his own fugal *voice*.

The barmaids' fugal voice is based on these words:

> Miss Douce . . . bronze . . . Miss Kennedy . . . gold . . . ladylike . . . eagerly

In the consonance of partial rhyme and alliteration, their sibilants and vowel sounds become repetitive stress patterns. Miss Kennedy's rhythm, like her surname, is dactyllic, and the barmaids' voices, though differentiated from each other, are not dissimilar as they disappear into the prose and reappear:

> flower . . . I'll . . . long . . . ladylike . . . she . . . teacup tea . . . teapot tea . . . reef . . . teas . . . teas . . .

The choice of "reef" suggests mermaids, the reiterated "teas" carries a double meaning, and Miss Kennedy's light front vowel "e," a soprano sound, becomes through the narrator's descriptive terms more firmly established as part of the barmaids' l-laden fugal voice. The opening passage concludes (as each successive statement does, following the musical convention) with a return to the tonic. Joyce repeats in a new intermixture the sounds and rhythms of the opening sentence, giving a sense of circular movement: "Yes, bronze from anear, by gold from afar, heard steel from anear, hoofs ring from afar, and heard steelhoofs ringhoof ringsteel."

In similar fashion Joyce selected for each of the "speaking" characters in the episode a pattern of sounds which, like the resonance of the barmaids' fugal voices, vibrate simultaneously in the ear and in the mind. These distinctive sound patterns, each one carefully introduced, are combined in duets, trios and quartets of mixed conversation, monologue and descriptive (presumably authorial) fact or comment. A narrative pattern is constructed on the fugal model of statement and restatement.

In the opening pages of the chapter, then, distinctive rhythms are established—like every verbal composition, the chapter is constructed of rhythms. Dante's Canto 5, on one poetic level, is composed of rhythms. Moreover, most admirers of Dante's poetry have noted that the determinants of rhythm are not the metronomic beats of absolute time but the phrasal rhythms and the movement of the line as a whole, in groupings of stresses which are related to the sense of the passage. As Bickersteth notes, in English verse also it is the relation of word-values accentually to one another that determines the rhythm. Joyce inspired Stuart Gilbert, in his book *James Joyce's Ulysses*, to call attention specifically to the importance of "the rhythm of the prose" in "Sirens." The first three pages of this section of Gilbert's exegesis are set off from the rest, and the introduction claims that these pages "reproduce word for word, information given me by Joyce."[12] Attention is called to "rhythm as one of the clues to the meaning," and to the fact that each character has "his appropriate rhythm." If Joyce was thus sensitive to the uses of rhythm it is hard to believe that he was unaware of its use to individuate the foremost personage of Canto 5. This is a complex matter.

*

Mode and tenor of discourse, and also choice of speaker, emerge from the hands of a craftsman like Dante or Joyce as an art of discrimination. Through many devices of style the reader is given wide ranging connections and contrasts, and delicate clues to meaning.

The modulations of speech in Dante's *Inferno* 5 are developed with some ambiguity. The story, told in melodious language while the great wind of Hell is stilled, seems out of place, an intrusion. Dante the traveler responds to the sad tale and to the inflections of the proud and gentle narrator with such compassion that at its conclusion he falls, fainting. Dante the poet has placed in eternal torment one of his most sympathetic portraits; in terms of the poem as a whole he has committed the lyric voice to the unfolding of a theme, the power of love, which seems not to belong to Hell since it is, for Dante, the force that draws man upward to Paradise. Linguistically as well as explicitly, love in the moral structure of the *Divine Comedy* is identified with Beatrice who brought Dante out of the Dark Wood.

Some of the linguistic subtleties of Dante's construction are also discernible in Joyce's "Sirens." First, modern critics have noted that "amore," a word reserved by Dante for the *Purgatorio* and *Paradiso*, appears a minimal number of times in the *Inferno* but is a key word in Francesca's story. This word, "love," is certainly a *voussoir* also in the rhetorical structure of the Sirens chapter. Joyce's manipulation of vocabulary in fact is as carefully precise as Dante's.[13]

Second, Joyce's selection of the fugue, with its potential for complicated interweaving of ideas and its recurrent summaries and restatements, becomes a powerful rhetorical implement. The fugue as a pattern offers a flexible verbal system in which the author can show his protagonist's thoughts moving back and forth between two poles—in this case, between the Dantesque themes of love and death. The chapter becomes a kind of dramatization of Dante's line, "e più di mille / ombre mostrommi, e nominommi a dito / ch'amor di nostra vita dipartille" ("and a thousand yet / and still more . . . he pointed to / and named, whom love from our life did separate"). Dante's meaning in this line is not, of course, simply physical death. It is the eternal death of the souls consigned to damnation. Joyce in this chapter invests the idea of death with multiple significance but always centers it on the *waste of life*: it may be the purposeless ending of life before one has fully lived; or the careless squandering of vitality in dissipation; or, especially, the moral death of despair which he associates with degradation, brutality, or venality.

These are matters of rhetoric, and in the Sirens episode Joyce's principal weapon is his use of the contrapuntal technique to pair contrasting aspects of his subject of discourse. Dante's line, "Amor condusse noi ad una morte" ("Love led us to one death") is the controlling idea of Joyce's Sirens as it is in the Francesca episode. It is not simply "Love" that is the object of inquiry, but the perverse aspect of willfully misguided love, through which men and women are drawn down to eternal death. It is *not* human passion that is punished in Canto 5, nor is it simple lust nor broken marriage vows. The mortal quality of the sin of Paolo and Francesca lay in their abandonment of reason, highest of human faculties, as a guide to action. Their punishment was to continue forever thus, losing their power of free movement and subject to their master "Amor" for all eternity.

Joyce's critical reading of this story is reflected in his identification of the Sirens' Song as the *mendacious* promise of love which leads men to death—literally in the Homeric original, morally in Joyce's view as also in Dante's. The Dantesque view is made explicit near the end of the novel, in the Eumaeus chapter, as Stephen Dedalus and Mr Bloom walk home together, "continuing their tête à tête . . . about sirens, enemies of man's reason" (*U* 649:25).

Third in Joyce's rhetorical maneuvers is the control of tone and atmosphere in the episode. Dante in Canto 5 has portrayed Francesca entirely by the suggestive potential of the lyric voice. Elsewhere in the *Divine Comedy*, in a striking simile or by some telling descriptive phrase, the poet sketches a character in brief decisive strokes, but he has not done so with Francesca. She appears to the reader as a presence, a gentle and modest noblewoman: we know her attributes through the tone of voice with which the poet has endowed her.

The two girls who are the sirens of Joyce's episode seem to present themselves to us directly; however, by subtle and sharp contrasts of tone, Joyce creates an ironic negative metaphor. In their self-image Miss Douce and Miss Kennedy resemble Francesca, but the reader sees them both through their own utterances and also in the private view where the spurious self-image is deflated. These two see themselves as "ladylike," but in fact they are vulgar in speech and action. They see themselves as generous and kindly, but in fact they are hostile and venal. Confidently they assume their feminine attractiveness; in fact their flirtatious relationship to the patrons of the Ormond is trivial and transient.

A similar but more ambitious effect is Joyce's portrait of Mr Bloom's mind, which is rendered without overt comment, by controlling the tone of his silent monologue and setting this in contrast to the conversations and remarks of the other patrons of the Ormond.

In the case of Mr Bloom, the resemblance to *Inferno* 5 stems from the moral and rhetorical uncertainties of Dante's construction, especially his placing of the gentle, proud, and loving Francesca in hell. Dante's awareness of the fatal flaw comes in the terzina where he asks Francesca how the lovers came to their sad plight:

> Ma dimmi: al tempo d'i dolci sospiri
>   a che e come concedette amore
>   che conosceste i dubbiosi disiri?

> . . . but tell me: in the time of the sweet sighs, by what and how did Love grant you to know the dubious desires? (*Inf.* 5:118-120, trans. Singleton)

Up to this point Dante has been altogether sympathetic. But now the tone changes: as Francesca recounts their mutual seduction through their reading of the tale of Lancelot, she enlarges the perspective, saying, "Our Galleotto [pander] was the book, and he who wrote it," "Galeotto fu il libro e chi lo scrisse," her words indicating her awareness of their mortal sin.

The pathos of Francesca's story is enhanced by the involvement of Paolo, which is minimal and thus more striking. At the end of the first part of her recital he appears, but only in the use of the plural pronoun, "da lor," "from them." Queste parole da lor ci fur porte" ("These words were borne to us from them"). The next line, set off from the preceding one by a full stop, is believed by some critics to be spoken by Paolo: "Caina attende chi a vita ci spense," "Caina waits for him who snuffed out our lives" (*Inf.* 5:108). The tone of this line, hostile and grim, has often been remarked upon as out of character for Francesca. Regardless of the speaker's identity, the *contrast of tone* of this line creates a powerful effect and one that seems essential in the characterization of Francesca. Rhetorically it is a basic element in the total effect. Finally, in the closing terzina, Francesca describes the lovers' first fatal kiss as Paolo silently weeps; and Dante faints in pity.

> Mentre che l'uno spirto questo disse
>   l'altro piangea sì, che di pietade . . .

> While the one spirit said this, the other wept, so that for pity I swooned . . . (*Inf.* 5:139-140, trans. Singleton)

Joyce, by a comparable modulation of tone, gives a sympathetic account of his protagonist's mind as it reflects on the same problem that Dante encounters in Canto 5—the causes and complications of guilty love. Mr Bloom asks himself, as Dante the traveler asks Francesca, "How does adultery come about?" The compassionate and humane quality of Bloom's reflections and conclusions are a kind of critical comment on *Inferno* 5; as Dante begins with compassionate curiosity ("l'affettuoso grido") but ends with a deep involvement of pity, *pietade*, so Mr Bloom exhibits something of Dante's unrelenting rationality. And the last line of the canto suggests Dante's familiarity with this sin: like Mr Bloom, Dante is *un homme moyen sensuel*.

Bloom's reflections center on his obsessive jealousy, fueled by the thought of his wife's probable infidelity with her concert manager, Blazes Boylan; his thoughts are counterpointed with his silent observations on the lives and personalities of the other patrons of the Ormond. At the core of the chapter is the tale of the deceived husband, the erring wife, and the wife's lover. Joyce's strategy uses the force of familiar songs to compel Mr Bloom to recall, one after another, circumstances associated with his wife. Extended by the development of Joyce's fugal web, the origins of Bloom's predicament unfold, as Francesca's tale unfolds, in a few sharply defined sequences.

Like the terza rima, the fugal form enriches while it constrains. The requirements, even when loosely observed, are a confining influence. (This is usually also true in musical compositions, of which the strictest canon compositions—e.g., "Three blind mice"—are the least interesting.) The form arrests the motion of language as the author concentrates on producing a verbal equivalent of imitative counterpoint. This effect in turn strengthens the inner movement. Within each statement—four in Joyce's chapter—an emotional climax is precisely built; a new aspect of Mr Bloom's dilemma is set forth as his silent monologue is related to the briefly summarized story of another character. The complexities of narration are firmly held by the fugal pattern.

More especially, the imitative quality of the fugal writing creates a resonance, a challenge recurrently suggested. The rigid form, that is, also holds in check the portrayal of complexities of personality. Contradictory glimpses are given of the principal voices, and especially of Mr Bloom. These are held in an undetermined state; they are invested with expectation. Precise meanings are never identified: they are examined but are presented as if not governed by the author.

Here the resemblance to Dante's Canto 5 calls up the three-line statement of Francesca which reveals that she and her lover were killed *in flagrante delicto* by her husband. It was this event, cutting off the guilty pair from any possibility of repentance of mortal sin, that determined their damnation.[14] This poses a moral problem that Dante deals with later in the poem and that is central to the artistic question of why he evokes our sympathy for Francesca. The suggestion is made that a force far more powerful than reason has been implanted in human nature; Dante contains this meaning in a single line, which he introduces first in Francesca's terzina:

Amor, ch' al cor gentil ratto s'apprende,
   prese costui de la bella persona
   che mi fu tolta; e 'l modo ancor m'offende.

Love, which is quickly kindled in a gentle heart, seized this one for
the fair form that was taken from me—and the way of it afflicts me
still. (*Inf.* 5:100-102, trans. Singleton)

The rather sordid and brutal particulars are stated with a gentle
reticence—almost the voice of innocence.

As in Dante's canto, Joyce's rhetoric shades the tone and atmosphere, creating emotional progressions. *Inferno* 5 begins with a storm:
as Francesca speaks the wind explicitly ceases, but within her tale, the
use of gentle terms such as "desire" and "peace" contrast with the brutality of the lovers' murder. There are two progressions, the first describing Francesca's birth and upbringing, her meeting with Paolo
and their love for each other, and their common death; the second
tells with great brevity and rising emotion how their love developed
into the sin of adultery. Both sections of the story, on different moral
levels, move from innocence to catastrophe, from love to death.

Joyce's four fugal statements within the chapter, taken either as a
whole or individually, are a progression from the simplicity of in-
genuous guile to the complex moral catastrophe of wasted life. First,
in a brief exposition of the fugal theme, the reader is introduced to
the siren barmaids and the ear is prepared for an apparent confrontation of Mr Bloom and his rival, the seducer Blazes Boylan. The fugal
technique requires repetition of the original theme, always with a difference. Thus, with the barmaids' flirtations as the "Subject" of the
fugue, Mr Bloom's version of the sirens' song will be the "Answer"
and Boylan's version the Countersubject. At once the dimensions are
widened by this formal pattern, of which the essence is contrast. The
reader is invited to look for resemblances that are *defined by the differences* that appear when things are set alongside each other.

The fugal web develops our knowledge of three Dublin characters
who, with Bloom, Boylan and the barmaids, are the major personages
of the chapter. Each is a study in failure; three lives have been ruined
by dissipation. Simon Dedalus, father of Stephen, once had talent and
still has charm, but we learn that conviviality was pursued at the ex-
pense of his family. His wife has died of overwork, his children are
ragged and hungry. Richie Goulding, Stephen's maternal uncle, is a
member of a Dublin business firm and carries himself as "a prince";
but in fact he is a spendthrift, is slowly dying of Bright's disease, and is
estranged from his brother-in-law, whom he nevertheless continues

to flatter. Ben Dollard, once a wealthy ships' chandler but now a resident in a home for derelicts, is an alcoholic bankrupt, the clearest example of failure through dissipation. Like Homer's original, the chapter's vehicle of enticement is music: all three men are notable in Dublin as vocal performers.

In the four fugal statements that make up the chapter's narrative, the intermingling of these characters becomes more complex and the account of failure and wasted life becomes increasingly specific. This progression is matched by the music (each of these characters "performs" in turn) which identifies and marks out each statement, and also by the internal rhetoric. Within each presentation there is also a movement, as the tale is told, from the idea of love to the idea of death.

While the singing of Dedalus and the conversation of Goulding elicits from Bloom a thin trickle of direct reply and a great deal of silent monologue, the reader watches the progress of Bloom's silent reflections about his wife. As Dante, the listener in *Inferno* 5, wishes to hear from Francesca what first steps led to the death of the lovers, Joyce's protagonist now reviews in his mind his courtship of Molly, their early love, and the circumstances of her involvement with Boylan. Joyce's passage is a kind of model, a demonstration of his admired predecessor's deployment of rhetorical devices. Observe the resemblances between the tone of Dante's request and the opening passages of Bloom's reminiscences. First there is a pattern of question and answer, speaker and listener, combined with a promise of revelation both in Dante's canto and in Joyce's passage.

Canto 5	"Sirens"
e cominciai: "Francesca, i tuoi martìri / a lagrimar mi fanno tristo e pio.	The voice of Lionel returned, weaker but unwearied. It sang again to Richie Poldy Lydia Lidwell also sang to Pat open mouth ear waiting, to
Ma dimmi: al tempo d'i dolci sospiri, / a che e come concedette amore / che conosceste i dubbiosi disiri?	wait.
"Francesca," I began, / "Your martyrdom calls forth compassion's tears: / But tell me, in the time of love's sweet sighs, / What stratagem of passion urged you on, / And wakened guilty yearning in your heart?" (*Inf.* 5:116-119)	How first he saw that form endearing, how sorrow seemed to part, how look, form, word, charmed him Gould Lidwell won Pat Bloom's heart. (*U* 270:36-40)

The fugal subject, answer and countersubject are set against each other as Bloom's monologue moves from the innocent joy of first love to the "loss" of love in estrangement, seduction, or death.

By shifting vocabulary, the change of atmosphere in the Ormond bar recalls the change of tone that introduces Francesca's story:

Canto 5	"Sirens"
Di quel che udire e che parlar vi piace / noi udiremo e parleremo a voi, / mentre che 'l vento, come fa, ci tace.	Through the hush of air a voice sang to them, low, not rain, not leaves in murmur, like no voice of strings of reeds [Mr Bloom's own words in italics] *or whatdoyoucallthem dulcimers*,
Of that which it pleases you to hear and to speak, we will hear and speak with you, while the wind, as now, is silent for us. (*Inf.* 5:94-96, trans. Singleton)	touching their still ears with words, still hearts of their each his remembered lives. (*U* 269:29-32)

The passage quoted from the *Divine Comedy* will be recognized as the one quoted earlier by Stephen Dedalus in the Aeolus chapter; it is notable that Mr Bloom hears the voice as a mediaeval instrument. The repetition of "still" and the associated terms, "hush," "low," and "murmur," suggest the change of tone in Canto 5 that comes at this point when the hellish blast, "la bufera infernal," ceases so that Dante may hear the lovers' story. Dante and Virgil listen to the tale of Francesca and Paolo; similarly the personal application of "Love's Old Sweet Song" will be recalled for each of the characters in the Ormond bar—especially for Mr Bloom.[15]

The song that Simon Dedalus sings, "M'appari," is rendered in English, but not fully, the title indicating that the translation comes from the Italian (the aria is from Flotow's opera *Martha*, originally written in German). As the song begins the word "love" is repeated three times in two lines. This suggests the triple repetition of "amor" in Francesca's story, as the initial word of three successive terzine:

Canto 5	"Sirens"
Amor, ch' al cor gentil ratto s'apprende,	Good, good to hear: sorrow from them each seemed to from both depart when first they heard. When
. . . . . .	first they saw, lost Richie, Poldy,
Amor, ch'a nullo amato amar perdona,	mercy of beauty, *heard from a person wouldn't expect it in the least* [Mr
. . . . . .	Bloom's own words in italics], her
Amor condusse noi ad una morte.	

Love which lays sudden hold on
gentle hearts
· · · · · ·
Love, which absolves no heart
beloved from loving,

· · · · · ·
Love led us both together to one
death. (*Inf.* 5:100, 103, 106)

first merciful lovesoft oftloved word.
Love that is singing: love's old sweet
song. . . . Love's old sweet *sonnez la
gold*. (*U* 269:32-38)

Joyce's language in the line, "Her first merciful lovesoft oftloved word," seems also to echo Dante's triple repetition, "Amor . . . amato amar," which heightens the emotional quality of the central terzina.[16]

The next sentence includes the Dantesque word "fourfold," and invites multiple interpretations as the complexity of Bloom's thoughts is suggested. The contrapuntal movement of the chapter is recapitulated by the use of musical terms: "Bloom wound a skein round four forkfingers, stretched it, relaxed, and wound it round his troubled double, fourfold, in octave, gyved them fast" (*U* 269:39).

The passage concludes with a restatement of Mr Bloom's fugal Answer. The note of death is struck as he imagines the breakup of his marriage and Molly's subsequent abandonment by her seducer.

> Thou lost one. All songs on that theme . . . Cruel it seems. Let people get fond of each other: lure them on. Then tear asunder. Death. Explos. Knock on the head. Outtohelloutofthat. Human life. . . . Gone. They sing. Forgotten. I too. And one day she with. Leave her: get tired. Suffer then. Snivel. Big Spanishy eyes goggling at nothing. (*U* 273:8-15)

He repeats the theme of the Sirens' Song, "Let people get fond of each other: lure them on," as the musical convention requires: but with the notable difference (which characterizes Mr Bloom as the fugal Answer) of the added element of compassion: "Cruel it seems." In the verbal counterpoint this "Answer" is juxtaposed with the fugal Subject, which at this stage in the development has become a batsqueak of sensuality: "Lydia for Lidwell squeak scarcely hear so ladylike the muse unsqueaked a ray of hope" (*U* 270:31).

The chapter as musical composition ends with a coda, introduced in Bloom's words by the the musical sign, "da capo." The brighteyed gallantry has whirled to a *stretto*; but it has been contradicted rhetorically, and the coda assumes a pensive tone. There is no longer any sound of piano or song; the chapter's sounds are now only thumps, taps, pom-poms, and growls. Mr Bloom, though he could not possibly quote Dante as Stephen Dedalus has done, nevertheless is allowed a Dantesque conclusion to his monologue. His digestion is disturbed by flatulence from his luncheon drink: "Gassy thing that cider" (*U* 283). With the musical signs of forte, *Ff*, and fortissimo, *Fff*, and the corresponding signs of *piano* and *pianissimo*, the growling "Rf" of Bloom's flatulence ends the chapter, as Dante ends a canto of the *Inferno*: "Ed elli avea del cul fatto trombetta" ("And he of his rump made a trumpet"). This line, moreover, is the line silently quoted by Stephen in *his* silent reflections in the National Library, the Scylla and Charybdis chapter. Joyce ends the Sirens chapter on a trumpeting triple forte:

Pprrpffrrppfff

with the last word being the Italian musical sign or direction, in its English translation, "Fine" ("Done").

*

If Joyce indeed meant to focus the Sirens episode on a narrative pattern that would reflect the Francesca story, the endeavor is in itself Dantesque. Dante gave a new ending to the Ulysses story in *Inferno* 26, and other traditional stories in the *Divine Comedy* are told with a new ending or from a unique point of view. Dante and Joyce assert their own vision. The triangular relationship that structures the narrative of *Ulysses* resembles the Francesca episode, but with some differences. In Dante's Canto 5, Virgil and the poet-pilgrim listen, Francesca speaks, and Paolo silently weeps; but the wronged husband is only a pronoun—"Caina attende chi a vita ci spense," "He who snuffed out our lives, for whom Caina waits." For their murder, and still more for encompassing their damnation, the jealous husband will be consigned to the deepest circle of hell—frozen Caina.

Joyce's twist gives the wronged husband the center of the stage. Mr Bloom, the principal voice in Joyce's fugue, has more than three times as many lines as any other character; his unspoken thoughts are the chapter's vehicle of narrative advance. Bloom's wife, Molly, is present—like Francesca's husband—only in the mind of her spouse and in the lazily scurrilous gossip of the patrons of the Ormond bar. The adulterous usurper, Boylan, does appear and speak in person, as the prospect of a confrontation opens the chapter. And there is a confrontation, but it takes place wholly in Bloom's mind. He and his rival are in adjoining rooms in these crucial moments before Boylan goes to the rendezvous. Mr Bloom stays out of sight, watches Boylan leave, considers going home to break it up, but in the end he does not do so.

Thus the chapter becomes an exploration in depth of the feelings of the wronged husband. As a rejection of the irrational wrath that produces murder, Sirens preserves the substance and moral stance of *Inferno* 5.

Joyce's novel is at its most un-Dantean in its exploration of domesticity. This is a matter to which Dante, whose own wife never appears in the *Divine Comedy*, makes only the most incidental reference. Dante has no encomium of the steadfast husband, no invective against the shrewish wife. In the Seventh cornice of Purgatory, the souls in the purging fire sing of husbands and wives who were chaste, "come virtute e matrimonio imponne" ("as virtue and strict wedlock point the way," *Purg.* 25:135). There are occasional references to the happiness of parenthood, as in Cacciaguida's account of old times and old families in Florence, but these focus on the parent-child rather than the husband-wife relationship; and except for Cacciaguida's remarks they are stated from the viewpoint of the child. Even the happiness of parenthood is qualified, as Dante notes that the fond, obedient child, who runs trustfully to the parent at the stage of lisping and babytalk, turns from his mother when he reaches the age of mature speech.

But the core of the narrative in *Ulysses* is the stripping away of sentimentality from the relationship of husband and wife. In the Sirens chapter, where a moment of crisis focuses the protagonist's action, it is revealed to Mr Bloom that he is a husband. He is the life-partner, Boylan the casual companion in lust.

*

Finally, there is the structural use of metaphor. Music as the art of the Sirens chapter is more than technique—it becomes an extended metaphor. Mr Bloom says, "Words? Music? No: it's what's behind." What he means, we learn from his silent monologue, is that music, the "language of love," is a vehicle of human communication. In this broader sense music has the functional importance in Joyce's chapter that literature holds for Dante's Canto 5.

The characters in this chapter of *Ulysses* respond to music with a mindless sentimentality that is revealed as being also their response to the problems of life. Music is seductive, but they meet it more than halfway, using music as a drug might be used. Their inadequacy in the musical dimension both stands for and is part of their other insufficiencies. The demonstration of this falsely sentimental quality of contemporary Dublin good-fellowship becomes the true business of the chapter.

Dante's lovers in *Inferno* 5 were enticed into adultery by reading together the story of Lancelot and Guinevere. By the use of this tale the Francesca episode invokes (as Dante does also in other parts of the poem) an older literary tradition, and Francesca's use of the cadences of Dante's own poetry invokes the *dolce stil nuovo* (which also is used in other parts of the *Comedy*). Present day readers are apt to overlook this aspect of *Inferno* 5 because, over seven centuries, Paolo and Francesca have themselves become legendary. But Dante makes these lovers, who were to him protagonists in a contemporary scandal, say that they were enticed into adultery by reading together an old fiction. The book was their pander, "and he who wrote it." Dante, poet as well as pilgrim, is shocked by the moral implications of this statement. The enchantment of literature is given a metaphorical extension to include the role of seducer, as Renato Poggioli first discovered.[17] This element of menace to his artistic authority, as well as his compassion for the lovers, increases Dante's personal involvement, as is evinced in his final fainting. The true business of the canto thus becomes the poet's broadened understanding of the nature of love and an adjustment of his art to express this knowledge.

In Joyce's chapter, music is the predominant art and is a seductive influence in exactly the way that literature is in *Inferno* 5. Mr Bloom's wife Molly is a concert artist, and Boylan, her seducer, has arranged concerts for her. Thus brought together in the first place by music, the ostensible purpose of their appointment on this fated day is a rehearsal for a forthcoming concert. On the piano in Bloom's house, the sheet music for "Love's Old Sweet Song" is, as Bloom himself sees at the end of the day, "open at the last page"; these words suggest the presence of a rhetorical model focused on the conclusion of Dante's little drama, and the word *page* directly connects Francesca's book with Molly Bloom's sheet music.

Again one observes the imitative movement of Joyce's design. The piano of the Ithaca chapter is functionally connected with the Sirens chapter by a descriptive term, *coffin* (*U* 259:20; 691:7), which also associates this passage with *Inferno* 5 by echoing a note of death. As the objects on the piano are enumerated, an emerging visual image of Boylan playing and Molly singing begins to resemble Dante's account of the seductive reading that entrapped Francesca—the song of love, the book of love. The convention of musical directions permits the Italian language to be used in Joyce's "final indications" of the musical duet; his chosen terms do not apply to the banal composition on the piano, but they do convey the emotional quality of Francesca's closing lines. Thus Joyce's final word, *close*, becomes a compressed expression of the equivalent moment in Canto 5, which Dante has emphasized by understatement and by setting it off grammatically in a separate statement occupying exactly one line: "quel giorno più non vi leggemmo avante," "that day we read no further" (*Inf.* 5:138).

Inferno 5	"Ithaca"
But if you have such great desire to know the first root of our love, I will tell as one who weeps and tells. One day, for pastime, we read of Lancelot, how love constrained him; we were alone, suspecting nothing. Several times that reading urged our eyes to meet, and took the color from our faces; but one moment alone it was that overcame us. When we read how the longed-for smile was kissed by so great a lover, this one, who never shall be parted from me, kissed my mouth all trembling. A Gallehaut was the book and he who wrote it; that day we read no farther in it. (*Inf.* 5:124-138, trans. Singleton)	What occupied the position originally occupied by the sideboard? A vertical piano (Cadby) with exposed keyboard, its closed coffin supporting a pair of long yellow ladies' gloves and an emerald ashtray containing four consumed matches, a partly consumed cigarette and two discoloured ends of cigarettes, its musicrest supporting the music in the key of G natural for voice and piano of *Love's Old Sweet Song* (words by G. Clifton Bingham, composed by J. L. Molloy, sung by Madam Antoinette Sterling) open at the last page with the final indications ad libitum, forte, pedal animato, sustained, pedal, ritirando, close. (*U* 691)

This particular arrangement of data, in its carefully composed sequence, tells the story of the exact moment of Molly's consent to her seducer; the visual image thus conveyed corresponds to the graphic recital by Francesca of the same moment in her story. It must be explained that this quotation is typical of the Ithaca chapter, which is rendered entirely in the narratorial voice and in which, throughout, information is given in the driest question-and-answer form. The song, of course, is a prominent feature of the Sirens chapter. Since Bloom has been told by Molly at an early stage of the novel that she is going to meet Boylan for a rehearsal of this song, when the reader reaches the Sirens episode he is aware that the mere thought of the title is enough to make Bloom think of the seduction enacted in his absence. As Dante connects *Inferno* 5 with other parts of his poem, so Joyce extends Sirens twice to establish important connections in the novel: first, by the talk between Bloom and Stephen about "Sirens, enemies of man's reason," in Eumaeus where Bloom and Stephen walk and talk together as Virgil and Dante do (*U* 649:24), and second, by this evocation of Molly in Bloom's mind, in Ithaca.

Bloom's recall of the title in Sirens comes at the beginning of Simon Dedalus's rendition of Lionel's aria, "M'appari." This is a passage which, as shown above, in placement and in rhetoric echoes *Inferno* 5, with an additional Dantesque implication in the use of "fourfold" to describe Bloom's winding of an elastic band round his fingers. This band later becomes a "musical instrument," when the singing has ended and Bloom has "ungyved his crisscrossed hands," but at this earlier point it must be intended as reinforcing imagery for the direction and complexity of Bloom's thoughts. It is an emotional climax both in the chapter and in the novel as a whole, where an unironic view is given—momentary but quite clear—of Bloom as he considers "Love's bitter mystery" with that knowledge of life which has thus far been denied to young Stephen Dedalus. And it is in this passage that Bloom articulates the metaphor of music as the "language of love."

Words? Music? No: It's what's behind.
Bloom looped, unlooped, noded, disnoded.   (*U* 270:21-22)

The verbs "noded" and "disnoded" seem almost to be Joycean inventions produced to fit the musical convention of his fugal pattern; but they also echo the *Divine Comedy*, where Dante twice uses "disnodare," a word taken directly from Latin, and as rare in Italian as "disnoded" is in English.

As Dante does with literature, so Joyce with music as his figurative vehicle builds a complex progression. The principal characters of the episode are presented in terms of the music they hear; the chapter explores the implications of the musical compositions that are presented and used in a variety of ways, always with extended significance. Both in the Francesca episode and in Sirens there are two sides to the metaphor, and in both works the negative and positive aspects are hedged with ambiguity. In Joyce's chapter, the negative thrust of the maneuver represents the music as seductive and weakening—not absolutely but potentially—but this is only part of the picture. As a vehicle of human communication music is also made to stand for an affirmation of vitality, of the deep wellsprings of life. To the extent that a parallel with Dante's metaphor can be accepted, this suggests a sensitive reading of *Inferno* 5. Dante's statement, "A Gallehaut was the book and he who wrote it," would have none of the force with which it comes through to the reader, placed as it is at the conclusion and climax of Francesca's tale, had it not been preceded by the moving and impressive representation in the lyric voice of the enchantment of the poet's art. Francesca's tale is given, not by a narrator but in her own words; and she utters a line of Dante's own poetry, for

"Amor, ch'al cor gentil ratto s'apprende" comes from Dante's sonnet, "Amore e 'l cor gentil sono una cosa," the tenth sonnet of the *Vita Nuova*.

In the positive dimension of the extended metaphor, the association of literature and music with love suggests that sensuality in human nature is not an evil impulse but rather one of the good things of life. It puts the sparkle in the eye, the spring in the step. It is God-given, and becomes reprehensible only when wrongly used: the line to be drawn between lust and love is a distinction to be made by man's reason. Not love, but Romantic Love is condemned.

Dante deals with this theme in more than one passage of the *Divine Comedy*. In Canto 26 of the *Purgatorio*, where Dante himself must undergo the purgation of lustful impulses, he requires the utmost urging from Virgil and Statius to enter the cleansing fire. Here he meets, not any of the great lovers of history, but the singers of love: Arnaut Daniel, the Provençal troubadour, and Guido Guinizelli, author of the poem, "Al cor gentil ripara sempre Amore," that inspired Dante's line in *Inferno* 5 and that led to the poetry of the "dolce stil nuovo," the sweet new style. The fire imagery, which extends into Canto 27, begins on the ascent to the Seventh cornice with Statius's explanation of the creation of the body and soul, heart and mind. Dante here describes man as the fair work of the Primal Mover, self aware and full of power, and he uses two strikingly sensuous figures: generation as the Sun's heat being turned into wine, and God's finished work as a little flame which follows the fire wherever it turns: "e simigliante poi a la fiammella / che segue il foco là 'vunque si muta" ("like the little flame which follows the fire / wheresoever it moves") (*Purg.* 25:97-98). The imagery is used by Joyce in the Sirens chapter, as noted above, at an emotional apex at which Bloom's reaction to the music reaches a peak of sensual excitement: "Braintipped, cheek touched with flame, they listened feeling that flow endearing flow over skin limbs human heart soul spine" (*U* 269). The association of ideas, of course, is not uncommon. But Joyce also used Dante's figure in a 1909 letter to his wife, Nora: "carrying always with her in her secret heart the little flame that burns up the souls and bodies of men."[18]

Dante's treatment of sensuality in the *Paradiso* extends this structure of meaning. Whom do we find in the Heaven of Venus? Not the chaste husbands and wives, but two carnal sinners who lived long enough to repent. The woman is Cunizza, and the man is Folquet de Marseille, another troubadour. The suggestion present in *Inferno* 5, that the lovers' damnation was determined less by their sin than by their lack of time to repent, is here explicitly reinforced by these happy souls of *Paradiso* 9.

The fire imagery of *Purgatorio* 25 is picked up in Cunizza's description of herself. She describes her ancestor as a firebrand and says that she "shines" here in the Heaven of Venus because on earth she had been conquered, "vinse" (Francesca says "prese," "seized") by the light of that star.[19] Nor is she ashamed to admit this, but gladly acknowledges it, Lethe having washed away all sense of guilt. She says, "ma lietamente a me medesma indulgo / la cagion di mia sorte, e non mi noia" ("Yet joyfully within me I approve / the occasion of my lot, nor am displeased") (*Par.* 9:34-35). Folquet makes the same point, and more strongly for after all he is a poet, saying that he is now stamped with the rays of this heaven as he was on earth, and that he blazed fiercely "infin che si convenne al pelo" ("so long as it matched my hair")—that is, until age overtook him (*Par.* 9:99).

Folquet's speech to Dante is a long one, more involved and obscure in its language than Folquet's poetry was on earth, in the Provençal tradition. At its conclusion the troubadour reveals to Dante that the spirit highest in this order of beatitude is Rahab, the harlot of Jericho, redeemed by her good deed in sheltering Joshua's spies. Following this train of thought Folquet remarks on the Pope's neglect of the Holy Land (at the end of his life Folquet became a bishop and a crusader), and Dante ends the canto with the word "l'avoltero" ("adultery") applied, with a decided reverse emphasis recalling the shock of finding the words "amor" and "pace" in *Inferno* 5, to the corruption of the papal curia. Thus Dante makes a strong rhetorical statement for sensuality, letting the adulterers be received into heaven, and describing as unlawful intercourse the actions of the papal regime.

In Joyce's chapter the association of music with love, and specifically with sensual love, is less explicit than Dante's association of love poetry with an affirmation of sensuality. The extended metaphor is perfectly clear in both, but Joyce's metaphor is encompassed by ironic qualifications. The ambiguities lie particularly in the role of Bloom in this paradoxical tension, and of course also in the underlying question of just how much of Joyce's construction depends on his reading of Dante.

Yet there are indications that Joyce's portrayal of Bloom, though extensively qualified, includes a positive role for his protagonist. First, Bloom is allowed to articulate the metaphor. We are thus encouraged to sympathize with him as we sympathize with Francesca. Joyce's chapter, like Dante's canto, could easily have been written otherwise, but both protagonists make this important point in voices that are recognizably their own. Second, to whatever extent music as the language of love is the chapter's controlling figure, there is much evidence to affirm Bloom's musicianship.

Joyce has used every kind of musical association, in this chapter, to convey meanings beyond the surface and setting. By implication, sensuality is represented as the underlying reality without which there can be no human "music," no real communication. The sirens, male and female, have their due measure of this. The vigorous rhythms of Blazes Boylan and the siren barmaids bring particular liveliness and color to the suggestion of sensuality in their briefly glimpsed actions. Joyce's best metaphors, like Dante's, continue to shine in the imagination long after the book has been closed.

It is Bloom who says that music is "all a kind of attempt to talk," and he is perceived as able to distinguish rationally between "music" and mere clamour. It is Bloom, cuckold but also "unconquered hero" (*U* 260:34), whose sensibility associates sensuality with the "language of love." Moreover, in his own words Bloom adds the dimension of joyfulness to sensuality, on the analogy of Mozart's Minuet from *Don Giovanni*:

> Nice, that is. Look: look, look, look, look, look: you look at us. That's joyful I can feel. Never have written it. Why? My joy is other joy. But both are joys. Yes, joy it must be. Mere fact of music shows you are. (*U* 277:34)

Bloom is also the channel of figurative expression through whom a progressive differentiation is made between the Sirens' song and the larger universe of discourse which is music: if the Sirens' song leads to death as drunkenness and brutality lead to degradation and despair, nevertheless sensuality transformed by kindness and steadfastness is on the side of life. Through adroit syntactical choices, the songs heard in the Ormond bar are made to suggest a counterpoint of brutality with compassion, mendaciousness with veracity, venality with benevolence and integrity, folly with reason, hatred and force with love, despair and death with hope and life.

Repeatedly the tones of the episode convey an impression of one sort which is contradicted by the appearance of the character in his own fugal voice; his individuating combination of words and rhythms is supplemented by direct discourse and by comment. Boylan's rhythms are consistently trochaic, a jaunty jingling, but there is a denial of this impression by what the reader learns elsewhere from description, comment, and Boylan's own flat tones in dialogue. Bloom says, "he can't sing for tall hats" (*U* 270); this might be only an indication that Bloom is an unreliable narrator; but another impression comes to us when Bloom says, "There's music everywhere. Ruttledge's door: ee creaking. No, that's noise," and we are thus reminded that one of Boylan's distinctive words is "creaking" (*U* 277; 260:29; 263:07; 272:04).

Other characters are portrayed with more straightforward irony. There is clearly less warm life in Simon Dedalus, Richie Goulding, Bob Cowley and Ben Dollard than in the portrayal of Boylan, the barmaids, and Bloom. And two minor characters, the deaf waiter, Pat, and the quarrelsome, grunting Boots, errand boy of the Ormond, suggest yet another kind of deprivation, an almost total inability to hear music and to make music.

As the question of Bloom's musicianship within the metaphor begins to seem important, evidence accumulates that he is sensitive and discriminating in his understanding of music; that he is, though untutored, in some sense musically competent. To begin with, Bloom is a careful listener with a good ear. He knows at once that the piano has been tuned, and he appreciates a competent performer. "Nice touch," he thinks. "Must be Cowley. Musical. Knows whatever note you play." Though he does not use the term "absolute pitch," the accuracy of Bloom's observation about Cowley is shortly confirmed when Simon Dedalus sits down at the keyboard: "No, Simon. Father Cowley turned. Play it in the original. One flat. The keys, obedient, rose higher . . . " (*U* 267). Still more important, Mr Bloom recognizes *the equivalent of perfect pitch in human communication*. He defines this as the instinctive response of person to person.[20] It is a quality that he associates with his erring wife: he realizes that she could comprehend the Italian hurdygurdy boy "without understanding a word of his language." "With look to look: songs without words . . . She knew he meant the monkey was sick. . . . Gift of nature" (*U* 281:13).

Bloom's preferred area of critical interest is the mechanics of music, and here his formulations seem knowledgeable and to the point. He rates above any mechanical instrument, "the human voice, two tiny silky chords. Wonderful, more than all the others." Though untrained, his understanding includes an intelligent interest in the theoretical basis of harmony: "Numbers it is. All music when you come to think. . . . Vibrations: chords those are. One plus two plus six is seven" (*U* 274). From this choice of words it is clear that Bloom recognizes, perhaps intuitively, the construction of a musical seventh: unison plus second plus sixth. He calls this "musemathematics" (*U* 274); his views are original and expressed with directness and vigor. When he thinks of girls learning the piano, playing scales up and down, he imagines the sound as "two together nextdoor neighbors" (*U* 274). His formulation, so comparable to Stephen Dedalus' description of rhymes as "two men dressed the same, looking the same, two by two," is surely a deliberate parallelism.

On the other hand, Bloom does have many deficiencies and weak points, most of them in the realm of musicology. He refers to the compositions he has heard in the Ormond as "all that Italian florid music" (*U* 273), apparently not realizing that "M'appari" and the minuet from *Don Giovanni* are the work of Germanic composers. He is also mistaken about the authorship of his favorite oratorio, "The Seven Last Words" which he attributes sometimes to Mercadante, sometimes to Meyerbeer. He expresses a preference for "the severe classical school such as Mendelssohn" (*U* 645), though that composer is a pillar of the romantic tradition. At the end of the day, as Bloom walks home with Stephen Dedalus, many such irrelevant and ridiculous comments are voiced. It becomes clear that Bloom is no scholar and could never win an argument about music.

But in the reader's wholly private view another hypothesis is offered, that Bloom's posturings are accident rather than substance. Music, despite all the ironic qualifications, seems to be Bloom's aesthetic métier. In comparison with his Dublin contemporaries, and still more in comparison with his own excursions into literature, he seems less of a purely comic figure when we share his desultory thoughts about music in the Ormond bar.

In the previous chapter Lenehan has said seriously. "There's a touch of the artist about old Bloom." Bloom's fund of intellectual curiosity has led him into exploration of scientific and philosophical questions, and he has had some slight and unmethodical literary ambitions. He has made an effort with literature, but he shows nowhere any literary discrimination comparable to the accuracy and sensitivity of his reflections about music. He is a comic figure as he daydreams of writing for a magazine or as he seeks earnestly in the works of Shakespeare a solution to the problems of life. In contrast, in the Sirens chapter he seems on firm ground of his own choosing when he says, "Words? Music? No: it's what's behind"—i.e., the human necessity.

The Sirens chapter has become something of a critical touchstone for the two major lines of interpretation of *Ulysses*. Dante continued his treatment of love into the *Purgatorio* and *Paradiso*, uniting this theme finally with the Beatific Vision. Joyce's treatment of love throughout his work is domestic and sensual. In *Ulysses* his protagonist, and still more his protagonist's wife, are personages humanly different from those of the *Divine Comedy*. It would take the most delicate and precarious art of the fulcrum, if indeed it is possible, to separate with finality the spiritual element from the sexual, in this experience we call love. Joyce's personal belief that the two aspects are inseparable is poignantly reflected in the intimate letters he wrote to his wife in 1909, letters given a partial echo in the final chapter of *Ulysses*. He knew from the *Rime Petrose* that Dante had known the violence of passion. Yet Dante created in Beatrice a lasting vision of the spiritual side of love. Joyce sought a more comprehensive and explicit treatment of the theme, and there will always be a difference of opinion about his success or failure. In *Ulysses* he claims for Bloom and Molly a sensibility on one level equal to that of Dante and Beatrice: that is, their common humanity. There are other levels, and they do not indeed compare in the expression of their love, but their possession of this important experience is sufficiently authenticated to suggest that Joyce selected Dante's theme in order to give it a deliberately revisionist treatment. Joyce does not say that Bloom is Dante (nor that Bloom is Joyce), but he suggests that all three have shared and given expression to a common human experience of love.

Dante and Joyce both censure and reject the romantic conception of love as an irresistible and ennobling force. Dante created in Beatrice the opposite of Francesca, a unique vision of spiritualized love. Joyce's modern vision took a different path, and in a letter to his brother (when he was twenty-four) he wrote, "Anyway my opinion is that if I put down a bucket into my own soul's well, sexual department, I draw up Griffith's and Ibsen's and Skeffington's and Bernard Vaughan's and St. Aloysius' and Shelley's and Renan's water along with my own. And I am going to do that in my novel (inter alia) and plank the bucket down before the shades and substances above mentioned to see how they like it: and if they don't like it I can't help them. I am nauseated by their lying drivel about pure men and pure women and spiritual love and love for ever: blatant lying in the face of the truth" (*Letters* II: 191-192). By the time he came to write *Ulysses*, Joyce had added Dante to his list. He removes the mystique from Romantic love by a naturalizing process, and so domesticates it, in the counterpoint of the sirens of the Ormond with the homeward-bound Mr Bloom.

Joyce gives the last word to Molly Bloom. The final chapter is written entirely in the first person, and it ends with a crescendo of rose symbolism that recalls the heavenly rose of Dante's *Paradiso* 32. Joyce has put Dante's great spiritual image of the love that moves the universe into this woman's mind. The closing, climactic, unpunctuated words of Molly's monologue develop strikingly their own tangled beauty. Molly is a sensualist, as is her husband, and her impulses and experiences have earlier in this final chapter been expressed by her in the crudest terms, the very nadir of lust. But Joyce with delicate verbal brushwork turns the tide of her soliloquy and moves her thoughts steadily upward until, as she recalls the details of "the day I got him to propose to me," her mind, like that of Dante's Cunizza, shows its highest sensibilities as it becomes possessed and absorbed by the knowledge and sensations no longer of lust but of love. Molly Bloom's acceptance of her greatest moment is characteristically offhand and unsentimental: "I thought well as well him as another" (*U* 768). But the impact of this remark is once more ironic rather than negative.

What is sometimes overlooked is the significance of Dante's continuing into Heaven his affirmation of the human fact of sensuality. It is no accident that Solomon is there. The effort to express with equal force the two faces of love is significantly present. Joyce's version is marked by an unpatronizing insistence that a degree of equality be granted to humble personages. They are full of faults, unintellectual, erring, and comical, but they are not brutish—Bloom and Molly are rational creatures, God's creatures, fully human. Joyce, we must conclude, understood that some of the lasting force of Dante's art in *Paradiso* 27 (where Beatrice and Dante together look down for the last time at "our little threshing floor" centered on Ulysses' narrow pass, the straits of Gibraltar, *Par.* 22:151) depends on the continued *human* quality of his protagonists even here in the highest spiritual realm.

Joyce's reading of Dante is indicated not only by his giving Stephen Dedalus the line, "che ' miei [occhi] di rimirar fé più ardenti" ("So that mine [eyes] became more ardent in their gaze"), which marks the point at which Dante finally passes beyond Beatrice, but still more by Joyce's decision to have Molly born in Gibraltar. This fact is surely an indication, as Ellmann suggests, that Joyce must very early have conceived the Dante parallels.[21] The Ulyssean reference in *Paradiso* 27 is a final reminder to the reader that Dante created his own version of this story; and *Paradiso* 27 must be connected geographically, for full understanding, with *Paradiso* 22. Similarly, in the last paragraphs of *Ulysses*, Molly remembers "Gibraltar as a girl" (*U* 768), and thinks of an adolescent love, "how he kissed me under the Moorish wall" (*U* 768). Minor loves here merge with the major love, her husband, exactly as occurs in Sirens at the climax of Bloom's thoughts about love. As the reader watches Dante and Beatrice looking down from Heaven, so also Joyce's reader receives from the close of the book a sense of Molly Bloom united with her husband and looking at life from the longest view of which she is capable.

Dante, by multiple references, emphasizes the connectedness of the separate cantiche in the poem's entirety, once again making imaginative use of pagan materials. Joyce underlines the interrelatedness of his separate episodes and also gives a final indication of the structural dependence of his work on the *Divine Comedy*. The effect of these verbal echoes, in both works, is reinforcement of meanings by the careful linguistic connection of parts with the whole.

It is not necessary to formulate a comprehensive judgment of *Ulysses* in order to recognize the seriousness of purpose with which Joyce absorbed Dante's treatment of *Amor* in the *Divine Comedy*. Manifestly, his assimilation of *Inferno* 5 was deep, and issued in wide-ranging imitative strategies. It was Joyce, after all, who once said, "I love Dante almost as much as the Bible; he is my spiritual food, the rest is ballast."[22]

DANTE begins and ends the *Purgatorio* with images of lustration. At the opening of Canto 1, he conveys to the reader his own delight in the mysterious gift of his expressive talent as he invites us to follow the "little skiff" of his poetic genius, "la navicella del mio ingegno."

In the first lines of the *Purgatorio*, Dante makes the reader aware of what it feels like to be a poet, in tropes that bring together all the associations of a spring morning at the edge of the sea:

L'alba vinceva l'ora mattutina
    che fuggia innanzi, sì che di lontano
    connobi il tremolar della marina.

The Dawn was vanquishing the early breeze
    of morn which fled away, so from afar
    I saw the sheen of sea crests by the shore.
                    (*Purg.* 1:115-117, trans. Bergin)

A joyous motion informs the lines; left behind are the painful plodding rhythms of that final climb "con fatica e con angoscia" in *Inferno* 34, where Dante and Virgil make their way "with labor and distress" out of the abyss (*Inf.* 34:78). Now the poet uses the trembling, dancing movement of the sea to set the terms of an equation between motion and good. Everything smiles, the heavens rejoice, and the rising of Venus in the east is a presentiment of the approaching sun, itself a figure of the "Love that moves the sun and the other stars." Thus the music of the closing line of the *Paradiso*, "l'amor che move il sole e l'altre stelle," is heard for the first time in the *Divine Comedy* in *Purgatorio* 1, as a song of the poet's delight in his exercise of skill.[1]

In this fresh and springtime world, where the smiling sea and sparkling waves are a song of love for the world's natural beauty, Virgil bends to the grass and with the dew on his hands he cleanses the tear-stained face of Dante. The Roman lustral rite is transformed by the simplicity of the gesture into a precursor of the Christian ceremonial; the unbaptized Virgil performs an action that he must have done many times in his own life. With reverent movements, the favor of spiritual forces is humbly, ceremonially, invoked.

At the end of Dante's journey through Purgatory he crosses Lethe, the pagan river. Virgil has disappeared; Dante is guided by a wholly imaginary figure, Matelda. The stream is narrow, so narrow that Dante could leap it, but he does not. He waits: a dramatic moment in the poem, a long moment prolonged from Canto 28 through Canto 31. The figure is finally completed only at the close of Canto 33, where Dante says, "Io ritornai da la santissima onda / rifatto." ("From that most holy wave I came away / refashioned.") These last nine lines of the *Purgatorio* are the poem's most direct description of Dante as the writer of a long poem, for he claims that composition stops here only because he has run out of space—the allotted number of lines have been used up.[2] Here and elsewhere in the sequence that begins at Canto 28:25, elements of the construction seem to be a reminiscence of Canto 1. One component is the lustration figure: the necessary cleansing before the journey can continue.

Images like these are found in abundance in Dante's poem and Joyce's fiction. What they have in common is, first, the picturing of a propitiatory act, and second, the use—by simple application or by immersion—of some healing substance, most frequently water. The presence of such an image places the text between poetry and religion; it comes from the writer's impulse to extend his thought toward an ideal conception.[3] The force of the analogy comes from association of the elements in the picture, now one and now another, with invocation of supernatural power. The metaphoric thrust is toward some kind of renewal, refreshment, even rebirth, coming initially from the Easter celebration of Christ's resurrection.

Singleton comments on the rhetorical and compositional elements by which Dante suggests the Resurrection in the opening scene of the *Purgatorio*. Dante's image would seem almost completely secularized, but for Cato's admonition which connects the cleansing of Dante's face with the journey's progress and its goal. Dante becomes a pilgrim, girded with a rush. Other elements of the pattern are nonspecific. Imaginative extension is thereby stimulated, as the poet selects from the range of attributes of water those that fit the renewal of nature: morning, spring, freshness, sparkle, movement. The localization of the incident on the seashore carries a suggestion of beginnings: Joyce uses many of the same elements at the close of *Finnegans Wake* to suggest death as a beginning, a metamorphosis.[4]

The ceremonies of Holy Week powerfully affected Joyce and he regularly attended them. In 1938 in Paris he invited Jacques Mercanton to go with him to St. Francis-Xavier's at 5 a.m. for the Office of the Easter Vigil. "He told me that Good Friday and Holy Saturday were the two days of the year when he went to church, for the liturgies which represented by their symbolic rituals the oldest mysteries of humanity."[5] The Office for which Joyce arose before dawn was traditionally one of the most important of the ecclesiastical year. It begins with the blessing of the Easter fire, and concludes with the blessing of the baptismal water, baptism of any new converts, and the solemn renewal of baptismal promises by the congregation. (This was the ceremony performed by St. Patrick, who by legend lit his first Easter fire on the Hill of Slane as a challenge to the Druids of the pagan king on the royal hill of Tara opposite, across the Boyne valley.) The liturgy of the Office includes readings from Exodus 14 and 15 that must have been the inspiration for Dante's choice of the Psalm sung by the arriving spirits.

Mercanton, however, arrived only at the end of the service, "at the moment of the benediction of the baptismal fonts;" he found Joyce in the baptistery, attending closely to the ceremony. They stayed until the procession returned to the sanctuary, where the Paschal Candle, symbol of the Easter fire, would be set in its special candlestick at the Gospel side of the altar and the Easter bells and the organ, silent since Holy Thursday, would burst forth in a great peal of joy. At this point, before the mass began, Joyce

> made a nervous, impatient gesture and murmured in English, "I have seen the rebirth of fire and of water. Enough until next year. The rest is without interest." And he walked rapidly away, his face set, while the Gloria burst out from the bell-towers.

Joyce in *Ulysses* reproduced specifically the departure from the Inferno and entrance onto the shores of Purgatory. Among the components he kept was the invocation of supernatural power and the pilgrim motif. He did not keep the aspect of morning freshness, nor the direct use of water, but he kept the implication of a propitiatory rite. His picture has the force, and his figure takes the direction, of Dante's lustration image, but with a difference. In the Ithaca chapter, a line from the 113th Psalm, "In exitu Israel de Aegypto," appears in a context that makes it seem one of the small number of direct quotations from the *Divine Comedy* that Joyce inserted into his novel. Dante uses the line three times. It figures in his Epistle to Can Grande, and also appears in its Latin form in the *Convivio*. In the *Purgatorio*, however,

Dante altered the last word to Italian to fit the rhyme; the line is sung by the spirits arriving at the mountain of Purgatory, while Dante, having made his exit from the Inferno, stands on the shore with Virgil.[6] It is Easter Sunday morning.

At the point in *Ulysses* where Joyce uses the quotation, Stephen and Bloom have emerged from Nighttown, have come into the garden of Mr Bloom's house, and are looking up at the stars. The time, as in the *Divine Comedy*, is the earliest dawn (*U* 682-683).

> *Joyce*: What spectacle confronted them when they, first the host then the guest, emerged silently, doubly dark, from obscurity by a passage from the rere of the house into the penumbra of the garden?
> The heaventree of stars hung with humid nightblue fruit.

> *Dante*: My leader and I entered on that hidden road to return into the bright world; and caring not for any rest, we climbed up, he first and I second, so far that through a round opening I saw some of the beautiful things that Heaven bears; and thence we issued forth to see again the stars. (*Inf.* 34:133-139, trans. Singleton)

These are the final lines of the *Inferno*. In the next passage, as the *Purgatorio* opens, Dante has Cato interrogate the travelers. They are identified by Virgil as pilgrims. Joyce (writing in the catechetical form of the Ithaca episode) asks and answers similarly, closing with the quotation from the Psalm, which is specifically indicated as "modus peregrinus"—the pilgrim mode:

> *Dante*: [The line is sung by the boatload of spirits arriving at the mountain, II:46; and Cato asks of Virgil and Dante:] Who has guided you, or what was a lamp to you issuing forth from the deep night that ever makes the infernal valley black? (*Purg.* 1:43-45, trans. Singleton)

> *Joyce*: In what order of precedence, with what attendant ceremony was the exodus from the house of bondage to the wilderness of inhabitation effected? [now Joyce's stage direction follows:]
> Lighted Candle in Stick borne by Bloom
> Diaconal hat on Ashplant borne by Stephen
> With what intonation *secreto* of what commemorative psalm?
> The 113th, *modus peregrinus: In exitu Israel de Egypto: domus Jacob de populo barbaro*. (*U* 682)

If confirmation of this Dantesque association be needed, it is found in the identifying term, "modus peregrinus." This is an echo of Virgil's reply when the newly arrived spirits ask him for directions. Virgil tells them, "ma noi siam peregrin, come voi siete," "but we are pilgrims (strangers) even as yourselves"[7] (*Purg.* 2:63). Leopold Bloom has a fatherly Virgilian role which is here affirmed. Ceremonially, however, Stephen's role as a poet who is also a Catholic is linked, by the structure and vocabulary of this little episode, to Bloom as a figure of the Hebrew religion. In part this is a parallel to the linkage that allows Dante, the Christian poet, to participate in the pagan lustral rite of Virgil. Dante could easily have written the scene so that Cato, who explains the cleansing action, would have performed it as well. Joyce makes Bloom a figure of the old law, a valid albeit a comic precursor.[8]

The processional of Stephen and Bloom is a ritual action, and it has a demonstrable connection with *Purgatorio* 1 and its notable image of lustration; but in Ithaca the cleansing action does not form an obvious part of the ritual. Where then is the connection? Joyce's little ceremony picks up the regenerative element of Dante's act of lustration. Not only does it end with micturition, possibly a comic equivalent of the liturgical asperges, but it suggests specifically the priestly rite of ordination which also contains brief acts of lustration.[9]

The account of this passage to the garden is written on two levels. Bloom carries a candle to get them to the doorway; in Stephen's mind, "secreto" (a liturgical term), the sight of the candle expands the incident into an ecclesiastical procession and he raises his "diaconal" hat on the point of his walking stick. It is in Stephen's mind also, "intonation secreto" (the descriptive term for passages in Catholic rites where the priest recites silently), that the line from Psalm 113 occurs, with the additional thought that connects it with Dante's poem, "modus peregrinus."

It is unlikely that Stephen sees Bloom as Virgil—it is James Joyce who does this—but it is a plausible inference that Stephen sees himself as a combination of Dante and the first deacon, the Stephen of Acts 6:1-5 and following, who appears in *Purgatorio* 15:107 as "un giovinetto," an example of meekness (Toynbee, p. 591). The processional is a comic moment in the narrative. At the same time, it marks Stephen's awareness of an element of mystery and even a sacred significance.

This young man has a complex mind that characteristically apprehends an event on several levels. If he were not so serious, one would say he sees the funny side of things: his reflections are a form

of comedy, which is his characteristic form. But the form that his reflections take is not straightforward comedy. His mind picks up the
bizarre element in everything—the extreme statement, the fantastic
image. His reflections therefore have a sardonic cast, and there is usually a bitter side to his jokes. Moreover, he knows too much. His
mind is a magpie's nest from which he draws the most unlikely bits of
information, from all kinds of sources, and connects these willy-nilly
with the event that strikes his consciousness.

Stephen, like the rest of us, has his preoccupations and obsessions.
One of these is the minutiae of doctrinal exposition and liturgical
worship in the Catholic Church. The first is an aspect of his interest in
the history of the Church, and of religion in general.[10] In this, he
seems to be following the lead of Renan, whose study for the priesthood led him to compare the early texts of the New Testament
and brought him to the conclusion that the New Testament was an
historical record without the supernatural sanction claimed by the
Church.[11] The second, Stephen's fixation on the intricate details of
ritual and liturgy, is partly an esthetic matter, insofar as he enjoys the
music and the dramatic form and the colorful spectacle generally. But
it is partly an intellectual matter, for Stephen is aware that drama and
poetry as we know it developed out of religious rites and spectacles.
The production of verbal art is Stephen's predominant concern, the
ambition on which all other preoccupations converge.[12]

While Stephen is with Bloom, he has one completely new experience; this is the conversation with Bloom as a Jew (in contrast to the
encounter with Bloom as a human being). This seems to be the first
time that Stephen has talked to a Jew about Judaism. Bloom is not as
closely connected with Judaism as Stephen is with Catholicism, but he
is a lapsed member of his religion and so is Stephen. Bloom thinks of
himself as an infidel, when he thinks of the matter at all (*U* 676:20).
Although he was baptized a Catholic (*U* 666:25), and married a
Catholic, Bloom does not think of himself as a Catholic. On this particular day he has been made uncomfortably aware of his Jewishness
in Catholic Dublin. His reflections and Stephen's converge on their
"racial differences."

The little processional takes its substance and its form from Bloom's
Jewishness and Stephen's fixation on Catholic rites. It is a comic moment in the narrative, because Bloom and Stephen are going outdoors to urinate. But they are also going outdoors to say goodbye to
each other. (The compositional mode of the farewell scene recalls, as
was discussed in Chapter Two, the leave-taking of Dante and Virgil.)
Stephen's thoughts, possibly including a recollection that Dante used

the line from Psalm 113, are extended by his author into a succinct picture that enlarges the existential moment by an implicit textual union linking the old and the new dispensation. Dante's syncretism becomes an aspect of Joyce's novel.

The suggestion of consecration comes from Stephen's association of the poet's role with the priestly role, the office of a mediator. The unbidden thought comes to him, with comic effect in this context, of "the sacerdotal integrity of Christ" (*U* 688:1). In the little procession, Stephen sees himself as one of the ordained, but yet a lesser figure; he is only a deacon, but still one of the minor orders, "sicut decet ministros Christi et dispensatores mysteriorum Dei" ("a minister of Christ and a dispenser of the mysteries of God").[13]

Joyce, at any rate, seems to have seen Virgil's action in *Purgatorio* 1 as an ordination of Dante, a laying-on of hands. Stephen Dedalus in such company would indeed be no more than a deacon. If Stephen is in fact thinking of Dante's use of Psalm 113, there may be a wry humility in his acceptance of the order below the priest's. The word "diaconal" helps to tie this passage to another sacerdotal vision, earlier in the book, with which it is in contrast: this is Stephen's desperate hallucination in Circe where he saw himself in hell as Cardinal Primate of all Ireland.[14]

The processional incident was a late addition to *Ulysses*, inserted as a unit in the proofs. Joyce intended from the outset to make the dialogue in the garden correspond in some way to the exit of Virgil and Dante from the *Inferno*; this is indicated by the presence in Joyce's original manuscript of the translated last line of *Inferno* 34: "the heaventree of stars hung with humid nightblue fruit" (*U* 683:4).[15] Although each of Dante's cantiche ends with the word "stars," "stelle," Joyce's placement of the line cannot be anything but a recall of *Inferno* 34, if there is any meaning to the lines immediately preceding, in which Bloom and Stephen "emerged silently, doubly dark, from obscurity by a passage from the rere of the house." Nothing in the concluding lines of the *Purgatorio* or *Paradiso* is suggested by the descriptive terms Joyce has selected; they reflect Dante's exit from Hell.

In the original manuscript of the Ithaca chapter the paragraphs immediately following these lines also give a somewhat more Dantesque version of Bloom's thought than appeared in the final version. His meditations are connected with astronomical phenomena: they range farther and farther out in the cosmos and associate the vastness of space with the brevity and vanity of human life. Dante does the same thing in *Paradiso* 22:148. "E tutti e sette mi si dimostraro / quanto son grandi e quanto son veloci / e come sono in distante

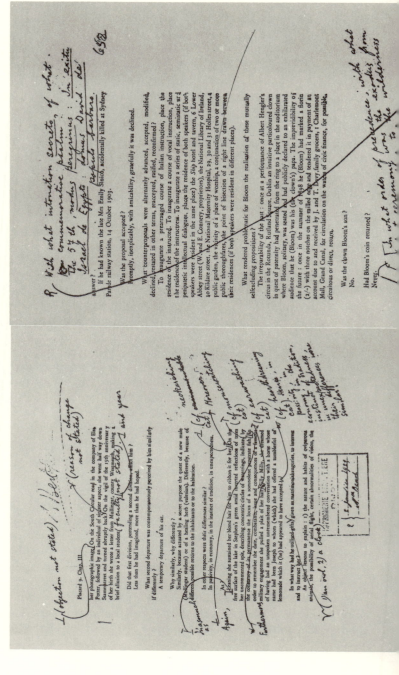

652

answer?

If he had known the late Mrs Emily Sinico, accidentally killed at Sydney Parade railway station, 14 October 1903.

Was the proposal accepted?

Promptly, inexplicably, with amicability, gracefully it was declined.

What counterproposals were alternately advanced, accepted, modified, declined, restated in other terms, reaccepted, ratified, reconfirmed?

To inaugurate a prearranged course of Italian instruction, place the residence of the instructress. To inaugurate a course of vocal instruction, place the residence of the instructress. To inaugurate a series of static, semistatic and peripatetic intellectual dialogues, places the residence of both speakers (if both speakers were resident in the same place), the Ship hotel and tavern, 6 Lower Abbey street (W. and E. Connery, proprietors), the National Library of Ireland, 10 Kildare street, the National Maternity Hospital, 29, 30 and 31 Holles street, a public garden, the vicinity of a place of worship, a conjunction of two or more public thoroughfares, the point of bisection of a right line drawn between their residences (if both speakers were resident in different places).

What rendered problematic for Bloom the realisation of these mutually self-excluding propositions?

The irreparability of the past : once at a performance of Albert Hengler's circus in the Rotunda, Rutland square, Dublin an intuitive particoloured clown in quest of paternity had penetrated from the ring to a place in the auditorium where Bloom, solitary, was seated and had publicly declared to an exhilarated audience that he (Bloom) was his (the clown's) papa. The impredictability of the future : once in the summer of 1898 he (Bloom) had marked a florin (2/-) with three notches on the milled edge and tendered it in payment of an account due to and received by J. and T. Davy, family grocers, 1 Charlemont Mall, Grand Canal, for circulation on the waters of civic finance, for possible, circuitous or direct, return.

Was the clown Bloom's son?

No.

Had Bloom's coin returned?

Never.

Placard 9, Chap. III

Her photographic image, On the South Circular road in the company of Elsa Potter, followed by an individual of sinister aspect, she went half way down Stamer street and turned abruptly back. On the vigil of the 15th anniversary of her birth she wrote a letter from Mullingar, county Westmeath, making a brief allusion to a local student (Frowsily text stated) and year.

Did that first division, portending a second division, afflict him?

Less than he had imagined, more than he had hoped.

What second departure was contemporaneously perceived by him similarly, if differently?

A temporary departure of his cat.

Why similarly, why differently?

Similarly, because actuated by a secret purpose the quest of a new male (Blephen student) or of a healing herb (valerian). Differently, because of different possible returns to the inhabitants or to the habitation.

In other respects were their differences similar?

In passivity, in economy, in the instinct of tradition, in unexpectedness.

leaning she sustained her blond hair for him to ribbon it for her. On the free surface of the lake in Stephen's green amid the reflections of trees her unconnected spit, describing concentric circles of liquid circles, indicating by the undulation of its first expansion the locus of a somnolent prostrate fish. In order to remember the date, combatants, issue and consequences of a famous military engagement she pulled a plait of her hair. Milly, in dream, telling passing, the time, eating, describing a forthcoming ...

of having had an unspoken unremembered conversation with a horse whose name had been Joseph to whom (which) she had offered a tumblerful of lemonade which it (he) had appeared to have accepted.

In what way had he utilised gifts given in the course of their matrimonial inquiries, to interest and to instruct her?

As object lessons to explain : 1) the nature and habits of oviparous animals, the possibility of aerial flight, certain abnormalities of vision, the secular process of imbalsamation : 2) the principle of the pendulum, exemplified in bob, wheelgear and regulator, the translation in terms of human or social regulation of the various positions of moveable indicators on an unmoving dial, the exactitude of the recurrence per hour of an instant in each hour, when the longer and the shorter indicator were at the same angle of inclination, *videlicet*, 5 5/11 minutes past each hour per hour in arithmetical progression.

In what manners did she reciprocate?

She remembered : on the 27th anniversary of his birth she presented to him a breakfast moustachecup of imitation crown Derby porcelain ware. She provided : at quarter day or thereabouts if or when purchases had been made by him not for her she showed herself attentive to his necessities, anticipating his desires. She admired : a natural phenomenon having been explained by him not for her she expressed the immediate desire to possess without gradual acquisition a fraction of his science, the moiety, the quarter, a thousandth part.

What proposal did Bloom, diambulist, father of Milly, somnambulist, make to Stephen, noctambulist?

To pass in repose the hours intervening between Thursday (proper) and Friday (normal) on an extemporised cubicle in the apartment immediately above the kitchen and immediately adjacent to the sleeping apartment of his host and hostess.

What various advantages would or might have resulted from a prolongation of such extemporisation?

For the guest : security of domicile and seclusion of study. For the host : rejuvenation of intelligence, vicarious satisfaction. For the hostess : disintegration of obsession, acquisition of correct Italian pronunciation.

Why might these several provisional contingencies between a guest and a hostess not necessarily preclude or be precluded by a permanent eventuality of reconciliatory union between a schoolfellow and a jew's daughter?

Because the way to daughter led through mother, the way to mother through daughter.

Inconsequent / polysyllabic

To what inspection of his host did the guest return a monosyllabic negative.

Did come *Spirit of / STEPHEN R*

Why would a recurrent frustration the more depress him?

Because at the critical turningpoint of human existence he desired to amend many social conditions, the product of inequality and avarice and international animosity.

He believed then that human life was infinitely perfectible, eliminating these conditions?

There remained the genetic conditions imposed by natural, as distinct from human law, as integral parts of the human whole ; the necessity of destruction to procure alimentary sustenance : the painful character of the ultimate functions of separate existence, birth and death : the monotonous menstruation of simian and (particularly) human females extending from the age of puberty to the menopause : inevitable accidents at sea, in mines and factories : certain very painful maladies and their resultant surgical operations, innate lunacy and congenital criminality, decimating epidemics : catastrophic cataclysms which make terror the basis of human mentality : seismic upheavals the epicentres of which are located in densely populated regions : the fact of vital growth, through convulsions of metamorphosis, from infancy through maturity to decay.

Why did he desist from speculation?

Because it was a task for a superior intelligence to substitute other *A more acceptable* phenomena in the place of the [phenomena] to be removed. *V less acceptable*

Did Stephen participate in his dejection?

He affirmed his significance as a conscious rational animal proceeding syllogistically from the known to the unknown and a conscious rational reagent between a microcosm and a macrocosm constructed upon the incertitude of the void.

Was this affirmation apprehended by Bloom?

Not verbally. Substantially.

What spectacle confronted them when they, first the host, then the guest, emerged silently, doubly dark, from obscurity by a passage from the rere of the house into the penumbra of the garden?

The heaventree of stars hung with humid nightblue fruit.

With what meditations did Bloom accompany his demonstration to his companion of various constellations?

Meditations of various constellation? *of the invisible moon in increscent / lunation, approaching perigee :*

---

5. Joyce's French printer, Darantiere, furnished "placards" with four pages to a sheet of proofs. Joyce added his transformation of *Purg.* 2:46, the processional of Bloom and Stephen in the Ithaca chapter of *Ulysses*, to the placards (*U* 682:14-24; *Purg.* 1:39-45; *Purg.* 2:46-48).

riparo." ("So all the seven to me were displayed; / I saw how great they are and how swift moving / And the vast distances between their gyres") (*Par.* 22:148-150). The manuscript version then asks whether Bloom was convinced of "the esthetic value of the spectacle," and answers with a reference to the "reiterated examples of poets" who invoke the constellations as a paradigm of love.

But Mr Bloom could not have read the *Divine Comedy*. Joyce's later additions in successive stages of proofreading enlarged the context of these paragraphs with language that enhanced the naturalistic element by making the "meditations" more strongly characteristic of the mind of Leopold Bloom. In these revisions, however, Joyce, while he obscured (without eliminating) the Dantesque component of Bloom's thoughts, also created the processional and gave to Stephen the silent remarks that suggest the parallel with the movements of Dante and Virgil.[16]

The lustration figure, closely related though it seems to be to the Christian rite of baptism, is historically wider and more complex than the sacramental pattern. The Church recognizes this, and has included some kind of "lustral" action, in the older sense of this word, in more than one of the sacraments. It is a part of almost every kind of liturgical rite. A ceremonial structure that identifies the propitiatory act with some visual element, some physical action, dramatically reinforces the basic idea of prayer. In recent reforms of the liturgy, many of these dramatic effects have disappeared from the Catholic service.[17] In Joyce's day they were still a powerful presence, and in his fiction, altars and sacrificial fires are sometimes explicitly present. In *Stephen Hero* the apprentice poet's sense of his art is expressed in terms appropriate to a pagan priesthood or a biblical prophet:[18]

> He spent days and nights gathering the first fruits and every peace-offering and heaping them upon his altar whereon he prayed clamorously the burning token of satisfaction might descend. . . . He would suddenly hear a command to begone, to be alone, a voice agitating the very tympanum of his ear, a flame leaping into divine cerebral life. (*SH* 30)

Such expressions became increasingly indirect and impacted in the narrative. In *Ulysses*, as Stephen and Bloom come into the house, one of Bloom's first actions is the laying and lighting of a fire.[19] On one level it is a bit of naturalistic detail. As a picture, however, it suggests a sacrificial altar: "A pyre of crosslaid resintipped sticks and various colored papers and irregular polygons of best Abram coal" (*U* 653). In Genesis I:7, a father of the Old Law, Abram, "built an altar and laid the wood in order," and Dante mentions Abraham in *Inferno* 4 as one of the figures of the Old Law who were translated to Heaven by Christ's harrowing of hell after the Crucifixion. Stephen thinks of "similar apparitions . . . others elsewhere in other times who, kneeling on one knee or on two, had kindled fires for him" (*U* 654:7-20). The event is shifted to a new plane, and a new prospect is offered.[20]

The lustration pattern depends on an ancient ritual and invokes a complex correlative. The archetypal propitiatory act is loaded with prior associations drawn from many and various areas. Religious practices and all their representations in art; the history of religions; anthropological studies of behavior patterns; folklore: all these help to establish connections.[21] Underlying this is the knowledge of unconscious mental processes that has developed out of psychoanalytic inquiry. Texts placed in a borderline region between religion and poetry offer a kind of para-metaphoric representation.

The ceremonial element in the lustration pattern is a matter of structure. The basic term includes all the methods of purification and expiation among the Greeks and Romans. The sacrificial altar would be approached only after some lustral action; human nature must purify itself from guilt before seeking communion with God, or even association with men.[22] A second idea can be distinguished: that guilt must be expiated voluntarily by certain divinely ordained processes, otherwise punishment will overtake it. The ceremonies might be performed in various modes, by sacrifice or procession; and the substances with which the ceremony was performed might be water, fire, air, earth, a branch of a sacred tree (especially laurel), or sulphur. Before sacrifice, participants usually bathed: salt water was better for this than fresh. In the Eleusinian mysteries, celebrants bathed in the sea. Water was more efficacious if a firebrand from the altar had been plunged into it. The asperges in all forms is a very old rite; before entering the temple the worshipper dipped a hand in a vase of lustral water at the door.

The Church recognized specifically that the ceremonials of the "old law" had a sacramental nature, and that in a still earlier state of innocence (the pagan era) there were no sacraments in the sense of the Church's definition. Thus such ancient rites as circumcision, the eating of the paschal lamb, the consecrating of priests, expiation ceremonies, and purification rites have always been considered in Catholic doctrine to have had a sanctifying nature. They produced grace, which is to say, supernatural favor.

Moreover, although the Council of Trent insisted that the sacraments were essential for salvation, Scholastic terminology found it useful to indicate an analogous relation between the life of the soul and the life of the body.[23] Even baptism (formally defined as the external ablution of the body by natural water, accompanied by the express invocation of the Holy Trinity), could be accomplished also by a perfect love of God, a state which the Church calls baptism of desire; and by martyrdom, a baptism of blood. Baptism signified spiritual regeneration, a new birth of the soul.

Dante made the most of distinctions such as these, which were still actively present in Catholic apologetics and doctrine when Joyce began to read the *Divine Comedy*.[24] The result was a syncretized and even secularized pattern of some quasi-sacramental act. The moment of consecration identifies the poet as an elected being; he and his imaginative act are something out of the ordinary. The lustration pattern becomes a confirmation of his special sensibility; it may also suggest a prophetic role. The poet's *mission* is ratified; as mythic truth takes charge, the poet's connection with his society is affirmed. To the sense of vocation is added the fictional embodiment of vocation with a mandate.

It is a strategy of indirection. Dante, at such times, protests his utter inability to convey in mere words the full experience: "Da quinci innanzi il mio veder fu maggio / che 'l parlar mostra, ch' a tal vista cede; / e cede la memoria a tanto oltraggio." ("From that point on my strength to see surpassed / our mortal speech which yields to such a sight / as memory must yield to such excess") (*Par.* 33:55-57). He also warns the reader of the difficulty of following him on these seas. "L'acqua ch'io prendo già mai non si corse; / Minerva spira, e conducemi Appollo, / e nove Muse mi dimostran l'Orse." ("The sea I range was never coursed before: / Minerva blows; Apollo guides me on / And the nine Muses point me out the Bears") (*Par.* 2:7-9, trans. Bergin). The pagan gods of poetic inspiration are his guides.[25]

Dante and Joyce were exploiting a venerable tradition. In the *Divine Comedy*, tropes of "cleansing" recapture possession of ancient practical wisdom. Poetry, beginning with the first cantos of the *Commedia* is metaphorically represented as a great stream, and this figure continues into the final cantos of the *Paradiso*. Virgil is a fount of speech (*Inf.* 1:79); the waters of Helicon, in the shadow of Parnassus, are clear springs; Dante's own poetry is a clear stream, as is the stream of memory. Even the Noble Castle of *Inferno* 4, the final home of the pagan sages and poets, is surrounded by "un bel fiumcello," a fair rivulet. Meanings exfoliate. Images of purification by immersion in some healing substance are associated with an increasing clarity of vision: this is the poem's central metaphor.[26] The "cleansing" of the corrupt Papacy adds the dimension of purge to purification.

Some part of the traditional association is maintained by Dante's use of Virgil to perform the lustral rite of *Purgatorio* 1, but then a second classical figure, Cato, explains its more localized connotation in the *Divine Comedy*. "For Rightful it were not with an eye befogged / By murky stain to stand before the first / Of our attendants, who is Heaven born" (*Purg.* 1:97-100). (Joyce brings this "murky stain" into *Finnegans Wake* as "Hellfeuersteyn," *FW* 225:24.) We are prepared for a later event by Cato's explanation of the earlier: that is, the cleansing of the vision of this individual, Dante, who is a poet like Virgil, but a Christian poet who will have the unique privilege of penetrating to the Divine Presence. The effect is cumulative. Virgil's action in washing Dante's face with the dew has a shaping effect on the passage of Dante across the river Lethe, many cantos later. This is a narrowing and deepening effect: in the classical tradition, Lethe conferred only a generalized oblivion of earthly existence on all souls.

The closing image of the *Purgatorio*, in which Dante comes away from "that most holy wave," the river Eunoè, contains the fulfilment of Cato's implied promise. These lines in turn are echoed by a parallel passage at the end of the *Paradiso*, when the river Dante has crossed is recalled to the reader's memory. The self-reflective images announce a poetic grasp of an inner coherence in human life. As *Purgatorio* 31 closes, after Dante's crossing of Lethe, he experiences the first of his divinely ordained visions. It is only a reflection (appropriately for this mid-point stage of the journey): Christ is not so much seen, as glimpsed in the eyes of Beatrice. Doctrine falls away as Dante the poet speaks.

O isplendor di viva luce eterna,
    chi palido si fece sotto l'ombra
    sì di Parnaso, o bevve in sua cisterna,
che non paresse aver la mente ingombra,
    tentando a render te qual tu paresti . . .

O glory of living light eternal,
    who, though he had waxed pale beneath the shade
    of high Parnassus or drunk of its well
Would not appear as one with memory dulled
    trying to render you as you appeared . . .
                    (*Purg.* 31:139-142, trans. Bergin)

The classical tradition is linked to the Christian, with echoes of *Purgatorio* 1, by the presence of the well of Apollo, where rose the springs of Helicon and where were invoked the pagan god of poetry and the muses of Parnassus. In the next two cantos Dante receives his poetic mission, a sacred charge, which now becomes the reason and the justification for the cleansing of his vision which began in *Purgatorio* 1 and was thereafter progressive. To the classical associations, Dante adds the Christian poet's vision (Dante's own invention) of the magical rivers of the Earthly Paradise, "welling up from one spring" ("veder mi parve uscir d'una fontana").[27] Lethe and Eunoè, in the geography of Dante's poem, are the source of the rivers below, earthly and infernal. Joyce summoned into action Dante's metaphor for the rivers with the final metamorphosis of river into sea, in the eighth chapter of *Finnegans Wake*, as Bernard Stambler first noticed:

> Dante's rivers seem always to be connected with great emotional outbursts. . . . *Purgatorio* 5 and 6 lead us directly into the great political invective at the end of Canto 6. In Canto 14 a natural history of Tuscan evil is given in terms of the course of the Arno (see also Canto 13:88-90). The immediate clue to this river question is of course in the twin rivers of the Earthly Paradise as sources not only of the stagnant rivers of Hell but also of the major rivers of earth; there results a great complex of ideas of purgation and metamorphosis not unlike (and possibly the source of) James Joyce's use of rivers and sea in *Finnegans Wake*.[28]

The process is metamorphosis; water is one of the efficient causes. Joyce made the river the agent of regeneration in *Finnegans Wake*. In Chapter 8, the book's feminine principle, Anna Livia Plurabelle, is the river Anna Liffey, winding through Dublin. (Old maps of Dublin show the river with this name.) Brendan O Hehir's *Glossary of the Gaelic in Finnegans Wake* notes that "Anna" does not come from the Gaelic *abha na*, "river," but derives either from *eanach-Life*, "Liffey-fen" or *ath na Life*, "Liffey Ford."[29] He demonstrates Joyce's decision for *eanach* by reviewing the book's other phonetic associations of the word, including "Fennyana" at *FW* 55:05. Two washerwomen on the bank call out to each other as they slap the items of laundry on the rocks to clean them. As Bernard Benstock has said, "The dirty linen of history has been washed throughout the night."[30] The washerwomen recognize the garments of all the inhabitants that have ever held the land through which the river flows: Celts, Jutes, Danes, Normans, and modern Dubliners. "Rinse them out and aston along with you! Where did I stop? Never stop! Continuarration!" (*FW* 205:14).

The Liffey in *Finnegans Wake* is like the river Lethe, not waxing and waning like an earthly stream but always magically replenished. The river carries away everything in its "several rinsings," making each

day a fresh start. "Clean" (*FW* 614:12). Metamorphosis in nature becomes a Viconian ricorso; river becomes sea, sea becomes cloud, cloud
becomes rain and fills the river once more. Water is the great instrument of change.

> Mopsus or Gracchus, all your horodities will incessantlament be
> coming back from the Annone Wishwashwhose, Ormepierre
> Lodge, Doone of the Drumes, blanches bountifully; and nightsend
> made up every article lathering leaving several rinsings so as each
> rinse results with a dapperent rolle. For nought that is has bane. In
> mournenlaund. Themes have thimes and habit reburns. (*FW*
> 614:1-8)

At the source of the Liffey, in the Wicklow hills, St. Kevin sits in the
cold water to reflect on this mystery. "He meditated continuously with
seraphic ardour the primal sacrament of baptism or the regeneration
of all man by affusion of water" (*FW* 606:10-12). This sentence was
drafted by Joyce in July 1923, at the very earliest stage of composition; such primacy is an indication of the importance he attached to
the pattern in his imaginative design.

In the final pages of *Finnegans Wake* the river seems to be the voice
of Eunoè, bidding man recall his good actions, so that "every good
deed it retrieves," "d'ogne ben fatto la rende" (*Purg.* 28:129). Now the
river is "a comforter as well" (*FW* 619:42). She reminds the man of all
the good things he has done, and although her wifely tone is acerbic,
she approves his ambitions (Tilltop, bigmaster! Scale the summit!"
FW 624:11) and his achievements, past and future. "How glad you'll
be I waked you! My! How well you'll feel! For ever after" (*FW*
625:33-34).

In *Finnegans Wake* the river speaks in its own voice, as a principal
character. Her daughter is Nuvoletta, the "little cloud." She looks
down "over the bannistars" at men in their solemn conclaves, debating the nature of knowledge ("their gnoses"). "As if that was their spi-
ration! As if theirs could duiparate her queendim!" (*FW* 157:08, 29).
The cloud reflects the sun, drawn by its warmth, and finally returns to
the river, the river returning to the sea.[31]

> Then Nuvoletta reflected for the last time in her little long life and
> she made up all her myriads of drifting minds in one. . . . She gave a
> childy cloudy cry: Nuee! Nuee! A lightdress fluttered. She was
> gone. And into the river that had become a stream (for a thousand
> of tears had gone eon her and come on her . . . and her muddied
> name was Missisliffi) there fell a tear, a singult tear, the loveliest of

all tears . . . But the river tripped on her by and by, lapping as
though her heart was brook. (*FW* 159:6-17)

One of Dante's terzine recapitulates the same process. The river, in
Dante's words,

> Infin là 've si rende per ristoro
> di quel che 'l ciel de la marina asciuga
> ond' hanno i fiumi ciò che va con loro . . .

> down to where it yields itself to replace that which the sky draws up
> from the sea, whence rivers have all that which flows in them . . .
> (*Purg.* 14:34-36, trans. Singleton)

Joyce has given the Liffey a more benign role in metamorphosis,
however, than Dante gave the Arno in *Purgatorio* 14. Both Dante and
Joyce specifically identify the river of their native city. The riverine
flow suggests change, an analogue of time and growth in Joyce's *Finnegans Wake*, of time and decay in Dante. As the Arno flows down-
stream the cities of Dante's Italy grow more evil, although with no
implication that the river is the agent of metamorphosis. The men
who live on the banks of the Arno have been as changed in their natures as if Circe had imprisoned them in her pasture. As the Arno
grows in its descent, evil also grows, especially envy which, with avarice, is the root of evil in society.[32]

Clusters of lustration images become themes of change and
metamorphosis.[33] "Themes have thimes" (*FW* 614:8). When the artist
becomes a central figure in the work, another dimension is added to
the process of metamorphosis, and additional uses are found for the
lustration image. The artist's development becomes a rebirth, his vocation becomes consecrated, and his mission has prophetic overtones.
Dante's protagonist in the *Divine Comedy* is not a consecrated being: he
remains fully human all through the poem. Joyce's poet experiences a
conscious act of dedication to vocation. Dante's poet recognizes with
humility the origin of his powers, while at the same time those powers
are sanctified and the poetic mission established more firmly. What
kind of humility is this? The pride of Stephen Dedalus and the humility of Dante may not be far apart. Despite affirmations of unworthi-
ness, Dante defines his own mission. He was self-selected, and he
makes certain that the permanence of his poetry and the righteousness of his political views are ratified at unimpeachable levels.[34]

Dante's *Vita Nuova* is an account of poetic sensibility in which poetry
is brought into relation with clear streams and with magical lustration.

The Beatrice of Dante's inspiration in the *Vita Nuova* reappears in the *Divine Comedy*.[35] Before Dante can be reunited with her, in *Purgatorio* 31, he must cross the clear stream and be immersed in it. When he does see her, he sheds tears of penitence for having abandoned her memory after she died. In both works Dante presents the artist as artist, not the lover alone.

The central metaphor of *A Portrait of the Artist as a Young Man* was identified by Ellmann as "the gestation of a soul," a metaphor in which Ellmann found the ordering principle for the images of water with which *A Portrait* abounds.[36] As critics have noted, each of the five chapters expresses a definite rhythm: the protagonist meets a challenging series of events, with which he comes to terms in one way or another, only to be undercut and in some sense forced to start over again.[37] Joyce's water images assist the narrative with metaphors that associate water with change, sometimes negatively. These may be images of sewers and effluvia, as the "foul green puddles" (*P* 63) of the countryside, or the "thick yellow scum" of the river at the Dublin quays (*P* 66). It may be a suggestion of fetid odors, as the description of the "square," or lavatory, at Clongowes; "there was a queer smell of stale water there. It was all thick slabs of slate and water trickled all day out of tiny pinholes" (*P* 43). It might also be the "ugly sound" of the dirty water, after he had washed his hands in the lavatory of the hotel and his father pulled the stopper up by the chain, "and the dirty water went slowly down through the hole in the basin" (*P* 11:25). It may be the unpleasant image of the quagmire, which Stephen hears in the retreat sermon, "your soul is a foul swamp of sin" (*P* 114), or his own thought of his condition as "a swamp of spiritual and bodily sloth." This sense of the image comes to Stephen in college; when he is disheartened by a stupid conversation, "the heavy lumpish phrase sank . . . like a stone through a quagmire," in his consciousness, a Dantean allusion (*P* 195:24; *Par.* 3:122-123). These and other negative associations of water are essential to the rhythm of the young man's development, the "slow and dark birth of the soul" (*P* 203:25).

The first chapter of the book moves from fear to fears overcome. The sensation of fear is connected with water: "he shivered as if he had cold slimy water next to his skin" (*P* 10). This comes from an unpleasant experience, one of the bigger boys having pushed Stephen into the "square ditch." It seems well established that the square ditch as it is described in *A Portrait* is Joyce's fictional invention. There is a little stream at Clongowes but it never had the direct connection with the "square," or lavatory, that seems to be suggested in *A Portrait*. The existing stream is slimy enough, and may well have had the "scum"

(*P* 10, 14) and the rat (*P* 10, 14, 22), as well as the other unpleasant qualities Joyce gives it by making it sound like a cesspool.

What gives these water images their force in the narrative is the accompanying sense of fear. Stephen "felt small and weak, and his eyes were weak and watery" (*P* 8); when Stephen is older and no longer small, the fear that comes from a sense of weakness continues. In successive chapters, there will be a movement toward non-physical weakness and fear. It begins with the child's reaction to the bigger boys' physical abuse but also his self-depreciation ("He felt small and weak. When would he be like the fellows in poetry and rhetoric?" *P* 17:03-04). Changes occur almost imperceptibly as the child's mind forms new images called up by his weakness in an illness and his sensations of awe and inexperience (*P* 21:05). The pattern of emotional development through image-forming is established in the first chapter.

Images of the sea, in combination with the child's sense of himself as small and weak, are in the first chapter vaguely frightening. "The sea was cold day and night: but it was colder at night. It was cold and dark under the seawall beside his father's house" (*P* 17:27-29). In the infirmary, as the sick boy listens to the infirmarian reading a newspaper aloud, he thinks of the dead Parnell in terms of the sea: "the dark waters, the light at the pierhead, and the moan of sorrow from the people when they had heard." The sea develops, more perceptibly than most of Joyce's water images, toward affirmation. Waves and tides, by the end of the book, are metaphors of thought, of language, and of a vital and creative force in life. While Stephen is in the infirmary, the voices he hears are "the noise of the waves. Or the waves were talking among themselves as they rose and fell." As he listens, "He saw the sea of waves, long dark waves rising and falling, dark under the moonless night" (*P* 26-27). Much later, when Stephen is in college, the dean of studies tells him that esthetic questions are very profound. "It is like looking down from the cliffs of Moher into the depths. Many go down into the depths and never come up. Only the trained diver can go down into those depths and explore them and come to the surface again" (*P* 187:4-7).

Between Chapter I and Chapter V, Stephen comes to terms with his fear of the sea. Wave images become less dark and fearful. At the thought of entering the university, "Pride after satisfaction uplifted him like long slow waves" (*P* 165:6). He thinks of his namesake, Daedalus the fabulous artificer; "he seemed to hear the noise of dim waves and to see a winged form flying above the waves and slowly climbing the air" (*P* 169:02). The fourth chapter ends, after the epiphany which has brought Stephen his sense of vocation, with an image of his own personal relation to the sea, now a more equable one.

> He climbed to the crest of the sandhill and gazed about him. Evening had fallen. A rim of the young moon cleft the pale waste of sky like the rim of a silver hoop embedded in the sand; and the tide was flowing in fast to the land with a low whisper of her waves, islanding a few last figures in distant pools. (*P* 173:4-9)

The close of Chapter IV seems to be a deliberate parallel to the ending of Chapters I and III; each is a short paragraph and each ends with a similar word. Dante, as noted above, closes each of the three main divisions of his poem with the same image, expressed in the word "stelle," "stars," which is the last word of the *Inferno*, the *Purgatorio*, and the *Paradiso*. Joyce's first chapter, with all its associations of water with weakness and fear, ends with the image of a fountain, its falling drops sounding like words to the child. He imagines the fountain first when, having broken his glasses, he watches the boys playing cricket at a greatly magnified distance and hears the sound of ball against bat; the broken glasses are the cause of the chapter's principal crisis, and when this has been successfully resolved by Stephen he imagines the fountain again as the chapter closes.

> The fellows were practicing long shies and bowling lobs and slow twisters. In the soft grey silence he could hear the bump of the balls: and from here and there through the quiet air the sound of the cricket bats: pick, pack, pock, puck: like drops of water in a fountain falling softly in the brimming bowl. (*P* 41:26; 59:22)

The three words, "bowl," "ciborium" and "pools," which respectively end Chapters I, III, and IV, are all containers of liquids. The bowl of Chapter I is a fountain; the ciborium (a drinking cup in classical usage) is the chalice that holds the Eucharist; and the tidal pools of Chapter IV are where Stephen Dedalus goes wading and discovers his vocation.

Cumulatively, the alternation and combined use of water images that are sometimes fearful and at other times vitally affirmative creates a sense of renewal and rebirth.

The second chapter opens with the Catholic asperges. Stephen goes for walks with his uncle Charles, who often pays a visit to the chapel (under English dominion, only the Protestants had 'churches' and all Catholic churches were 'chapels'). "As the font was above Stephen's reach, the old man would dip his hand and then sprinkle the water briskly about Stephen's clothes and on the floor of the porch" (*P* 61:34). This action is the act of lustration which the images foreshadow, a religious act of propitiation. It has become automatic in modern times and has ceased to have any significance. Uncle Charles would not have thought at all about what he was doing, or why. It functions in this chapter as an invocation of protection for Stephen, but unsuccessfully. The chapter ends with tears, and in this context they are a less benign asperges.

The true business of Chapter II is Stephen's first encounter with the flesh and its seductions, one of the three dangers his Church warns against. Tides are the metaphor. When he and his girl are together as children, "his heart danced upon her movements like a cork upon a tide" (*P* 69:22). But within a few years, adolescence has forced its way into his body, and his mind has been taken over by "monstrous reveries," which "abase his intellect." He tries to "build a breakwater":

> to dam up, by rules of conduct and active interests and new filial relations, the powerful recurrence of the tides within him. Useless. From without as from within the water had flowed over his barriers: their tides began once more to jostle fiercely above the crumbled mole. (*P* 98:21-25)

The chapter had begun with an "unsubstantial image" from his romantic reading, a female figure with whom, "in a moment of supreme tenderness" he would be magically transformed. "Weakness and timidity and inexperience would fall from him in that magic moment" (*P* 65:13). At the end of the chapter his actual encounter is with a prostitute. "In her arms he felt that he had suddenly become strong and fearless and sure of himself." The lustration image that opened the chapter closes it with an asperges of tears, as Stephen "all but burst into hysterical weeping. Tears of joy and relief shone in his delighted eyes" (*P* 101:06).

Chapter III of *A Portrait* has been called by Hans Gabler "literally and structurally the dead center of the novel." His conclusion, based on a study of the sequence of composition of the five chapters of the novel as it emerged from Joyce's revision of *Stephen Hero*, is that Joyce made a momentous "decision to abandon the sequential or cyclic narrative by episodes as used in *Stephen Hero* in favor of a chiastic center design."[38] Gabler sees Chapters I and V as "exact symmetrical counterpart(s)," the former centered on the Christmas dinner scene and the latter on the composition of the villanelle. Chapters II and IV, however, are "basically narrated in a linear sequence of episodes"; in Chapter III, "the sequential progression is stayed by the unifying and centralizing effect of a concentration on the single event of the religious retreat."

Thematically there is some support, at least within this chapter, for the notion of a structure that moves downward to the moment when Stephen's 16-year-old imagination convicts him of mortal sin, the death of the soul. The rhetorical movement is one of contrast; refreshment comes only after thirst. Images of lustration move from vitality to stagnation; from the fountains of sanctifying grace (dried up) to desert dryness that finally explodes in hellish fire. The sea's waves provide the first metaphor:

> At his first violent sin he had felt a wave of vitality pass out of him and had feared to find his body or his soul maimed by the excess. Instead the vital wave had carried him on its bosom out of itself and back again when it receded; and no part of the body or soul had been maimed but a dark peace had been established between them. (*P* 103:21-23)

But the narrative action is focused on Stephen's imaginative reaction to three retreat sermons. The image now develops into "waves of fire" (*P* 125:07), and the language of the chapter becomes dry and parched, as Stephen's heart "withered like a flower of the desert" (*P* 108). Images of thirst increase in intensity (parched lips and aching throat, *P* 123; his flesh shrank . . . dried up, *P* 125; his tongue cleaving to his palate, *P* 135), with waves of fire sweeping through Stephen's brain until his brain begins to glow and his skull to crack. These culminate in the descriptive terms for hell, as a lake of fire and a burning ocean (*P* 121:21, 24). Spiritual aridity is finally relieved with images of tears and, as the chapter ends, healing rain.

The poetic center of *A Portrait of the Artist* is the last of the retreat sermons, with its horrible picture of the soul's death. The *Vita Nuova* has a similar center, the 23d of its 42 sections (not of equal length, but marked off by the author as divisions the author considered significant), in which Dante has an apocalyptic vision of the death of Beatrice.[39]

The square ditch returns in Chapter III, with appropriate associations of fetid streams, scum, and filthy swamps. Stephen's sins, as he confesses them, "trickled in shameful drops . . . a squalid stream of vice. . . . The last sins oozed forth, sluggish, filthy" (*P* 144). He thinks of his soul as a foul swamp of sin; he is caught in a swamp of spiritual and bodily sloth (*P* 106, 114). A thick scum of fearfulness is in his mouth (*P* 111), and "thick fog" accompanied by fear darkens his mind (*P* 111).

There are five explicit references to baptism, which functions in Chapter III as the asperges did in Chapter II (*P* 106:25; 107:36; 108:03; 122:04). Of the eight times the word is used in the novel, all but one occur in this chapter. It is made part of the retreat sermon: "As the waters of baptism cleanse the soul with the body, so do the fires of punishment torture the spirit with the flesh" (*P* 122). St. Francis Xavier's prodigies of baptizing make him a "great fisherman of souls." The correlative image is the tears of repentance that relieve Stephen's thirsty soul after his repentance begins, and a flooding rain that relieves his spiritual aridity (*P* 116:15; 129; 139:10). Before his repentance is complete, however, rain becomes in his mind a fearful image of the deluge.

> Rain was falling on the chapel, on the garden, on the college. It would rain for ever, noiselessly. The water would rise inch by inch, covering the monuments and the mountain tops. All life would be choked off, noiselessly: birds, men, elephants, pigs, children: noiselessly floating corpses amid the litter of the wreckage of the world. Forty days and forty nights the rain would fall till the waters covered the face of the earth.
> It might be: Why not? (*P* 117:1-10)

The most terrifying of the retreat sermons follows, after which Stephen's overheated imagination brings up nauseating bestial figures of sin: "God had allowed him to see the hell reserved for his sins" (*P* 138). If there is indeed a "dead center" to the narrative movement, on one level it can plausibly be located here, at the point where Stephen is so parched that he cannot weep (*P* 136:32). Thereafter, the rhetoric moves toward the rebirth associated with baptism. The image of the deluge was Stephen's; the freshening rain placed here is Joyce's.

> The rain had drawn off. . . . Heaven was still and faintly luminous and the air sweet to breathe, as in a thicket drenched with showers: and amid peace and shimmering lights and quiet fragrance he made a covenant with his heart. (*P* 138:23-29)

Joyce's novel, of course, uses other images as well as the general associations of water and the more specific images I have called lustration. *A Portrait of the Artist as a Young Man* was not the first symbolist novel, but it is a model of its kind. It is not surprising to find in it, along with a great volume of aqueous figures, other designs involving fire, colors, music, birds, caves, and many more. The special Joycean invention, in Ellmann's words, is the collation of specific detail raised to rhythmic intensity.[40] The sequences in *A Portrait* are not linear;

they do not progress in simple chronology; it is not easy to define the mode of progression. Clusters of images accompany Joyce's agglomeration of narrative detail; it is a layering effect. Lustration imagery contributes to one identifiable perception, a sense of growth by regeneration. The rudimentary meanings of Chapter I move toward more complex ones, and in Chapters II and III the terrors of childhood and sin move toward a relatively more secure confidence as the embryo artist develops a sense of vocation.

Chapter IV describes yet another water-assisted rebirth. After the infernal echoes of Chapter III, this chapter is purgatorial in tone. Waves and tides continue. Stephen's amendment of life, with which the chapter opens, fails at last and leaves him with "a sense of spiritual dryness." This comes when he realizes that temperamentally he cannot merge his life in "the common tide of other lives." To the asperges in Chapter II and baptism in Chapter III, Joyce now adds the metaphor of the sacraments as fountains or springs of grace (*P* 152:3). Sensuality also returns, as an advancing tide, in small, timid, noiseless wavelets of temptation (*P* 152:28).

But the experience of sin, repentance and amendment of life has left Stephen with a Dantesque vision of the whole world forming one vast symmetrical expression of God's power and love; like Dante in the *Vita Nuova*, Stephen broods on this great mystery and feels within him a warm movement "like that of some newly born life." In Chapter IV, after he has rejected the Jesuits' invitation to join their order, he crosses two bridges: one over the squalid little stream of the Tolka, to reach his home. Here he acknowledges that his choice as an artist cannot be the secure but sterile order of the repressed religious life, and he accepts the disorder, misrule and confusion, and even vegetable stagnation, of everyday life "in his father's house."

Before Stephen crosses the second bridge, he thinks of "wild creatures racing, their feet pattering like rain" (*P* 165:18). The second bridge brings him to an epiphany of vocation, an image that forms in his mind as he goes wading in a tidal pool. An unknown girl suddenly looks like a miraculous visitant, an "envoy from the fair courts of life, to throw open before him in an instant of ecstasy the gates of all the ways of error and glory" (*P* 172:10-13). An image of rebirth precedes this vision: "his soul had arisen from the grave of boyhood" (*P* 170:3). The call of life comes as "a faint noise of gently moving water . . . low and faint and whispering . . . hither and thither" (*P* 171:30-33).

There are Dantesque echoes in these climactic paragraphs. Joyce's phrase, "her image had passed into his soul forever," seems to be a transcription of Dante's line in the *Vita Nuova*, "la sua imagine, la quale continuamente meco stava," "her image, which remained constantly with me" (*VN* II). More striking, however, is the Dantesque rose that Stephen imagines as he falls asleep on the beach.

> A world, a glimmer, or a flower? Glimmering and trembling, trembling and unfolding, a breaking light, an opening flower, it spread in endless succession to itself, breaking in full crimson and unfolding and fading to palest rose, leaf by leaf and wave of light by wave of light, flooding all the heavens with its soft flushes, every flush deeper than other." (*P* 172:31-36)

The heavenly rose of *Paradiso* 30 appears to Dante out of the water imagery of the great river of light; Beatrice is about to take her place in the rose, which is the "world," "nostra città" of the saved souls. The close parallel is seen in the reflective phrasing of Joyce's figure which, as Barbara Seward noted (also remarking on the association of water imagery with rebirth in this passage and in *Paradiso* 30), seems to pick up Dante's "si specchia," "mirroring," as well as the more obvious rhetorical resemblances of the design.[41]

Chapter V of *A Portrait*, which is much longer than the others, opens with an account of Stephen washing himself before leaving for his University lecture. His ablutions correspond to the asperges of Uncle Charles that opened Chapter II; both are placed at the beginning of the chapter, as the liturgical asperges is made the opening action of the Mass and other rites. As imagery, it is a construction that comes from Joyce's mind, not Stephen's; the two cannot always be disentangled, since Stephen's habit of thinking in images, a trait demonstrated continually throughout the book, is so much a part of his characterization. As in Chapter IV, narrative elements that suggest a poetic vocation for Stephen (whether or not these may have ironic significance) are attached to images of water in ways that call up the idea of rebirth. They are also accompanied by Dantesque allusions.

The second and last of the lustration images in Chapter V that can be identified as the author's construction comes at the end of the first section, where Joyce has placed a silent reproduction of the *Vita Nuova*. Stephen, like Dante, sees his beloved in a group of ladies; he stands silently against a wall, looking up at her. Joyce adds to this a shower of rain, in which Stephen stands, "heedless of the rain which fell fast, turning his eyes towards her from time to time" (*P* 215:35-36; *VN* XIV).

In the next section, which follows immediately, Stephen writes a poem, a villanelle. The suggestion of rebirth is strongest here, the second of the chapter's three divisions. The discovery by Gabler that the villanelle section was a late addition to the manuscript of *A Portrait*, inserted in its final form when all the rest of Chapter V had been written in fair copy, invites close inspection of whatever patterns Joyce may have put into this section that may relate to the chapter and to the book as a whole. One of these is clearly the lustration image with which the section opens. Stephen wakes up; the inspiration for a poem comes into his mind.

> His soul was all dewy wet. Over his limbs in sleep pale cool waves of light had passed. He lay still, as if his soul lay amid cool waters, conscious of faint sweet music. His mind was waking slowly to a tremulous morning knowledge, a morning inspiration. A spirit filled him, pure as the purest water, sweet as dew, moving as music. (*P* 217:1-5)

These images of pure water and dew, here and at the end of the villanelle section, are Stephen's; but in the larger pattern of the chapter and the book, the consistency of association of rain, dew, and other clear natural waters with poetic inspiration and with language is Joyce's, and is part of a pattern also found in Dante's poetic imagery.

Resemblances between Dante's *Vita Nuova* and Joyce's *A Portrait of the Artist as a Young Man* begin with the choice of title. The "new life" in Dante's book is that of a young man learning to be a poet; the qualifying phrase in Joyce's title, *"as a Young Man,"* identifies the limits of the book as those that Dante chose for himself. The shape of Joyce's patterns also suggests the *Vita Nuova*.

Joyce's water images came from his general reading as well as from his study of Dante, and from the *Divine Comedy* rather than the *Vita Nuova*. Joyce did not always take his metaphors and images directly from Dante's poetry, but he learned there how to construct them. The traces of Dante's lustration images in *A Portrait* indicate a close study of the range of Dante's expressive means.

In *Ulysses*, Joyce depicts Bloom as a mind untouched by the religious influences that molded, and that still hold, the mind of Stephen Dedalus. Near the end, in the Ithaca chapter, the author brings together in one paragraph a catalog of water's metaphorical applications (*U* 654). It is a prolonged, obsessively precise, and apparently comprehensive sequence. The narrator asks, "What in water did Bloom, waterlover, drawer of water, watercarrier returning to the range, admire?" The answer, a grossly inflated explanation of a routine action, is gently ironic. It lists 43 ways in which Leopold Bloom might consider the properties of water.[42] Five of the items in this list contribute directly to the formation of lustration images of the kind that have here been discussed. These include its "secrecy" in springs and in latent humidity; its healing virtues; its cleansing, thirst-quenching, fire-quenching, and nourishing properties; its metamorphoses in mist, cloud, and rain; the noxiousness of its effluvia, in which the narrator mentions marshes, fens, faded flowerwater, and stagnant pools in the waning moon (*U* 656). Another 24 items in the list have contributed to Joyce's more generalized use of water imagery. The thirty-third item on the list identifies as one of the properties of water, "Its infallibility as paradigm and paragon": that is, as a pattern or model for imitation, and also a model of supreme excellence. Even without this descriptive term, the text at that point emphasizes some metaphorical aspects of water. In the narrative, after Bloom lights a fire in the grate, he puts a kettle of water on the range and then washes his hands. He suggests that Stephen do likewise; Stephen refuses.

> What reason did Stephen give for declining Bloom's offer? That he was hydrophobe, hating partial contact by immersion or total by submersion in cold water (his last bath having taken place in the month of October of the preceding year), disliking the aqueous substances of glass and crystal, distrusting accquacities of thought and language. (*U* 657:5-10)

These negatives stand in contrast to the 43 affirmatives of Mr Bloom. The sentence contains echoes of Chapter V of *A Portrait of the Artist*. Stephen tells his friend Cranly, "I fear many things: dogs, horses, firearms, the sea, thunderstorms, machinery, the country roads at night," and when asked why, he replies, "I imagine that there is a malevolent reality behind those things I say I fear" (*P* 243:17, 20). There are several minor indications of Stephen's dislike of cold water, some of these a holdover from his early experience with the square ditch at Clongowes. But there are also indications that Stephen does not necessarily avoid things he fears.

> He passed from the trembling bridge [in Chapter IV, just before his epiphany of vocation] on to firm land again. At that instant, as it seemed to him, the air was chilled and looking askance towards the water he saw a flying squall darkening and crisping suddenly the tide. A faint click at his heart, a faint throb in his throat told him once more of how his flesh dreaded the cold infrahuman odour of the sea: yet he did not strike across the downs on his left but held straight on along the spine of rocks that pointed against the river's mouth. (*P* 167:5-12)

It is the narrator who gives this description; the picture in the text is not one of Stephen's images, although some of the descriptive terms come from his mind. The descriptive words are so colorful, however, that the context set up by the words given to the narrator is easily overlooked. A hasty reading can easily enough lead to the conclusion that, if there is a connection between water and art in the author's design, Stephen's future as an artist is dubious because he hates contact with water.[43] Fear of the sea, in the terms of this book, is a metaphoric reflection of Stephen's fearfulness confronting the oceans of humanity and the tides of life, "the common tide of other lives."

But Stephen's physical reactions are one thing, his rational and intellectual operations are another.

In the Ithaca chapter, Stephen's dread of water, his description of himself as a "hydrophobe," is attached to something quite different: his sensitivity to *the power of water as a metaphor*. Moreover, his fear (or dislike) is attached very loosely: the clauses of the sentence are separable. In this respect, as the long list indicates and as the thirty-third item specifies, water is indeed the model of excellence, a paragon. Stephen's answer has singled out just two qualities, both negatives of the metaphor. These are two barriers, the first to understanding (aqueous substances of glass and crystal, which impede vision), and the second to expression (aquacities, or wateriness, of thought and language). Glass, in these terms, is not transparent; the power of language, in these terms, is not enhanced but diminished. Stephen's idea may come from St. Paul: "For now we see through a glass, darkly . . . now I know in part, but then shall I know even as I am known" (I *Corinthians*, xiii:12). But Stephen puts his idea in watery terms.

Stephen's own metaphors are affirmative in tone as well as negative. Some of these, finding in water a metaphor for language, have been seen in the Proteus chapter. At least a dozen of these are clearly parallel, and another dozen have a more tenuous connection with the list in Ithaca. For example, item 19, "its alluvial deposits," is reproduced as "These heavy sands are language tide and wind have silted here" (*U* 45:34); item 18, "its slow erosion of peninsulas and promontories," appears as "a bank of dwindling sand" (*U* 47:02); item 5, "the restlessness of its waves and surface particles," is embedded in a series of metaphors using waves as speech: "sighs of leaves and waves," "four-worded wavespeech," and "wavenoise: many crests, breaking, splashing."

In structure and in a general way in vocabulary, the list of water's properties in Ithaca is reminiscent of Dante's little work, *Questio de Aqua et Terra*. This is now believed to have been a thesis expounded by

6. Two similar uses of the same allusion connect *Ulysses* and *Finnegans Wake*. Joyce finished *Ulysses* in the late months of 1921; in the summer of 1923 he began work on a fragment of *Finnegans Wake*. We find parallel Dantean allusions in the Ithaca chapter at this late stage of *Ulysses*, and in the "St. Kevin fragment," at the earliest stage of composition in the *Wake*. Joyce is using the nine concentric circles of Dante's *Paradiso*: "On that point the heavens and all nature are dependent." In Ithaca he writes, "the upcast reflection of a lamp

of Kevin, of Increate God the servant of the Lord Creator
a filial fearer, the miracles, death and life are these.   27

Procreated on the ultimate island of Ireland in the
encyclical Irish archipelago, come their feast of precreated
holy whiteclad angels, voluntarily poor, Kevin, having
been granted the privilege of a priest's postcreated portable
altare cum balneo, when espousing the one true cross,
invented and exalted, in celibate matrimony, at matin
chime arose and westfrom went and came in alb of
cloth of gold to our own midmost Glendalough-le-Vert
by archangelical guidance where amiddle of meeting
waters of river Slaney and Liffey river on this one love
navigable lake piously Kevin, lauding the Triune
trishagion, amidships of his conducible altar super
bath, rejected centripetally the diaconal servant of orders
Hibernian midway across the subject lake surface to
its supreme epicentric lake isle, whereof its lake is the
centrifugal principality, whereon by prime powerful in
knowledge Kevin came to where its centre is among
the circumfluent watercourses of Ishgapramia and
Ishgadectera an enisled lakelet islanding a
lacustrine islet whereupon with beached raft
subdiaconal bath propter altar, with oil extremely

anointed, accompanied by prayer, holy Kevin hides
till the third morn hour but to build a rubric penitential
honeybeehivehut in whose enclosure to live in
fortitude, a colyte of cardinal virtues whereof the arenary
floor most holy Kevin excavated as deep as to a depth
of a seventh part of one full fathom, which excavated,
venerable Kevin anchorite, taking counsel, proceeded
towards the lakeside of the isletshore whereat seven
several times he eastward genuflecting, in entire
obedience at sextnoon collected gregorian water
sevenfold and with Ambrosian eucharistic joy of
heart as many times receded carrying that oriviledged
altar unacumen bath which severally seven times
into the cavity excavated, a lector of water levels,
most venerable Kevin then effused thereby letting
there be water where was theretofore dryland by him
so concreated who now confirmed a strong perfect
christian, blessed Kevin, exorcised his holy sister
water, perpetually chaste, so that well understanding
she should fill to midheight his tubbathaltar
which handbathtub most blessed Kevin ninthly
enthroned in the interconcentric centre of the
translated water whereamid, when violet vesper
vailed Saint Kevin Hydrophilus, having girded
his sable cappa magna as high as to his
chemical toins, set in his seat of wisdom, that
at solemn compline

and shade, an inconstant series of concentric circles of varying gradations of light." In the rough draft of the *Wake* fragment, the allusion comes into his mind as he inserts the word "ninthly" and a short time later, in the fair copy, the allusion is very nearly in final form: "ninthly enthroned in the interconcentric center of the translated water." The only change made in the published version was the removal of "inter" (*U* 721:21; *FW* 606:3; *Par.* 28:33-34).

Dante in Verona, on the question whether water, being "nobler" than earth, stands higher than land on the earth's circumference.[44] Some of its ideas found their way into *Paradiso* 16, in remarks about the tides, and *Paradiso* 2, Dante's explanation of the spots on the moon. Besides the appearance of tides here and in Joyce's Ithaca list, the two books have in common also the sea as the source of all waters; its center an element of universality; the question why, from the sea, mountains appear lower than the surface of the water, an idea that Joyce expresses as "its vast circumterrestrial ahorizontal curve" in item 26 of his list; and the idea that the sea's surface is never higher than the land, which contains the sense of item 2, "democratic constancy to its nature in seeking its own level."

The lustration image, in Dante's poem and in Joyce's fiction, is part of a much larger body of expressive devices, the use of water imagery on the one hand, and on the other hand the representation by other means of ideas of renewal, regeneration, and rebirth. In Joyce's work, without the lustration image and its centripetal impetus, images of water and metaphors involving water would be an unfocused and even an amorphous mass. There is also another dimension to the use of the lustration image by Joyce and by Dante: this is the movement of their work toward myth. Walton Litz has defined this component as it appears in the Ithaca chapter:

> It was Joyce's unique gift that he could turn the substance of ordinary life into something like myth, not only through the use of "parallels" and allusions but through direct transformation: and the ending of Ithaca like that of 'Anna Livia Plurabelle' would seem to vindicate his method. Most of *Ulysses* can be understood by the same methods one applies to *The Waste Land*, where the manipulation of a continuous parallel between contemporaneity and antiquity 'places' the contemporary action, but the ending of 'Ithaca' consists of metamorphosis rather than juxtaposition.[45]

One of the things that Joyce learned from his reading of the *Divine Comedy* was the imaginative expression and manipulation of polarities. Dante allows the trope to extend itself in a widening metonymy of purpose (in Honig's phrase), by which it contributes to the creation of a symbolic fiction. Both Dante and Joyce, placing the artist at the center of their work, made poetic invention itself the subject and tested the limits of their art.

... method which bends upon these present things and so works upon them and fashions them that the quick intelligence may go beyond them to their meaning, which is still unuttered. (Joyce, "James Clarence Mangan," 1902)

... Le presenti cose col falso lor piacer volser miei passi.

present things, with their false allurement, turned my steps aside.
(*Purg.* 31:34)

WE now return, by a somewhat different different approach, to the agenda of the opening chapter. Joyce's eclectic treatment of Dante's images has been described in the three central chapters of this book as a poetic configuration of intermingled theme, style and form. It is now appropriate once more to resume a chronological sequence and to inspect Joyce's writing as a series of individual works intimately related and connected with each other, in order to make a final examination of his allusions to Dante in this perspective. The immediate purpose of the inquiry is to fix more precisely the character of Joyce's allegorical mode as it relates to Dante.

Readers have made some of the same assumptions about the allegorical aspect of Joyce's fictions that were made in previous centuries about Dante's.[1] Narrowing the definition of allegory, the medieval tradition argued that fictions existed to express a truth. Fiction and truth must not be confused: *this* fiction, the story told or the experience related, always had to stand for *that* conceptual or spiritual reality. But Dante made two different statements about poetry, and, in the second, took his *Commedia* out of the medieval category of lying fictions. Thus it has been felicitously said that the fiction of the *Divine Comedy* is that it is not fiction.[2]

Joyce, when he made one of his infrequent defenses of his method of writing, indicated the presence in his work of a broadly conceived type of allegory, and thus of a poetic method similar to Dante's. Writing of *Dubliners*, Joyce said, "He is a very bold man who dares to alter in the presentment, still more to deform, whatever he has seen and heard."[3] Such a statement coming from Joyce is like Ibsen saying of himself, "I only write about people; I don't write symbolically." *Dubliners* was taken by some (not all) reviewers as a slice of life in the naturalistic tradition.[4] But, as John Kelleher says, Joyce "may have regarded the surface story with an even more uncompromising realism than his critics have allowed" at the same time that he created successive levels of meaning by insistent symbolism.[5] Ibsen furnished *The Wild Duck* with stage directions that placed in the attic specific props he remembered from the attic of his own childhood; Joyce embedded in his stories a multitude of local and private references which, rediscovered, enlarge the meanings of the work. Something of this process can be found also in Joyce's use of literary materials, especially in that gratuitous and minimal "parody of parody" that Robert Adams found also in Pope's satire, where the allusion "simply uses the same word, touching off the very minimum reverberation of a parallel."[6] Joyce's economical use of Dante often involves an echo so very minute and spare, or so remotely connected, that it seems almost to be a private reference, like the quotation from *Inferno* 5 (described above in Chapter Three) that Joyce placed below a photograph of a withered old woman.

Parody and quotation, always a useful adjunct to metonymy, in Joyce's hands move toward the construction of literary allegory. Flickering echoes, remote but clear, build a context that is akin to Dante's in style and in substance. Dante became a presence in all the areas of Joyce's writing. Joyce made use of the *Divine Comedy* and the *Vita Nuova* in *Exiles*, his only play, and there are traces of Dante in *Dubliners* and in Joyce's poetry. The dates of composition and publication are significant. As noted above in Chapter One, there are discernible stages in Joyce's use of Dante's themes and imagery. *Chamber Music* (1907), *Dubliners* (published in 1916 but actually finished in 1907-1909), and *Exiles* (published in 1918 but composed before 1915) all represent an earlier reading of the *Divine Comedy* and the *Vita Nuova*, a reading that was certainly less intensive and resulted in an imitation less assured of its purpose and direction.

*

Joyce's first volume of verse, *Chamber Music*, is a sequence of thirty-six love poems; in *Stephen Hero* (174) the poet's early verses are arranged as a *Vita Nuova*. In Poem XXI, "He who hath glory lost," Joyce sees himself as an exiled Dante, "That high unconsortable one;" dedicated "To Nora" (Sept. 30, 1904), it was put first in a 1905 MS arrangement. Poem XXVIII begins, "Gentle Lady," an echo of Dante's *donna gentil*. The published sequence ends with a lost love.

Joyce's second volume of poetry, however, contains two of Dante's images, in two poems. One of these is the poem called "Tilly," the first one in the collection, and the other is "A Memory of the Players in a Mirror at Midnight." The allusions in these two poems require description and comment, despite problems of dating and uncertainties of historical context. Because the poetic form demands a compressed use of allusion, the mechanism of reference is often more visible than that which appears in the more leisurely and discursive constructions of prose. Most definitions and critical distinctions that govern our conception of how allusion works have come from poetic effects rather than from an inspection of prose mechanisms. Joyce's two poems represent his most economical use of Dante's poetry, and they set in perspective a pattern of allusion that governed his artistic choices and decisions also in the prose fictions. The poems show clearly and in a narrow compass the dramatic effects he could achieve by inserting a Dantean context. By forcing on the reader a doubleness of vision, the allusion focused attention on the speaker not only by the dramatically indicated distance, but also by the radical transformation that gave a new voice to the poem.

The poem "Tilly" has been given extended critical discussion. The Dante allusion was first noticed by Robert Scholes, who also gave a comprehensive account of the manuscript evidence that suggests that the printed version of 1927 was a late revision of a poem originally written in Dublin and mentioned in the diary of Stanislaus Joyce in 1903.[7] The poem's theme, a comparison of the Irish people to a driven herd, patient and unthinking, remains the same in both versions. (An intermediate manuscript shows a change in title from "Cabra," a place-name, to the more thematic "Ruminants.") In the first version the speaker is not particularized, and the only departure from a tone of simple pastoral description comes in the final words, "the door made fast."

Cabra

He travels after the wintery sun
Driving the cattle along the straight red road;
Calling to them in a voice they know,
He drives the cattle above Cabra.

He tells them home is not far.
They low and make soft music with their hoofs.

He drives them without labour before him,
Steam pluming their foreheads.

Herdsman, careful of the herd,
Tonight sleep well by the fire
When the herd too is asleep
And the door made fast.

In the second version the poet speaks quietly in the third person
until, in the last two lines, there is a sudden change to the first person.
A striking contrast is created.

Tilly

He travels after a winter sun,
Urging the cattle along a cold red road,
Calling to them, a voice they know,
He drives his beasts above Cabra.

The voice tells them home is warm.
They moo and make brute music with their hoofs.
He drives them with a flowering branch before him,
Smoke pluming their foreheads.

Boor, bond of the herd,
Tonight stretch full by the fire!
I bleed by the black stream
For my torn bough!

The allusion is to *Inferno* 13 and to Dante's account of Pier della
Vigna, another poet who is bleeding and torn. Dante has just crossed
the black river of blood to reach this evil wood, which is a darker reminiscence of the *selva selvaggia* he escaped in *Inferno* 1. Here in the
Wood of the Suicides, a broken branch speaks to Dante:

Allor porsi la mano un poco avante
  e colsi un ramicel da un gran pruno;
  e 'l tronco suo gridò: "Perché mi schiante?"

Then I stretched my hand a little forward and plucked
  a branch from a great thorntree; and the trunk of it
  cried, "Why dost thou rend me?"   (Inf. 13:31-33)

Joyce uses Dante's personification to create an effect of explosive
bitterness.

I bleed by the black stream
For my torn bough!

Dante's figure is radically displaced, for the bleeding speaker of Joyce's poem is at a greater distance, though it is unspecified, from his "torn bough" than the branch is distant from the thorntree in *Inferno* 13. The closing lines are far more demanding than the closure of the first version.

The speaker is recalling with nostalgia an identifiable scene and figure, the cattle-driver in Cabra—Cabra being a north-Dublin suburb, in which even today a common sight is the cattle being driven to the open cattle-market in the northwest section of the city. The poem develops, through image and tone, an ambiguous involvement of the speaker with his own remembered home. Note the words, "home is warm," and the contrasting vision of the herdsman, "bond of the herd / Tonight stretch full by the fire!" But the speaker bleeds by the black stream. Why should the poet associate himself thus with a cattle-driver? The nexus is Dante's torn bough, a very old image which Joyce here puts into a new and different yet wholly appropriate context, making it one of the "images independent of life or fact" like Yeats's great-rooted blossomer.[8]

The broken branch was not Dante's exclusively or originally: the tree losing its branch is in the language. There is a similar event in Spenser's *Faerie Queene* (I.ii); before that we find it in Ovid, and especially in Virgil, when the broken branch speaks to Aeneas. But we recognize that Joyce's lines refer to Dante's, and that Joyce's true subtext is *Inferno* 13, because of the words, "black stream." If the reader knows nothing at all about the poem, the psychic effect of being transposed to an infernal scene sets a tone of profound estrangement even if the source is unrecognized.

Moving from the image of the broken branch to the context, we discover why this Dantean construction appealed to Joyce. In *Inferno* 13, Pier della Vigna is a man with a grievance, which he relates in full to Dante. He was banished from his honorable post at the court, brought down as he insists by the false innuendo of jealous enemies. Here a biographical connection is suggested, for Joyce's voluntary exile from Ireland, which began in 1904, remained tentative for some years. In 1912, after a couple of brief visits to Dublin, he left Ireland for good, a man with a real grievance, believing that his book of short stories, *Dubliners*, had been denied publication by a silent censorship in which the literary establishment had acquiesced.[9] The Dantean context, as Scholes suggests, thus makes the poem more specifically a song of betrayal and exile.

Going further into *Inferno* 13, the reader finds Pier insisting to Dante that he is innocent of the charges and did not commit the treason for which he was banished. Dante, although he does not say so explicitly, accepts Pier's version of the matter. In the *Divine Comedy* Minos hears every soul's full confession and sends the sinner to his proper region of hell, and if Pier della Vigna had indeed been a traitor he would have been in the lowest circle where Brutus and Cassius and other traitors are frozen in ice; he is here only because of his suicide.[10] Undoubtedly Joyce noticed the self-identification of Dante with this unfortunate spirit, represented by Dante's grieving silence when the torn bough has finished its tale. A similar self-identification, not with the suicidal ending but with the story of undeserved betrayal and despair that led to the suicidal impulse, must have been in Joyce's mind when he made the final revision of his poem, with its echo of Dante's episode.

Restoration of the Dantean context brings all the images of the poem into focus. The cattle driver and his docile herd were the young Joyce's wry vision of his country and its leaders, including its intellectual leadership. Introduction of the "flowering" branch adds a dimension to the analogue, making the final two lines a more radical version of the theme of exile, voluntary or involuntary, as the artist's fated lot.[11]

It is not the personification of the broken branch that "matters" in Joyce's little poem, but rather the introduction of a literary element, an allusion in which small details are manipulated to set up effects of likeness and opposition, that has charged with meaning the poem's reference to two contrasted individuals. It is the presence of a prior context that enlarges and deepens that meaning. Joyce's allusive structure has created an urgent voice that was not present in the first draft, and a play of likeness and difference between his construction and Dante's. The speaker bleeds in both; the speaker is a poet in both. One is a suicide, the other is not; both are homesick exiles. The originality of Joyce's transformation makes the reader search with close attention for the element of artistic choice that determines the new context. Manifestly it lies within the tensions implicit in "he" and "I" as the poet develops his striking opposition between the herdsman and the speaker, the violent "gridò" of the speaker and the complacent voice of the "boor" who holds the flowering branch.

The second allusion in Joyce's *Pomes Penyeach* comes from Dante's *Vita Nuova* III; this is "A Memory of the Players in a Mirror at Midnight," in which the central image of Dante's third chapter is transformed by Joyce into a midnight vision of death. In Dante's story the poet is awakened "in the fourth hour of the night" by an apparition of the god of Love, holding a nude sleeping figure that Dante recognizes as Beatrice, and bearing in his hands a fiery object, Dante's heart. The vision is followed by a poem:[12]

> The first three hours of night were almost spent
> The time that every star shines down on us,
> When Love appeared to me so suddenly
> That I still shudder at the memory.
> Joyous Love looked to me, the while he held
> My heart within his hands, and in his arms
> My lady lay asleep wrapped in a veil.
> He woke her then and trembling and obedient
> She ate that burning heart out of his hand;
> Weeping I saw him then depart from me.   (trans. Musa)

From Dante's poem Joyce takes the startling nature of the vision, the meditative tone of midnight solitariness, and the striking image of the poet's heart being eaten. He combines these in a vision that captures the full force of Dante's fourth line, "Cui essenza membrar mi da orrore," "That I still shudder at the memory," a form truly terrifying to remember. The allusion to the *Vita Nuova* was first noted by Richard Ellmann, who also remarked the connection with Hamlet's players.[13]

A Memory of the Players in a Mirror at Midnight

> They mouth love's language. Gnash
> The thirteen teeth
> Your lean jaws grin with. Lash
> Your itching and quailing, nude greed of the flesh.
> Love's breath in you is stale, worded or sung,
> As sour as cat's breath,
> Harsh of tongue.
> This grey that stares
> Lies not, stark skin and bone.
> Leave greasy lips their kissing. None
> Will choose her what you see to mouth upon.
> Dire hunger holds his hour.
> Pluck forth your heart, saltblood, a fruit of tears,
> Pluck and devour!

As in "Tilly," the Dantesque image is contained in the last two lines, where the desperate hungers of love are evoked. But under the masks of the players is the grim grey visage of death. Joyce, as will be seen below, was sensitive to the presence of death in the *Vita Nuova*. But the requirements of his novels did not allow a direct treatment of death as Joyce, on the evidence of this poem, confronted the theme. In *Ulysses*, the recollection by Stephen Dedalus of his mother's deathbed scene offers a near approach to the images of "A Memory of the Players." Insofar as Stephen's reaction to this event (often dismissed as over-reaction) represents a portrayal of the poet's sensibility, the disposition of imagery also resembles somewhat the pattern in the poem. Dante in the *Divine Comedy* also speaks of life as "a race toward death," and occasionally summons up such forbidding aspects as the "fangs of death," or its chill grip, or its inexorable net. In this little poem, however, Joyce expresses directly what elsewhere he has treated with humorous wit and always more benignly: that is, the sense of life as shadowed by death, a baleful reality underlying all the representations of the artist, whether "worded or sung."

*

Dubliners, the book that altered the art of the short story, was written between 1904 and 1907, although censorship and other publishing difficulties delayed publication until 1914. Joyce wrote the stories of *Dubliners* in the mood and manner of Dante's abrasive denunciations of faction-ridden Florence, the city Dante describes as "piena d'invidia," full of envy and every sort of iniquity. "Rejoice, O Florence," he says in the canto of *Ulysses*, "in being so great that thy name resounds throughout Hell" (*Inf.* 26:1-3). Joyce's chosen term for the description of his native city in his own book, "paralysis," is a metaphor for the "static lifelessness of unrelieved viciousness" that Beckett, under Joyce's inspiration, describes as the essence of Dante's Hell.[14]

Dubliners was also the first of Joyce's published books to carry a suggestion of Dantean structure. When Joyce sent the collection to Grant Richards in late November 1905, the first story, "The Sisters," was still in the form of its first publication in *The Irish Homestead* (*Archive* 4:xxx). But in the revised version, as Jackson Cope discovered, the first story opens with the words Dante set above the gate of hell in *Inferno* 3: "There was no hope," while the final story, "The Dead," concludes with a disembodied vision of a frozen Ireland that imitates Dante's image of a frozen world, "where the shades were wholly covered (là dove l'ombre tutte eran coperte)" (*Inf.* 34:11), from the final canto of the *Inferno*.[15] Joyce's last sentence and first sentence were written, as Professor Cope comments, in deliberate emulation of the *Divine Comedy*. The last words of "The Dead" recall frozen Cocytus, Dante's last image of despair: "His soul swooned slowly as he heard the snow falling faintly through the universe and faintly falling, like the descent of their last end, upon all the living and the dead." The allusive pattern of *Dubliners* is signaled by rhetorical clue.

Joyce wrote in the margin of the manuscript, "End of the story The Dead" opposite the words, "She was fast asleep" (*Archive* 4:497). This seems a quite gratuitous action unconnected with publication of the story. The final section is set off in the printed version by extra spacing; without it, the ending of the story would closely resemble the inconclusive ending of "A Little Cloud," "Counterparts," and others in the collection. As a coda that epitomizes the dialectic of living death and thus significantly stands for the book as a whole, the final section also echoes the lines in which at a comparable stage of the work Dante addresses the reader.

> How frozen and faint I then became, ask it not, reader, for I do not write it, because all words would fail. I did not die and I did not remain alive.

> Com'io divenni allor gelato e fioco,
>   nol dimandar, lettor, ch'i' non lo scrivo,
>   però ch'ogne parlar sarebbe poco.
> Io non mori'e non rimasi vivo . . .
> > (*Inf*. 34:22-25, trans. Singleton)

From *Dubliners* on, each of Joyce's works would carry a Dantean pattern. Joyce's decision to do this can be dated as well as established by an examination of Joyce's manuscripts. The manuscript evidence fixes with some precision the point at which Joyce first began to think of the stories as a book, early in 1905. This must have been between March 15, when he finished Chapter 18 of *Stephen Hero*, and June, when he wrote "The Boarding-House" and "Counterparts." The first stories written were the three published in Russell's *Irish Homestead*: "The Sisters" in its first version, "Eveline," and "After the Race." The revision of "The Sisters" came very late indeed, and whatever Dantesque implications we find in the themes and arrangement of the stories must reckon with the belatedness of that revision, which made the theme of simony the central focus of *Dubliners*. The fourth story was "Hallow Eve," for which no manuscript exists except in the final form as "Clay." Joyce took a new direction, it is clear, with the writing of the fifth and sixth stories; thereafter he wrote very fast and brought the collection to its first-stage conclusion by December 4, when the manuscript was first sent to Grant Richards.

But I believe that the Dantean conception as such first entered his mind at the moment in which he realized that his stories of Dublin might form a narrative pattern similar to the scheme that makes Dante's *Inferno* a drama of passion and action shaped as a moral critique of society; and I believe the conception first entered Joyce's mind as early as February 1905. This was the month in which he finished Chapter 18 of *Stephen Hero*. As originally written the chapter began with an episode deliberately constructed as a detailed parallel to *Inferno* 15. It has been thought of as a separate chapter, having been so labeled by Theodore Spencer because of a misinterpretation of notes in the manuscript at MS pages 609 and 610 (*Archive* 8:239-241). Joyce obviously intended to use his pastiche of *Inferno* 15 as an episode in the final chapter of the revised *Portrait of the Artist*: at some time after 1907, and probably closer to 1911-12, he wrote in red crayon at the bottom of the page, obscuring four lines of his manuscript, "End of second Episode of V." (He added the four lines to the margin of the next page, writing "Chapter XVIII" at the top of the page.) Thus when he says he has finished Chapter 18, in a letter of March 15, 1905, Joyce is referring to a much longer piece of work—to a chapter that deals with Dante and Aquinas and describes a work, a critique of society, in terms that fit both the *Inferno* and *Dubliners* (*Letters* II: 82, 86; RE:*JJ* 200).

The early critics were right, then, up to a point, in seeing the *Dubliners* stories as realistic. Joyce himself saw them thus at the outset. But he changed his mind about the direction of his work in 1905. Joyce's symbolic mode, which appeared in published form for the first time in *Dubliners*, must be recognized as an aesthetic decision closely connected with his judgment in favor of a Dantean structure.

When the titles are set in parallel columns showing both the order Joyce assigned the stories in the book and also the order of their composition, a new light is thrown on the last six stories Joyce wrote for the book. They are, in order: "Araby," "Grace," "Two Gallants," "A Little Cloud," "The Dead," and finally the massive revision of "The Sisters." These are the stories most plainly and specifically associated with cantos of the *Inferno*. To make a full demonstration of all Joyce's connections is matter for another book. What is readily apparent, however, is the progress of Joyce's imaginative vision.

Another set of parallel columns, showing the order in which Dante placed sins and sinners in his *Inferno*, will allow the titles of the *Dubliners* stories to be arranged to show the Dantean moral order of Joyce's

7. *THE DANTEAN DESIGN OF JOYCE'S DUBLINERS*

DANTE'S HELL (The Damned)	JOYCE'S DUBLIN	*Divine Comedy*
Circles		
The Indifferent .... "Eveline"		*Inferno* 3
River Acheron, boundary of Hell (ferryman, Charon)		
1st — Limbo: The Unbaptized		
2d — The Lustful .... "Araby"		*Inferno* 5
3d — The Gluttonous		
4th — The Avaricious and Prodigal . "After the Race"		*Inferno* 7
5th — The Wrathful		
River Styx (ferryman, Phlegyas)		
THE WALLS OF DIS		
6th Heretics		
River Phlegethon		
7th The Violent:		
against one's neighbor .... "Counterparts"		*Inferno* 8, 12
against one's self .... "A Painful Case"		*Inferno* 13
against God .... "An Encounter"		*Inferno* 15
THE ABYSS OF MALEBOLGE (*ferryman, Geryon*)		
8th Panders and Seducers ..... {"Two Gallants"		} *Inferno* 18
{"The Boarding House"		} *Inferno* 18
Simonists .... {"The Sisters"		*Inferno* 19
{"Grace"		*Inferno* 19
Soothsayers .... "Clay"		*Inferno* 20
Grafters and Barrators ...... "Ivy Day"		*Inferno* 21
Hypocrites		
Thieves		
False Counselors .... "A Little Cloud"		*Inferno* 26
Sowers of Discord .... "A Mother"		*Inferno* 28
Counterfeiters and Falsifiers		
THE GIANTS' WELL		
Frozen Lake of River Cocytus (ferryman, Giant Antaeus)		
9th Traitors:		
to family; to guests;		*Inferno* 32
to benefactors; to country; . "The Dead"		*Inferno* 33
to Church and State		*Inferno* 34

(Vertical labels along left margin: INCONTINENCE for circles 1st–5th; VIOLENCE for circle 7th; FRAUD for circle 8th region.)

The Schema for Dante's Hell is adapted from Thomas G. Bergin, *Dante* (Orion Press, 1965), p. 218. Permission of the author and publisher is gratefully acknowledged.

book. It is not Dante's precise order, but it shows a very close "fit" of the stories to the stages in his moral hierarchy. In fact every story in *Dubliners* can be matched with an episode in the *Inferno*, either by subject matter or incident, in a catalogue of moral death.

Since Joyce specifically described his ordering principle as a chronology from childhood to "public life," let us look at his stories in the Dantean order. The strong reminiscence of Dante's *Vita Nuova* in "Araby" makes that story preeminently a little narrative of love, and its position at such an early stage in the book is surely related to the comparable position of Francesca in Dante's love story in *Inferno* 5. The protagonist of "Eveline," as a lukewarm sluggard incapable of making a positive decision, is reminiscent of the sinner who made the great refusal, "il gran rifuto," that condemned him to the vestibule of hell in Canto 3. An example of prodigal waste, which Dante saw punished along with avarice in *Inferno* 7, is found in Joyce's story, "After the Race." The story "Counterparts" is Joyce's equivalent of Dante's Fifth Circle, the wrathful sinners of *Inferno* 8. Farrington is the epitome of the violent man: "A spasm of rage gripped his throat"; "His heart swelled with fury"; "His fury nearly choked him." At the end of the tale we find that "he jumped up furiously," seized a walking stick, and beat his child, "striking at him viciously." No one is killed, but in his raging frenzy Farrington would qualify for the Seventh Circle of the violent as well as the Fifth Circle of the wrathful (*Inferno* 8:22-24; 12:49).

The mortal crime of suicide, punished in *Inferno* 13, has its turn in "A Painful Case." Sodomy, the matter of the fourteenth and fifteenth cantos, is the subject of "An Encounter." With "The Boarding-House," the first story written as an element in the Dantean pattern, we enter Joyce's equivalent of Malebolge, the vast expanse of hell where the fraudulent are found. Mrs. Mooney, the "Madam" who "deals with moral problems as a cleaver deals with meat," (*D* 63) is quite clearly one of the panders of *Inferno* 18. In "Two Gallants" the seducers of *Inferno* 18 are seen in action. The simoniacs of *Inferno* 19 are represented in *Dubliners* by two stories. The first is the revised version of "The Sisters," with its terrible vision of the simoniac priest enticing the young boy into "some pleasant and vicious region" (*D* 11). The second is the story "Grace," Joyce's classic portrayal of simony—a dramatic and explicit rendering of the Irish clergy's exchange of spiritual benefits for worldliness and gain.

The story of Maria, "Clay," is a story that turns on fortunetelling, a parallel to Dante's account of the soothsayers and fortunetellers in Canto 20. "Ivy Day in the Committee Room" deals with grafters, the Dublin ward heelers whose corruption is the equivalent of the barrators in *Inferno* 21. "A Little Cloud" takes its title from *Inferno* 26:39, "sì come nuvoletta," Dante's simile of the little cloud by which he describes the flame hiding Ulysses and the other false counselors of this canto. Ignatius Gallaher, whose fraudulence is stressed, and whose bad counsel has helped to ruin the life of Little Chandler, is described as similarly hidden, "emerging after some time from the clouds of smoke in which he had taken refuge" (*D* 78). His story, suitably adjusted by Joyce, resembles a capsule history of the protagonist of *Inferno* 26:

> Of course he did mix with a rakish set of fellows at that time, drank freely and borrowed money on all sides. In the end he had got mixed up in some shady affair, some money transaction: *at least that was one version of his flight*. (Italics mine.)

The last words remind the reader that Dante in this canto created a new version of the last voyage of Ulysses, described as a "mad flight," "il folle volo" in *Inferno* 26:125, and "il varco folle" in *Par.* 27:82. Finally, "A Mother" shows the disruption created by the greedy and quarrelsome Mrs. Kearney, who, as a fomenter of discord, resembles the sinners Dante saw in *Inferno* 28.

And what of the last story, "The Dead"? The final section of Dante's *Inferno* is reserved for traitors, who are buried in the eternal cold of frozen Cocytus. Dante shows the reader examples of traitors to family, traitors to guests, traitors to benefactors, traitors to their country. All these aspects of betrayal can be found in the last story of *Dubliners*. Joyce's setting, a Christmas feast which calls attention to food as dramatically as Dante's tale of Ugolino portrays starvation, is in this respect an ironical inversion of *Inferno* 33. The central figure at the feast, and in the story, is Gabriel Conroy; as John Kelleher discovered, Gabriel's misfortune in the final incident, which forms the climax of the story, is a punishment—a reprisal for having sinned against his kinfolk and his country.[16] The story, as Kelleher has shown, is a ghost story. Gabriel's middle class forefathers, to whom he owes his education and his present position as a well-to-do Catholic teacher in Protestant-dominated Ireland, are ridiculed by Gabriel, and they punish him for his temerity and hubris. He denies his country: "Well, said Gabriel, if it comes to that, you know, Irish is not my language" (*D* 189). When baited by Miss Ivors, one of the guests, he retorts even more strongly: "O, to tell you the truth, . . . I'm sick of my own country, sick of it." These indiscretions continue, and he makes a disrespectful salute to the statue of Daniel O'Connell, who brought about the repeal of the Catholic penal laws. The action is a denial of his origins, as his inward contempt for his aunts and his family is also a spiritual betrayal. Worst of all, he makes sport of his hardworking grandfather, whose starch mill brought the Conroy family to the place Gabriel thoughtlessly takes as his due—the middle-class security and respectability of a house in the sanctum of Protestant Ascendancy Dublin, Ushers Island. Gabriel's funny story makes everyone laugh at the old man's horse that plods round and round the hated statue of King Billy (William of Orange, conqueror at the Battle of the Boyne), as the subject Irish for many centuries had been forced to trudge and toil in a meaningless round under their masters' rule (*D* 208).

The similarities and differences between the *Inferno* and *Dubliners* become most interesting and significant when one considers the moral structure of the two works. Dante used the seven deadly sins as the structure of his Purgatory, but not in his Hell. There are striking omissions from the list of sins punished in Dante's Hell, and his ordering of distinctions in the gravity of moral error is his own. It is not in conflict with doctrine but it reflects subjectively Dante's own point of view. As Professor Bergin has noted, Dante considers flattery a graver moral fault than seduction, and simony more serious than either, but he gives little attention to pride and envy, "without whose vigorous collaboration the Adversary would be all but helpless against the children of Eve."[17]

Joyce saw that Dante had taken a moral and philosophical (basically Aristotelian) pattern rather than a Christian and doctrinal pattern or even a purely religious basis for his structure. Both Dante and Joyce see their *Inferno* in the nonsectarian terms expressed by Father Foster for the *Inferno*, "mainly as an outline of *human* evil drawn by human wit."[18] (Italics mine.) Only the heretics and simoniacs in Dante's hell are "Christian" sinners in the sense that their transgression implies the standards of a specifically Christian world. (And even here, the chosen heresy is the Epicurean denial of personal immortality, a form of unbelief that does not presuppose Christianity.) Most striking of all is the conception of Dante's Limbo, where the great pagans are shown as intellectually rather than morally inadequate; the presence of Virgil there, having lost heaven only for lack of faith and naught else— "non per altro rio"—implies, as Father Foster says, "a natural order morally independent of the supernatural."

In some such reading of the *Divine Comedy* Joyce must have found his warrant for creating his own imaginative pattern and his own hierarchy of moral depravity. His *Dubliners* comes closest to Dante's construction in its strong emphasis on the anti-social quality of injustice in human malice and fraud. His idea of *frode* (fraud), which governs the design of thirteen cantos—the vast region of the Malebolge between *Inferno* 17 and *Inferno* 30—is closely parallel to Dante's. Joyce's stories emphasize malicious injury *to one's fellow-man*; the disposition to inflict injustice and injury is central to his design, found somewhere in every story and dominant in several. But Joyce also follows Dante in allowing his narrative skills a free run. Joyce wished to call the attention of his city to its own moral condition, and to do this required a vigorous play of personality and dramatic action. Hence the mixture in his stories of good and evil, faults and mere weaknesses, humor and anger and pathos. They are full of ambiguities, such as, in "Clay," Maria's unacknowledged isolation, which is disclosed through a fortune-telling game that is harmless in itself and dangerous only when a whole society falls prey to superstition. From the same origin also comes the inevitability of the chosen central action, which in each story is completely integrated with the personalities portrayed, and so sparely and so accurately drawn that it seems to preclude any alternative solution. In the note of complacence—the tranquil and arrogant self-satisfaction of the characters in the last four stories of the book—Joyce is extremely close to Dante's portrayal of souls in the grip of mortal sin. Dante's sinners are true to their natures: they are embodiments of the fault for which they are imprisoned in hell.

The fourteen stories are epiphanies of frustration, broadening from private to public scope, in the words of Harry Levin.[19] Joyce announced for the book a basically tripartite structure: childhood, youth, and maturity, with three additional stories representing public life in Dublin, and a final novella, "The Dead." This chronological arrangement allowed Joyce to suggest, as Dante does, a progression from the less culpable forms of moral failure to the most unregenerate evil: in Joyce's view the evil in the last chapters is far more culpable, because it is unconscious of wrongdoing and utterly self-confident. A venal ruling establishment is portrayed, operating under clerical guidance in a simoniacal pattern. Dublin life has become a frozen conformity under this perverted control. This is the angry vision that issued in Joyce's arrangement of the stories of *Dubliners*.

There has been a good deal of critical comment on the Dantean aspects of *Dubliners*, with illuminating incidental discussions of liturgical motifs in the stories, the use of biblical allegory, their connections with *Ulysses* and *Finnegans Wake*, and their symbolic extension of images of movement or inertia to spiritual conditions.[20] Joyce's brother Stanislaus, who was no Dantist, and who was genuinely irreligious and far more bitterly anticlerical than his brother James, spoke of the arrangement of *Dubliners* as "an obvious touch of parody on the *Divine Comedy*." Stanislaus Joyce also announced that the three parts of the story "Grace" corresponded to the three cantiche of the *Divine Com-*

edy.[21] Marvin Magalaner, in *The Time of Apprenticeship*, saw the story "Grace" as "a gentle juxtaposition of a public and universal mythical structure . . . with a sordid contemporary narrative," and herein found a type of parody that was a preparation for the Dantean effects of *Ulysses*.[22] Father Robert Boyle proposed an elaborate four-level diagram for "Grace": he arranged the liturgical, doctrinal, historical, pastoral and pietistic elements of the story in "four levels of meaning of Joyce's Dantean parody," to correspond with the fourfold method described in Dante's letter to Can Grande: literal, moral, allegorical, anagogical.[23] A common interpretation of the story accepts the version of Joyce's brother:

> There is in the story a parody of the *Divina Commedia*: in the underground lavatory *l'Inferno*; in bed at home convalescing, *il Purgatorio*; in church listening to a sermon, *il Paradiso*. The parody in no way detracts from my brother's almost boundless admiration for the *Divina Commedia* . . .[24]

There is, however, no evidence attaching this interpretation to Joyce himself. Stanislaus Joyce in this critique of *Dubliners* chided the critics for strained interpretations of the stories, but it is difficult to apply his own comment to Dante's poem in any meaningful way.

In conclusion let us review the more directly allusive echoes of Dante that Joyce placed in "Araby," written late in the sequence of composition, only a few weeks before he sent off the first manuscript of twelve stories. As an account of a young boy's agitated worship of an idealized feminine figure, it resembles the *Vita Nuova*. Analogies of action, of phrasing, and of diction build up the allusion. The boy sees his distant loved one as he walks down the street; "I did not know whether I would ever speak to her or not, or, if I spoke to her, how I could tell her of my confused adoration." This parallels Dante's line in *Vita Nuova* III: "While walking down a street she turned her eyes to where I was standing faint-hearted."

Dante describes the effect of the first greeting of Beatrice: ". . . she greeted me so miraculously that I felt I was experiencing the very summit of bliss" (*Vita Nuova* III). Joyce reproduces the event in less exalted prose: "At last she spoke to me. When she addressed the first words to me I was so confused that I did not know what to answer" (*D* 31).

Dante's repeated statements of his inability to approach Beatrice or to speak to her are echoed also; the unnamed boy of "Araby" says, "I had never spoken to her except for a few casual words, and yet her name was like a summons to all my foolish blood" (*VN* II). And

Dante's description of the first instant of recognition seems to be reproduced by Joyce:

"Araby"	*Vita Nuova*
All my senses seemed to desire to veil themselves and, feeling that I was about to slip from them, I pressed the palms of my hands together until they trembled, murmuring, O Love! O Love! many times. (*D* 31)	At that moment I say truly that the vital spirit, the one that dwells in the most secret chamber of the heart, began to tremble so violently that even the least pulses of my body were strangely affected; and trembling, it spoke these words: "Here is a god stronger than I, who shall come to rule over me." (tr. Musa)

The tears shed by Dante at so many points in the story, especially at
VN III, XV, and XXII, are also present in Joyce's account of the boy's
emotion. "My eyes were often full of tears (I could not tell why) and at
times a flood from my heart seemed to pour itself out into my bosom."

The minor Dantean effects reproduced in "Araby" are evidence of
a fictional event that is rarely present in Joyce's work—a straightforward and un-ironic description of love. That is, the boy's
emotion is genuine enough: irony is present in the contrast between
Joyce's authentically Dantesque portrayal of an emotion that produced immortal poetry, and the Dublin setting in which he places it.
Joyce's "Araby" provides a background for the accounts of emotional
starvation in the succeeding stories of men and women grown older in
Dublin, where love is known only by its absence or diminution or distortion.

*

Exiles, composed in 1914-15 (Herbert Gorman said the first months
of 1914[25]) from notes written down in the spring of 1913 (*Archive*
11:xxiv-xxv), reproduces in part the closing episode of Dante's *Purgatorio* and marks an important stage in Joyce's use of Dante. In *Purgatorio* 30 and 31, Dante is reunited with Beatrice and receives from
her the assurance that his poetic mission has divine validation. Dante's
meeting with the lady who inspired his youthful poems, the *Vita
Nuova*, becomes a return to his origins: this event is mirrored in *Exiles*
by a comparable revisiting by the protagonist of his youthful self.
Richard Rowan, the artist-hero of *Exiles*, defines a conception of love
in a dialectic of moral freedom, and Joyce here deliberately constructs
a modern and relativist interpretation of Dante's sequence.

There are a substantial number of echoes of the Dantean Beatrice in the first act of *Exiles*. These, however, are only a part of the Dantean dimension of the play. When the fragmentary correspondences are observed as a unit it becomes apparent that some are identifiable references to the Beatrice of the *Vita Nuova*; and others are references to the reunion episode in the *Purgatorio*. A third element of allusion, related to the first two but also distinctly different from them, refers to the Dantean imagination and personality and to the Catholic structure of scholastic theology that was Dante's inheritance and nurture. In the totality of a tacit Dantean context, which begins as an imitation but ends as something entirely new, the reader sees the originality of Joyce's use of *Purgatorio* 30 and 31.

The dramatic shape of *Exiles*, as well as the presence of a Dantean structure, was announced in *Stephen Hero*. Stephen Daedalus says, "Renan says a man is a martyr only for things of which he is not quite sure" (*SH* 175:16). Stephen and Cranly have been arguing about the *Vita Nuova*, and Stephen takes the position that the modern lover, lacking the faith and purpose of Dante, is "compelled to express his love a little ironically." Cranly, speaking as "a cynical romanticist," insists that human nature is a constant quantity, and that the "faith and purpose" of medieval man can be preserved in the modern world. But Cranly's cynical view of human nature reduces love to an empty phrase. The young men argue whether a changeless passion can be expressed, and Stephen decides that Love is a name "for something inexpressible," but at once he exclaims, "But no! I won't admit that," and says that a test of love might be to see what exchanges it offers (*SH* 174-175). Such a test of love informs the three acts of Joyce's play, which ends with Richard Rowan's decision for uncertainty as a principle of life.

In the *Divine Comedy*, *Purgatorio* 30 describes Dante's emotion at the first sight of his long-dead lady, and Canto 31 describes their actual meeting. The place of reunion is the Earthly Paradise, Eden, where Virgil, Dante, and Statius have arrived at the summit of the mountain. The site of man's original sin is now seen by the poet, in a scene described almost as an annunciation, "as if sent from Heaven." ("quasi da ciel messo" *Purg.* 30:10.) The words used combine the Old Testament with the New: "Benedictus qui venit." But it is Beatrice who comes, in a cloud of flowers, her face veiled and invisible. The cloud of flowers, "nuvola di fiori" (*Purg.* 30:28), recalls the "nuvoletta" of *Inferno* 26 and *Vita Nuova* XXIII, the first sight of Beatrice thus being associated with the poet's earlier work. Here at the mid-point of his poem he brings back the *Vita Nuova*. As he promised in that book, he will write of Beatrice that which has never been written of any other lady.

Joyce seems to have been thinking of this poetic promise and fulfillment when he represented the young Stephen Daedalus refusing to admit that any human passion can be "inexpressible." The printed text of *Stephen Hero* fails to show here an exclamation mark which is present in the manuscript and indicates intended emphasis: "But no! I won't admit that."[26] (*Archive* 8:583.) Joyce decided to embody the ideas expressed by the immature college student in a dramatic portrayal of an older artist. Richard Rowan constructs, in *Exiles*, the test of love that Stephen first imagines.

In *Purgatorio* 30, before Beatrice is unveiled to Dante's sight she greets him sternly and reproaches him severely for having forgotten her memory. With echoes of the *Vita Nuova*, she says that this man, Dante, "was such in his new life that every right disposition would have made marvelous proof in him" ("questi fu tal ne la sua vita nova / virtualmente, ch'ogne abito destro / fatto averebbe in lui mirabil prova" (*Purg.* 30:115-117, trans. Singleton). Instead, when Beatrice had ascended from flesh to spirit, "and beauty and virtue were increased in me" ("Quando di carne a spirto era salita / e bellezza e virtù cresciuta m'era," *Purg.* 30:127-128), Dante turned his steps along another way, pursuing false images of the good. Having been saved only by the miraculous intervention of Beatrice, now he must show penitence before crossing Lethe. Thus in Canto 31, with the river still between them, Dante confesses, weeping, that the things of the present with their false pleasures turned him away from the memory of Beatrice as soon as the sight of her had been lost. In a dramatic reminiscence of the *Vita Nuova*, the poem here recalls the donna gentil who consoled the young Dante. In *Vita Nuova* XXXVII he confessed that the sight of the compassionate lady, "young and very beautiful," so moved him that "My eyes began to delight too much in seeing her."

Dante's self-reproach in the *Vita Nuova* is echoed in *Purgatorio* 31, Finally the penitent is drawn across the water by Matelda and the taste of Lethe removes all memory of sin, all sense of guilt. Dante is brought to Beatrice's side, and in a final reminiscence of the *Vita Nuova* he says that a thousand desires hotter than flame held his eyes. The lyrical force and focus of the early poem have been recapitulated, as John Freccero says, in the vision of Beatrice as Dante originally saw her.[27]

The Beatrice of this reunion scene is not an allegorical or symbolical figure. Her charges of broken faith are personal to Dante as an individual. Their meeting is the reunion of one human personality with another. Dante remains human through the rest of the poem, but when he joins Beatrice across the river she takes on a symbolical meaning. Freccero notes that subtle changes in the framing of the scene accomplish this symbolical transformation. First Beatrice turns away to gaze fixedly at the Griffin, the figure of Christ as head of the Church. Then she moves to the foreground in front of the chariot, becoming a figure of Revelation leading the Church. In the *Paradiso* we must assume that Beatrice, like all the other blessed souls, is a point of light with no human physical characteristics, but at this earlier point in Dante's poem her eyes are emeralds and she has the regal dominance of an admiral on the bridge, or the severity of a stern mother. The reproaches of Beatrice have been given an allegorical reading by many critics, but others have seen the episode in primarily human terms. De Sanctis, whose interpretation was read by Joyce, said:

> It is the time-worn battle between the senses and reason, the old tragic struggle of the soul, sunk among the errors and assaults of the senses. Here it turns into comedy, through the victory of the spirit. The concept is perfectly clear, shown in direct theological language. But it has come down into the reality of life, and produces a real dramatic scene: Heaven and earth, reason and passion, abstract and concrete, are all so marvellously fused that we find in it the stuff that gave birth to the Spanish drama.[28]

Joyce saw these cantos both in their human dimension and metaphysically. He creates a reunion episode, going so far as to name one of his characters Beatrice, and he dramatizes the struggle of the soul between passion and reason in a little drama of jealousy mastered, or accepted. *Exiles* thus brings to the Dantean theme of love a modern relativism. Eternity, which was such a compelling conception for Dante, cannot dominate the modern imagination. "We cannot swear or expect eternal fealty because we recognize too accurately the limits of every human energy," says Stephen Daedalus (*SH* 174:25). Joyce's artist is the heir of intellectual movements unknown to Dante, and he is shown by his author as Kantian and Rationalist. His intellectual inheritance, however, also includes specifically and actively the scholasticism that informs Dante's theology. This strengthens his will. Richard is a man of strong feeling who will nevertheless not allow his feelings to control his moral decisions and actions. Richard's reunion, like Dante's, is with his younger self, a Romanticism rejected now and portrayed by Joyce in the play through two characters, Robert and

Beatrice, who were the companions of his youth. The fourth character, Bertha, is his wife and the mother of his child, and Francis Fergusson's definitive reading of the play has identified in this dimension
the tragic flaw in Richard's metaphysical situation.[29] "Bertha is a hos-
tage to the others and to the disorderly world of concrete experience
. . . in this relation the split between his intellectual integrity and his
love becomes truly tragic." Richard embraces doubt almost to the
point of martyrdom.

The interview between the principal figures of *Purgatorio* 30-31 is
reproduced by Joyce in a reversal of roles that maintains the tenor
and structure of the original. Where Beatrice sternly queries Dante's
actions since their last meeting, and forces from him an admission of
fault, in Joyce's play Beatrice is pursued by Richard with assertions of
her inadequacy in love: "You could not give yourself freely and
wholly. . . . You would try, yes. You were drawn to him as your mind
was drawn towards mine. You held back from him. From me too, in a
different way. You cannot give yourself freely and wholly." This
Beatrice is ethically incomplete. Joyce apparently wanted to suggest,
by placing a negative stress on his Beatrice's Protestant upbringing,
the importance of Richard's Catholic background for his moral position and, by implication, for his art. The play stresses more explicitly,
in references to Richard's dead mother, the value of a scholastic
foundation for Richard's present views on free will and moral choice.
Richard describes his mother as a bigoted Catholic but he also invokes
for himself her "hardness of heart." The lines recall Joyce's comparison of himself with "that motley crew," his Protestant contemporaries,
in "The Holy Office" (1904):

> Those souls that hate the strength that mine has,
> Steeled in the school of old Aquinas.   (*CW* 152)

Extended insights into Richard, Robert and Bertha are found in
the author's notes, and in the text of the play all four are fully developed characters. In performance, the richness of character development and subtlety of interrelations between the characters becomes
apparent.

Let us observe briefly some of the details of parallel construction.
One of the two feminine characters is named Beatrice. The hero of
Exiles, Richard Rowan, is a writer who has corresponded with this
Beatrice and sent her chapters of his book "for nine long years," dur-
ing which he has been a voluntary exile from Dublin. Beatrice
responded: his first letter

was answered at once by you. And from then on you have watched
me in my struggle . . . did you feel that what you read was written
for your eyes? Or that you inspired me? (Act I; *E* 18-19)

The nine year hiatus and the suggestion of inspiration significantly
reflect the *Vita Nuova*. In the *Divine Comedy* the journey of Dante is
made possible by the miraculous intervention of Beatrice, who from
heaven has watched Dante's struggle and who sends Virgil to help
him. The Dantean Beatrice is echoed also in an allusion to her
illness—"I nearly died,"—and to the change that came from her illness. "I did not suffer; only I was changed . . . It brought me near to
death. It made me see things differently." There is also a suggestion
of feudal poetic practice in the "secret engagement" of Beatrice to
Robert, especially in the granting of her garter—the lady's token to
the knight. But this Beatrice is so different from Dante's, in the terms
of the play, that the use of the name becomes a significant symbol of
the past. (*E* 20-21)

In a reversal of Dante's pattern, the reproaches of Beatrice to Dante
become in Joyce's play the reproaches of Richard Rowan to Beatrice.
The critical originality of Joyce's reading appears in his perception of
Dante as the poet who so markedly wishes us to see his visible presence and identity in the closing cantos of the *Purgatorio*—the pilgrim's
last moments in the temporal dimension. A momentary reminder is in
order, not only that Dante is dramatically and uniquely named here
but also that he closes the final canto of the *Purgatorio* with an address
to the reader claiming that the poem stops because all the allotted
lines have been used up.[30] In the calling of Dante's name by Beatrice,
who also pronounces Virgil's name before and after the naming of
Dante, a new poetic identity is established in *Purgatorio* 30.[31] This aspect of Dante's Reunion in Eden appears in *Exiles* in the confrontation
of Richard with the ideas of his youth, represented, as Fergusson has
shown, by Robert and Beatrice. Out of that encounter emerges an artistic personality rooted in a new morality.[32]

This artist-hero of *Exiles* is not Dante, but he is clearly a Joycean
interpretation of the artist-pilgrim of the *Divine Comedy*. Richard
Rowan is exiled, in Joyce's play, by "the old mother," a figure of the
Catholic Church. "She drove me away. On account of her I lived years
in exile and poverty too, or near it" (Act I; *E* 24). The reason given for
his exile has no connection with the political reasons for Dante's exile,
but it may reflect the common assumption that the "Dark Wood" of
Inferno I represents an intellectual and spiritual impasse following
upon the philosophical studies that resulted in the *Convivio*. Richard

Rowan's "exile" is attributed more loosely than this to a conflict with the Church's claim to supernatural authority over men's minds: "I fought against her spirit while she lived to the bitter end. It fights against me still—in here." This Blakean phrase is echoed in *Ulysses*, when Stephen says, "It is here I must kill the priest and the king." (*U* 589.28)

The most important element of alignment with Dante's *Purgatorio* is Richard's return to his origins. Joyce situates his artist between two modes, Classicism and Romanticism. He is the author of a successful book, an "Irish writer," who is described (in Act I; *E* 51) as imbued with "fierce indignation": this recalls not only Swift but also the "alma sdegnosa" of Dante. Throughout the play Richard's identity is increasingly defined. He dominates the others, moving Robert and Bertha like puppets, forcing Robert and Beatrice to see themselves from his point of view, and refusing to impede his wife's freedom of action by any word of encouragement or discouragement or advice. Thus he dissociates himself from Robert's Romanticism.

> *Robert*
> . . . The blinding instant of passion alone—passion, free, unashamed, irresistible—that is the only gate by which we can escape from the misery of what slaves call life. Is not this the language of your own youth that I heard so often from you in this very place?
>
> *Richard*
> (Passes his hand across his brow.) Yes. It is the language of my youth. (Act II; *E* 89)

Richard's dissociation of himself from Beatrice is also a confrontation with his origins. The play's theme is enunciated when she says, "It is a terribly hard thing to do . . . to give oneself freely and wholly—and be happy." Richard replies: "But do you feel that happiness is the best, the highest that we can know?" and then he adds:

> O if you knew how I am suffering at this moment! And how I pray that I may be granted again my dead mother's hardness of heart! For some help, within me or without, I must find. And find it I will. (Act I; *E* 22)

Although Richard's predicament does not resemble Dante's, his state of mind at this moment in the play, and the action of clasping his hands, suggests strongly the sacramental moment of Dante's confession—an appeal for the Divine Grace that comes from receiving the Church's sacraments—in *Purgatorio* 31.

Moreover, Richard is stating the metaphysical conflict at the core of the play. The actual dramatic problem, focused on the possible seduction of Bertha by Robert, has not yet arisen at this early point in the action. That existential problem clearly is meant to stand for the larger conflict within Richard, which is between his desire to return home to Ireland as an Irish writer, and his clear vision of the compromising effect on his artistic integrity that would be involved in such a return. His sense of himself is at stake on both levels. It is a drama of identity.

Richard does find the strength he needs, but only in himself, and only by accepting "a deep wound of doubt," the closing words of the play. He is not a martyr, but he fits the statement attributed in *Stephen Hero* to Renan. By this secular treatment of the theme of Dante's *Purgatorio* episode, Joyce gives a modern restatement of Virgil's charge to Dante, "Free, upright and whole is your will . . . wherefore I crown and mitre you over yourself" (*Purg.* 27:140-142).

The writing of *Exiles* was Joyce's first move toward a mature syncretism. Despite its weakness, the play's complex Dantean dimension shows Joyce's firm reading of the *Divine Comedy* and his subtle transformation of its patterns into his own fiction. In his exploration of motives in the dramatic confrontation of the principal characters, he repeatedly marks the distance between Dante and the modern artist. Where Dante's exploration of the "struggle of the soul" is theologically-directed, Joyce's comes near to being psychoanalytically directed. The play carries Oedipal overtones, and Joyce's comments in the Notes on the unconscious motivation behind Richard's refusal of intervention in the possible seduction of Bertha by Robert show an anticipation of post-Freudian revisionism.

The sequence of composition is relevant to an understanding of Joyce's use of Dante in *Exiles*. The play was written between November 1913 and April 1, 1915, in the same period in which the revision of *Stephen Hero* into *A Portrait of the Artist* was completed. The first three chapters of *Ulysses* had also been drafted before June 1915.[33] The date of Chapter XXII of *Stephen Hero*, approximately May 1905 (*Letters* II:89-90), marks the earliest appearance of the conception of a Dantean model for *Exiles*. [This is Chapter XXII by Joyce's numbering in the Manuscript, which differs from Theodore Spencer's numbering in the printed text (*SH* 164; *Archive* 8:543).] A group of letters written by Joyce to his wife in 1909 show how very personal to him was the theme of jealousy he developed in *Exiles*. These set in sharp relief the difference between the feelings of the Joyce of 1909 and the idea of the character in *Stephen Hero* who suggests that "it might be a test of love to see what exchanges it offers" (*SH* 175:22). There may be an oblique allusion to his emulation of Dante in a reference these letters contain, to "those boundless ambitions which are really the leading forces in my life" (*Letters* II:256).

An intermediate work, the little sketch of a love affair to which he gave the title *Giacomo Joyce*, contains echoes of Dante that surface again in *Exiles*. Ellmann as editor comments on the relation of the story's heroine to the Beatrice in *Exiles*, where one sentence appears unchanged: "Why? Because otherwise I could not see you" (*GJ* 16; *E* 18). This line forms part of the dialogue between Richard and Beatrice in the opening scene of the play. The heroine of *Giacomo Joyce* is an explicit Beatrice: "So did she walk by Dante in simple pride." Now of course Dante's Beatrice was worshipped from a distance. Joyce, we observe, has made a modern correction of focus. The "Beatrice" who shares the life of the lover of *Exiles* is Bertha, whose simple pride Joyce portrays, who was willing to love without counting the cost. The critical comment begun in *Stephen Hero* is thus continued in *Exiles*, and would be continued further in *Ulysses*. "Modern love, losing somewhat of its fierceness, gains also somewhat in amiableness" (*SH* 174:24). The narrator of *Giacomo Joyce* goes on to describe the Dantean Beatrice: "She speaks. A weak voice from beyond the cold stars. Voice of wisdom. Say on! O, say again, making me wise! This voice I never heard" (*GJ* 15).

The conception of *Exiles* that was foreshadowed in *Stephen Hero* is now seen taking shape, in the play of Joyce's imagination over the facets of Dante's art.[34] In *Giacomo Joyce* there is a single heroine. In *Exiles*, two women are required to express a dual contribution to the composition in which we can identify Joyce's revisionist version of the unique relationship that was attached by Dante forever to the name of Beatrice. Joyce writes, in *Giacomo Joyce*, "My words in her mind: cold polished stones sinking through a quagmire" (*GJ* 13). The apothegm which thus deflates both lover and mistress uses, with a modern irony, a famous Dantean image from *Paradiso*. To stand for the "mental intercourse" (*U* 721:5) of man and woman, Joyce goes to the canto of Piccarda:

> Thus did she speak . . . and then began to sing,
>   and, singing, vanished as through deep water
>   some heavy thing. (trans. Singleton)

> Così parlommi, e poi cominciò "*Ave,*
>   *Maria*" cantando, e cantando vanio
>   come per acqua cupa cosa grave.   (*Par.* 3:121-123)

In *Exiles* the conception alone, without the image, appears in the reiterated attraction of Richard's mind for Beatrice.

But this is not a simple matter, and the notes to *Exiles* suggest the dimensions of the split conception. "Bertha is fatigued and repelled by the restless, curious energy of Richard's mind." Beatrice, however, is not. Joyce plays with the tensions he discovered in the writing of *Giacomo Joyce*. Richard asks Beatrice, "Then it is my mind that attracts you? Is that it?" but when she replies—hesitatingly—"Why do you think I come here?" he affects not to understand, and with the invocation of their long acquaintance from childhood the lines from the unpublished work are repeated. "Why, then?" says Richard, and Beatrice replies, "Otherwise I could not see you." The play's ironic mistrust of the possibility of sublimated mental intercourse comes into Joyce's work again in *Ulysses*, with fuller restatement of pattern, when the narrator of the Ithaca chapter describes the Blooms' estrangement in terms of a suspension of both mental and carnal intercourse. (*U* 720-721; *E* 158, *E* 18).

The distance that Dante's heroine has traveled is indicated not only by her name in this inauspicious setting but by making her a Protestant. In the notes to the play the mind of this Beatrice is described as "an abandoned cold temple in which hymns have risen heavenward in a distant past but where now a doddering priest offers alone and hopelessly prayers to the Most High."[35] Joyce transfers to Richard Rowan the Catholic values of spiritual strength and force that are portrayed in the Beatrice of *Purgatorio* 30. The modern world's break with its Catholic past enters the play with the negative image implied in the naming and characterization of Beatrice, while the other half of the conception is Joyce's distinctive reservation for his artist-hero of the values associated with the intellectual discipline of scholasticism. In *Exiles* for the first time Joyce begins to make Dante stand for a Catholic presence in Irish life and in the imagination of the artist.

Chapter Six
Between Time and Eternity

Trasumanar significar *per verba* / non si poria; però l'essemplo basti . . .

To pass beyond humanity may not be set forth in words; wherefore let the example suffice. (*Par.* 1:70-71)

Dante tires one quickly; it is like looking at the sun. (Joyce to Georges Borach)[1]

EVERY great imaginative writer moves back and forth between the real world and the creations of his fantasy, and nothing is more interesting than to watch him deploying his metaphorical skills and devices. Dante's characters became part of Joyce's fictional world along with "real" people, and in much the same way. From both, he selected recognizable characteristics. Individuals Joyce had known as a student in Dublin often recognized themselves in a novel, sometimes with dismay. More often, however, the sitter could not recognize himself, although another reader might well do so, because the "real" individual's distinctive features had been blurred by an infusion of traits and circumstantial particulars taken from some fictional model. Other writers had made similar combinations, but in Joyce's novels the metaphoric mode became a significant dimension of the work. Joyce did not thereby bring literary experience into the province of "real" experience, but he calls attention to the presence of an original reality behind the literary allusion.

Joyce's symbolic imagination in combination with his power of dramatic narrative produces verbal linkages which, though fragile, are as strong for their purpose as the spider's web. What Joyce learned about Dante's imagery became a central poetic principle in Joyce's own work, influencing and assisting metaphoric construction. Like T. S. Eliot, Joyce was crucially affected by his reading of the *Divine Comedy*.[2]

Studies of Dante's imagery have made readers aware of the ways that figurative language is used to tie the cantos into a closely knit artistic construction.[3] It was Dante's ability to produce a complex structure of poetic discourse that attracted Joyce to Dante's poem, as we see from the shape of his allusions to the *Divine Comedy*. Many of Dante's images of intellect and poetic imagination as light are linked by the slenderest of verbal resonances. For example, in the second canto of the *Paradiso* Beatrice discourses to Dante on the differences in luminosity among the heavenly bodies, as a figure of "unity in substance with multiplicity in virtue." Her argument is one of considerable subtlety, scholastic in content and deriving from Aristotle and Aquinas, but in its form poetic and carried forward by a sequence of light imagery. In this poetic dimension Dante carries the image forward to the final cantos of the *Comedy*, recalling at the same time the images of mirrored light that have brightened the *Purgatorio*. One small resonance comes through forcefully in Canto 2 at lines 109-112, where Beatrice has concluded one stage of the argument and makes a new start. She says to Dante,

> così rimaso te ne l'intelletto
> voglio informar di luce sì vivace.
> che ti tremolerà nel suo aspetto.

In translation, the promise of Beatrice is:

> You, in your understanding likewise stripped
> I would endow with such a vivid light
> that it will shimmer as you gaze upon it.
> (*Par*. 2:109-111; trans. Bergin)

This recalls, principally by the verb "tremolare," but also by the image contained in "di luce sì vivace," the moment of cleansing of Dante's vision at the opening of the *Purgatorio*:

> L'alba vinceva l'ora mattutina
> che fuggia innanzi, sì che di lontano
> conobbi il tremolar de la marina.

> The dawn was vanquishing the early breeze
> of morn which fled away, so from afar
> I saw the sheen of seacrests by the shore.
> (*Purg*. 1:115-117, trans. Bergin)

The Bergin translation renders the poetic effect of the word "tremolar," used as a verb in the *Paradiso* ("shimmer") and as a noun ("sheen") in the *Purgatorio*; literally rendered as "tremble," or "quiver," it conveys a sense of light in motion, glimpsed far off. The

word is so placed by the poet that it exercises musical control over the
terzina; it is this musical quality that provides mnemonic effect. In
both cantiche, the context is Dante's increasing vision, an advance in
his capacity to "see" the things of pure intellect. At the opening of the
Purgatorio the pilgrim sees the quivering light of the dawn-reflecting
ocean; now in the *Paradiso* the reader realizes more fully and more
forcefully that this distant glimpse of the reflected light of the rising
sun had been part of the great metaphor first announced by the rising
sun on the mountaintop in *Inferno* 1:17.

*

As we turn now to Joyce's novels, the allusions to Dante appear as
an allegory of art. In *Ulysses* especially, the allusions assist in display-
ing both uniqueness and universality in the Dantesque Bloom and the
Dantesque Stephen. It is a design in which the true analogue is the
mind of the artist. His versions of that experience, the dynamics of
the artist's world, are illuminated by the metaphorical connections
made in Joyce's radical experiments with style.[4]

The posthumously published *Stephen Hero* demands special appraisal, for it must be noted that Joyce deliberately preserved this
manuscript, or a surviving fragment of the manuscript, although he
could have destroyed it, as he evidently did destroy other drafts and
early works.[5] In a very real sense, it is a separate novel. Joyce called it
a "first draft" of *A Portrait of the Artist as a Young Man*, but it made a
significant contribution in *Ulysses*, as well, to the portrait of Stephen
Dedalus as still a *young* man (as Joyce emphasized) who is still in the
process of becoming an artist. In this early work the influence of
Dante is expressly identified, openly displayed, and discussed as it
never was again in Joyce's writing. But it is *not* altogether unconcealed. Along with the several instances of Stephen Daedalus
openly quoting, interpreting, and paraphrasing Dante's lines, there is
the single covert instance of an ambitious metamorphosis by the author, James Joyce, when *Inferno* 15 is transformed into a discrete unit,
fully integrated into the chapter and the book. Joyce's *modus operandi*
is prophetically identified.

Other authors as well—Shakespeare, D'Annunzio and Ibsen—
appear in *Stephen Hero*, and their influence is shown in some detail.[6]
Here also Joyce's artist figure grapples with problems of aesthetics
and produces a significant statement, however tentative and incomplete it may be, in the notion of epiphany. The character of Stephen
Dedalus is a constant in three of Joyce's books: although *Stephen Hero*

is outside the canon, as an incomplete fragment, to neglect its evidence would be a crippling omission. In his review of the esthetics of Stephen Daedalus in the unfinished novel, S. L. Goldberg called for closer scrutiny of the range of Joyce's work and raised the question of *why* Stephen uses Shakespeare for his illustrations (*SH* 184-185).[7] These questions must be raised again in an appraisal of the contribution of Dante to *A Portrait of the Artist* and to *Ulysses*.

In *A Portrait of the Artist*, Joyce's reading of Dante's *Vita Nuova* entered into the book's design through the relation of the writing of love poetry to the artistic development of the poet. To understand the design in relation to Dante we may first examine, as separate elements of the work, the fact of the young man's feelings of love, on the one hand, and on the other the fact of his impulse to write in a familiar tradition. The writing of love poetry becomes a transaction of aesthetic significance as the event is explored and queried by the young man. The literary groundwork appears first in *Stephen Hero*, connected with Dante and tacitly also with D'Annunzio. Because it was greatly altered in revision, it is useful to examine the circumstances of composition.

After a close study of the Dublin holograph manuscript of *A Portrait of the Artist*, Hans Walter Gabler concludes that Joyce made a radical revision of the book between the spring of 1912 and the summer of 1914.[8] The inferences drawn by Gabler about the sequence of these assumed revisions suggest that Joyce gave the book at this time a new structure which coincides remarkably with the poetic structure of the *Vita Nuova*.

Joyce's copy of the *Vita Nuova* was published in 1911, and was bought by him second hand in Trieste soon after that. Joyce certainly knew Dante's *Vita Nuova* long before this date, but it is likely that a connection exists between the purchase and Joyce's final revision of *A Portrait of the Artist*. The copy of the *Vita Nuova* that Joyce bought in Trieste was a deluxe illustrated version of the first pre-Raphaelite edition of 1902, for which Antonio Agresti, the son-in-law of W. M. Rossetti, contributed as a preface essays on the *Vita Nuova* and on the Rossetti illustrations. Of all Dante's interpreters, Rossetti and his group were the least likely to appeal to Joyce himself. But in 1912 Joyce was drawing a portrait showing the "poet in action." The more closely we examine his construction the more convincingly it appears that this was not just any young poet but one most carefully placed. The young man of the fifth chapter of *A Portrait* is writing in Ireland at the turn of the century, with Dante in his baggage, and he is casting a critical eye on his age and his origins. His author daringly shows this

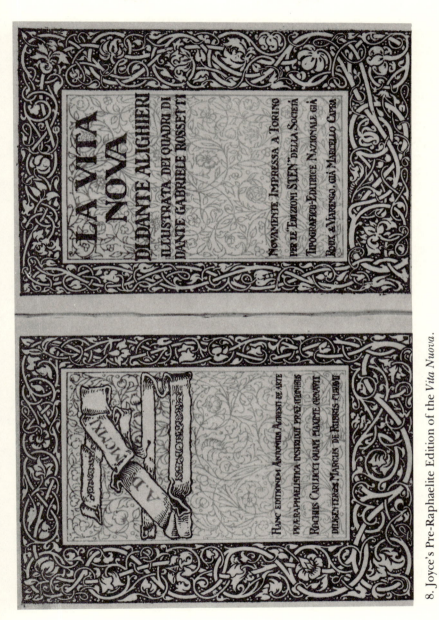

8. Joyce's Pre-Raphaelite Edition of the *Vita Nuova*.

young man in the act of writing a poem which is supplied in full text—almost a unique literary event—and fully glossed, thus marking forever a moment in the zenith of the literary movement that Joyce described elsewhere as "the backwash of that tide which has advanced from Flaubert through Jakobsen to D'Annunzio" (*CW* 71). The youthful Joyce saw the established writers of his day, especially Yeats and Moore, as aesthetes "with a floating will," and his essay sardonically locates aestheticism off the highroad of art, a diversion from its central concerns. But his first novel suggests obliquely the involvement of a young Catholic poet with the artistic influences of his time. Aestheticism therefore had to be present, and was present, however ambiguous its final rendering might be.

Gabler's evidence indicates that in 1912 Joyce wrote Chapter Five of *A Portrait of the Artist*; at the start of this operation the manuscript known as the Dublin Holograph included all of Chapter Four and the first three manuscript leaves of Chapter Five. The observed sequence finds, as the first stage, all of Chapter Five except the villanelle episode (*i.e.*, the last one-third of the book) being written, in final form. In a second stage, Chapters One, Two, and Three were revised and recopied; here, Gabler infers that a new structural plan had emerged from the writing of Chapter Five and that changes were made in the first three chapters to fit the new structure. In 1913 the title page was dated; in the summer of 1914 the villanelle episode was added to Chapter Five as the last act of composition.[9] Gabler's hypothesis supports the argument for a direct connection between the writing of Chapter Five, the re-writing of earlier chapters to fit a new design, and the purchase of Joyce's edition of Dante's *Vita Nuova*.

I suggest that Joyce, the selfconscious modernist, owed to his reading of Dante the decision, first of all, to use a construction that would portray his artist, Dublin's Dante, in two separate works. Second, in writing *A Portrait* Joyce would transform *Stephen Hero* into an internally focused and chronologically limited portrayal. In *A Portrait of the Artist as a Young Man* Joyce brings the reader wholly inside the mind of his artist, as Dante does in the *Vita Nuova*. Third, in *Ulysses* Joyce would restore the external perspective. This view of Stephen had been so strikingly displayed in *Stephen Hero* that the publication of the "first draft" radically changed the critical perception of *A Portrait*. This sequence of decisions by Joyce has, of course, been previously identified. But the attachment to Dante has not been observed. Joyce carried out his new purpose, I believe, by creating a second figure of Dante. Bloom as well as Stephen could carry the image and likeness of Dante, author and protagonist of the *Divine Comedy*, man as well as artist. The sardonic humor of Stephen Dedalus balances, in *Ulysses*, with the humanely comic perspective of Leopold Bloom. Comedy is the attribute of maturity. Joyce's comic mode (which sharply differentiates *Ulysses* and *Finnegans Wake* from the manner and atmosphere of the early works) came into his epic when he realized that the mind of Mr Bloom (in addition to all the other artistic chores performed by this character for his author) could portray the humanistic equivalents for Dante's sense of unity, his vision of perfection, and his affirmation of life.

When the presence of Dante in *A Portrait of the Artist* is compared with a similar presence in *Stephen Hero* and in *Ulysses*, an interesting series of observations emerges. These observations center on the use Joyce made in the three books, not only of Dante but of the three other authors that principally influenced the mind of Stephen Dedalus: Shakespeare, Ibsen and D'Annunzio. It then becomes apparent that Joyce had consciously developed a mode of literary allusion which he directed to specific fictional purposes, beginning with the 1912-1914 revisions.

All four authors are significantly called up in *Stephen Hero*, and overtly presented as influences on the young poet. In *A Portrait of the Artist* and in *Ulysses*, Ibsen is given only a single mention (*P* 176; *U* 598). D'Annunzio is not mentioned by name in *Stephen Hero* nor in *A Portrait*, but he furnishes the model for the villanelle section of Chapter Five, a brief mimetic episode in which, according to Gabler, the poem was inserted after all the rest of the book had been faircopied.[10] D'Annunzio takes the same role, which is to say he (not Pater or Yeats) stands for the Aesthetic position generally, in both the "first draft" and the finished novel. He is the unnamed inspiration for a short poem which is made part of the text in *Stephen Hero* (*SH* 37), and for a later effort, a villanelle which is not shown (*SH* 211). And again, in chapter V of *A Portrait*, Gabriele D'Annunzio's first novel is the original of a nearly identical episode in Joyce's first novel, without explicit comment but quietly named ["Gabriel . . . had come to the virgin's chamber" (*P* 217:23)] D'Annunzio completely disappears from *Ulysses*.

Shakespeare, however, becomes the presiding genius of Stephen's intellectual development in *Ulysses*, and *Hamlet* becomes a significant structural element in that book in the same way that the *Vita Nuova* does in *A Portrait of the Artist*. Nothing, surely, is more striking than the nearly complete absence of quotations from Shakespeare in *A Portrait*, compared with their presence in *Stephen Hero* and their proliferation in *Ulysses*. William Schutte attributes to Stephen (out of 202

Shakespeare quotations in *Ulysses* as a whole) 42 quotations from *Hamlet* and 76 from other plays. Moreover, Schutte has counted in this table only direct or paraphrased quotations, leaving aside the way in which Joyce organized the Shakespeare material. Schutte concludes, I think wrongly, that "Shakespeare was not one of Stephen's early heroes."[11] He believes that, between the date of the end of *A Portrait of the Artist* (presumably 1902; marked in crayon across the manuscript of *Stephen Hero* are the words "Departure for Paris") and June 16, 1904, Stephen has "immersed himself in Shakespeare's works, Shakespeare criticism, and Shakespeare biography."[12] But this view, and Schutte's excellent study, ignores the substantive differences between *Stephen Hero* and *A Portrait*, in the aspect of a Shakespearean presence, and since he makes only selective use of the Shakespeare references in *Stephen Hero* in the text of his book, Schutte gives less than a full account of the development of Stephen's ideas of Shakespeare, and does less than full justice to Joyce's representation of this complex phenomenon.

In *Stephen Hero*, the references by Stephen Daedalus to Dante and to Shakespeare are almost equally significant both in bulk and in the manner of their use.[13] It looks as though Joyce made a crucial decision about the manner of presenting his artist's development at the time, whenever it was exactly, that he wrote Chapter Five of *A Portrait of the Artist* and re-wrote the other chapters to fit his new plan. We know, however, that any such decisions were made before the end of 1914. By the time he left Trieste for Zurich, Joyce had settled the characterization of Stephen Dedalus, for he had not only finished *A Portrait of the Artist* but had also drafted the first three chapters of *Ulysses*.

The pattern of Joyce's decision seems to have been as follows. First, he would focus on Shakespeare and Dante as the significant poetic influences in his artist's development, reducing the visibility of Ibsen and D'Annunzio.[14] He would use Dante and Shakespeare both covertly and openly in both books, but not again in the didactic manner of *Stephen Hero*.[15] Instead, he would follow the example of Dante (and Shakespeare as well) in not only putting the artist into the work as a character, but also *creating a voice for the book itself*. For this he would use the works of Dante and Shakespeare (as well as those of other authors). Second, he would remove Shakespeare from *A Portrait of the Artist as a Young Man*, probably in order to emphasize and more fully establish the medieval quality of Stephen's upbringing. The Scholastic foundations of Stephen's thought, which were immensely important to Joyce, would have been grievously diluted by the intro-

duction of a second influence so important and (especially) so generally well-known as Shakespeare. Third, he would give to Stephen's
diary, at the end of *A Portrait of the Artist*, poetic lessons learned from
both Dante and Shakespeare, as these had been represented in *Stephen
Hero*,[16] and he would allow Stephen no more than this statement in
his own voice, holding back for *Ulysses* the elements of critical theory
which had been formulated as early as Chapter XIX of *Stephen Hero*.[17]
Critical attention has focused on the *content* of the epiphanies in Stephen's diary: it is surely more important, in the sequence of artistic
development represented by the book, to recognize these entries as
evidence that Stephen's is, both intentionally and self-consciously, an
epiphany-producing mind. Fourth, Joyce must have decided at this
time (and with conscious reference to Ibsen, D'Annunzio and Shakespeare) to use Dante's *Vita Nuova* as a significant structural element in
A Portrait of the Artist, and to use the *Divine Comedy* in a similar way in
Ulysses.

*

It is time to examine Dante's contribution to *A Portrait of the Artist as
a Young Man*, to *Ulysses*, and to *Finnegans Wake*. The first two will be
considered together, or as a unit; they are linked as Dante's *Vita
Nuova* and *Divine Comedy* are linked. The crucial connecting element
between Dante's *Vita Nuova* and Joyce's *A Portrait of the Artist* is the relation of the writing of love poetry to the artistic development of the
protagonist—in both books a young poet.

The poems of the *Vita Nuova* are related to the prose account by a
progression in which the poet is a *persona* of Dante as Stephen Dedalus is a *persona* of Joyce. The *Vita Nuova* as a work of art is unique,
and, as Vossler and others have said, it will always inspire a variety of
interpretations. It shows the young Dante writing within a tradition in
order consciously to surpass it. He gives the stylized conventions in
which he learned his craft not merely a new treatment but a new direction, "highly personal, approaching the realistic." Yet despite a
vivid description of events occurring in a definite place at a definite
time, and despite the particularity of experiences that happen to (and
within) a specific young man, who is identified and named, Dante's
little book describes the poet's lady with sufficient ambiguity, and in
terms so apocalyptic, that we cannot be wholly certain of her identity.
Some readers will see her as a real woman, others as a symbol or an
abstraction or a parable.

The *Vita Nuova* is a retrospective search for meaning, as Mark Musa has said. "In the course of his Three Movements in Love Dante learns that true happiness, which is the goal of all men, lies above and beyond the material world, and that only by experience, failure, and continuous struggle for meaning and understanding, which is the movement of the *Vita Nuova*, can man hope to attain his goal" (Musa, *VN*, 1962, xviii). The Dante of the story passes through successive stages in understanding love, and through this inquiry he becomes a poet.

At first Dante is a composer of facile verses, in the prevailing literary convention—the Stilnovistic reworking of a poetic tradition established by William of Poitou, the lyric traditions of courtly love. Love, for the troubadours, was a force beyond human control and beyond the resistance of the lovers. For the young Dante, however, as a result of having had a vision of love at the early age of nine, there exists at the back of his mind a secret ideality that makes him veil his true feelings. The Beatrice of his childhood vision represents this sense of a higher love; he does not approach her directly but only through his verses. He addresses his poetry to other ladies so that his real attachment will be concealed, but after a time he finds himself writing so ardently that Beatrice, disappointed, refuses to speak to him. Dante now realizes that the sense of ideality as an element in sexual love is what really matters to him. He is a man of strong and deep passions, for whom this is nothing less than a matter of life and death. The father of Beatrice dies, and Dante has a nightmare vision of the death of his beloved. In the end he realizes that the experience of ideal love, represented by Beatrice, is the best part of his nature. What began as an abstraction is finally admitted as a personal and individual attachment.

The central figure of the book is, of course, not Beatrice but Dante himself, a poet who is describing the making of poetry. Joyce's reading of the *Vita Nuova* especially reflects the young Dante's use of scholarly elements and psychological understanding in that work. Dante's account provides a full description of the development of his craft. The little book reveals Dante's mind and sensibility, giving an account of his aesthetic principles and of his reading both directly and indirectly. Dante places himself, as protagonist, in a succession stretching back to Virgil, Ovid, Horace; he displays his scholastic training; he makes effective allusion to the Bible and to his Stilnovistic predecessors; *his* poet, in sum, is an intellectual whose development is presented in a carefully structured sequence.[18] Joyce, whose first reading of the *Vita Nuova* is described in *Stephen Hero*, similarly made a retrospective discovery of the significance of his youthful experience. This was, of course, different from Dante's. But Joyce, with a similar deliberateness, embarked on the construction of a portrait of the "poet in action."

There are inevitably features of Joyce's portrayal that emphatically separate his book from Dante's. Joyce has drawn his portrait in the round, giving the impression that he has dealt with all the significant aspects of his young artist's development. Dante's book, on the other hand, "has no other subject than the growth of love in the heart and mind of the poet."[19] Dante's love for Beatrice has from the outset a moral and religious character that, though not wholly absent from Joyce's treatment, is displayed and developed in quite a different manner in *A Portrait of the Artist as a Young Man*. One cannot deny the presence of religious and moral elements in Stephen's sensibility, and these indeed become the fabric of the poem he writes in the final chapter. But these elements remain aspects of Stephen's religious upbringing and the shape of his imagination, not directly but ambiguously attached to the individual girl for whom the verses are written.

Another distinguishing feature is the figure of Beatrice, who is the key to Dante's pattern in a way that is wholly absent from *A Portrait of the Artist*. Yet the economy of Joyce's novel owes a good deal to his reading of *La Vita Nuova*. Dante's sensibility and his development form the material of the book, and his treatment of other characters—the God of Love, the screen ladies, and the beautiful precursor Giovanna—serves only to identify and illuminate important stages in the poet's progressive understanding. The emotions of the poet (whom Dante presents in his book as a being of extraordinary sensibility, all tears, sighs, and dreams, and wearied to exhaustion by his emotions) are the wellsprings of poetry. The poet's art progresses and develops and deepens, *not by extending the love affair* but by deepening the poetic sensibility that he has first discovered in this dimension. He is indeed thereby deepening his capacity to love, for this is another way of describing the capacity to feel. In these aspects Joyce's hero has a basic similarity to Dante's.

J. E. Shaw has remarked on " . . . the scarcity of concrete details, and the fact that it (the *Vita Nuova*) is an account of mental rather than physical experience.[20] While the book is the story of Dante and Beatrice, the paramount fact in our knowledge of Beatrice is that she was the object of Dante's love. So also with the girl for whom Stephen Dedalus writes verses; she is identified only by initials, "E____ C____," or by the term "your beloved." The principal difference between the books, if we consider only the central relationship of the poet and the woman for whom he writes verses, is Joyce's admission of sensuality into his story. The sensuality of Dante's "Petra" is wholly absent from the *Vita Nuova*. In the early draft, *Stephen Hero*, Joyce gave a more factual account of the "love affair," and provided a detailed narrative of the relationship between the young protagonist and the girl who, by attracting him physically, awakened his emotions (*SH* 67-68; 154-156; 158; 188-189). Joyce's closer study of the full range of Dante's poetry in relation to the *Vita Nuova* is revealed in the changes he made in the construction of *A Portrait of the Artist as a Young Man*. We shall return to these interesting resemblances after examining the contribution of Dante to Joyce's *Ulysses*.

*

In *Ulysses* Joyce confronts, more methodically than elsewhere, both style and substance in Dante's poem, with results that appear in the treatment of theme and construction of character. These matters have been displayed in earlier chapters and do not require restatement, but a final comment is needed on the Dantean journey.

Joyce gave the role of protagonist in his transformation of the *Odyssey* to Leopold Bloom, and modeled one aspect of Stephen Dedalus on Dante's Ulysses. The latter is a character markedly different from Homer's wanderer—he is a proud man, determined to push toward the frontiers of knowledge at all costs. Such a pattern, a double focus on two major figures, allowed Joyce to hold in aesthetic tension for the reader's enlightenment those qualities that unite and those that fragment the social community. He conjoined the elements of continuity and of recklessness.[21] Homer's Ulysses is a rover of the seas from necessity rather than choice; like Leopold Bloom, he is a reluctant wanderer. Irresistibly drawn homeward to wife, to connubial bed, to things known and familiar, both Bloom and Homer's Ulysses, as W. B. Stanford says, display the centripetal force that holds society together. Dante's Ulysses, by contrast, allows no bond to hold him: "neither fondness for my son, nor reverence for my aged father, nor the due love which would have made Penelope glad, could conquer in me the longing that I had to gain experience of the world, and of human vice and worth" (*Inf.* 26: trans. Singleton). In the character of Stephen Dedalus, this quality of the Dantean version appears as a constant. As an aspect of Stephen's personality it explains quite straightforwardly why he declines ["Promptly, inexplicably, with amicability, gratefully" (*U* 680)] Bloom's well-meant offers of asylum:

> How did the centripetal remainer afford egress to the centrifugal departer?

By inserting the barrel of an arruginated male key in the hold of an unstable female lock, obtaining a purchase on the box of the key and turning its wards from right to left, withdrawing a bolt from its staple, pulling inward spasmodically an obsolescent unhinged door and revealing an aperture for free egress and free ingress.

How did they take leave, one of the other, in separation?

Standing perpendicular at the same door and on different sides of its base, the lines of their valedictory arms, meeting at any point and forming any angle less than the sum of two right angles.

What sound accompanied the union of their tangent, the disunion of their (respectively) centrifugal and centripetal hands?

The sound of the peal of the hour of the night by the chime of the bells in the church of Saint George. (*U* 688:13-27)

The paragraph notably does not illustrate the *reason* for departure but only imparts to the event a certain character and an embodiment by the emphatic use of those two adjectives, "centripetal" and "centrifugal." Like Dante's Ulysses, Stephen represents the heterodox element in conflicts between orthodoxy and heresy, conservatism and progressivism, which were a manifestation of intellectual ferment in Dante's time and also in Joyce's.[22]

Stanford, in *The Ulysses Theme*, thus borrows Joyce's terms to describe the two major versions of the Ulysses tradition, reintegrated in Joyce's novel:

In general Dedalus-Telemachus represents the centrifugal, rebellious, destructive, home-abandoning element in the homo uluxeanus. . . . Like Dante's Ulysses, he will be deterred by no love of family or home from travelling into the unknown world to find new knowledge and experience. Bloom, on the other hand, like the Ulysses of Homer, Shakespeare, and Giraudoux, represents the centripetal, conservative, and constructive element in society. Dedalus rejects and struggles to overthrow; Bloom accepts and tries to improve. Dedalus denies; Bloom affirms. . . . In this way Dedalus marks the negative pole of the Ulyssean character, Bloom the positive. Between them they encompass the whole cosmos of the tradition.[23]

However, in addition to the two figures of Ulysses, Joyce invested his two protagonists with recognizable aspects of Dante: the man as he was born, and the man he became in the writing of the *Divine Comedy*. Stephen Dedalus, whose "entire aptitude is for the composition of prose and verse" (*SH* 232), is a figure of Dante at the time of his going into exile—the man whose pride and scorn would not allow him to

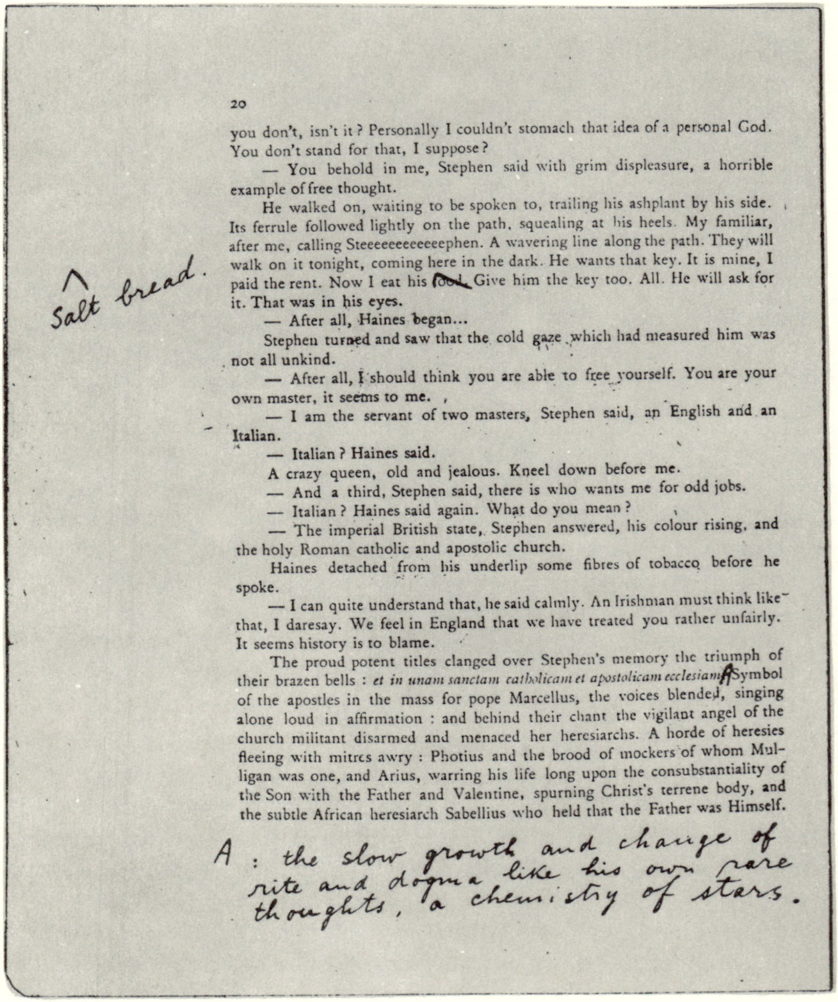
20

you don't, isn't it? Personally I couldn't stomach that idea of a personal God. You don't stand for that, I suppose?

— You behold in me, Stephen said with grim displeasure, a horrible example of free thought.

He walked on, waiting to be spoken to, trailing his ashplant by his side. Its ferrule followed lightly on the path, squealing at his heels. My familiar, after me, calling Steeeeeeeeeeeephen. A wavering line along the path. They will walk on it tonight, coming here in the dark. He wants that key. It is mine, I paid the rent. Now I eat his ~~food~~. Give him the key too. All. He will ask for it. That was in his eyes.

Salt bread.

— After all, Haines began...

Stephen turned and saw that the cold gaze which had measured him was not all unkind.

— After all, I should think you are able to free yourself. You are your own master, it seems to me.

— I am the servant of two masters, Stephen said, an English and an Italian.

— Italian? Haines said.

A crazy queen, old and jealous. Kneel down before me.

— And a third, Stephen said, there is who wants me for odd jobs.

— Italian? Haines said again. What do you mean?

— The imperial British state, Stephen answered, his colour rising, and the holy Roman catholic and apostolic church.

Haines detached from his underlip some fibres of tobacco before he spoke.

— I can quite understand that, he said calmly. An Irishman must think like that, I daresay. We feel in England that we have treated you rather unfairly. It seems history is to blame.

The proud potent titles clanged over Stephen's memory the triumph of their brazen bells : *et in unam sanctam catholicam et apostolicam ecclesiam* A Symbol of the apostles in the mass for pope Marcellus, the voices blended, singing alone loud in affirmation : and behind their chant the vigilant angel of the church militant disarmed and menaced her heresiarchs. A horde of heresies fleeing with mitres awry : Photius and the brood of mockers of whom Mulligan was one, and Arius, warring his life long upon the consubstantiality of the Son with the Father and Valentine, spurning Christ's terrene body, and the subtle African heresiarch Sabellius who held that the Father was Himself.

A : the slow growth and change of rite and dogma like his own rare thoughts, a chemistry of stars.

9. In the same run of galley proofs Joyce added two small allusions to make both Stephen Dedalus and Leopold Bloom figures of Dante in exile. In the sentence, "Now I eat his food," Joyce adds the words "salt bread" to replace "food," thus making the sentence an echo of Cacciaguida's prophecy: "You shall come to know how salt is the taste of another's bread" (*U* 38:8; *Par.*

read it nearer, the title, the blurred cropping cattle, the page rustling. A young
white heifer. Those mornings in the cattlemarket the beasts lowing in their
pens, branded sheep, flop and fall of dung, the breeders in hobnailed boots
trudging through the litter, slapping a palm on a ~~meaty~~ hindquarter, there's
a prime one, unpeeled switches in their hands. He held the page aslant patiently, bending his senses and his will, his soft subject gaze at rest. The crooked
skirt swinging whack by whack by whack.

    The porkbutcher snapped two sheets from the pile, wrapped up her sau-
sages and made a red grimace.

    — Now, my miss, he said.

    She tendered a coin, smiling boldly, holding her thick wrist out.

    — Thank you, my miss. And one shilling threepence change. For you,
please?

    Mr Bloom pointed quickly. To catch up and walk behind her if she went
slowly, behind her moving hams. Hurry up, damn it. She stood outside the
shop in sunlight and turned lazily to the right. He sighed down his nose : they
never understand. Sodachapped hands. Crusted toenails too. Brown scapulars
in tatters, defending her both ways. The sting of disregard glowed to weak pleasure within his breast. For another : a constable off duty cuddled her in Eccles
Lane. *They like them sizeable. O please, Mr Policeman,*

    — Threepence, please. —————— *I'm lost in the wood.*

    His hand accepted the moist tender gland and slid it into a sidepocket.
Then it fetched up three coins from his trousers' pocket and laid them on the
rubber prickles. They lay, were read quickly and quickly slid, disc by disc, into
the till.

    — Thank you, sir. Another time.

    A speck of eager fire from foxeyes thanked him. He withdrew his gaze
after an instant. No : better not : another time..

    — Good morning, he said, moving away.

    — Good morning, sir.

    No sign. Gone. What matter?

    He walked back along Dorset street, reading gravely. Agendath Netaim :
planters' company. You pay eight marks and they plant a dunam of land for
you with olives, oranges, almonds or citrons. Olives cheaper : oranges need
artificial irrigation. Every year you get a sending of the crop. Your name
entered for life as owner in the book of the union. Can pay ten down and the
balance in yearly instalments. Bleibtreustrasse 34, Berlin, W, 15.

*A To purchase waste sandy tracts from
Turkish government and plant with
eucalyptus trees. Excellent for shade, fuel
and construction. Orangegroves and
immense melonfields north of Jaffa.*

[margin annotations: ripeneated / Pleasant to see first thing in the morning.]

17:58-59). Then Joyce adds a line to Mr Bloom's silent monologue: "I'm lost
in the wood" is a reminiscence of the opening lines of the *Inferno*, where
Dante says, "I found myself in a dark wood, for the straight way was lost" (*U*
59:41; *Inf.* 1:2-3).

return to his native city except on his own terms. Stephen's silent reflection, as he relinquishes the Tower key to Mulligan, is "Now I eat his salt bread" (*U* 21:40), reflecting Cacciaguida's chilling prophecy of Dante's future.

> You shall leave everything beloved most dearly; and this is the arrow which the bow of exile shoots first. You shall come to know how salt is the taste of another's bread . . . (trans. Singleton)

> Tu lascerai ogne cosa diletta
>   più caramente, e questo è quello strale
>   che l'arco de lo essilio pria saetta.
> Tu proverai sì come sa di sale
>   lo pane altrui . . .   (*Par.* 17:55-59)

Like Dante, Stephen Dedalus is a Catholic, and his enemy Mulligan sees this as a crucial handicap, a bar to success in the writing of serious poetry because "they drove his wits astray . . . by visions of hell." Stephen, however, in the private view given us by the author, has a fellow-craftsman's knowledge of Dante's poetry. His ability to remember in coherent patterns a selection of Dante's rhyme-words pulled together from all three cantiche is a guarantee that he has absorbed the poem. Like Dante, Stephen is preoccupied with the tragic violence of his country's history and, again like Dante, Stephen has written love-verses. The Stephen Dedalus of *Ulysses*, however, has no Beatrice. His acute sensitivity to emotional impressions shows itself primarily in his reactions to his mother's death, through which the reader is made aware of Stephen's capacity to love. Apart from this, on the 16th of June, 1904, Stephen is represented as loveless.

Leopold Bloom, however, is also a figure of Dante: "It was now for more than the middle span of our allotted years that he had passed through the thousand vicissitudes of existence" (*U* 400:42). He makes, though only in his mind, the pilgrimage toward contemplation that Dante makes through the three realms, until at the end, in the Ithaca chapter, Bloom is able to look down upon his disturbing world with the perspective Dante has achieved in *Paradiso* 27:[24]

> So that I saw beyond Cadiz the mad way which Ulysses took. . . .
> And further had the site of this threshing-floor been unfolded to me . . . (trans. Singleton)

> Sì chi'io vedea di là da Gade il varco
>   folle d'Ulisse . . .
>
>   . . . . . .

E più mi fora discoverto il sito
  di questa aiuola . . .   *(Par.* 27:82-86)

It is Dante himself as author of the *Comedy* who has made the journey
Ulysses wanted to make, "to gain experience of the world and of
human vice and worth" (" . . . a divenir del mondo esperto / e de li vizi
umani e del valore") *(Inf.* 26:98-99). Dante himself had the quality of
pride of intellect that is such a striking feature of his Ulysses, but the
Dante of *Paradiso* 27 recognizes the passage taken by Ulysses as "il
varco folle," a mad way. Bloom is inherently reasonable and prudent;
Bloom, like the Dante of *Paradiso* 27, has journeyed to equanimity
through reflection.

As Joyce through his basic strategies of characterization brought
together the poles of the Ulysses tradition, so also he maneuvers characters and events, fusing the histories of Stephen and Bloom. Such a
fusion made it possible to give the opening chapters of the Tele-
machiad some aura of the opening cantos of the *Inferno*, while the progressions of the central chapters convey the sense of hard-won understanding that marks a reading of the *Purgatorio*, and the final
chapters of the Nostos and Penelope achieve, without any novelistic
resolution, a satisfying completion of period so distinct that it carries
something of the final sublimity of the *Paradiso*. As Marilyn French
has observed (and demonstrated, in a reading of *Ulysses* that invokes
the *Divine Comedy*), Bloom embodies the principle of *caritas*.[25] Bloom's
small, inconspicuous acts of generosity during the day add up "to the
ancient and most exalted of Christian virtues, *caritas*. Bloom's possession of this virtue makes him a superior being, as superior in the
moral sphere as is Stephen in that of the intellect."

                                 *

The Dantesque thrust of this aspect of Joyce's writing will be further clarified by a brief return to Dante's *Vita Nuova*. The center of
the *Vita Nuova* is death, the event which no one can experience. As
Singleton has decisively argued, the death of Beatrice is the instrument that allows Dante, as author, to move from the poetic conventions of the first half of the *Vita Nuova* to the love represented in the
exalted poetry of the *Divine Comedy*: a Christian poetry because it was
imbued with *caritas*, which now became "The love that moved the sun
and the other stars."[26] Dante solved in a new fashion the problem of
reconciling love of woman with love of God. For the Provençal poet,
there was no place in poetry for an object of love higher than the lady.

For the Christian, there can be no object of love higher than God, and all other loves must show their subordinate status. The result of these opposite demands was an irreconcilable conflict of poetic purpose. Usually the poet made a timely recantation, taking no chances with his salvation and expressing his repentance well before his death. Petrarch, after several sonnets of repentance, closes his *Rime* with the most powerful of his palinodes; because the conflict of poetic purpose is still apparent in the *Rime*, Singleton calls him the last of the troubadours.[27]

Dante demonstrates certain conventions of troubadour love in the first part of his little book, and in the prose commentary explicitly attaches his verse to the Stilnovistic tradition which followed the Provençal.[28] But Dante finds a way out of the dilemma that is posed in the question, "Must love die with the death of the object of love?" Dante invokes an older tradition still, the theological tradition of *caritas* expressed by Augustine and the mystics of the early Church. Augustine makes the crucial distinction:

> I mean by charity that affection of the mind which aims at the enjoyment of God for His own sake, and the enjoyment of one's self and one's neighbor in subordination to God; by lust I mean that affection of the mind which aims at enjoying one's self and one's neighbor and other corporeal things without reference to God.[29]

God *is* love; love *is* God. It is uncreated being; "the love that moves the sun and the other stars." Dante's effort to move whole-heartedly toward this ideal makes his love for Beatrice unique.

Dante, in the *Vita Nuova*, makes poetic use, in *peripetaea*, of the *vision* of Beatrice dead. He comes to his understanding of *caritas* as inseparable from love of woman, not with the actual death of Beatrice, but with brooding upon a dream in which he has imagined her dead.[30]

> Dante found a way to go beyond the conflict of love of woman with love of God, bringing to the thesis and the antithesis of the one and the other that synthesis which managed to reject neither the one or the other but to keep both in a single suspension—in a single theory of love. The *Vita Nuova* is that theory . . . in a first sense of the word: a *beholding of* how certain things may be.

By means of the prose glosses on his poems, Dante prepares the reader for the gradual revelation of the true nature of Beatrice, whose name is spelled both with and without the capital letter. She has been sent to him miraculously, indeed she is a miracle. Through her he reaches understanding. Joyce must have been aware that the larger understanding was not portrayed and not present in the *Vita Nuova*. There, only the love of man and woman, albeit in an idealized form, is presented. In the *Divine Comedy*, love in every form is shown. The *Vita Nuova* in this respect is potentiality moving toward actuality. The crucial artistic event is the death of Beatrice.

Joyce, continuing into *Ulysses* the portrait of his young artist, followed this aspect of Dante's design. He made a similar division, not following Dante's pattern but observing and using its principle. In both books he increased the intensity by restricting the focus of attention. Thus, in *Ulysses*, Stephen Dedalus is not seen in relation to any woman except his mother and his sister, and the former association is further restricted to memory and hallucination. In *A Portrait*, however, Stephen is seen definitively, though always briefly, in relation to a number and a variety of women.

There is no death in *A Portrait of the Artist* (there was such a chapter in *Stephen Hero*), but in *Ulysses* the death of Stephen's mother is an important element. It is unlikely that Joyce would have missed the aesthetic significance in the *Vita Nuova* of Dante's double treatment of the death of Beatrice. In *VN* XXIII, after the poet's apocalyptic vision of her death, he writes a long canzone; but in *VN* XXVIII and XXIX, when Beatrice actually dies, no poem is written. The emotional wellsprings are checked, in a discontinuance that becomes progression.

A similar configuration can be found in *A Portrait of the Artist as a Young Man*—not in a reproduction of Dante's pattern of writing a poem as a response to the experience of death, but in Joyce's similar creation of a discontinuous sequence of emotional climaxes as the register of his poet's sensibility. This movement reaches its high point with the actual writing of a poem; but the parallel with the *Vita Nuova* is found in the principle of design rather than in substance. Joyce's poet, like Dante's, writes in the dominant tradition of his time. Both Dante and Joyce give a number of subtle and ambiguous indications of alliance with, as well as departure from, tradition and poetic inheritance.

The presence of Dantesque elements in the early chapters of *A Portrait* argues that these parallels are volitional. Barbara Seward found in the rose-symbolism of Joyce's book "perceptible Dantesque hues" (of the *Divine Comedy*, not the *Vita Nuova*) which establish the rose in Dante's poem as the flower of Beatrice. Seward sees the roses of Stephen's childish song in the opening section of Chapter I as "hints of Stephen's artistic leanings."[31] Rose associations accumulate with mounting intensity to the point at which Stephen writes his villanelle, after which the mention of roses abruptly stops. Dante had created the metaphor of a white rose as the heavenly city of souls in Paradise, a final extension of the medieval rose of love. Joyce transformed the figure: "A world, a glimmer, or a flower?" As a fictional event, the rose here (*P* 172:35, 173:2) expresses the adolescent Stephen's vision of his artistic vocation. The allusion brings into the fiction Dante's heavenly city, but with the very important difference that sensuality has now not been excluded. Such a fusion of sensuousness and religiosity was typically Pre-Raphaelite.[32]

In his Symbolist novel generally, but most markedly in the second section of Chapter Five, the villanelle episode, Joyce made a subtle combination of substance and style that reflects the intricate history of theory and practice. An important indication of the change in his plans is the note written across the MS of *Stephen Hero* at page 609: "End of second episode of V" (*Archive* 8:609). He intended to bring Dante into his portrayal of "the poet in action," as *Stephen Hero* puts it, and in his first plan for revision he apparently meant to use at this point his parodic transformation of *Inferno* 15. Instead, it appears that the purchase of the Pre-Raphaelite edition of the *Vita Nuova* stimulated him to put at this place in his new structure a mimetic episode indeed, and one with Dantesque overtones, but not taken from the *Divine Comedy*. Instead, he appropriated as a model the Symbolist novel of D'Annunzio, *The Child of Pleasure*, which is preeminently D'Annunzio's novel of the Decadence, and is focused wholly on the life and loves of a young poet, Andrea Sperelli. As the second episode of Chapter Five of *A Portrait*, Joyce re-wrote the short chapter in D'Annunzio's novel in which a sonnet sequence is written and its origins are fully explained. With Dante's *Vita Nuova*, these seem to be the principal and at the time of Joyce's writing the only instances of fictional portrayal of the inner life of the poet with a full example of the resulting poetry.[33]

The villanelle itself collects and organizes all the images of woman in the limited experience of Stephen Dedalus. A brief review of the feminine image in *A Portrait*, omitting details, will be useful here. In the first four chapters the book has shown brief vignettes, or epiphanies, of woman in childhood, youth, maturity, and old age in Stephen's own family, in the markedly narrow range of his acquaintance, and in his observation of the life around him. All this is of course a Catholic experience and it leaves out of account the Anglo-Irish aspect of Dublin. Stephen's is not a rich or a rewarding experience of woman. Indeed, the pattern conveys a contrary impression and this design is clearly volitional. The images of the book are sharp, their fewness telling its own story. They are set in a design of sharp contrasts.

The memory of E____ C____ dancing, lightly as an apple-blossom on the breeze, is set against the feminine figures Stephen sees elsewhere: the "frowsy girls" of the streets (*P* 140); the flowerseller with "young blue eyes" who accosts him, ragged and hoydenish, with damp coarse hair; and of course the prostitute whom he encounters in the full tide of adolescent sexuality. These are distinctly not the images of woman in Swinburne, Huysman, or D'Annunzio. Alongside these various impressions drawn from life Joyce places two figures from the unsubstantial world of art and religion. The dominant figure is the Blessed Virgin Mary, who represents a mediator and comforter like Stephen's own mother. But she is a virgin mother and sinless from her conception, the "Refuge of sinners," and to the young Stephen "the morning star, bright and musical." These are Newman's words; she is a literary as well as a religious influence. No feminine figure from secular literature is allowed to enter the novel except Mercedes, the Count of Monte Cristo's love. None, that is, until the last sight of Stephen in the closing pages of the novel, where Dante's Beatrice appears. She is emphatically not the idealized Pre-Raphaelite Beatrice. Altogether absent are the religious associations of the villanelle. This is a secularized Beatrice.

> Met her today pointblank in Grafton Street. The crowd brought us together. We both stopped. She asked me why I never came, said she had heard all sorts of stories about me. This was only to gain time. Asked me, was I writing poems? About whom? I asked her. This confused her more and I felt sorry and mean. Turned off that valve at once and opened the spiritual-heroic refrigerating apparatus invented and patented in all countries by Dante Alighieri. Talked rapidly of myself and my plans. In the midst of it unluckily I made a sudden gesture of a revolutionary nature. I must have looked like a fellow throwing a handful of peas into the air. People began to look at us. She shook hands a moment after and, in going away, said she hoped I would do what I said.
>
> Now I call that friendly, don't you?
>
> Yes, I liked her today. A little or much? Don't know. I liked her and it seems a new feeling to me. Then, in that case, all the rest, all that I thought I thought and all that I felt I felt, all the rest before now, in fact . . . O, give it up, old chap! Sleep it off! (*P* 252)

The allusion to Dante connects this passage unmistakably with the villanelle episode, in which Stephen echoed the *Vita Nuova*: "He had

written verses for her again after ten years" (*P* 222.9). She is the inspiration of his verses, as Beatrice was for Dante. Now they are about to
part, as Dante was parted from Beatrice. The concluding section of
the *Vita Nuova* (*VN* XLII) encapsulates Dante's book as a whole, and
the diary entry similarly recapitulates the appearances of E____ C____
in *A Portrait* by the reminder of Stephen's "plans" and the announcement of his "new feeling" with a suggestion of prelude in "all the rest
before now."

> After this sonnet there appeared to me a miraculous vision in which
> I saw things that made me resolve to say no more about this blessed
> one until I should be capable of writing about her in a more worthy
> fashion. And to achieve this I am striving as hard as I can, and this
> she truly knows. So that, if it be the wish of him in whom all things
> flourish that my life continue for a few years, I hope to write of her
> that which has never been written of any other lady. (*VN* XLII,
> trans. Musa)

Joyce has domesticated the revelations of the *Vita Nuova*; Stephen
Dedalus speaks to this Beatrice and even treats her casually.

Thus the striking rhetorical connection of the diary entry with the
villanelle episode requires comment. Each time that E____ C____ has
come into the story, reference has been made to poems that Stephen
has written for her (*P* 69-70, 77, 115-116, 215-224, 252). The first occasion is a children's party, and ten years later (in the *Vita Nuova*
Dante connects the first two poems by a precise nine-year interval) Stephen writes the villanelle. This event is preceded by an incident that
echoes *Vita Nuova* III, when Stephen stands with Lynch watching his
girl among her friends. "Your beloved is here," says Lynch
(*P* 215:33).

We know, however, that Joyce's model for the discrete seven-page
episode (set off by asterisks at beginning and end) was the short chapter of D'Annunzio's novel. The choice of Parnassian verse form and
the rhythms of the episode would tend to mark the section as a reflection of Aestheticism even without any knowledge of the D'Annunzian
original. Yet it is an ambiguous rather than a straightforward parody,
for the protagonist of Joyce's novel does not at all resemble D'Annunzio's hero, and the handling of imagery in the villanelle is counter-
D'Annunzio. There can be no doubt that Joyce wrote the villanelle
specifically to fit the chapter, and wrote the account of composition to
direct attention to whatever in the poem marks these differences.

The true author of the poem makes Stephen take a direction that
marks a crucial departure from the D'Annunzian original. Stephen is

thus placed at a distance from Aestheticism even though he is not aware of his situation. The reason for this important difference is indicated proleptically in the discussion of aesthetic theory that immediately precedes the poem. It is a complex construction in which the key must be seen as Joyce's decision, in revising *Stephen Hero*, to focus his design on the development of Dante's poetic art rather than on his love for Beatrice.

Let us look briefly at the similarities and differences. In Stephen's villanelle and in Andrea Sperelli's sonnet sequence, the central image of ritual and celebrant is evocative rhetorically of the Christian Mass:

> *Andrea*: But, at the circle's summit, see a fair
> White woman, in the act of worship, holds
> In her pure hands the sacrificial Host.
> *Stephen*: While sacrificing hands upraise
> The chalice flowing to the brim,
> Tell no more of enchanted days.

The religion of beauty and the priesthood of art have passed from Flaubert to D'Annunzio's hero; the celebrant of this rite is a woman, revealed in the poem as the Madonna, and the artist is a suppliant seeking forgiveness for a dissolute life. Joyce's poet has a more rigorous view of *both* religion and art. Woman is no priestess in the villanelle, and the man asks no forgiveness. It is indeed a fleeting thought of the priesthood of art that supplies the central image of Stephen's poem, but this comes in the middle of composition and was written by Joyce quite obviously as a variation on D'Annunzio's chapter.

A striking similarity is seen in the break in composition that comes when Stephen's search for a rhyme leads his subconscious mind to a jarring and unpoetic recollection that destroys inspiration and threatens the poem (*P* 218:16-18). A similar event occurs in *The Child of Pleasure*, but without an explanation of the interruption; D'Annunzio's hero simply continues composing with practiced, mechanical skill. In Joyce's episode quite to the contrary, the "poet in action" tells in his unspoken thoughts exactly where the poem came from, and exactly how the rhythm of composition is recaptured. "The radiant image of the Eucharist united again in an instant his bitter and despairing thoughts . . . in a hymn of thanksgiving" (*P* 221:17).

At this point Stephen does not look like an apprentice Decadent, however much the verse-form and imagery may owe to Aestheticism. Stephen's priesthood is quite different from Andrea's. For Andrea, what matters is the intensity of the vision:

"For I, she saith, "am the unnatural Rose,
I am the Rose of Beauty. I instil
The drunkenness of ecstasy . . . "

This is Art for Art at its most unconcealed. In contrast, Stephen concentrates on the *communication of the vision*: on the expression of a reality unfathomable save for the brief instant of transfixing by the poet's candor and his art. Stephen's metaphor makes the artist more truly a priest, a mediator. The groveling of D'Annunzio's artist makes his sonnet sequence, in comparison, a narcissistic exercise:

So be it, Madonna; and from my heart outburst
The blood of tears, flooding all mortal things . . .
Let the depths swallow me, let there as at first
Be darkness, so I see the glimmerings
Of light that rain on my unconquered soul!

The trope in which Stephen's villanelle achieves completion is distinctly different from the superficially analogous figure in D'Annunzio's poem. The hiatus which establishes a decisive similarity between D'Annunzio's construction and Joyce's, as a central feature of the chapter and the episode, is also the element that constitutes the difference between them. It is a deliberate and significant artistic decision by Joyce. Not only does the hiatus furnish the trope that rescues the poem, it also is made to display, in Stephen's thoughts, the presence of a vital relation between the poem and its origins. "And yet he felt that, however he might revile and mock her image, his anger was also a form of homage" (*P* 220:34). Regardless of any judgment about the level of its artistic quality, the villanelle must be valued in Joyce's novel as an authentic instance of "imagination saturated with the results of 'real' experience." The pattern of the episode argues for a decision by Joyce to make Stephen represent a young man passing through what Joyce himself called the "two eras," of Aestheticism and Decadence, though he may not yet have emerged on the far side.[34]

We now observe that the elements of the unfinished *Stephen Hero* have been re-arranged in a new sequence. The significance of the new pattern is apparent in the placement of the villanelle episode immediately after Stephen's discussion of aesthetics, with a momentary glimpse of Dante's *Vita Nuova* between the two. Where the "scattered love verses" of *Stephen Hero* (*SH* 174:9) had been given an explicit but vague connection with the *Vita Nuova*, in the finished novel Stephen is silently made a figure of the young Dante. The similarity, however, is not in the quality of his love or of his art; rather, in his role as a young man for whom poetry-writing is a way of life, an individual with an epiphany-producing mind. Stephen's poem, critics have observed, does not match his grasp of poetic theory. Joyce, in *A Portrait*, anticipated the Neo-Scholastic philosophers in attaching a theory of beauty to Aquinas, but his hero is certainly no philosopher and not really a Neo-Scholastic thinker either. He takes St. Thomas's remarks out of context, whether deliberately or inadvertently. But this is irrelevant to *Joyce's fictional context*, where an important connection is made that shows the presence of Dante and the importance of Scholasticism in the development of his artist.

*

Joyce's most sophisticated knowledge of the *Divine Comedy* went into his last work, *Finnegans Wake*. For this book his method of composition was entirely different from his earlier works. *Dubliners, A Portrait of the Artist as a Young Man*, and *Ulysses* had all gone through conventional stages of composition and revision, chapter by chapter. The writing proceeded, if not strictly in sequence, at least one segment at a time. *Finnegans Wake* was written by a process of accretion, starting with brief sketches that were gradually enlarged, fitted together (in a design that apparently was in Joyce's mind at a very early date), and enlarged again. The first sketches for the book were written in 1923 but were not inserted in the book until 1938, just before publication (*Selected Letters* 296 n.).

Joyce's decision to cast the entire book in the shape of a dream may owe something to his reading of Dante's *Paradiso*. The representation of a dream is the largest challenge to the imagination of the artist, for there is no original on which it can be based. One can represent fictionally a marriage, or an automobile accident, or even death—which the writer cannot have experienced even vicariously—with more assurance and with less originality than is required for the imagining of "a dream," for which in the nature of things there can be no objective correlative. Dante's originality reached its highest point in the *Paradiso*, markedly transcending the medieval tradition of dreams and visions.

Dante creates a solid reality from the first lines of his poem. Thus we forget, or are not aware, that as the Pilgrim and his escorts go through hell and purgatory they are in a bodiless world; the individuals met are shades, Dante alone casts a shadow. By the time he reaches Heaven (and in contrast to the transition from hell to purgatory, he does not tell us how he got there), the spirits are wholly points of light; yet the vividness of the account, including the description of just how the spirits of La Pia, Cacciaguida, St. Peter and Adam make themselves known to Dante, by some poetic magic carries the reader into full acceptance of the vision as a real event.

In the opening cantos of the *Paradiso* Dante warns those who would follow him to turn back to their own shores, avoid the risk of deeper waters unless they can follow steadily the track of Dante's "navicella," the little ship of his genius that now travels a sea never traveled before. To Joyce, after finishing *Ulysses*, this may have seemed a challenge to be taken up. By the time he started writing *Finnegans Wake* Joyce had grasped the full implication of Dante's lines, "Trasumanar significar *per verba* / non si poria" ("The passing beyond humanity may not be set forth in words"), which express with poignance the artistic endeavor of the *Paradiso*. The poetry of Canto I, in which the time is high noon and Dante in obedience to Beatrice looks straight at the sun, is echoed in Joyce's statement, quoted by his Zurich friend Georges Borach: "Dante tires one quickly. It is like looking at the sun." *Finnegans Wake*, which is not a novel, not a poem, but a poetic fiction in prose, embodies Joyce's most ardent pursuit of the example of Dante's poem.

The construction of a dream-language, and its consistent use throughout a book almost as long as *Ulysses*, was Joyce's most ambitious technical undertaking. Unquestionably this decision grew out of Joyce's close study of Dante's linguistic achievement, his awareness that Dante had been a conscious innovator, a pioneer, as Thomas G. Bergin says, who came very close to anticipating the basic principles of modern nineteenth-century Romance philology.[35] Samuel Beckett's essay, "Dante . . . Bruno . . . Vico . . . Joyce," spoke of "this attractive parallel between Dante and Mr. Joyce in the question of language."[36]

The essay by Beckett was one of twelve, published in 1929 while the new book was appearing in fragmentary form in *transition* under the title, "Work in Progress." Parts of chapters had also been published as small books. Joyce became aware that the technique and meaning of *Finnegans Wake* were glimpsed by readers and critics only faintly, if at all. He encouraged the writing of critical essays, and later admitted to Valery Larbaud that he had directed the work of "those twelve apostles," Samuel Beckett and other friends (*Letters* I: 283-284).

> My impression is that the paper cover, the grandfather's clock on the title page and the word Exagmination itself . . . inclined reviewers to regard it as a joke, *though these were all my doing* (italics mine) but some fine morning . . . some enterprising fellow will discover the etymological history of the orthodox word examination and begin to change his wavering mind on the subject of the book, whereupon one by one others will faintly echo in the wailful choir,

"Siccome i gru van cantando lor lai" ("As the cranes go, chanting their lays") (*Inf.* 5:46).

The morning did not dawn; contemporary critical opinion remained impervious to these efforts at bringing external evidence of the author's intentions to bear on the understanding of Joyce's book.

The essays of this symposium are valuable as evidence that Joyce built his book on a pattern that he believed could be discerned in a careful reading. The twelve writers were really engaged in a general defense of Joyce's art. In one of the best of the essays, strategically given the final position in the book, William Carlos Williams answered the malicious strictures of Rebecca West's review of *Ulysses* at the same time that he responded to her comments on *Finnegans Wake*. Williams wrote that "defect" in Joyce's writing "is a consequence of the genius which, to gain way, has superseded the restrictions of the orthodox field." Williams had obviously been encouraged by Joyce to discuss the broad design of the book's linguistic maneuvers, and he wrote: "Writing is made of words . . . in just this essential Joyce is making a technical advance . . . breaking with a culture older than England's when he goes into his greatest work. . . . He is a writer broken-hearted over the world. . . . As literature, Joyce is going on like French painters by painting, to find some way out of his sorrow—by *literary* means. . . . As a writer he is trying for new means. He is looking ahead to find if there be a way, a literary way (in his chosen category) to save the world—or call it (as a figure) to save the static, worn out language."[37]

Joyce also encouraged Beckett to put forward a view that combined Vico and Dante to explain "The circular structure of the book, in which the incidents described are to be considered as happening over and over again." Beckett writes:

> In what sense then is Mr. Joyce's work purgatorial? In the absolute sense of the absolute. Hell is the static lifelessness of unrelieved viciousness. Paradise the static lifelessness of unrelieved immaculation. Purgatory a flood of movement and vitality released by the conjunction of these two elements. . . . On this earth that is Purgatory, Vice and Virtue—by which you may take to mean any pair of large contrary human factors—must in turn be purged down to spirits of rebelliousness. Then the dominant crust of the Vicious or Virtuous sets, resistance is provided, the explosion duly takes place, and the machine proceeds.[38]

This is neither Vico nor Dante, nor is it Joyce; but it indicates the presence, as Joyce saw it, of a Dantean pattern. Vico and Dante are linked, according to Thomas McGreevy's essay, "The Catholic Element in Work in Progress," in which McGreevy says, "The conception of the story as a whole is influenced by the *Purgatorio* and Vico, the Dante of the Counter Reformation." The absence of context for remarks such as these, left dangling as *obiter dicta*, suggests that they were directly quoted without being fully understood, from statements made by Joyce as his young friends wrote their essays.

The linkage of Vico and Dante in Joyce's Examination, however, closely parallels the points made by Vico himself, in "Discovery of the true Dante," a brief critique undoubtedly known to Joyce. The *Divine Comedy* is best understood, Vico says, "as a history of the period of barbarism in Italy, as a source of the fairest Tuscan speech, and as an example of sublime poetry." Vico does not describe the sublimity he finds in Dante's poem, but rather its sources in loftiness of mind and the historical process that brought it forth. Vico's Dante is an innovator: "For human talents are like those of the earth which, if brought under cultivation after fallow centuries, produce at the outset fruits marvelous for their perfection . . ."[39]

Beckett's essay was based on conversations with Joyce; it seems clear that Joyce had read both the *De Vulgari Eloquentia* and the *Convivio* and saw himself as Dante's disciple particularly in the area of linguistic innovation. What compelled Joyce's interest was, however, nothing so simple as word coinage or the fracturing of syntax; it was a concern with the ultimate reality of language, with its most fundamental and most general principles. This was what led Joyce to create the language of *Finnegans Wake*, which, as one realizes immediately on hearing the recorded voice of the author reading his own work, is English in syntax, Irish in cadence, and multilingual in vocabulary; and in all this it is a continuation of experiments begun in *Ulysses* and even earlier—a fulfilment of tendency. Beckett writes that between Dante and Joyce "there exists considerable circumstantial similarity. They both saw how worn out and threadbare was the conventional language of cunning literary artificers; both rejected an approximation to a universal language.' . . . If English is not yet so definitely a polite necessity as Latin was in the Middle Ages, at least one is justified in declaring that its position in relation to other European languages is to a great extent that of medieval Latin to the Italian dialects."[40]

Beckett made the point that Dante's development of a vernacular adequate to encompass the range of his poem's design followed from his decision, or gradual realization, that Latin did not provide for his purposes an adequate literary form; and the phrase, "circumstantial similarity" obviously reflects Joyce's view of his own problems in fashioning a verbal medium which would render the night-time life of the mind. Dante's ultimate mastery of language came with his narration of an experience which is not a dream yet is somehow beyond the mind's waking life. Joyce, who once said, "I can do anything with words,"[41] also saw the dreaming consciousness as a challenge and sought a literary form in which he could represent it. Joyce worked for seventeen years on *Finnegans Wake* constructing a fiction which, like the *Divine Comedy*, could be called "the Strangest Dream that was ever Halfdreamt" (*FW* 307:12). Certainly he wished it to be read; he considered his dream-language to be difficult (in the way that Hart Crane is difficult or Wallace Stevens), but not totally obscure.

Thus it is interesting to find the youthful Beckett, under Joyce's inspiration, writing of Dante's conclusion that, "he who would write in the vulgar must assemble the purest elements from each dialect and construct a synthetic language that would at least possess more than a circumscribed local interest . . . that *could* have been spoken by an ideal Italian who had assimilated what was best in all the dialects of his country."[42]

To Joyce's cosmopolitan outlook this approach to language was irresistible. As he began the writing of his universal history, his hero—Universal Man—was endowed with all languages, classical and modern, Indo-European and non-European as well. Scholars have assembled glossaries of Gaelic, Scandinavian, German, Malay, Hebrew, Chinese, and Swahili elements in *Finnegans Wake*.[43] The book is among other things a vocabulary of mutations. Joyce's compounds in *Ulysses* were recognizably English, in *Finnegans Wake* they are polyglot. Of this vocabulary Beckett writes, "It is reasonable to admit that an international phenomenon might be capable of speaking it, just as in 1300 none but an inter-regional phenomenon could have spoken the language of the *Divine Comedy*."[44] Leaving aside the many arguable features of Joyce's book, this determination to force language into a new range is testimony to Joyce's most ambitious and deliberate imitation of Dante.

Acknowledgment of the connection comes from Joyce himself, in a comment reported by Ettore Settanni. Work had begun on an Italian translation of two fragments of the Anna Livia Plurabelle chapter (the first pages, 196-201:21, and the final pages, 215-216); Joyce read some lines aloud to Settanni and asked what he thought of it. His friend (who had confessed bewilderment) reports:

> Joyce took a copy of the *Divine Comedy* and pointed out Dante's line, "Papé Satàn, papé Satà aleppe!" [Inf. 7:1] "May Father Dante forgive me," he said, "but I took this technique of deformation as my

point of departure in trying to achieve a harmony that vanquishes our intelligence as music does."

The Italian translation had been made with Nino Frank, in 1937.[45] It was an extremely important event because this was, as we now know, Joyce's own translation. He was enthusiastic about the result, and Louis Gillet reports having seen Joyce absorbed in it at St. Gerand-le-Puy in 1939, in its first publication in the Italian review, *Prospettivi*. Nino Frank published the story of his collaboration with Joyce in 1967, and in 1973 a comprehensive essay by Jacqueline Risset gave the full publishing history with the text of the fragments (substantially as published by Settanni in 1955), and an analysis of the achievement. Mme. Risset displays brilliantly the Dantesque dimension of Joyce's translation. Joyce inserted into the translated passages many allusions to the *Divine Comedy*, some of which bore little if any relation to his published text. It seems that the occasion thus given him to write in Dante's language stimulated Joyce to make a strong statement of indebtedness in these few pages. Mme. Risset describes the effect as Joyce translating Joyce under the sign of Dante, "remaking in the Italian language the experience of Dante." Joyce, she says, "is the sole 'disciple' of Dante, in the sense that he is the only one who truly engages him [Dante] at the level of the act of writing."

The modes of the Italian version are the same as those of the published book. Joyce creates portmanteau words: one of the most striking is the successful addition of one more river to his river chapter by his use of the word *mosa* in "Come disse El Negro quando vide che mosa la Plata gli fe." ("As El Negro winced when he wonced in La Plate" *FW* 198:13; Settanni 38.) The word *mosa* here combines *muovere* (move) with *muso* (grimace), and *Mossa* is the Italian designation for the river Meuse. Joyce also "creates" a new word by altering a single letter: thus 'panitostati' (toast) becomes 'panicostati' (*FW* 199:26; Settanni 39). He includes private jokes, "E barone Collesse" reminding the reader that Joyce used the pseudonym, "Monico Colesser" and rhymed "Herr Collessor" with "Professor" as a teaching device in the Berlitz School in Trieste. Joyce keeps the effect of lively untutored diction which is always characteristic of the speaker in *Finnegans Wake*, and particularly so in this chapter of the washerwomen, by grammatical distortions and errors in syntax, by slang, and by the occasional Neapolitan spelling and Triestine dialect word. He also makes complex literary allusions: from "the gran Phenician rover" (*FW* 197:31), he produces "il gran fenicio lope de mara," an echo of Lope de Vega (1562-1635) who was sometimes called the great Phoenix.

As the Italian translation in general mirrors Joyce's methods of constructing *Finnegans Wake*, so also does it reflect accurately his use of Dante both in the *Wake* and elsewhere. Joyce puts direct quotations from Dante, only slightly altered, into these pages. From *Inferno* 5 he takes "e ciò sa il suo [*sic*] dottore" ("and that's what his doctor knows" *Inf.* 5:123; Settanni 36). Dante's magic formula, "ciò che si vuole, e più non dimandare," with which Virgil gets the travelers safely past the guardians of hell, emerges in Joyce's translation as "ciò che si suole a non dimandare," from Dante's "Thus it is willed: and ask no more" (*FW* 200:23; *Inf.* 3:96; 5:24; Settanni 41). Joyce renders his original line, "And what was the wyerye rima she made!" as "Ma come suona la torza rima" (*FW* 200:33; Settanni 41). Dante's angelic messenger of Purgatory 2, "Da poppa stava il celestial nocchiero," becomes "Ma dov'era colui, l'alto nocchier?" (*FW* 197:33; *Purg.* 2:43; Settanni 37).

One of Joyce's favorite lines, the "salt bread" of Cacciaguida's prophecy in *Paradiso* 17, is probably present as "focaccia," a word for hard breakfast bread, which Joyce put into the portmanteau word *fuocacciarore* as a combination of bread, fire, and cheese or cheesemaker. As a more subtle configuration, Joyce suggests a Dantesque world by the line, "Diresti che i suoi fur per paradefungere, in tal sogno dormiva trapassecolato" ("with such a dream did he sleep over the centuries"), especially by the conflation of enjoyment and Paradise in *paradefungere*. And finally, the addition of one conspicuously Dantesque word (la maschia) to a distorted version of the phrase, "Was Paris worth a Mass," provides an echo of Dante's City of Dis in *Inferno* 8:70, where the travelers see in the distance the "mosques," "le sue meschite," of hell itself. The image thus called forth, of a looming ecclesiastical structure, in the context suggests the dome of St. Peter's in Rome (*FW* 199:8, Settanni 39; *FW* 199:9, Settanni 39; *FW* 198:5, *Par.* 17:59, Settanni 37).

Joyce also wished to represent language in its relationship to varying human situations and changing environments—its capacity for change—as an essential element in his universal history. Here again he comes close to Dante, who in *Inferno* 31 gives us the unintelligible language of Nimrod and his fellow Titans, and in *Paradiso* 26 explains through the voice of Adam how the diversity of human languages came about. When we find a fragment, Joyce's book tells us, "even a written on with dried ink scrap of paper," the mere fact of its survival is so remarkable an event that we should "cling to it as with drowning hands" (*FW* 118-119:03). *Finnegans Wake* echoes the lines from *Paradiso* 26, "The tongue which I [Adam] spoke was all extinct before the people of Nimrod [i.e., those who built the Tower of Babel] attempted their unaccomplishable work; for never was any product of reason durable forever, because of human liking, which alters, following the heavens" (*Par.* 26:124-126; trans. Singleton). Joyce's chapter says: "Soferim Bebel . . . every person, place and thing in the chaosmos of Alle . . . was moving and changing every part of the time" (*FW* 118:18-21).

Dante's entire poem records his belief that, despite time and change, one voice speaks to another across the gulf of centuries, as Virgil's voice is heard in Dante's lines and as Virgil's poem echoes Ovid. The poetics of the work are its imperishable vehicle. Joyce gives a comic turn to a serious idea, describing the almost undecipherable "letter" dug up from a midden of garbage by a domestic hen. Yet Joyce's "letter" is not far from Augustine's Word. In every verbal artifact can be found the mark of its maker, "whether it be thumbprint, mademark or just a poor trait of the artless" (*FW* 114.32).

Dante in *Paradiso* 26 gives an unobtrusive demonstration of the process of linguistic change by choosing for Adam's speech a word of Dante's own coinage developed from the Provençal—a word, moreover, which is given to Arnaut Daniel in the concluding lines of *Purgatorio* 26. The rhyme word "v'abella," which closes Adam's terzina, and brings Dante's thought to a strong conclusion (as so often with the closing words of a terzina), is a word unknown in any Italian dialect, Thomas M. Greene tells us, having evidently been taken over from the Provençal by Dante. The use of a different tongue by Dante's poetic ancestors is linked rhetorically to Adam's account of the development of language. Professor Greene adds, "There may also be a punning secondary meaning in Adam's discourse, to become or to appear beautiful."[46] Joyce was sensitive to the punning elements in the *Divine Comedy*, and he may have recognized the etymological linkage of the two words, "m'abellis" (trans. "adorn myself") in *Purgatorio* 26:140 and "v'abella" (trans. "please yourself") in *Paradiso* 26:132, for his edition of the *Commedia* carries a footnote calling attention to the identity of meaning in the two words.

The title of Beckett's essay, which was inspired and assisted by Joyce, combined Dante's name with Vico's and is an additional indication that Joyce had marked for his own use Dante's poetic treatment of the origins of language. The rhetorical unit, migrating across centuries and across cultural barriers, is the vehicle of every kind of utterance. Not only literary language but every level of speech and address survives somewhere, making up the great amorphous mass of linguistic utterance from which, moment by moment and day by day, meanings are extracted. Ideas survive, despite the randomness of human speech, because of verbal art. An idea begins its existence when it has been given a shape. Through the study of language, as Vico knew, we recover a past reality; Vico came to his understanding of language through Dante, and Joyce built *Finnegans Wake* on their combined insights.

"The word is an historical artifact," Greene writes, "which comes into being, endures, and changes, turns back upon itself, uses and repudiates its past in ways that affect any utterance of any text, however cut off ostensibly from temporal process."[47] In *Finnegans Wake* Joyce set out to represent fictionally, but systematically, the conception we know as linguistic survival. His strategic tool is etymology; his protagonist is the book itself, and he embodies in the fiction a voice for the book as it is being written.

In the last pages of *Finnegans Wake* the falling leaves of Anna Livia's final soliloquy are the words of the great book pictured in the closing lines of Dante's poem, "the scattered leaves of the universe, bound with love in one volume." Professor Greene has displayed the connection of Dante's figure with an earlier canto, *Paradiso* 26, where (in the dialogue with Adam) Dante invokes the highest supernatural authority for reflections, which are of course Dante's own, on that fundamental human phenomenon, language. "That man should speak is nature's doing, but whether thus or thus, nature then leaves you to follow your own pleasure" (*Par.* 26:130). Joyce's close study of Dante's poetic praxis fixed on the figure of the falling leaf: "the usage [i.e., the babel of linguistic variety] of mortals is as a leaf on a branch, which goes away and another comes" (*Par.* 26:136-138). An early chapter of *Finnegans Wake* contains the conception expressed in Adam's statement to Dante: ideas perish with the disappearance of the language in which they have been expressed.

Dante is present in *Finnegans Wake* by name, by paraphrased quotation, and by the implications of the text. Characteristically, the Dante allusions are fragmentary, disguised, and mixed with allusions to other authors and other works; even final attribution may sometimes seem ambiguous. A recognizable allusion taken out of context may lose its aura and emerge in Joyce's dream language sounding mechanical and laboured—an effect that is familiar to anyone who has tried to recapture a dream faithfully but without artificial expression. Joyce was operating, as he said, "outside of discourse." He told Jan Parandowski, "I took literally Gautier's dictum, 'The inexpressible does not exist.' With this hash of sounds I am building the great myth of everyday life."[48] Parandowski, a novelist, met Joyce in Paris in 1937 while he was working on *Finnegans Wake*. When Joyce learned of Parandowski's love of Homer he gave the Polish novelist an account of the writing of *Ulysses* that also applies to *Finnegans Wake* as a description of Joyce at work, in one of the most penetrating and comprehensive reminiscences that have come down to us.

> Ah, how wonderful that was to get up early in the morning . . . and enter the misty regions of my emerging epic, as Dante once entered his selva oscura selva selvaggia. Words crackled in my head and a multitude of images crowded around, like those shades at the entrance to the Underworld when Ulysses stood there awaiting the spirit of Tiresias. I wrote the greater part of the book during the war. There was fighting on all fronts, empires fell, kings went into exile, the old order was collapsing with a crash; and I had, as I sat down to work, the conviction that in the midst of all these ruins I was building something for the most distant future. (trans. Willard Potts)

James Atherton noticed a concentration of Dante allusions in the "Night Lessons" chapter (Book II.ii, pp. 260-308), the tenth (and central) section.[49] Cast in the form of a running commentary on book-learning, represented by children studying lessons, this chapter suggests a compendium of knowledge and summons up the ghosts of all mankind's written texts. Within it, and dominating the last third, is a geometry problem complete with a diagram of two intersecting circles, in which two triangles have been inscribed. Joyce told Adolph Hoffmeister, "Number is an enigma that God deciphers."[50]

> I have discovered the importance of numbers in life and history. Dante was obsessed by the number three. He divided his poem into three parts, each with thirty-three cantos, written in terza rima. And why always the arrangement of four—four legs of a table, four legs of a horse, four seasons of the year, four provinces of Ireland. . . . The significance of the same number varies, depending on where it occurs and what it refers to.

Dante allusions in the geometry lesson point to circular patterns that connect Dante's *Paradiso* with the tenth chapter specifically, and also with the book's larger design.[51]

Joyce described this centrally placed chapter in simplistic terms. But we now know that it received a disproportionate share of authorial effort and time, "composed backward over a period of approximately six years" according to David Hayman. Joyce wrote to Frank Budgen describing his construction: "The technique here is a reproduction of a schoolboy's (and schoolgirl's) old classbook complete with marginalia by the twins, who change sides at half time, footnotes by the girl (who doesn't), a Euclid diagram, funny drawings, etc. It was like that in Ur of the Chaldees too, I daresay" (*Letters* I: 405-406). Hayman, who edited the voluminous manuscripts of this section, interprets the author's remarks more broadly: "This is by design a scrapbook unit dealing with aspects of the learning or maturation process of the youthful male and female psyches, set against the background of an ominous mature world" (*Archive* 52:vii).

Artistic invention constructs, within the pattern thus described, a surface text with an encyclopedic range of reference. A massive structure of literary allusions conjures up those compelling intellects who have set down in words some great vision of history and human destiny. The geometry problem closes the chapter, and the dominant voices at that point are quite clearly those of writers whose work is remembered for the effort to penetrate into the ultimate mystery of being: Plato, Euclid, Dante, Blake, and an Irishman, Yeats. These come to stand for the greatest effort of mind and imagination.

Meanwhile the comments that Joyce described as "marginalia by the twins" provide a running comment on the text. Right and left margins are distinct voices, identified typographically and strikingly different in tone. The copious footnotes are a third voice; while left and right margins dispute and restate each other, the footnotes argue discursively with the author's text. In combination, these three give a Talmudic appearance to the chapter, as of a text endlessly and exhaustively glossed. The three voices are provocative, pedantic, disrespectful; the vision is thus mocked, in the chapter, but not by Joyce. The mockery represents other minds and other voices within the author's larger construction.

The marginal comments and footnotes were not present in the first printing of the chapter, which was in *transition* Number 11, February 1928; they first appeared in the 1935 printing of two short sections from the beginning and the end of the chapter. After at least five laboriously composed drafts had been written and re-worked, Joyce found his design, and produced in 1935 the fragment *Storiella As She Is Syung*, which quickly became the pattern for the full chapter. At an intermediate stage of composition, in 1929, Joyce added the phrase, "a daintical pair of accomplasses," to register the presence of Dante in the section of the geometry problem.

Other writers have used geometry as the poetic expression of an ultimate vision. To do so was not Dante's invention, and indeed the symbolic use of circle and triangle is a worldwide phenomenon far older than Christianity. Dante transforms these symbols into a passionate, poetic apotheosis (*Par.* 33:133-135). In *Paradiso* 33 the poet describes his vision as three spinning "giri"—circlings, rather than circles.[52] The canto opens with St. Bernard's prayer to Mary, "Virgin mother, daughter of thy Son." (Joyce uses this line in *Ulysses*: he gives it to Stephen Dedalus as a direct quotation.) Dante's image of the geometer who sets himself to square the circle, and cannot find the principle he needs, becomes in this canto a statement of the inability of man to express deity in terms of humanity. It is the Trinity, a representation of the mystery of pure intellect, that appears to Dante as three circling "giri," reflected one by the other, with the third seeming to be a fire "breathed equally from the one and the other."

> Ne la profonda e chiara sussistenza
> de l'alto lume parvermi tre giri
> di tre colori e d'una contenenza;

> In the deep subsistence of
> the lofty Light, three whirling gyres appeared
> having three colors and one measurement;
>
> (*Par.* 33:115-117)

The circling is seen as reflecting light, mirrored. This culminating vision of the poem is given to Dante after St. Bernard, at the opening of Canto 33, prays to the Blessed Virgin that the supreme vision may be granted:

> Qui se' a noi meridiana face
> di caritate, e giuso, intra' mortali,
> se' di speranza fontana vivace.

> For us here thou art as the meridian torch
> of love, and for the mortals down below
> Thou art the living fountain of their hope.   (*Par.* 33:10-12)

Bernard prays for divine grace for Dante, "Who hath seen one after one / The spirit lives, from out the deepest pit / Of all the universe upwards to here." ("Or questi, che da l'infima lacuna / de l'universo infin qui ha vedute / le vita spiritali ad una ad una." *Par.* 33:22-24). The poetry, as Singleton comments, expresses an action, the completion of a circle.[53] This dextrous achievement in Dante's style is responsible in part for the circularity in form that characterizes *Finnegans Wake*, a book whose opening sentence picks up from the last words of the last page, and that also carries internal hints of its own circularity.

Dante conveys poetically the nostalgic recording of a memory—all that is retained of his vision of having penetrated to the central truth of Creation, and having known as one whole the substance and accidents of all the universe. In *Finnegans Wake*, Dante's lines make a new appearance; his recollection of the experience, "almost wholly fails my vision, while yet the sweetness born thereof is in my heart distilled," becomes Joyce's line, "I can almost feed their sweetness at my lisplips" (*FW* 276:n. 6). In the final pages of *Finnegans Wake* Joyce puts a Dantean allusion in the last thoughts of Anna Livia, the river, as she meets the sea and dies, to be reborn. "Avelaval. My leaves have drifted from me. All. But one clings still. I'll bear it on me. To remind me of. Lff!" These fragmentary words remind the reader of a terzina from the *Paradiso* that Joyce has also placed in the tenth chapter: "To book alone belongs the lobe [i.e., love]," an echo of one of Dante's famous images: "I saw ingathered, bound by love in one volume, the scattered leaves of all the universe" (*FW* 305:31, 628:6-7; *Par.* 33:57-66; 85-87).

Dante's line, "di speranza fontana vivace," "living fountain of hope," is reproduced in *Finnegans Wake* as a dual occurrence of the Italian word *speranza*. First it appears in the eighth chapter, the "river chapter," which is Anna Livia's domain; here it is one item in a long list of her gifts to her children. Then it is used again in the tenth chapter as a footnote in the geometry section: "the chape of Doña Speranza of the Nacion." (Doña Speranza was a pseudonym of Lady Wilde, who was the mother of Oscar Wilde, and wrote patriotic verse for *The Nation* in the 1840's.) Anna Livia, as the mother of the twins, is the focus of attention in the geometry problem. Her sign is the triangle, the river's delta. The geometric figure of the chapter shows two triangles drawn inside two intersecting circles, the triangles labeled ALP in Roman and in Greek letters. A voice in the text says, "Now . . . I'll make you to see figuratleavely the whome of your eternal geomater." (In the early drafts this line read, "Now I'll show you whom your geometer is"; in revision, "geometer" became feminine, and "whom" was changed to "whome.") Adaline Glasheen's *Third Census* picks up the etymology of "geomater" to remark on the suggestion of Earth-Mother;[54] the word is also an equivalent of Dante's "geomètra."

> Qual è 'l geomètra che tutto s'affige
>   per misurar lo cerchio . . .
>
>   .   .   .   .   .   .
>
> as the geometer who sets himself
> to measure the circle . . .   (*Par.* 33:133-134)

The geometer is measuring the circle in the attempt, never yet successful, to square it. In *Finnegans Wake*, while the geometric figure is explained in the text, a marginal comment says, "All Square." Circle and square have been combined in all ages by philosophers, mathematicians and poets. Donne, finding geometry acceptable in poetry, wrote of "Round earth's imagined corners." In the *Divine Comedy*, the wheel is Dante's primary image of universal order in action.

Joyce's perception of Dante's wheel (a conception not exclusively Dante's, but perhaps most finely his) was set down on paper with apparent casualness, in an Easter postcard to Harriet Shaw Weaver.

> Dear Miss Weaver: I wish you a pleasant Easter up in the north. I finished my revision and have passed 24 hours prostrate more than the priests on Good Friday. I think I have done what I wanted to. I am glad you liked my punctuality as an engine driver. I have taken this up because I am really one of the greatest engineers, if not the greatest, in the world besides being a musicmaker, philosophist and heaps of things. All the engines I know are wrong. Simplicity. I am making an engine with only one wheel. No spokes of course. The wheel is a perfect square. You see what I am driving at, don't you? I am awfully solemn about it, mind you, so you must not think it is a silly story about the mooks and the grapes. No, it's a wheel, I tell the world. *And* it's all square. (*Selected Letters* 321; 16 April 1927)

Joyce's geometry problem becomes grotesque when Kev and Dolph, the twins of the Night Lessons chapter, seek the mystery of creation by lifting the skirt of Anna Livia to see her "muddy old triagonal delta," the first of all "usquiluteral threeingles." [There is an echo here also of Stephen's rambling remarks in Eumaeus: "Dante and the isosceles triangle, Miss Portinari, he fell in love with . . ." (*U* 621:31).] The attachment of such associations to Dante's final vision cannot be left unremarked. In part, the interweaving of such incongruous elements, such a ludicrous distortion, can be traced to the free-association configuration of the dream, and in part it is a reminder that Dante's own sublimity includes and poetically uses grotesque components. Joyce called McGreevy's attention to the monogram page in the Book of Kells on which the detail of the illumination shows two rats tearing the Host from each other with their teeth. Like the gargoyles on Notre Dame, such unnerving images have been comfortably absorbed into the view we now take of medieval Catholicism. For Joyce, the medieval images were living presences, concrete evidence of the symbolic imagination at work. His modern vision found in Dante the full range of the medieval imagination, from the most spiritual to the most grotesque, and embodied this in *Finnegans Wake*. He used a deliberate disharmony to rewrite Dante's vision of harmony, exploiting in a new and original way "the unresolved clash of incompatibles." An important dimension of *Finnegans Wake* is its consistent heterogeneity; its novelty lies in the mixture Joyce produces of uncanny and comic effects in which the comedy depends on a mundane context and the resonances of a Dublinesque diction, while the uncanny sensations become "an uneasy revisiting of the subconscious."[55] The images of the *Divine Comedy* identified an individual, Dante, for Joyce. The geometry lesson of the *Wake*'s tenth chapter is the voice of the imagination that saw Vico's "barbarous sublimity" in the *Divine Comedy*, and that transformed Dante's lines as they can be seen in *Finnegans Wake*. Joyce explained to Adolph Hoffmeister his belief that anyone could read the book and could understand it if he were only willing to return to the text again and again. He said that the book has "a significance completely above reality; transcending humans, things, senses, and entering the realm of complete abstraction."[56]

*

Joyce's allusions to the *Divine Comedy* and the *Vita Nuova* cover the whole range of those works, and also cover the whole range of literary analogy. They appear as parallels of situation, structure, and incident; as verbal mannerisms and stylistic artifice; as personification, as direct quotation and as tags of quotation. The allusions appear in all areas of Joyce's work, in his poems and his play as well as his fiction. Let us look briefly at Joyce's view of Dante's art.

Joyce was a careful reader, staying always close to Dante's text. His allusions open the poem to new understandings, partly by encouraging his readers to make their own close reading of the passage he has used. He gives minute attention to details of image construction. Not only does he note the shape of the configuration and the verbal details that give it life; he also penetrates to its essential quality, identifying aesthetic decisions that mark Dante's placement of a verbal construction with the lineaments we find. Dante's original conceptions survive their transformation, though sometimes showing the strain of a wild ride with Joyce's imagination, and usually they are given a modernist revision that results in some incongruous juxtaposition and otherwise alters the context. The parallels reveal to the reader the dynamic quality of Dante's cantos and convey an increased sense of Dante's dramatic and compositional skills. The contrasts make an unforgettable impression—Dante's image will be remembered longer and more forcefully for its striking appearance in Joyce's mimetic version.

Joyce appreciated Dante's art in all its aspects. His humor presents Dante's characters and scenes with a robust vitality, and many of his incongruous transformations have the value of presenting Dante's realism as an important element of the poem's surface that is easily overlooked. His art is less visual than Dante's, possibly because of his lifelong eye trouble, yet the Dantesque patterns have the realism of the original in their instinct for that telling detail that infuses life into scene and personality. Incongruity often brings forward the most significant details, and even provides a sharper focus for a re-reading of the original.

Sometimes such fantastic juxtapositions identify in the original the crucial element of comparison. Joyce's patterns reflect the presence of humor in the *Divine Comedy*; this is especially characteristic of the *Inferno* and is an element also in the *Paradiso*, although surprisingly faint or scant in the *Purgatorio*. Dante's Cacciaguida is most authentically human when he is allowed to say of Dante's enemies, "If it (Dante's account of their wrongdoing) itches, let them scratch" (*Par.* 17:127-129). Joyce identifies an element of unconscious humor when he exploits the description of Cacciaguida's descent from the Cross of Mars, "e pare stella che tramuti loco," the effect of a falling star coasting down the radial line of the figure in the heavens in order to come down to Dante's level. The black humor of Dante's devils was turned to account by Joyce in several places, and the last line of *Inferno* 21 appears at least twice in his work.

Sometimes the Dantesque allusions are a form of ironic moralising, and occasionally they suggest that the literal level of Dante's text contrasts and even conflicts at times with the religious assumptions that underlie the *Commedia*. Dante's inversions are always striking, and Joyce's awareness of this was heightened by his own background of Catholic dogma and traditional practice. The emotional force of the final hallucination in the Circe episode of *Ulysses* is increased by the line that parodies Dante's similar parody, changing one word in the opening of the hymn sung at Vespers in Holy Week and making this the first line of the final canto of the Inferno. Dante's "Vexilla Regis prodeunt *inferni*" becomes Joyce's "Introibo ad altare *diaboli*," unquestionably as a reminder that Dante's inversions sometimes have the tone of blasphemy. Such inversions usually form the most striking and memorable aspect of the larger pattern for which, unmistakably, they were invented. The simoniacal popes upside down in fiery pits in the *Inferno* are remembered in the *Paradiso*, when St. Peter declares his chair on earth vacant while a chair is reserved in Heaven for the still-living emperor. A like effect is seen in the presence of the tenth canto of the *Paradiso*, beside St. Thomas Aquinas, of the man whose doctrines he expressly and extensively refuted, Siger of Brabant (who is present in *Finnegans Wake*: "And eachway bothwise glory signs. What if she love Sieger less though she leave Ruhm moan?" *FW* 281:23). Dante ran great risks in his challenges to the contemporary Papacy; I have seen in one fifteenth-century Spanish copy of the *Divine Comedy* a single line completely burned out of the text by the Inquisition. I believe that Joyce was particularly attracted by equivocal and ambivalent areas of the poem.

Joyce's most significant critical insights identify the connections, often minute and always subtle, that tie Dante's figures into the poem's larger structures. His reading of the *Divine Comedy* was literary and secular, based on habits of mind and artistic sympathies (and repeated re-readings of the poem) that gave him a fellow-craftsman's understanding of the working operations of Dante's allegorical and historical mode. Dante's own allusions furnished a demonstration and a rich store of examples to be drawn upon and imitated. Joyce of course knew the *Aeneid* in Latin and must have read it, as well as the *Divine Comedy*, with the critic's eye. Thus we see him deliberately comparing the two poems in order better to understand Dante's use of Virgil.

Joyce had a particular interest in Dante's portrait of the poet. Virgil's fictional personality in the *Divine Comedy* is reproduced in the subtle touches that make Leopold Bloom a Virgil figure, thus calling attention to the qualities of the original and fixing the impression made by Dante's beloved pagan guide. Professor Bergin and others have commented that Dante also created a figure of "Dante" within the poem, not an empirical identification (although often so interpreted), but a poetic voice in the first person. As J. E. Shaw and Charles Singleton have notably shown, there are at least three and perhaps four distinguishable voices; not just one "Dante" in the *Vita Nuova* and the *Commedia*, but the pilgrim, the poet, and other identities as well.[57] Joyce's compositional mode shows his interest in this construction: he too appears in his own fiction, speaking similarly with more than one voice, and from time to time named or described or otherwise identified. As Singleton says of Dante's poet and speaker, the multiple voices organically blend in one single fiction: "To follow the poem in its own terms is to follow these voices into and through that very welding illusion."[58]

There are also negative aspects of Joyce's Dantesque patterns.

Joyce's runaway imagination encourages over-expansion of Dante's figures: he seizes on a crucial element of visual detail or humor to make his point, but sometimes runs it into the ground. When his imitative passages become grotesque he may be accused of failures in taste and lack of discriminating sensitivity. But the greatest artists are those who draw from life, as Dante drew Cacciaguida, and these artists are not over-concerned with taste. Dante himself was often enough (particularly in the seventeenth century) charged with being unpoetic—crude, morbid, even barbaric. Joyce answered such charges against his own work by saying, "If *Ulysses* isn't fit to read, then life isn't fit to live."[59]

Dante's naturalistic effects come into Joyce's fiction sometimes as a flat-toned reproduction that faithfully echoes the original in a new idiom, but rides roughshod over any delicacies of diction that may be in the way. Joyce runs the risk of reducing the sublime to the merely facetious, and at the least he loses some of the pathos or solemnity of the original without making his own purpose clear. Thus in *Finnegans Wake* he brings Francesca's story down to the level of a teacher seducing his pupil. "Still he'd be a good tutor two in his big armchair lerningstoel and she be waxen in his hands. Turning up and fingering over the most dantellising peaches in the lingerous longerous book of the dark. Look at this passage about Galilleotto! I know it is difficult but when your goche I go dead" (*FW* 251:26). When he "shifts the register of the original," as Lowry Nelson aptly describes the process, Joyce is not always sensitive to the danger of creating "a gross discrepancy between the borrowed theme and the play of variation."[60] Another risk is the possibility of *over-subtilizing* when his allusion is not an obvious parody, or when he creates a fiction that has Dantesque overtones yet is not overtly or consistently ironical.

Joyce's scatalogical proclivities are a dangerous area of his Dantesque allusions, as they are with his use of Swift and other writers. This aspect is more prominent in *Finnegans Wake* than elsewhere for the sound artistic reason that most people do have just such an undercurrent of distracting random thoughts, which Joyce wished to reproduce. But in the Dantesque allusions the distracting effect may take over, as Joyce's demands on the reader become too great. When he embodies the closing effects of the *Paradiso* in what Kenner rightly calls a "lewd grammatical exegesis," one may wish that Joyce had exercised less (Kenner's phrase again) indiscriminate energy.[61] Yet one cannot quarrel with the passage on grounds of misinterpreting the original. As we come to understand his books we see that Joyce took many risks, as Dante also did, both of them with a willingness that will be acknowledged with gratitude by generations of their readers.

The Dantesque patterns, whether more successful or less, always reveal the uniqueness of Joyce's imaginative vision. They are an important dimension of the originality of his work, showing his unrivaled capacity for finding new and unsuspected possibilities in old themes. Joyce called Dante "the first poet of the Europeans," and said that in him "a human personality had been found united with an artistic manner which was itself almost a natural phenomenon" (*SH* 41:16). The same could be said of Joyce himself. His transformations of Dante reveal the interaction of his personality with his art.

The Dantean allusions, taken as a statement of Joyce's ideas about Dante, place Joyce in the critical tradition begun by Benvenuto da Imola, who was the first writer to produce a comprehensive commentary on the *Divine Comedy*, in the generation of Boccaccio (who was Benvenuto's friend) and Petrarch. Benvenuto's lectures at Bologna made the *Divine Comedy* at this early date, as Louis La Favia says, "for the first time a standard work in the repertoire of university studies, on a par with any of the great classic authors of antiquity."[62] Benvenuto is the founder of the tradition that reads the *Divine Comedy* as *literary* allegory; this critical approach focuses on the "many passages in the poem clearly intended to tell us something about Dante the artist."[63] Attention may center on Dante's view of his craft, or it may extend to the widest range of aesthetic mode and purpose in the poem. There is something of it in almost every serious study that has been made of the poem, as Louis Rossi has abundantly demonstrated.

Benvenuto deals with every canto, line by line. To him we owe a wealth of documentation of doctrinal meanings and local references in the *Commedia*. His talent and his interests produced a critical reading completely different from the symbolical and didactic commentary of his seven predecessors in the fourteenth century. Benvenuto explicated everything in the *Divine Comedy* in terms of his own personal experience, giving endless examples and illustrations in a realistic running commentary that often becomes vulgar or merely anecdotal, taking the mysticism out of the original, and rejecting or ignoring the doctrinal framework to emphasize the gross naturalism. This, however, is to state all his faults at once. Louis Rossi, in his fine study of the Benvenuto *Commentary*, more justly characterizes it as a creative work, a parallel work that is a consciously creative effort, in which the commentator identifies himself with the poet in his attitude toward his own creation.[64]

In rejecting the narrowly allegorical interpretations of his predecessors, Rossi says, Benvenuto brought the *Divine Comedy* all the way into the Renaissance; he insists on understanding Dante's characters historically. Benvenuto emphasizes Dante's own role in the figure of the poet, in the poem; he makes the reader see this as a struggle, even to the point of over-emphasis. Rossi's account shows that Benvenuto interprets so many passages as Dante's account of difficulties in writing the poem that he projects his own views into the text, and many times reads into it unwarranted references to Dante's personality or his experience. But to all this, and transcending it, we owe the critical tradition of interpreting the *Commedia* as literary allegory, finding in the work what Rossi calls a myth of the poet. Momigliano, who has the credit for rediscovering Benvenuto in our own day, gives a favorable appraisal of his aesthetic perceptions and calls him not only the clearest and most attentive commentator but also a reader who illuminates poetically Dante's art. Later and less comprehensive commentaries that follow Benvenuto's fundamental insight are valuable additions to our understanding of Dante.[65]

Joyce's critical perceptions of Dante are his own; they did not come to him by way of the Benvenuto commentary, directly or indirectly. The vast commentary of Lord Vernon, which its subtitle describes as "Based on the Commentary of Benvenuto da Imola," is the principal source of Benvenuto's work in English. A new edition came out in 1905, but it is most unlikely that Joyce saw this work, or that he would have read it had he been aware of it. Joyce's own copy of the *Divine Comedy* is an edition prepared before the Benvenuto commentary received its first full editing in 1871; the footnotes in Joyce's edition do include contributions taken from Benvenuto, but only from an older and quite fragmentary edition.

Far more likely is the circumstance that Joyce's temperament and artistic proclivities directed him independently toward interpretations that coincide with the Benvenuto critical tradition. In Joyce's Trieste notebook, which contains notes made for *A Portrait of the Artist* between 1907 and 1909, there is this fragmentary entry under the heading. "Cavalcanti (Guido):"[66]

His father Cavalcante Cavalcanti asks Dante where he is (*Inf.* X). Dante hesitates before he replies.

This was something Joyce noticed without requiring anyone's assistance; it is the kind of naturalistic detail that appealed to him. It is also, however, precisely the *kind* of annotation that has come down to us from Benvenuto.

However, in his account of Stephen's musings about Dante in the

Aeolus chapter of *Ulysses*, Joyce gives Stephen a critical formulation which, as Tibor Wlassics has discovered, could very well have come directly from Benvenuto. Under the heading of "Rhymes and Reasons," the reader observes Stephen thinking of Dante's terza rima:

> He saw them three by three, approaching girls, in green, in rose, in russet, entwining . . . (*U* 138:4)[67]

Professor Wlassics points out that one of Benvenuto's many anecdotes concerns Dante's rhymes presented as "so many lovely maidens," and furthermore that this story was retold by Paget Toynbee in his little book on the life of Dante. Here is the story in Toynbee's translation.[68]

> Another commentator, Benvenuto da Imola, in connection with Dante's extraordinary facility in the matter of rimes, repeats a quaint conceit, which had been imagined, he says, by an ardent admirer of the poet: "When Dante first set about the composition of his poem, all the rimes in the Italian language presented themselves before him in the guise of so many lovely maidens, and each in turn humbly petitioned to be granted admittance into this great work of his genius. In answer to their prayers, Dante called first one and then another, and assigned to each its appropriate place in the poem; so that, when at last the work was complete, it was found that not a single one had been left out."

It may indeed be the case that Joyce saw this little book of Toynbee's, for it was acquired by the National Library in Dublin soon after publication. Or Joyce might have read it in Trieste or Zurich, or conceivably in Paris in 1902. But Joyce's allusion is a specific and directly relevant image of the terza rima, and it probably came directly from his own imagination's moving on the same lines as Benvenuto's, some five centuries later.

Neither Dante nor Joyce are political philosophers as that phrase would be applied to St. Augustine, or to Hobbes, Locke, Rousseau or Machiavelli. But the impact of the *Divine Comedy* and of *Ulysses* owes its force in part to aspects in which Dante and Joyce deal with the questions that a political philosopher must consider. They both focus on society, presenting a broad or narrow view of the life of man under contemporary political and social institutions. Both have placed their work deliberately in a philosophical and literary tradition. Each of them both sums up his age and takes the reader beyond it. Each mounted an attack which, as we now see, was successful partly because of its passionate sincerity and its technical competence, partly because of its solid intellectual underpinning. Each brought to his work an artistic impulse new in spiritual direction as well as in its ordering of language.

Dante's *Divine Comedy* makes his readers aware simultaneously of an extraordinary display of poetic force and a loosely associated disclosure of his own personal experience. It was this mode of imaginative expression, subtle, complex and authoritative, that chiefly interested Joyce. When Joyce set out, as he says in *Stephen Hero*, to portray "the poet in action," Dante became his model. "The Divine Comedy dramatizes in a fundamental way the activity of interpretation; it recounts the efforts of the poet-exegete to read the book of the world."[69] For Dante, history was God's book; for Joyce, the world was "signatures of all things I am here to read" (*U* 38:2). Giuseppe Mazzotta argues persuasively that the activity of interpretive reading is a central element in the design of the poem, and that in the working out of his design Dante "abolishes the boundaries between theology and poetry." Six centuries after Dante, Joyce would portray his Dantean artist as saying, "History is a nightmare from which I am trying to awake" (*U* 35:19).

Joyce, who called his philosophical principles "applied Aquinas," traversed the same path that Dante had followed. The orthodoxy of Joyce's Catholic educational experience, in the Dublin of 1900, was a closed world. It was, intellectually, as though there had been no Reformation. The weight of the social machinery was skilfully brought to bear to enforce conformity of thought. The *idea* of heresy flourished in Dublin as in Dante's Florence, under a subtle inquisitorial power.

For Joyce to assert in this context a conception of the artistic process as a "natural process" was, at least potentially, revolutionary. He claimed for the artistic process an autonomy comparable to the freedom implicitly demanded for "Lady Philosophy" by Dante's *Convivio*. To be sure, in Joyce's Dublin neither books nor men were burned. The reach of the Dublin ecclesiastical establishment was shorter than the power of the medieval Church over ideas in Dante's time. But the everyday influence of ecclesiastical control was probably not very different, so long as one chose, as Joyce did, to remain within its operational sphere. The fact that Joyce persisted in developing his ideas within the scholastic framework directly relates his achievement to that of Dante. The timeless quality of Joyce's later fiction derives in large part from the mature extension of his early secularism into a larger Dantean vision of society.

Joyce's achievement gave a fresh and luminous depth to our critical perception of the poetic structures in which imaginative genius manifests itself. The fiction of Dante's poem is that it is not fiction. Joyce's

Dublin and its citizens are not fictional but are, as Stephen Dedalus says, "life recreated out of life" (*P* 172:9), veritable creations of the artist. Not only Stephen Dedalus but all the characters who move through *Dubliners, A Portrait, Exiles,* and *Ulysses* can echo Stephen's words (in Proteus), "He willed me and now may not will me away or ever" (*U* 39:13). Not only the childish memories of *A Portrait,* or the drama of jealousy enacted by Leopold Bloom in *Ulysses* and by Richard Rowan in *Exiles,* but all the incidents of all Joyce's books are in some measure a reclaimed reality, events that Joyce has "drawn out of his own long pocket" (*U* 202:14). Dante's Cacciaguida and Virgil, as well as his Brunetto, came from his own mind and his own life, and were brought by his imagination into a new and more lasting life. Dante, so goes the tale, was looked upon by those who saw him in the streets as one who had literally come back from hell. Joyce, through all his travels, never left Dublin. His fictions never leave his own life, as he "bends upon these present things and so works upon them and fashions them that the quick intelligence may go beyond them to their meaning, which is still unuttered" (*CW* 74). From such "fictions," we as readers experience a special kind of reality. It is not a form of knowledge but rather a form of being, described by Coleridge as the reciprocal interaction of the artist's imagination and his world: "A repetition in the finite mind of the eternal act of creation." Joyce identified unerringly the inward truth of the "shaping imagination" when he wrote that, in Dante, "a human personality had been found united with an artistic manner which was itself almost a natural phenomenon" (*SH* 41:16). In writing this of Dante, Joyce was describing himself.

⤝ Appendix: Joyce's Allusions to Dante

IN this list of allusions, taken as a whole, the evidence of the manuscripts becomes an Ariadne's thread—a clue to the labyrinthine processes by which Joyce's reading of one author entered his art. Often the holograph entry provides vital confirmation of the Dantean source. In a single run of page proofs, for example, Joyce makes two additions that have a subterranean connection with each other: he makes his two chief characters in *Ulysses* resemble for an instant Dante as the lost exile of *The Divine Comedy*. The first allusion is sufficiently obvious: Stephen is made to say, "Now I eat his salt bread." But the second, Bloom's recollection of an obscure Irish popular song, is far from obvious: "O Please Mr Policeman I'm Lost in the Wood." The last five words seem to be an echo of Dante's statement in *Inferno* 1:3, "I found myself in a dark wood where the straight way was lost," but certainty comes only with the evidence of the page proofs that Joyce thought of the two additions at the same time. (See p. 188 above.)

In another allusion and in a different context, the manuscript evidence corroborates an intuitive hypothesis that the word "sheepfolds" in the sixteenth chapter of *Finnegans Wake* came from Joyce's reading of *Paradiso* 25:5, where Dante describes his native city as "fair sheepfold, where slept I as a lamb." The early draft shows Joyce's mind at work; he crosses out "what he holds in his hand" and substitutes "whose heel he sheepfolds in his wrought hand," thereby attaching Dante's distinctive word to the sleeping twin, Jerry, who will grow up to be Shem the Penman.

Taken chronologically, the list is massive testimony for the consistency of Joyce's interest in Dante, and the dating of the manuscripts shows Joyce's deliberate repetition of favorite lines as well as his revision of Dantesque themes and patterns between one work and the next. For example, as *Ulysses* neared completion in 1921, Joyce wrote for the Ithaca chapter the passage that describes "an inconstant series of varying degrees of light and shadow." *Ulysses* was published in

1922. In 1923 Joyce wrote the first fragmentary passages for a new work that later became *Finnegans Wake*. The early manuscript draft of one of these fragments shows Joyce making as an addition the Dantean allusion, "ninthly enthroned, in the concentric center," thus linking his two last works to Dante's great conception, in *Paradiso* 27 and 28, of a universe of nine revolving heavens moved by intellection and love (*FW* 606:3).

Joyce may construct his allusion either in the original Italian, or in a freely adapted English equivalent; he may use a striking single word or phrase, or a larger allusion or a Dantean context. I have therefore assembled the allusions list on a broad base and in a uniform format. For each allusion I give in the left-hand column the page and line of Joyce's text; in a second column the corresponding line of Dante's text; and in a third column the words of the texts themselves, first Joyce's and then Dante's in both Italian and English. The Italian text follows the modern Petrocchi edition, and the translation throughout is the prose translation by Charles Singleton.

In the left-hand column, under the page and line reference to Joyce's text, I have identified the manuscript evidence (when available) of the allusion's first appearance in Joyce's work. Citations of Joyce's works refer to the American standard editions as listed in the front of this volume; where a choice of editions was available I have used the edition that is the basis for the Concordance to that work. Citations to the manuscripts identify the volume and page of the facsimile edition of Joyce's manuscripts for the work in question. Not all of Joyce's manuscripts have survived, but a very large proportion of them is now available in *The James Joyce Archive*, issued in 63 volumes by Garland Publishing, Inc. For each allusion I have recorded the earliest manuscript evidence available, usually the first holograph entry. Where significant alteration of the allusion was made in various stages of revision, I have tried to identify both the earliest appearance and the stage at which the allusion took final form.

In the case of *Ulysses* a second major facsimile edition is necessarily involved. This is the autograph fair copy commonly known as the "Rosenbach Manuscript," which was already available in facsimile and therefore was not included in the Garland edition. For *Ulysses*, therefore, I have recorded the allusions that make a significant appearance in this manuscript, using the notation developed by the editor, Clive Driver.

An entry reading "*Arch.* 14:272" will direct the reader to Volume 14 of the *James Joyce Archive*, p. 272. (A short-title list of the volumes in the Garland *Archive* is given below.) An entry reading "*Ros. MS.* P688" will direct the reader to page 688 of the first Paris edition of *Ulysses* (reproduced as one of the three volumes of the Rosenbach facsimile edition, and used as the key to the manuscript itself), and also to the page of the manuscript of *Ulysses* carrying the identification "P688-689 L870-871 *VN* 737." An entry giving both *Ros. MS* and *Archive* reference numbers means that the allusion is present in the Rosenbach manuscript but received some alteration at another stage of composition.

Joyce's methods of composition, and the sequence of development of individual works, cannot be described here, but the subject is highly relevant to any account of his literary allusions. Each section of the Garland *Archive* carries an editor's preface summarizing the most recent conclusions about the composition and dating of each of Joyce's works: Michael Groden, general editor: associate editors, Hans Walter Gabler, David Hayman, A. Walton Litz, and Danis Rose. The Rosenbach facsimile gives a useful account of the composition of *Ulysses*, but later evidence has changed our knowledge of the dating and use of some sections of the Rosenbach manuscript. Interested readers should consult, for all works, the relevant sections of the definitive biography, *James Joyce*, by Richard Ellmann (Oxford University Press, 1959); for *Ulysses* and *Finnegans Wake*, A. Walton Litz, *The Art of James Joyce* (Oxford University Press, 1961); for *Ulysses*, Michael Groden's definitive work on the composition of the book, Ulysses *in Progress* (Princeton University Press, 1977); the two volumes by Phillip F. Herring, *Joyce's* Ulysses *Notesheets in the British Museum* (University Press of Virginia, 1972), and *Joyce's Notes and Early Drafts for* Ulysses: *Selections from the Buffalo Collection* (University Press of Virginia, 1977); and *James Joyce Quarterly*, Textual Studies Issue, vol. 12, nos. 1/2 (1974-75).

Many of the Dante allusions here presented have appeared in the broadly comprehensive allusions lists collected by James S. Atherton in *The Books at the Wake* (Viking Press, 1960); Weldon Thornton, *Allusions in Ulysses* (Simon and Schuster and University of North Carolina Press, 1961, 1973); Don Gifford, with the assistance of Robert Seidman, *Notes for Joyce* (E. P. Dutton and Co., 1967); Don Gifford with Robert J. Seidman, *An Annotation of James Joyce's Ulysses* (E. P. Dutton and Co., 1974); Adaline Glasheen, *Third Census of* Finnegans Wake (University of California Press, 1977), with previous editions in 1963 (*Second Census*) and 1956 (*A Census of* Finnegans Wake); Luigi Schenoni, "Amaro in *FW*," and "Further Notes on Amaro," *AWN* XI.4 (Aug. 1974), pp. 68-70 and *AWN* XIII.2 (April 1976), pp. 32-36; "Italian Words and References in *FW*.II.1," *AWN* XV.4 (August 1978), pp.

51-55; Rosa Maria Bosinelli, "The Relevance of Italian in *FW* with Reference to I.18," *AWN* XIII.2 (April 1976), pp. 19-32; Roland McHugh, *Annotations for* Finnegans Wake (Johns Hopkins Press, 1980); Richard Ellmann, *James Joyce, passim*; and in individual critical studies. I have tried to give credit for significant early identifications in the chapters above; for those I have missed, I regret the inadvertent omission.

The James Joyce Archive (New York: Garland Publishing): a short-title listing

Vol.
1. *Poems*
2. *Critical Writings*, Part I.
3. *Critical Writings*, Part II.
4. *Dubliners*: Drafts and MSS
5. *Dubliners*: Proofs, 1910 Ed.
6. *Dubliners*: Proofs, 1914 Ed.
7. *A Portrait*: Epiphanies, Notes, MSS, TS
8. *Stephen Hero*, MS
9. *A Portrait*: Part I, Dublin Holograph
10. *A Portrait*: Final Holograph MS, Part II.
11. *Exiles*

ULYSSES
12. *Ulysses*: Notes for the Book and MSS for Episodes 1-9
13. *Ulysses*: Drafts, MSS and TS for Episodes 10-13
14. *Ulysses*: Drafts, MSS and TS for Episodes 14-15, Part I.
15. *Ulysses*: MSS and TS for Episodes 15 (Part II) and 16
16. *Ulysses*: MSS and TS for Episodes 17 and 18

GALLEY PROOFS
17. *Ulysses*: Placards (galley proofs) for Episodes 1-6
18. *Ulysses*: Placards for Episodes 7-10
19. *Ulysses*: Placards, Episodes 11-14
20. *Ulysses*: Placards, Episodes 15-16
21. *Ulysses*: Placards, Episodes 17-18

PAGE PROOFS
22. *Ulysses*: Page proofs, Episodes 1-6
23. *Ulysses*: Page proofs, Episodes 7-9
24. *Ulysses*: Page proofs, Episodes 10-11
25. *Ulysses*: Page proofs, Episodes 12-14

26. *Ulysses*: Page proofs, Episode 15
27. *Ulysses*: Page proofs, Episodes 16-18

> *Archive* vols. 28-43, Finnegans Wake: *The Buffalo Notebooks*:
> not used for this Appendix

FINNEGANS WAKE, BOOK I

44. *Finnegans Wake*: Drafts, TS and Proofs, Book I, Chap. 1
45. *Finnegans Wake*: Drafts, TS, Proofs, Book I, Chaps. 2-3
46. *Finnegans Wake*: Drafts, TS, Proofs, Book I, Chaps. 4-5
47. *Finnegans Wake*: Drafts, TS, Proofs, Book I, Chaps. 6-7
48. *Finnegans Wake*: Drafts, TS, Proofs, Book I, Chap. 8
49. *Finnegans Wake*: Galley Proofs, Book I (Part 1)
50. *Finnegans Wake*: Galley Proofs, Book I (Part 2)

BOOK II

51. *Finnegans Wake*: Drafts, TS, Proofs, Book II, Chap. 1
52. *Finnegans Wake*: Drafts, TS, Proofs, Book II, Chap. 2, Part I.
53. *Finnegans Wake*: Drafts, TS, Proofs, Book II, Chap. 2, Part II.
54. *Finnegans Wake*: Drafts, TS, Proofs, Book II, Chap. 3, Part I.
55. *Finnegans Wake*: Drafts, TS, Proofs, Book II, Chap. 3, Part II.
56. *Finnegans Wake*: Drafts, TS, Proofs, Book II, Chap. 4

BOOK III

57. *Finnegans Wake*: Drafts, TS, Proofs, Book III, Chaps. 1 and 2
58. *Finnegans Wake*: Drafts, TS, Proofs, Book III, Chap. 3, Part I.
59. *Finnegans Wake*: Drafts, TS, Proofs, Book III, Chap. 3, Part II.
60. *Finnegans Wake*: Drafts, TS, Proofs, Book III, Chap. 4
61. *Finnegans Wake*: *transition* pages, Book III, Chaps. 1-4
62. *Finnegans Wake*: Galley proofs, Book III.

BOOK IV

63. *Finnegans Wake*: Drafts, TS, Proofs, Book IV.

Paging of *Finnegans Wake* Chapters

Chapter	Book/Episode	Pages
1	I.i	3-29
2	I.ii	30-47
3	I.iii	48-74
4	I.iv	75-103
5	I.v	104-125
6	I.vi	126-168
7	I.vii	169-195
8	I.viii	196-216
9	II.i	219-259

Chapter	Book / Episode	Pages
10	II.ii	260-308
11	II.iii	309-382
12	II.iv	383-399
13	III.i	403-428
14	III.ii	429-473
15	III.iii	474-554
16	III.iv	555-590
17	IV	593-628

Paging of *Ulysses* Episodes

Chapter	Episode	Pages Mod.Lib.	Vintage ed.	To convert †
1	Telemachus	5-24	3-23	− 1†
2	Nestor	25-37	24-36	− 1
3	Proteus	38-51	27-51	− 1
4	Calypso	55-69	55-70	− 1 to 1
5	Lotos Eaters	70-85	71-86	+ 1
6	Hades	86-114	87-115	+ 1
7	Aeolus	115-148	116-150	+ 2
8	Lestrygonians	149-181	151-183	+ 2
9	Scylla & Charybdis	182-215	184-218	+ 2 to 3
10	Wandering Rocks	216-251	219-255	+ 3 to 4
11	Sirens	252-286	256-291	+ 4 to 5
12	Cyclops	287-339	292-345	+ 5 to 6
13	Nausicaa	340-376	346-382	+ 6
14	Oxen of the Sun	377-421	383-428	+ 6 to 7
15	*Circe	422-593	429-609	+ 7 to 16*
16	Eumaeus	597-649	613-665	+ 16
17	Ithaca	650-722	666-737	+ 16 to 15
18	Penelope	723-768	738-783	− 15

† To find reference add or subtract
* Circe pages

422-429	+ 7
430-449	+ 7.5
450-469	+ 8
470-499	+ 9.75
500-524	+ 10.25
525-549	+ 11.5
550-574	+ 13
575-593	+ 15.50

Critical Writings

CW 74:22-23

. . . any method which bends upon these present things and so works upon them and fashions them that the quick intelligence may go beyond them to their meaning which is still unuttered. ("James Clarence Mangan," 1902)

Purg. 31:34-36

Piangendo dissi: "Le presenti cose / col falso lor piacer volser miei passi, / tosto che 'l vostro viso si nacose."

Weeping I said, "The
present things, with
their false pleasure, turned my steps
aside, as soon as your countenance was
hidden."

CW 79:4-5

Vittoria Colonna and Laura and Beatrice . . . embody one chivalrous idea, which is no mortal thing . . . ("James Clarence Mangan," 1902)

[Dante's Beatrice]

CW 81:11-12

Those whom the flames of too fierce love have wasted on earth become after death pale phantoms among the winds of desire . . . ("James Clarence Mangan," 1902)

Inf. 5:31-33

La bufera infernal, che mai non resta, / mena li spirti con la sua rapina; / voltando e percotendo li molesta.

The hellish hurricane, never resting, sweeps along the spirits with its rapine; whirling and smiting, it torments them.

CW 82:23

The philosophic mind inclines always to an elaborate life—the life of Goethe or of Leonardo da Vinci; but the life of the poet is intense—the life of Blake or Dante—taking into its centre the life that surrounds it and flinging it abroad again amid planetary music. ("James Clarence Mangan," 1902)

CW 101:15-16

And Ibsen has united with his strong, ample imaginative faculty a preoccupation with the things present to him. ("Catalina," 1903)

Purg. 31:34

Le presenti cose

These present things

CW 101:21-26

But meanwhile a young generation which has cast away belief and thrown precision after it, for which Balzac is a great intellect and every sampler who chooses to wander amid his own shapeless hells and heavens a Dante without the unfortunate prejudices of Dante, will be troubled by this preoccupation, and out of very conscience will denounce a method so calm, so ironical. ("Catalina," 1903)

CW 109:18-22

at the present time, when the scientific specialists and the whole cohort of Materialists are cheapening the good name of philosophy, it is very useful to give heed to one who has been wisely named 'maestro di color che sanno' ("Aristotle on Education," 1903)

Inf. 4:130-132

Poi ch'innalzai un poco più le ciglia, / vidi 'l maestro di color che sanno / seder tra filosofica famiglia.

When I raised my eyes a little higher, I saw the Master of those who know, seated in a philosophic family.

CW 150:9-14 (*Arch*. 1:278, 284)   For every true-born mysticist / A Dante is, unprejudiced, / Who safe at ingle-nook, by proxy / Hazards extremes of heterodoxy, / Like him who finds a joy at table, / Pondering the uncomfortable. ("The Holy Office." 1904)

CW 154:15-21 (*Arch*. 2:85-86)   the passage in Dante's *Inferno* where his mentor points to one of the Celtic magicians tormented by infernal pains and says:] Quel' altro, che ne fianchi è così poco, / Michele Scotto fu, che veramente / Delle magiche frode seppe il gioco. ("Ireland, Island of Saints and Sages," 1907)

Inf. 20:115-117   Quell' altro che ne' fianchi è così poco, / Michele Scotto fu, che veramente / de le magiche frode seppe 'l gioco.

That other who is so spare in the flanks was Michael Scot, who truly knew the game of magic frauds.

CW 183:1-3 (*Arch*. 2:136)   There is only one chivalrous idea, only one male devotion that lights up the faces of Vittoria Colonna, Laura, and Beatrice . . . ("James Clarence Mangan," 1907)

[Dante's Beatrice]

CW 183:6-7 (*Arch*. 2:136)   . . . the peaceful oriflamme of the Florentine theologian. ("James Clarence Mangan," 1907)

Par. 31:127   così quella pacifica oriafiamma

so was that pacific oriflamme

CW 186:15 (*Arch*. 2:140)   one who has expressed in a worthy form the sacred indignation of his soul . . . ("James Clarence Mangan," 1907)

Inf. 8:44-45	. . . "Alma sdegnosa, / benedetta colei che 'n te s'incinse!
	"Indignant soul, blessed is she who bore you!
CW 219:20-22 (*Arch.* 2:225)	He [Blake] began to study Italian in order to read the *Divina Commedia* in the original and to illustrate Dante's vision with mystical drawings. ("William Blake," 1912)
CW 221:34-36 (*Arch.* 2:232)	Eternity, which had appeared to the beloved disciple and to St. Augustine as a heavenly city, and to Alighieri as a heavenly rose . . . ("William Blake," 1912)
CW 236:5-6, 9-10 (*Arch.* 2:699)	. . . the visionary Saint Fursa, described in the hagiographic calendar of Ireland as the precursor of Dante Alighieri. . . . This vision would have served as a model for the poet of the *Divine Comedy*, who, like Columbus, is honoured by posterity because he was the last to visit and describe the three regions of the soul. ("The Mirage of the Fisherman of Aran," 1912)
Padua essay	Mettete *Tristano ed Isolta* accanto all' *Inferno* e v' accorgerete come l'odio del poeta segue la sua strada d'abisso in abisso nella scia un idea che s'intensifica; e più intensamente il poeta si consuma nel fuoco dell' idea dell' odio, più truce diventa l'arte colla quale l'artista ci communica la sua passione. L'una è un'arte di circostanze, l'altra è ideativa.
	Place *Tristan and Isolde* next to the *Inferno* and you will notice how the poet's hate follows its path from abyss to abyss in the wake of an idea that intensifies; and the more intensely the poet consumes himself in the fire of the idea of hate, the more

violent becomes the art with which the artist communicates his passion. One is the art of circumstance, the other is ideational. ("L'influenza letteraria universale del rinascimento" "The Universal Literary Influence of the Renaissance," 1912 trans. Louis Berrone New York: Random House, 1977, pp. 10-11, 16, 22.)

Defoe Essay

La letteratura inglese durante i secoli che seguirono la conquista francese andava a scuola ed i suoi maestri erano Boccaccio, Dante, Tasso e messer Lodovico. . . . Il [sic] *Paradiso Perduto* di Milton è una trascrizione puritanica della *Divina Commedia*.

English literature, during the centuries which followed the French conquest, was at school, and its masters were Boccaccio, Dante, Tasso, and Messer Lodovico . . . Milton's *Paradise Lost* is a Puritan transcript of the *Divine Comedy*. (*Daniel Defoe*, edited and translated by Joseph Prescott. State University of New York at Buffalo, 1964, p. 7.)

Collected Poems

CP 47 (*Arch.* 1: 202-203, 251-254) "Tilly":
I bleed by the black stream
For my torn bough!

Inf. 13:31-35 Allor porsi la mano un poco avante / e
colsi un ramicel da un gran pruno; / e 'l
tronco suo gridò: "Perché mi
schiante?" / Da che fatto fu poi di sangue
bruno, / ricominciò a dir: "Perché mi
scerpi?"

Then I stretched my hand a little forward and plucked a twig from a great
thornbush, and its stub cried, "Why do
you break me?" And when it had become
dark with blood, it began again to cry,
"Why do you tear me?" [Dante and Virgil
have just crossed the river of blood, described at *Inf.* 12:117-132, to arrive at the
Wood of the Suicides.]

CP 57 (*Arch.* 1:194, 195, 270, 271) "A Memory of the Players in a Mirror at
Midnight":
Pluck forth your heart, saltblood, a
fruit of tears,
Pluck and devour!

VN III E nell' una delle mani mi parea che questi
tenesse una cosa, la quale ardesse tutta; e
pareami che mi dicesse queste parole:
Vide cor tuum. E quando egli era stato alquanto, pareami che disvegliasse questa
che dormia; e tanto si sforzava per suo
ingegno, che le facea mangiare quella
cosa che in mano gli ardeva, la quale ella
mangiava dubitosamente. Appresso ciò,
poco dimorava che la sua letizia si conver-
tia in amarissimo pianto: e così piangendo
. . . e trovai che l'ora, nella quale m'era
questa visione apparita, era stata la quarta
della notte . . .

In one of his hands he held a fiery object,
and he seemed to say these words: "Behold your heart." After spending a short
while with me, he seemed to awaken the
sleeping one, and through the power of
his art made her eat this glowing object in
his hand. Hesitantly, she ate it. It was only
a short while after this that his happiness turned into bitterest weeping . . . I
realized that the vision had appeared to
me in the fourth hour of the night.
(trans. Musa, 5-6)

Chamber Music

XXI

He who hath glory lost, nor hath
   Found any soul to fellow his,
Among his foes in scorn and wrath
   Holding to ancient nobleness,
That high unconsortable one—
   His love is his companion.

(*Chamber Music*, ed. W. Y. Tindall.
Columbia Univ. Press, 1954, p. 149;
Arch. I:36, 38, 61, 78, 135, 175)

Dubliners

"THE SISTERS"

D 9:1 (*Arch.* 4:353)　　　　　　　There was no hope for him this time.

　　　Inf. 3:9　　　　　　　Lasciate ogne speranza, voi ch'intrate.

　　　　　　　　　　　　　　　Abandon every hope, you who enter.

D 9:12 (*Arch.* 4:353)　　　　　　It had always sounded strangely in my
　　　　　　　　　　　　　　　ears, like . . . the word *simony* in the
　　　　　　　　　　　　　　　Catechism.

　　　Inf. 19:1　　　　　　　O Simon mago, o miseri seguaci / che le
　　　　　　　　　　　　　　　cose di Dio, che di bontate / deoń essere
　　　　　　　　　　　　　　　spose, e voi rapaci / per oro e per argento
　　　　　　　　　　　　　　　avolterate . . .

　　　　　　　　　　　　　　　O Simon Magus! O you his wretched fol-
　　　　　　　　　　　　　　　lowers that, rapacious, prostitute for gold
　　　　　　　　　　　　　　　and silver the things of God which ought
　　　　　　　　　　　　　　　to be the brides of righteousness!

D 11:30-31 (4:359-361)　　　　　　It began to confess to me in a murmuring
　　　　　　　　　　　　　　　voice. . . . I felt that I too was smiling fee-
　　　　　　　　　　　　　　　bly as if to absolve the simoniac of his sin.

　　　Inf. 19:49-50　　　　　　Io stava come 'l frate che confessa / lo
　　　　　　　　　　　　　　　perfido assessin . . .

　　　　　　　　　　　　　　　I was standing there like the friar who
　　　　　　　　　　　　　　　confesses the perfidious assassin . . .

"AN ENCOUNTER"

D 24:7-8 (*Arch.* 4:285)　　　　　　when we reached the field we made at
　　　　　　　　　　　　　　　once for a sloping bank.

　　　Inf. 15:1; 10-12　　　　　Ora cen porta l'un de' duri margini; /
　　　　　　　　　　　　　　　. . . / a tale imagine eran fatti quelli, /
　　　　　　　　　　　　　　　tutto che né sì alti né sì grossi, / qual che si
　　　　　　　　　　　　　　　fosse, lo maestro félli.

Now one of the hard margins bears us on;
. . . in like fashion were these banks made,
except that the builder, whoever he was,
made them neither so high nor so thick.

D 24:17-18, 20, 32 (*Arch.* 4:287)　　I saw a man approaching. . . . When he
passed at our feet he glanced up at us
quickly and then continued his way. . . .
He stopped when he came level with us
and bade us good-day.

Inf. 15:16-18; 23　　. . . incontrammo d'anime una schiera /
che venian lungo l'argine, e ciascuna / ci
riguardava . . . / . . . / . . . fui conosciuto da
un . . .

we met a troop of souls that were coming
alongside the bank, and each looked at
us. . . . I was recognized by one . . . (The
canto of the sodomites)

D 28:1 (*Arch.* 4:297)　　saying that I was obliged to go, I bade him
good-day.

Inf. 15:115-116　　Di più direi; ma 'l venire e 'l sermone /
più lungo esser non può . . .

I would say more, but my going and my
speech must not be longer . . .

D 28:10 (*Arch.* 4:297)　　he came running across the field to me!
He ran as if to bring me aid.

Inf. 15:121-124　　. . . parve di coloro / che corrono a Verona il drappo verde / per la campagna;
e parve di costoro / quelli che vince, non
colui che perde.

. . . he seemed like one of those who run
for the green cloth in the field at
Verona, and of them seemed he who
wins, not he who loses.

"ARABY"

D 30:32-34 (*Arch.* 5:37)

I had never spoken to her . . . and yet her name was like a summons to all my foolish blood.

VN III

e però che quella fu la prima volta che le sue parole si mossero per venire alli miei orecchi, presi tanta dolcezza, che come inebriato mi partii dalle genti.

And since that was the first time her words had entered my ears, I was so over-come with ecstasy that I departed from everyone as if intoxicated. (trans. Musa)

D 31:1 (*Arch.* 5:37)

Her image accompanied me even in places the most hostile to romance.

VN II

Ed avvegna che la sua imagine, la quale continuamente meco stava, fosse bal-danza d'amore a signoreggiarmi.

Her image, which remained constantly with me, was Love's assurance of holding me. (trans. Musa)

D 31:11 (*Arch.* 5:37)

Her name sprang to my lips at moments in strange prayers and praises which I myself did not understand. My eyes were often full of tears (I could not tell why) and at times a flood from my heart seemed to pour itself out into my bosom. I thought little of the future . . . my body was like a harp and her words and ges-tures were like fingers running upon the wires.

VN XI

E chi avesse voluto conoscere Amore, far lo potea mirando lo tremore degli occhi miei . . . non che Amore fosse tal mezzo che potesse obumbrare a me la intol-lerabile beatitudine, ma egli quasi per soperchio di dolcezza divenia tale, che lo mio corpo, lo quale era tutto allora sotto il

suo reggimento, molte volte si volgea
come cosa grave inanimata.

And whoever had wished to know Love
might have done so by looking at my
trembling eyes. . . . Love was no medium
capable of shadowing my unbearable
bliss, but rather, as if possessed with an
excess of sweetness, he changed so that
my body, which was completely under his
rule, often moved like a heavy inanimate
object. (trans. Musa)

D 31:26-29 (*Arch.* 5:37)

All my senses seemed to desire to veil
themselves and, feeling that I was about
to slip from them, I pressed the palms of
my hands together until they trembled.

VN II

In quel punto dico veracemente che lo
spirito della vita, lo quale dimora nella
segretissima camera del cuore, cominciò a
tremare sì fortemente, che apparia nelli
menomi polsi orribilmente;

At that moment I say truly that the vital
spirit, the one that dwells in the most secret chamber of the heart, began to tremble so violently that even the least pulses
of my body were strangely affected;
(trans. Musa)

D 31:30-31 (*Arch.* 5:38)

At last she spoke to me. When she addressed the first words to me I was so confused that I did not know what to answer.
. . . I forgot whether I answered yes or no.

VN III

Poichè furono passati tanti dì, che
appunto erano compiuti li nove anni
appresso l'apparimento soprascritto di
questa gentilissima, nell' ultimo di questi
dì avvenne, che questa mirabile donna
apparve a me . . . e passando per una via,
volse gli occhi verso quella parte dov' io
era molto pauroso; . . . mi salutò vir-
tuosamente tanto, ch'elli mi parve allora
vedere tutti i termini della beatitudine.

After so many days had passed that precisely nine years had been completed
since the appearance I have just described of this very gracious lady, it happened that on the last day the miraculous
lady appeared to me . . . and while walking down a street she turned her eyes to
where I was standing faint-hearted, and
. . . she greeted me so miraculously that I
felt I was experiencing the very summit
of bliss. (trans. Musa)

"AFTER THE RACE"

D 44:32; 45:27-28

he was about to stake the greater part of
his substance! It was a serious thing for
him. . . . A certain pride mingled with his
parents' trepidation, a certain eagerness,
also, to play fast and loose . . .

Inf. 7:40-42

"Tutti quanti fuor guerci / sì de la mente
in la vita primaia, / che con misura nullo
spendio ferci."

"Each and all of these were so asquint of
mind in the first life that they followed
there no right measure in their spending." (The canto of the profligates)

"TWO GALLANTS"

D 60:24-30 (*Arch.* 5:84)

Lenehan . . . was baffled and a note of
menace pierced through his voice.
—Can't you tell us? he said. Did you try
her?
Corley halted at the first lamp and stared
grimly before him. Then with a grave
gesture he extended a hand towards the
light. . . . A small gold coin shone in the
palm.

Inf. 18:62-66

". . . e se di ciò vuoi fede o testimonio /
rècati a mente il nostro avaro seno." /
Così parlando il percosse un demonio /

de la sua scuriada, e disse: "Via, / ruffian! qui non son femmine da conio."

"and if of this you wish assurance or testimony, recall to mind our avaricious nature." As he spoke thus, a demon smote him with his lash, and said, "Off, pander! There are no women here to coin."

"THE BOARDING-HOUSE"

D 63:5-10, 24 (*Arch*. 4:19, 21)

As Polly was very lively the intention was to give her the run of the young men.... Polly, of course, flirted with the young men but Mrs. Mooney, who was a shrewd judge, knew that the young men were only passing the time away: none of them meant business.... Things went on so for a long time . . . when she noticed that something was going on between Polly and one of the young men.... At last, when she judged it to be the right moment, Mrs. Mooney intervened. She dealt with moral problems as a cleaver deals with meat.

Inf. 18:86-97

Quelli è Iasón . . . / Ello passò per l'isola di Lenno / poi che l'ardite femmine spietate / tutti li maschi loro a morte dienno. / Ivi con segni e con parole ornate / Isifile ingannò, la giovinetta / che prima avea tutte l'altre ingannate. / Lasciolla quivi, gravida, soletta; . . . / Con lui sen va chi da tal parte inganna . . .

That is Jason.... He passed by the isle of Lemnos when the bold and pitiless women had given all their males to death. There, with tokens and with fair words, he deceived the young Hypsipyle who first had deceived all the rest. He left her there pregnant and forlorn.... With him go all who practice such deceit; (The canto of the seducers and panderers)

"A LITTLE CLOUD"

D 70:1 (*Arch.* 5:185)

A Little Cloud

Inf. 26:39

sì come nuvoletta, in sù salire:

like a little cloud ascending

D 78:9-10 (*Arch.* 5:193)

Ignatius Gallaher, emerging after some time from the clouds of smoke in which he had taken refuge . . .

Inf. 26:47

E 'l duca . . . disse: / "Dentro dai fuochi son li spirti; / catun si fascia di quel ch'elli è inceso." /

And my leader said: "Within the fires are the spirits: each swathes himself with that which burns him."

D 81:7-9 (*Arch.* 5:197)

I'm going to have my fling first and see a bit of life and the world before I put my head in the sack—if I ever do.

Inf. 26:94-99

né dolcezza di figlio, né la pieta / del vecchio padre, né 'l debito amore / lo qual dovea Penelopè far lieta, / vincer potero dentro a me l'ardore / ch'i' ebbi a divenir del mondo esperto / e de li vizi umani e del valore . . .

neither fondness for my son, nor reverence for my aged father, nor the due love which would have made Penelope glad, could conquer in me the longing that I had to gain experience of the world, and of human vice and worth. (the canto of Ulysses)

"COUNTERPARTS"

D 87:26-27 (*Arch.* 4:51)

A spasm of rage gripped his throat for a few moments

Inf. 12:14-15

e quando vide noi, sé stesso morse, / sì come quei cui l'ira dentro fiacca.

And when he saw us he bit himself, like one whom wrath rends inwardly.

D 90:25-26, 28-31 (*Arch.* 4:65)

He longed to execrate aloud, to bring his fist down on something violently. . . . He felt strong enough to clear out the whole office single-handed. His body ached to do something, to rush out and revel in violence. All the indignities of his life enraged him.

Inf. 12:15-50

sì come quei cui l'ira dentro fiacca. / . . . / Qual è quel toro che si slaccia in quella / c'ha ricevuto già 'l colpo mortale, / che gir non sa, ma qua e là saltella, / vid' io lo Minotauro far cotale . . . / . . . / Oh cieca⌐ cupidigia e ira folle, / che sì ci sproni ne la vita corta . . .

like one whom wrath rends inwardly. / . . . / As a bull that breaks loose in the moment when it has received the mortal blow, and cannot go, but plunges this way and that, so I saw the Minotaur do. . . . O blind cupidity and mad rage, which in the brief life so goad us on . . .

"CLAY"

D 99:10-11; (*Arch.* 5:227)
D 101:13-14; (*Arch.* 5:229)
D 105:8-9 (*Arch.* 5:234-235)

Maria was a very, very small person indeed but she had a very long nose and a very long chin . . . when she laughed her grey-green eyes sparkled with disappointed shyness and the tip of her nose nearly met the tip of her chin; . . . The two next-door girls had arranged some Hallow-Eve games. . . . They insisted then on blindfolding Maria and leading her up to the table to see what she would get; and, while they were putting on the bandage Maria laughed and laughed again until the tip of her nose nearly met the tip of her chin.

Inf. 20:52-55, 82-86

E quella che ricuopre le mammelle, / che tu non vedi, con le trecce sciolte, / . . . / Manto fu. . . . / . . . la vergine cruda / . . . / ristette con suoi servi a far sue arti . . .

And she that covers her bosom, which you cannot see, with her loose tresses . . . was Manto. The cruel virgin . . . there stopped with her servants to practice her arts.

Inf. 20:121-123

Vedi le triste che lasciaron l'ago / la spuola e 'l fuso, e fecersi 'ndivine; / fecer malie con erbe e con imago.

See the wretched women who left the needle, the spool, and the spindle, and became fortune-tellers; they wrought spells with herbs and with images.

"A PAINFUL CASE"

D 114:3-6 (*Arch.* 4:117, 165)

as the train was about to start he observed a woman attempting to cross the lines. He ran towards her and shouted but, before he could reach her, she was caught by the buffer of the engine and fell to the ground. [Mrs. Sinico's suicide]

Inf. 13:94-95

Quando si parte l'anima feroce / dal corpo ond'ella stessa s'è disvelta . . .

When the fierce soul quits the body from which it has uprooted itself [the suicides]

"IVY DAY IN THE COMMITTEE ROOM"

D 125:8, 17-20; 127:18-20 (*Arch.* 197-198, 199, 205, 244-245, 249.)

Do you know what my private and candid opinion is about some of those little jokers? I believe half of them are in the pay of the Castle . . . That's a fellow now that'd sell his country for fourpence—ay—and go down on his bended knees and thank the Almighty Christ he had a country to sell. . . . There's some deal on in that quarter, said Mr. O'Connor thoughtfully. I saw the three of them hard at it yesterday at Suffolk Street corner.

Inf. 21:37-42

... "O Malebranche, / ecco un de li anzian di Santa Zita! / Mettetel sotto, ch'i torno per anche / a quella terra, che n' è ben fornita: / ogn' uom v'è barattier, fuor che Bonturo; / del no, per li denar, vi si fa *ita*."

"O Malebranche, here's one of Saint Zita's elders! Thrust him under, while I go back for more, to that city where there's a fine supply of them: every man there is a bar- rator . . . there they make Ay of No, for cash."

"A MOTHER"

D 149:12-13, 18-20, 23-25
(*Arch.* 4:331)

Mrs. Kearney stood at the door, haggard with rage, arguing with her husband and daughter, gesticulating with them. . . . She stood still for an instant like an angry stone image. . . . As she passed through the doorway she stopped and glared into Mr. Holohan's face. "I'm not done with you yet," she said.

Inf. 28:34-35

E tutti li altri che tu vedi qui, / seminator di scandalo e di scisma / fuor vivi . . .

all the others whom you see here were in their lifetime sowers of scandal and of schism. . .

"GRACE"

D 173:26-30; 174:6-9

Father Purdon developed the text with resonant assurance. . . . It was a text which might seem to the casual observer at variance with the lofty morality elsewhere preached by Jesus Christ. . . . He designed to give them a word of counsel, setting before them as exemplars in the religious life those very worshippers of Mammon who were of all men the least solicitous in matters religious.

Inf. 19:90-93, 112-114

"Deh, or mi dì: quanto tesoro volle / Nostro Segnore in prima da san Pietro / ch'ei ponesse le chiavi in sua balìa? / Certo non chiese se non 'Viemmi retro.' / . . . / Fatto v'avete dio d'oro e d'argento . . ."

"Pray now tell me how much treasure did our Lord require of Saint Peter before he put the keys into his keeping? Surely he asked nothing save: 'Follow me.' . . . You have made you a god of gold and silver . . ." (The simoniacs)

"THE DEAD"

D 188: 3-5, 16, 20-22 (*Arch.* 4:515)
D 189:21-22, 30-31 (*Arch.* 4:516)
D 192:26-27 (*Arch.* 4:519)

—Well, I'm ashamed of you, said Miss Ivors frankly. To say you'd write for a rag like that. I didn't think you were a West Briton. . . . He did not know how to meet her charge. . . . He continued blinking his eyes and trying to smile and murmured lamely that he saw nothing political in writing reviews of books. . . .

—Well, said Gabriel, if it comes to that, you know, Irish is not my language. . . . —O, to tell you the truth, retorted Gabriel suddenly, I'm sick of my own country, sick of it! . . . What did he care that his aunts were only two ignorant old women?

D 177:16-17 (*Arch.* 4:463, 506)
D 223:17-18 (*Arch.* 4:501, 559)
D 224:2-4 (*Arch.* 4:503, 560)

A light fringe of snow lay like a cape on the shoulders of his overcoat. . . . His soul had approached that region where dwell the vast hosts of the dead. . . . His soul swooned slowly as he heard the snow falling faintly . . . like the descent of their last end, upon all the living and the dead.

Inf. 32-34, e.g., 32:70-72, 75, 110-111

. . . vid' io mille visi cagnazzi / fatti per freddo; onde mi vien riprezzo, / e verrà sempre, de' gelati guazzi. . . . / e io tremava ne l'etterno rezzo; / . . . / malvagio traditor; ch'a la tua onta / io porterò di te vere novelle.

. . . I saw a thousand faces made purple by the cold, whence a shuddering comes over me and always will, at frozen fords . . . and I was shivering in the eternal chill . . . "accursed traitor, . . . to your shame will I carry true news of you." (Cantos 32-34; traitors to kindred, to country or party, and to benefactors, are frozen in ice)

Stephen Hero

SH 41:14-19 (*Arch.* 8:131-132)

Here [*i.e.*, in Ibsen] and not in Shakespeare or Goethe was the successor to the first poet of the Europeans, here, as only to such purpose in Dante, a human personality had been found united with an artistic manner which was itself almost a natural phenomenon.

SH 70:9-14 (*Arch.* 8:223)

Stephen was . . . much surprised one evening as he was walking past the Christian Brother's School in North Richmond St to feel his arm seized from behind and to hear a voice say somewhat bluntly:
—Hello, Daedalus, old man, is that you?

Inf. 15:23-24

fui conosciuto da un, che mi prese / per lo lembo e gridò: "Qual maraviglia!"

I was recognized by one who took me by the hem, and cried, "What a marvel!"

SH 70:14 (*Arch.* 8:223)

—Hello, Daedalus, old man, is that you?

Inf. 15:30

"Siete voi qui, ser Brunetto?"

"Are you here, ser Brunetto!"

SH 71:3 (*Arch.* 8:225)

—See me down a bit of the way, will you?

Inf. 15:31-33

"O figliuol mio, non ti dispiaccia / se Brunetto Latini un poco teco / ritorna 'n dietro e lascia andar la traccia."

"O my son, let it not displease you if Brunetto Latini turns back a little with you and lets the train go on."

SH 71:6 (*Arch.* 8:225)

So they walked on side by side.

Inf. 15:40	Però va oltre: i' ti verrò a' panni;
	Therefore go on: I will come at your skirts,
SH 71:7 (*Arch.* 8:225)	Well, and what have you been doing with yourself?
Inf. 15:46-47	El cominciò: Qual fortuna o destino / anzi l'ultimo dì qua giù ti mena?
	He began, "What chance or destiny brings you down here before your last day?
SH 72:15-16 (*Arch.* 8:229)	—When you're a great writer yourself— as the author of a second Trilby, or something of that sort . . .
Inf. 15:55-56	Ed elli a me: "Se tu segui tua stella, / non puoi fallire a glorioso porto,
	And he said to me, "If you follow your star you cannot fail of a glorious port,
SH 72:25-26 (*Arch.* 8:231)	For the most part the students were walking in little groups through the grounds, . . . Some of the students saluted Wells . . .
Inf. 15:16	quando incontrammo d'anime una schiere / che venian lungo l'argine, e ciascuna / ci riguardava . . .
	when we met a troop of souls that were coming alongside the bank, and each looked at us . . .
SH 73:10-12 (*Arch.* 8:233)	Wells wished Stephen to gather that he despised his fellow students . . .
Inf. 15:103-104, 110-114	Ed elli a me: "Saper d'alcuno è buono; / de li altri fia laudabile tacerci, / . . . / . . . anche; e vedervi, / s'avessi avuto di tal

tigna brama, / colui potei che dal servo de' servi / fu trasmutato d'Arno in Bacchiglione . . .

And he to me, "It is well to know of some of them; about the rest it is well that we be silent, . . . and you could also have seen there, had you hankered for such scurf, him who was transferred by the Servant of Servants from Arno to Bacchiglione, . . .

SH 74:13,23-24 (*Arch.* 8:235, 237) A little band of students passed. . . . The little band went down the path. In a few minutes another little band passed . . .

Inf. 15:37-42

qual di questa greggia / s'arresta punto, giace poi cent' ani /
. . . i' ti verrò a' panni; / e poi rigiugnerò la mia masnada, / che va piangendo i suoi etterni danni."

whoever of this flock stops even for an instant must then lie a hundred years. . . . I will come at your skirts, and then will rejoin my band who go lamenting their eternal woes."

SH 74:33-35 (*Arch.* 8:237) The vagrant bands of students were all turning their steps towards the college.

Inf. 15:40-41

. . . i' ti verrò a' panni; / e poi rigiugnerò la mia masnada . . .

I will come at your skirts, and then will rejoin my band . . .

SH 75:8-9 (*Arch.* 8:239) The lodge woman opened the side-door and Wells looked out for a second or two almost enviously.

Inf. 15:119-120

Sieti raccomandato il mio Tesoro, / nel qual io vivo ancora . . .

Let my *Treasure*, in which I yet live,
be commended to you . . .

SH 75:10-12 (*Arch.* 8:239) —Well, goodbye, old man. Must run now.
. . . I must run. Goodbye.

Inf. 15:115-116 Di più direi; ma 'l venire e 'l sermone /
più lungo esser non può,

I would say more, but my going and my
speech must not be longer.

SH 75:13-14 (*Arch.* 8:239) As he tucked up his soutane high and ran
awkwardly up the drive he looked a
strange, almost criminal, fugitive in the
dreary dusk.

Inf. 15:121-124 Poi si rivolse e parve di coloro / che corrono a Verona il drappo verde / per la
campagna; e parve di costoro / quelli che
vince, non colui che perde.

Then he turned back, and seemed like
one of those who run for the green cloth
in the field at Verona, and of them
seemed he who wins, not he who loses.

SH 78:31-34 (*Arch.* 8:249) The classical temper . . . chooses rather to
bend upon these present things and so to
work upon them and fashion them that
the quick intelligence may go beyond
them to their meaning which is still unuttered.

Purg. 31:34 . . . "Le presenti cose / col falso lor piacer
volser miei passi,

Present things, with their false pleasure,
turned my steps aside,

SH 92:5-6 (*Arch.* 8:297) —Why not for the poet too? Dante surely
examines and upbraids society.

SH 156:4-5 (*Arch.* 8:511) He remembered almost every word she had said from the first time he had met her . . .

VN II la sua imagine, la quale continuamente meco stava, fosse baldanza d'amore a signoreggiarmi . . .

her image, which remained constantly with me, was love's assurance of holding me . . .

SH 158:16-17 (*Arch.* 8:521) Stephen's way through self examinations had worn him out so much that he could not but long to repose himself in the neighborhood of her beauty.

VN XXXVIII Io venni a tanto per la vista di questa donna, che li miei occhi si cominciaro a dilettare troppo di vederla; onde molte volte me ne crucciava nel mio cuore . . .

When, once again, I returned to see this lady, the sight of her had such a strange effect on me that often I thought of her as someone I liked too much. (trans. Musa)

SH 158:33-36 (*Arch.* 8:523) he went on repeating to himself a line from Dante for no other reason except that it contained the angry disyllable "frode." Surely, he thought, I have as much right to use the word as ever Dante had.

Inf. 11:25-26 Ma perché frode è de l'uom proprio male, / più spiace a Dio . . .

But because fraud is an evil peculiar to man, it more displeases God . . .

SH 159:1-3 (*Arch.* 8:523) The spirits of Moynihan and O'Neill and Glynn seemed to him worthy of some blowing about round the verges of a hell which would be a caricature of Dante's.

SH 159:3-6 (*Arch.* 8:523-525)

The spirits of the patriotic and religious enthusiasts seemed to him fit to inhabit the fraudulent circles where hidden in hives of immaculate ice they might work their bodies to the due pitch of frenzy.

Inf. 32:22-24

Per ch'io mi volsi, e vidimi davante / e sotto i piedi un lago che per gelo / avea di vetro e non d'acqua sembiante.

At this I turned and saw before me, and under my feet, a lake which through frost had the semblance of glass and not of water.

SH 159:7-11 (*Arch.* 8:525)

The spirits of the tame sodalists, unsullied and undeserving, he would petrify amid a ring of Jesuits in the circle of foolish and grotesque virginities and ascend above them and their baffled icons to where his Emma, with no detail of her earthly form or vesture abated, invoked him from a Mohammadan paradise.

Inf. 9:52-53

"Vegna Medusa: sì 'l farem di smalto," dicevan tutte . . .

"Let Medusa come and we'll turn him to stone," / they all cried . . . /

Purg. 30:32-33

donna m'apparve, sotto verde manto / vestita di color di fiamma viva.

a lady appeared to me, clad, under a green mantle, with hue of living flame. [Dante reunited with Beatrice in the Earthly Paradise]

SH 169:21-22 (*Arch.* 8:563)

He chose Italian as his optional subject, partly from a desire to read Dante seriously.

SH 174:7-10 (*Arch.* 8:579)

The *Vita Nuova* of Dante suggested to him that he should make his scattered

love-verses into a perfect wreath and he
explained to Cranly at great length the
difficulties of the verse-maker.

SH 174:13-21 (*Arch.* 8:579)

. . . in his expressions of love he found
himself compelled to use what he called
the feudal terminology and as he could
not use it with the same faith and purpose
as animated the feudal poets themselves
he was compelled to express his love a
little ironically. This suggestion of relativity, he said, mingling itself with so im-
mune a passion is a modern note: . . . It
is not possible for the modern lover to
think the universe an assistant at his love-
affair and modern love, losing somewhat
of its fierceness, gains also somewhat
in amiableness.

SH 175:4-8 (*Arch.* 8:583)

As for the scheme of making a wreath of
songs in praise of love he [Cranly]
thought that if such a passion really
existed it was incapable of being
expressed.—We are not likely to know
whether it exists or not if no man tries to
express it, said Stephen.

A Portrait of the Artist as a Young Man

MS Notebook (1909) (*Arch*. 7:91)	His [Christ's] two interpreters: Blake and Dante. (Edited by Robert Scholes and Richard M. Kain, *The Workshop of Daedalus*, Northwestern Univ. Press, 1965, p. 72)

MS Notebook (1909) (*Arch*. 7:114) Cavalcanti (Guido)
      His father Cavalcante Cavalcanti asks Dante where he is (Inf. cant X). Dante hesitates before he replies.
      Betto Brunelleschi and his brigade railed at him one day as he was coming in from Orsanmichele. He (being near [in] a burial ground) said to them: *Signori, voi mi potete dire a casa vostra ciò che vi piace*. His speculations (he held the views of Epicurus) *eran solo in cercare se trovar si potesse che Iddio non fosse* (Bocc 6.viii)
(Scholes and Kain, *Workshop*. p. 94)

P 8:4-9

His mother said.
—O, Stephen will apologise.
Dante said:
—O, if not, the eagles will come and pull out his eyes.
          Pull out his eyes,
          Apologise,

Purg. 9:19-30

in sogno mi parea veder sospesa / un' aguglia nel ciel con penne d'oro / con l'ali aperte e a calare intesa; / . . . / Poi mi parea che, poi rotata un poco, / terribil come folgor discendesse, / e me rapisse suso infino al foco.

I seemed to see, in a dream, an eagle poised in the sky, with feathers of gold, its wings outspread, and prepared to swoop.

... Then it seemed to me that, having wheeled a while, it descended terrible as a thunder bolt and snatched me upwards as far as the fire.

P 137:31 (*Arch.* 10:687-689)

Creatures were in the field; one, three, six: creatures were moving in the field, hither and thither. [Stephen's nightmare of his own death and damnation.]

VN XXIII

E però mi giunse uno sì forte smarrimento, ch'io chiusi gli occhi, e cominciai a travagliare come farnetica persona, ed imaginare in questo modo: che nel cominciamento dell'errare che fece la mia fantasia ...

I went so out of my head that I closed my eyes and became convulsed as one in a delirium and began to have these imaginings. ... certain faces, strange and horrible to behold, saying to me: "You are dead." [Dante's dream of the death of Beatrice]

P 142:25-28 (*Arch.* 10:715-717)

Had it been any terrible crime but that one sin! ... Little fiery flakes fell and touched him at all points, shameful words, shameful acts. Shame covered him wholly like fine glowing ashes falling continually.

Inf. 14:28-30

Sovra tutto 'l sabbion, d'un cader lento / piovean di foco dilatate falde, / come di neve in alpe sanza vento.

Over all the sand huge flakes of fire were falling slowly, like snow in the mountains without a wind.

P 145:25-27 (*Arch.* 10:729)

He knelt to say his penance ... and his prayers ascended to heaven from his purified heart like perfume streaming upwards from a heart of white rose.

Par. 31:1-2	In forma dunque di candida rosa / mi si mostrava la milizia santa . . .
	In form then of a pure white rose the saintly host was shown to me . . .
Par. 30:124-126	Nel giallo de la rosa sempiterna, / che si digrada e dilata e redole / odor di lode al sol che sempre verna . . .
	Into the yellow of the eternal Rose, which rises in ranks and expands and breathes forth odor of praise unto the Sun which makes perpetual spring. [The heavenly rose : The heavenly city]
P 148:2-3 (*Arch.* 10:745)	Every part of his day, divided by what he regarded now as the duties of his station in life, circled about its own centre of spiritual energy.
Par. 28:41-45	. . . da quel punto / depende il cielo e tutta la natura. / Mira quel cerchio che più li è congiunto; / e sappi che 'l suo muovere è sì tosto / per l'affocata amore ond' elli è punto.
	On that point the heavens and all nature are dependent. Look on that circle which is most conjoined to it, and know that its motion is so swift because of the burning love whereby it is spurred.
P 149:6-9 (*Arch.* 10:751)	The imagery through which the nature and kinship of the Three Persons of the Trinity were darkly shadowed forth. . . . The Father contemplating from all eternity as in a mirror His Divine Perfections.
Par. 33:115-119	Ne la profonda e chiara sussistenza / de l'alto lume parvermi tre giri / di tre colori e d'una contenenza; / e l'un da l'altro come iri da iri / parea reflesso . . .
	Within the profound and shining subsistence of the lofty Light appeared to me

three circles of three colors and one magnitude; and one seemed reflected by the other, as rainbow by rainbow . . .

P 149:10-11 (*Arch.* 10:751)   the Father begetting eternally the Eternal Son and the Holy Spirit proceeding out of Father and Son from all eternity . . .

Par. 10:1-3   Guardando nel suo Figlio con l'Amore / che l'uno e l'altro etternalmente spira, / lo primo ed ineffabile Valore . . .

Looking upon His Son with the love which One and the Other eternally breath forth, the primal and the ineffable Power . . .

P 149:33-34 (*Arch.* 10:755)   Gradually, as his soul was enriched with spiritual knowledge, he saw the whole world forming one vast symmetrical expression of God's power and love.

Par. 33:85-92   Nel suo profondo vidi che s'interna, / legato con amore . . . / . . . / sustanze e accidenti e lor costume / quasi conflati insieme, . . . / . . . / La forma universal di questo nodo credo ch'i' vidi, . . .

In its depth I saw ingathered, bound by love in one single volume, . . . substances and accidents and their relations, as though fused together. . . . The universal form of this knot I believe that I saw, . . .

P 150:1-3 (*Arch.* 10:755-757)   The world for all its solid substance and complexity no longer existed for his soul save as a theorem of divine power and love and universality . . .

Par. 33:133-136   Qual è 'l geomètra che tutto s'affige / per misurar lo cerchio, e non ritrova, / pensando, quel principio ond' elli indige, / tal era io a quella vista nova . . .

As is the geometer who wholly applies himself to measure the circle, and finds not, in pondering, the principle of which he is in need, such was I at that new sight.

P 159:32 (*Arch.* 10:799)

and he would be a priest for ever according to the order of Melchisedec . . .

Par. 8:124-126

per ch'un nasce Solone . . . / altro Melchisedèch e altro quello / che, volando per l'aere, il figlio perse.

so that one is born Solon . . . one Melchizedek and another he who flew through the air and lost his son.

P 159:35-36 (*Arch.* 10:799)

And let you, Stephen, make a novena to your holy patron saint, the first martyr . . .

Purg. 15:106-108

Poi vidi genti accese in foco d'ira / con pietre un giovinetto ancider, forte / gridando a sé pur: "Martira, martira!"

Then I saw people, kindled with the fire of anger, stoning a youth to death, and ever crying out loudly to each other, "Kill, kill!"

P 172:6-7 (*Arch.* 10:855)

Her image had passed into his soul for ever and no word had broken the holy silence of his ecstasy.

VN II

Ed avvegna che la sua imagine, la quale continuamente meco stava, fosse baldanza d'amore a signoreggiarmi, tuttavia era di sì nobile virtù, che nulla volta sofferse che Amore mi reggesse senza il fedele consiglio della ragione, in quelle cose là dove cotal consiglio fosse utile a udire.

And though her image, which remained constantly with me, was Love's assurance of holding me, it was of such a pure qual-

ity that never did it permit me to be over-
ruled by Love without the trusted counsel
of reason. (trans. Musa)

P 172:10 (*Arch.* 10:855)

A wild angel had appeared to him, the
angel of mortal youth and beauty . . .

VN II

Egli mi comandava molte volte, che io
cercassi per vedere quest' angiola
giovanissima . . .

Often he commanded me to seek out this
youngest of angels . . . (trans. Musa)

P 172:26-31 (*Arch.* 10:857)

His soul was swooning into some new
world, fantastic, dim, uncertain as under
sea, traversed by cloudy shapes and
beings.

Par. 2:19-36

La concreata e perpetua sete / del
deiforme regno cen portava / veloci quasi
come 'l ciel vedete / . . . / Parev' a me che
nube ne coprisse / lucida, spessa, solida e
pulita, / quasi adamante che lo sol
ferisse. / Per entro sé l'etterna
margarita / ne ricevette, com' acqua
recepe / raggio di luce . . .

The inborn and perpetual thirst for the
deiform realm bore us away, swift almost
as you see the heavens. . . . It seemed to
me that a cloud had enveloped us, shin-
ing, dense, solid and polished like a dia-
mond smitten by the sun. Within itself the
eternal pearl received us, as water
receives a ray of light . . .

P 172:31-36 (*Arch.* 10:857-859)

A world, a glimmer, or a flower? . . . a
breaking light, an opening flower, it
spread in endless succession to itself . . .
leaf by leaf and wave of light by wave
of light . . .

Par. 30:94-117

così mi si cambiaro in maggior feste / li fiori e le faville, sì ch'io vidi / ambo le corti del ciel manifeste . . . / Lume è là sù, che visible face / lo creatore a quella creatura / . . . / E se l'infimo grado in sé raccoglie / sì grande lume, quanta è la larghezza / di questa rosa ne l'estreme foglie!

so into greater festival the flowers and the sparks did change before me that I saw both the courts of Heaven made manifest. . . . A Light is thereabove which makes the Creator visible to every creature. . . . And if the lowest rank encloses within itself so great a light, how vast is the spread of this rose in its outermost leaves!

P 195:25 (*Arch.* 10:1051)

The heavy lumpish phrase sank slowly out of hearing like a stone through a quagmire.

Par. 3:121-123

. . . vanio / come per acqua cupa cosa grave.

. . . vanished, as through deep water some heavy thing.

P 215:28-30 (*Arch.* 10:1049)

They found many students sheltering under the arcade of the Library. Cranly, leaning against a pillar . . .

VN XIV

Allora dico che io poggiai la mia persona simulatamente ad una pintura, la quale circondava questa magione . . .

Then, so as not to attract attention, I leaned against a painting that ran along the walls of that house . . . (trans. Musa)

P 215:31-33 (*Arch.* 10:1051)

Some girls stood near the entrance door. Lynch whispered to Stephen:
—Your beloved is here

VN XIV

avvenne che questa gentilissima venne in parte, ove molte donne gentili erano adunate; alla qual parte io fui condotto per amica persona, credendosi fare a me gran piacere in quanto mi menava là dove tante donne mostravano le loro bellezze. . . . Sì che io, credendomi far il piacere di questo amico, proposi di stare al servigio delle donne nella sua compagnia . . .

it happened that my most gracious lady went to a place where many worthy ladies were gathered. I was taken there by a friend who believed he was giving me great delight by taking me to such a place where many ladies displayed their beauty. . . . So I, thinking that I should please my friend in so doing, decided to remain with him in attendance upon the ladies. (trans. Musa)

P 215:34-216:1 (*Arch*. 10:1051)

Stephen took his place silently on the step below the group of students . . . turning his eyes towards her from time to time. She too stood silently among her companions.

VN XIV

. . . levai gli occhi, e mirando le donne, vidi tra loro la gentilissima Beatrice.

I raised my eyes and, gazing at the ladies, I saw among them the most gracious Beatrice. (trans. Musa)

P 217:1-14 (*Arch*. 10:1055)

Towards dawn he awoke. . . . In a dream or vision he had known the ecstasy of seraphic life.

VN III

E pensando di lei, mi sopraggiunse un soave sonno, nel quale m'apparve una maravigliosa visione . . . lo mio deboletto sonno non potè sostenere, anzi si ruppe, e fui disvegliato.

In my reverie a sweet sleep seized me, and a marvelous vision appeared to me.

. . . My sleep could not endure but rather it was broken and I awakened. (trans. Musa)

P 217:19-27 (*Arch.* 10:1057)

The instant of inspiration seemed now to be reflected from all sides at once. . . . The instant flashed forth like a point of light and now from cloud on cloud of vague circumstance confused form was veiling softly its afterglow. . . . An afterglow deepened within his spirit, whence the white flame had passed, deepening to a rose and ardent light. That rose and ardent light was her strange, wilful heart.

VN III

che a me parea vedere nella mia camera una nebula di colore di fuoco, dentro alla quale io discernea una figura d'uno signore. . . . E nell' una delle mani mi parea che questi tenesse una cosa, la quale ardesse tutta; e pareami che mi dicesse queste parole: *Vide cor tuum*.

I seemed to see a cloud the color of fire in my room and in that cloud a lordly man. . . . In one of his hands he held a fiery object, and he seemed to say these words: "Behold your heart." (trans. Musa)

P 222:9,20 (*Arch.* 10:1081)

He had written verses for her again after ten years. . . . Ten years from that wisdom of children to his folly.

VN III

Poichè furono passati tanti dì, che appunto erano compiuti li nove anni appresso l'apparimento soprascritto di questa gentilissima . . . proposi di fare un sonetto.

After so many days had passed that precisely nine years had been completed since the appearance I have just described of this very gracious lady . . . I resolved to compose a sonnet. (trans. Musa)

P 232:8-9 *(Arch.* 10:1125)

She passed out from the porch of the library and bowed across Stephen in reply to Cranly's greeting.

VN X

E per questa cagione, cioè di questa soperchievole voce, che parea che m'infamasse viziosamente, quella gentilissima . . . passando per alcuna parte mi negò il suo dolcissimo salutare, nel quale stava tutta la mia beatitudine.

For this reason, namely the scandalous rumors that stripped me of my good name, the most gracious Beatrice . . . passing along a certain way, denied me her most sweet greeting in which lay all my bliss. (trans. Musa)

P 233:25-30 *(Arch.* 10:1131-1133)

It was not thought nor vision though he knew vaguely that her figure was passing homeward through the city. Vaguely first and then more sharply he smelt her body. A conscious unrest seethed in his blood.

VN XIV

Allora furono sì distrutti li miei spiriti per la forza che Amore prese veggendosi in tanta propinquitade alla gentilissima donna che non mi rimase in vita più che gli spiriti del viso; e ancor questi rimasero fuori de' loro strumenti, . . . E avvegna ch'io fossi altro che prima, molto mi dolea di questi spiritelli, che si lamentavano forte . . .

. . . Then were my spirits so disrupted by the strength that Love acquired when he saw himself so close to the most gracious lady, that none remained alive except the spirits of sight; and even these remained outside their instruments, because Love usurped their enviable seat to view the marvelous lady. And even though I was not myself, I was still greatly moved by these little spirits that bitterly protested. (trans. Musa)

P 250:30-32 (*Arch.* 10:1207)   O life! Dark stream of swirling bogwater on which appletrees have cast down their delicate flowers.

Purg. 32:73-75   Quali a veder de' fioretti del melo / che del suo pome li angeli fa ghiotti / e perpetue nozze fa nel cielo . . .

As when brought to see some of the blossoms of the apple tree that makes the angels greedy of its fruit and holds perpetual wedding feasts in Heaven . . .

P 252:5-13 (*Arch.* 10:1211-1213)   *15 April:* Met her today pointblank in Grafton Street. The crowd brought us together. We both stopped. She asked me why I never came, said she had heard all sorts of stories about me. This was only to gain time. Asked me, was I writing poems? About whom? I asked her. This confused her more and I felt sorry and mean. Turned off that valve at once and opened the spiritual-heroic refrigerating apparatus, invented and patented in all countries by Dante Alighieri. Talked rapidly of myself and my plans.

Exiles

EX 16:5 (*Arch.* 11:97)

[Richard]   I had begun to think you would never come back . . .
[Beatrice]   . . . But I have come.

Purg. 30:34-39

E lo spirito mio, che già cotanto / tempo era stato ch'a la sua presenza / non era di stupor, tremando, affranto, / sanza de li occhi aver più conoscenza, / per occulta virtù che da lei mosse, / d'antico amor sentì la gran potenza.

and my spirit, which now for so long a time trembling with awe in her presence had not been overcome, without having more knowledge by the eyes, through occult virtue that proceeded from her, felt old love's great power.

EX 17:13 (*Arch.* 11:98)

[Richard]   Because it is about yourself?
[Beatrice]   Yes. But not only that.
[Richard]   Because it is written by me?

VN XLII

. . . vidi cose, che mi fecero proporre di non dir più di questa benedetta, infino a tanto che io non potesse più degnamente trattare di lei. E di venire a ciò io studio quanto posso, sì com' ella sa veracemente.

. . . I saw things that made me resolve to say no more about this blessed one until I should be capable of writing about her in a more worthy fashion. And to achieve this I am striving as hard as I can, and this she truly knows. (trans. Musa)

EX 18:26 (*Arch.* 11:99)

[Richard]   . . . I sent you from Rome the chapters of my book as I wrote them; and letters for nine long years . . .
[Beatrice]   Yes, it was nearly a year before your first letter came.

VN XXVIII

Tuttavia, perchè molte volte il numero del nove ha preso luogo tra le parole dinanzi, onde pare che sia non senza ragione e nella sua partita cotale numero pare che avesse molto luogo, conviensi qui dire alcuna cosa, acciò che pare al proposito convenirsi. Onde prima dirò come ebbe luogo nella sua partita . . .

Nevertheless, since the number nine has appeared many times among the preceding words, which clearly could not happen without a reason, and since in her departure this number obviously played a part, I think it fitting that I say something here concerning this, inasmuch as it seems pertinent to my theme. Wherefore, I shall tell first the part it played in her departure . . . (trans. Musa)

EX 18:31 (*Arch.* 11:99)

[Beatrice]   . . . it was nearly a year before your first letter came.
[Richard]   It was answered at once by you. And from that on you have watched me in my struggle. [*Joins his hands earnestly*] Tell me, Miss Justice, did you feel that what you read was written for your eyes? Or that you inspired me?

Inf. 2:61-72

l'amico mio . . . ne la diserta piaggia è impedito / sì nel cammin, che vòlt' è per paura; / e temo che non sia già sì smarrito, / ch'io mi sia tardi al soccorso levata, / per quel ch'i' ho di lui nel cielo udito. / . . . I' son Beatrice . . . / amor mi mosse, che mi fa parlare.

my friend . . . finds his way so impeded on the desert slope that he has turned back in fright; and, from what I have heard of him in Heaven, I fear he may already have gone so astray that I am late in arising to help him . . . I am Beatrice. . . . Love moved me and makes me speak. [Beatrice, watching Dante from Heaven, sends Virgil to aid him]

EX 21:5 (*Arch.* 11:101)

[Beatrice]   I always knew you would go some day. I did not suffer; only I was changed. . . .
[Richard]   Yes. I saw that you had changed when I received your first letter after a year; after your illness, too. You even said so in your letter.
[Beatrice]   It brought me near to death. It made me see things differently.

Purg. 30:124-135

Sì tosto come in su la soglia fui / di mia seconda etade e mutai vita, / questi si tolse ·a me, e diessi altrui. / Quando di carne a spirto era salita, / e bellezza e virtù cresciuta m'era, / fu' io a lui men cara e men gradita; / e volse i passi suoi per via non vera. / . . . / Né l'impetrare ispirazion mi valse, / con le quali e in sogno e altrimenti / lo rivocai: sì poco a lui ne calse!

So soon as I was on the threshold of my second age and had changed life, this one took himself from me and gave himself to others. When from flesh to spirit I had ascended, and beauty and virtue were increased in me, I was less dear and less pleasing to him and he turned his steps along a way not true. . . . Nor did it avail me to obtain inspirations with which, both in dream and otherwise, I called him back, so little did he heed them.

EX 24:14 (*Arch.* 11:105)

[Richard] . . . I lived years in exile and poverty too,

Par. 17:55-60

Tu lascerai ogne cosa diletta / più caramente; e questo è quello strale / che l'arco de lo essilio pria saetta. / Tu proverai sì come sa di sale / lo pane altrui, e come è duro calle / lo scendere e 'l salir per l'altrui scale.

You shall leave everything beloved most
dearly; and this is the arrow which the
bow of exile shoots first. You shall come
to know how salt is the taste of another's
bread, and how hard the path to de-
scend and mount by another man's stairs.
[Dante's exile predicted]

Giacomo Joyce

GJ 11:3-4 (*Arch.* 2:297)

She walked before me along the corridor ... So did she walk by Dante in simple pride ...

VN III

e passando per una via volse gli occhi verso quella parte dov'io era molto pauroso;

While walking down a street, she turned her eyes to where I was standing faint-hearted,

GJ 13:1-2 (*Arch.* 2:302)

My words in her mind: cold polished stones sinking through a quagmire.

Par. 3:121

Così parlommi, e poi cominciò *"Ave, / Maria"* cantando, e cantando vanio / come per acqua cupa cosa grave.

Thus did she speak to me, and then began to sing *Ave Maria*, and, singing, vanished, as through deep water some heavy thing.

GJ 15:4-6 (*Arch.* 2:306)

E col suo vedere attosca l'uomo quando lo vede. I thank you for the word, Messer Brunetto.

Inf. 15:119

Siete raccomandato il mio Tesoro, / nel qual io vivo ancora ...

Let my *Treasure* in which I still live be commended to you. [Brunetto Latini]

GJ 15:4-6, 27-29 (*Arch.* 2:307)

She speaks. A weak voice from beyond the cold stars. Voice of wisdom. Say on! O, say again, making me wise! This voice I never heard.

Par. 2:124-126

Riguarda bene omai sì com'io vado / per questo loco al vero che disiri, / sì che poi sappi sol tener lo guado.

Observe well now how I advance through this pass to the truth which you seek, so that hereafter you may know how to take the ford alone. [Beatrice, instructing Dante as they journey through the *Paradiso*.]

Ulysses

U 21:41 (*Arch*. 22:70)	Now I eat his salt bread
Par. 17:58-59	Tu proverai sì come sa di sale / lo pane altrui . . .
	You shall come to know how salt is the taste of another's bread . . .

U 22:30 (*Arch*. 12:233; *Ros.MS* P.21)	Sabellius
Par. 13:127	sì fé Sabellio e Arrio e quelli stolti
	Thus did Sabellius, and Arius, and those fools

U 27:8 (*Ros.MS* P.26)	Through the dear might of Him that walked the waves
Par. 24:38-39	per la qual tu su per lo mare andavi.
	concerning the Faith by which you did walk upon the sea.

U 29:12 (*Ros.MS* P.28)	Averroës
Inf. 4:144	Averoìs che 'l gran comento feo
	Averroës, who made the great commentary.

U 38:8 (*Ros.MS* P.32; *Arch*. 12:239)	*maestro di color che sanno*
Inf. 4:131	vidi 'l maestro di color che sanno
	I saw the Master of those who know,

U 46:28 (*Arch*. 12:250)	the courtiers who mocked Guido
Inf. 10:63	forse cui Guido vostro ebbe a disdegno
	whom perhaps your Guido had in disdain

U 59:42 (*Arch.* 22:177)

O please, Mr. Policeman, I'm lost in the wood.

Inf. 1:2-3

mi ritrovai per una selva oscura / che la diritta via era smarrita.

I found myself in a dark wood, for the straight way was lost.

U 95:20 (*Arch.* 17:220)

Yet sometimes they repent too late. Found in the riverbed clutching rushes.

Purg. 5:82-108

"Corsi al palude, e le cannucce e il braco / m'impigliar sì ch' i caddi . . . / . . . / . . . a piè del Casentino / traversa un'acqua c'ha nome l'Archiano, / . . . Là 've 'l vocabol suo diventa vano, / arriva' io forato ne la gola, / fuggendo a piede e sanguinando il piano. / . . . / . . . e quivi / caddi, e rimase la mia carne sola. / . . . / l'angel di Dio mi prese, e quel d'inferno / gridava: 'O tu del ciel, perché mi privi? / Tu te ne porti di costui l'etterno / per una lagrimetta che 'l mi toglie; / ma io farò de l'altro altro governo!' "

"I ran to the marsh, and the reeds and the mire so entangled me that I fell . . . At the foot of the Casentino a stream crosses, named the Archiano. . . . To the place where its name is lost I came, wounded in the throat, flying on foot and bloodying the plain. . . . The Angel of God took me, and he from Hell cried, 'O you from Heaven, why do you rob me? You carry off with you the eternal part of him for one little tear which takes him from me; but of the rest I will make other disposal!' " (Buonconte da Montefeltro and his companion, the late-repentant)

U 98:10 (*Arch.* 17:239)

to row me o'er the ferry . . . to heaven by water

Inf. 3:86

i' vegno per menarvi al l'altra riva . . .

I come to carry you to the other shore . . .
[Charon speaking]

Purg. 2:41-42

. . . un vasello snelletto e leggero, / tanto
che l'acque nulla ne 'nghiottiva. / Da
poppa stava il celestial nocchiero . . .

A vessel so swift and light that the water
took in naught of it. At the stern stood the
celestial steersman . . .

U 102:29 (*Arch.* 22:384)

Must be an infernal lot of bad gas round
the place

Inf. 18:106-108

Le ripe eran grommate d'una muffa, /
per l'alito di giù che vi s'appasta, / che con li
occhi e col naso facea zuffa.

The banks were crusted over with a mold
from the vapor below that sticks on them
and that did battle with the eyes and with
the nose.

U 108:10 (*Arch.* 12:281)

Now who is that lankylooking galoot
over there in the macintosh? Now who is
he I'd like to know? Now, I'd give a trifle
to know who he is. Always someone
turns up you never dreamt of.

[Dante, cf. 108:23; 251:5-6; 327:34.]

U 109:32 (*Arch.* 17:266)

Out of the fryingpan of life into the fire
of purgatory.

Purg. 26:148

Poi s'ascose nel foco che li affina.

Then he hid himself in the fire that
purifies them.

U 112:22-23 (*Arch.* 12:283:
Ros. MS P. 109)

How many! All these here once walked
round Dublin. Faithful departed. As you
are now so once were we.

Inf. 3:55-57 e dietro le venìa sì lunga tratta / di gente, ch'i' non averei creduto / che morte tanta n'avesse disfatta.

and behind came so long a train of people that I should never have believed death had undone so many.

U 113:28 (*Arch.* 17:254) There is another world after death named hell.

Inf. 18:1 Luogo è in inferno detto Malebolge ...

There is a place in Hell called Malebolge ...

U 136:28 (*Arch.* 18:61) RHYMES AND REASONS

[Dante's precise choice of rhyme-words.]

U 136:37 (*Arch.* 12:296; *Ros.MS* P. 132) two men dressed the same, looking the same, two by two.

Purg. 29:134-135 vidi due vecchi in abito dispari, / ma pari in atto e onesto e sodo.

I saw two old men, unlike in dress but alike in bearing, venerable and grave.

U 137:1-3 (*Ros.MS* P.132; *Arch.* 12:296) . . . . *la tua pace*
. . . . *che parlar ti piace*
mentreche il vento come fa, si tace.

Inf. 5:92,94,96 noi pregheremmo lui de la tua pace, / . . .
Di quel che udire e che parlar vi piace, /
. . . mentre che 'l vento, come fa, ci tace.

We would pray Him for your peace, . . .
of that which it pleases you to hear and
to speak, . . . while the wind, as now, is silent
for us.

U 137:4-5 (*Ros.MS* P.133; He saw them three by three, approaching
Arch. 12:296) girls, in green, in rose, in russet, entwining . . .

      Purg. 29:121-128 Tre donne in giro da la destra rota /
venian danzando; l'una tanto rossa / ch'a
pena fora dentro al foco nota; / l'altr' era
come se le carni e l'ossa / fossero state di
smeraldo fatte; / la terza parea neve testé
mossa; / e or parean da la bianca tratte, /
or da la rossa . . .

Three ladies came dancing in a round at
the right wheel, one of them so ruddy
that she would hardly have been noted in
the fire; another was as if her flesh and
bones had been of emerald; the third
seemed new fallen snow; and they seemed
to be led, now by the white, now by the
red . . .

U 137:5 (*Ros.MS* P.133; *per l'aer perso*
Arch. 12:296)

      Inf. 5:89 per l'aere perso

through the black air

U 137:6 (*Ros.MS* P.133; *quella pacifica oriafiamma*, in gold of
Arch. 12:296 oriflamme . . .

      Par. 31:127 così quella pacifica oriafiamma / nel
mezzo s'avvivava . . .

So was that pacific oriflamme quickened
in the middle . . .

U 137:6-7 (*Ros.MS* P.134; *di rimirar fé più ardenti*.
Arch. 12:296)

      Par. 31:142 che' miei di rimirar fé più ardenti.

he made mine eyes more ardent in their
gazing.

U 137:8 (*Ros.MS* P.134; Arch. 12:296)	But I old men, penitent, leadenfooted
Inf. 23:59,65	che giva intorno assai con lenti passi, / [ma] . . . dentro tutte piombo, e gravi tanto,
	who were going round with very slow steps [but] within, all of lead, and so heavy
U 137:8-9 (*Arch*. 18:69)	underdarkneath the night . . .
	[Dante's poem-vision: Stephen's imagination encapsulates the *Divine Comedy*]
U 137:23 (*Arch*. 18:69)	LINKS WITH BYGONE DAYS OF YORE
	[the Dantean allusions in Stephen's mind]
U 138:8 (*Arch*. 18:70)	ITALIA, MAGISTRA ARTIUM
	[Dante's *Divine Comedy*]
U 142:42; 143:2 (*Arch*. 18:73)	Dublin. I have much, much to learn. . . . —I have a vision too, Stephen said.
	[Stephen sees himself as Dublin's Dante after reviewing Dante's rhymes]
U 168:22 (*Arch*. 18:124)	Harpooning flitches
Inf. 21:55-57	. . . i cuoci a' lor vassalli / fanno attuffare in mezzo la caldaia / la carne con li uncin . . .
	cooks make their scullions plunge the meat down into the cauldron with their forks . . .

U 182:37 (*Ros.MS* P.176;   *Ed egli avea del cul fatto trombetta*
Arch. 12:350)

     Inf. 21:139   ed elli avea del cul fatto trombetta

                                  and he had made a trumpet of his arse

U 192:11 (*Ros.MS* P.186;   A basilisk. *E quando vede l'uomo l'attosca.*
Arch. 12:356)   Messer Brunetto, I thank thee for the
                                  word.

     Inf. 15:119-120   Sieti raccomandato il mio Tesoro, / nel
                                  qual io vivo ancora . . .

                                  Let my *Treasure*, in which I yet live, be
                                  commended to you . . .

U 204:33 (*Ros.MS* P.198;   *nel mezzo del cammin di nostra vita*
Arch. 12:364

     Inf. 1:1   Nel mezzo del cammin di nostra vita

                                  Midway in the journey of our life

U 205:37-38 (*Ros.MS* P.199;   nature, as Mr. Magee understands her,
Arch. 12:364)   abhors perfection

     Par. 13:76   ma la natura la dà sempre scema,

                                  But nature always gives it defectively

U 209:25-26 (*Ros.MS* P.203;   in the middle of his life
Arch. 12:367

     Inf. 1:1   Nel mezzo del cammin di nostra vita

                                  Midway in the journey of our life

U 225:19-20 (*Ros.MS* P.219;   *Eppoi mi sono convinto che il mondo è*
Arch. 13:3, 13)   *una bestia.*

     Inf. 15:73-74   Faccian le bestie fiesolane strame / di lor
                                  medesme . . .

Let the Fiesolan beasts make fodder of
themselves . . .

U 225:24-25 *(Ros.MS* P.219;   *Ma, dia retta a me. Ci refletta . . . Ci riflet-*
Arch. 13:3-4)   *terò, Stephen said . . .*

      Inf. 15:55-57, 70   Ed elli a me: Se tu segui tua stella, / non
                                        puoi fallire a glorioso porto, / . . . / La tua
                                        fortuna tanto onor ti serba . . .

                                        And he to me: "If you follow your star
                                        you cannot fail of a glorious port. . . .
                                        Your fortune holds for you such honor
                                        . . .

U 225:42-226:1 *(Ros.MS* P.220;   Almidano Artifoni . . . trotted on stout
Arch. 13:4, 14)   trousers after the Dalkey tram. In vain he
                                        trotted, signalling in vain . . .

      Inf. 15:121-123   Poi si rivolse e parve di coloro / che cor-
                                        rono a Verona . . . / . . . e parve di
                                        costoro / quelli che vince, non colui che
                                        perde.

                                        Then he turned back, and seemed like
                                        one of those who run . . . at Verona, and
                                        of them seemed he who wins, not he who
                                        loses.

U 245:25 *(Ros.MS* P.239;   They drove his wits astray, he said, by
Arch. 13:27)   visions of hell . . .

                                        [Stephen's Catholicism and Dante's
                                        Inferno]

U 251:5-6 *(Ros.MS* P.244;   a pedestrian in a brown macintosh, eating
Arch. 13:30)   dry bread, passed swiftly and unscathed
                                        across the viceroy's path.

      Par. 17:58-59   Tu proverai sì come sa di sale / lo pane
                                        altrui,

                                        You shall come to know how salt is the
                                        taste of another's bread.

Inf. 9:79-81

vid' io più di mille anime distrutte / fuggir
così dinanzi ad un ch'al passo / passava
Stige con le piante asciutte.

I saw more than a thousand ruined souls
flee before one that strode dry-shod over
Styx.

U 269:36 (*Ros.MS* P.263;
Arch. 13:70

her first merciful lovesoft oftloved word

Inf. 5:103

Amor, che a nullo amato amar

Love, which absolves no loved one from
loving

U 269:37-38 (*Ros.MS* P. 263;
Arch. 13:70)

Love that is singing: love's old sweet
song. . . . Love's old sweet *sonnez
la gold*.

Inf. 5:100,103,106

Amor, ch' al cor gentil ratto s'apprende /
. . . / Amor, ch'a nullo amato amar
perdona / . . . / Amor condusse noi ad
una morte.

Love, which is quickly kindled in a gentle
heart. . . . / Love, which absolves no loved
one from loving. . . . / Love brought us to
one death.

U 270:22 (*Ros.MS* P.263;
Arch. 13:70)

Bloom looped, unlooped, noded,
disnoded.

Par. 28:58

Se li tuoi diti non sono a tal nodo

If your fingers are insufficient for such
a knot

U 273:16 (*Arch*. 24:210)

her wavyavyeavyheavyeavyevyevy
hair un comb: 'd.

Par. 31:128

nel mezzo s'avvivava . . . / . . . / . . . allen-
tava la fiamma;

quickened in the middle . . . / . . . / . . .
tempering its flame

U 286:16-18,23 (*Arch.* 13:54)

Prrprr. Must be the bur. Fff. Oo. Rrpr.
Nations of the earth. No one behind.
She's passed. *Then and not till then.* Tram.
Kran, kran, kran. Good oppor. Coming
Krandlkrankran. I'm sure it's the bur-
gund. Yes. One, two. Let my epitaph be.
Karaaaaaaa. Written. I have.
Pprrpffrrppff. Done.

Inf. 21:139

ed elli avea del cul fatto trombetta

and he had made a trumpet of his arse

U 291:38 (*Arch.* 25:16)

Dante Alighieri, Christopher Columbus,
S. Fursa, S. Brendan, . . .

U 327:29 (*Ros.MS* P.319;
Arch. 13:161)

Love loves to love love.

Inf. 5:103

Amor ch' a nullo amato amar perdona

Love, which absolves no loved one from
loving.

U 327:33-34 (*Ros.MS* P.319;
Arch 13:161-162)

The man in the brown macintosh loves a
lady who is dead.

[Dante and Beatrice, *cf.* 108:10; 108:23;
251:5-6; and 420:10, "Walking Mackin-
tosh of lonely canyon."]

U 339:17/22 (*Ros.MS* P.330;
Arch. 13:168)

When, lo, there came about them all a
great brightness and they beheld the
chariot wherein He stood ascend to
Heaven. And they beheld Him in the
chariot, clothed upon in the glory of the
brightness, having raiment as of the sun,
fair as the moon and terrible that for awe
they durst not look upon Him. . . . And
they beheld Him, even Him, ben Bloom
Elijah, amid clouds of angels, ascend to
the glory of the brightness at an angle of
forty-five degrees over Donohoe's in Little Green Street like a shot off a shovel.

Inf. 26:34-39

E qual colui che si vengiò con li orsi / vide 'l carro d'Elia al dipartire, / quando i cavalli al cielo erti levorsi, / che nol potea sì con li occhi seguire, / ch'el vedesse altro che la fiamma sola, / si come nuvoletta, in sù salire . . .

And as he who was avenged by the bears saw Elijah's chariot at its departure, when the horses rose erect to heaven—for he could not so follow it with his eyes as to see aught save the flame alone, like a little cloud ascending . . .

U 383:38 (*Ros.MS* P.372; *Arch.* 14:76)

according to the opinions of Averroes

Purg. 25:62-63

. . . quest' è tal punto, / che più savio di té fé già errante.

this is such a point that once it made one wiser than you [Averroes] to err.

U 383:39 (*Ros.MS* P.372; *Arch.* 14:77)

He said also how at the end of the second month a human soul was infused

Purg. 25:68-72

sì tosto come al feto / l'articular del cerebro è perfetto / lo motor primo a lui si volge lieto / sovra tant' arte di natura, e spira / spirito novo, di vertù repleto . . .

so soon as in the foetus the articulation of the brain is perfect, the First Mover turns to it with joy over such art of nature, and breathes into it a new spirit replete with virtue . . .

U 385:5-6 (*Ros.MS* P.373; *Arch.* 14:23)

Desire's wind blasts the thorntree but after it becomes from a bramblebush to be a rose upon the rood of time.

Par. 13:133-135

ch'i' ho veduto tutto 'l verno prima / lo prun mostrarsi rigido e feroce, / poscia portar la rosa in su la cima;

for I have seen first, all winter through,
the thorn display itself hard and stiff, and
then upon its summit bear the rose.

U 385:20 *(Ros. MS* P.373;
Arch. 14:23)

vergine madre figlia di tuo figlio

    Par. 33:1

"Vergine Madre, figlia del tuo figlio,

Virgin Mother, Daughter of thy Son,

U 388:34-35 *(Ros.MS* P.377;
Arch. 14:178)

Master Bloom, at the braggart's side,
spoke to him calming words to slumber
his great fear,

    Purg. 20:134-135

. . . 'l maestro inverso me si feo, / dicendo:
"Non dubbiar, mentr' io ti guido."

my master drew toward me, saying, "Do
not fear while I guide you."

U 400:41-42 *(Ros.MS* P.388;
Arch. 14:115)

It was now for more than the middle span
of our allotted years

    Inf. 1:1

Nel mezzo del cammin di nostra vita

Midway in the journey of our life

U 402:31 *(Ros.MS* P.389;
Arch. 14:120)

A very pelican in his piety

    Par. 25:112-113

"Questi è colui che giacque sopra 'l
petto / del nostro Pellicano . . .

"This is he who lay upon the breast of our
Pelican . . .

U 405:18 *(Ros.MS* P.392;
Arch. 14:128, 149)

The inferno has no terrors for me.

U 406:6 *(Ros.MS* P.393;
Arch. 14:127)

a retrospective arrangement, a mirror
within a mirror

Par. 29:144	speculi fatti s'ha in che si spezza
	mirrors wherein it is mirrored

U 407:32 (*Ros.MS* P.394; *Arch.* 14:131)	the penultimate antelucan hour
Purg. 27:109	E già, per li splendori antelucani,
	And now before the splendors which precede the dawn,

U 424:11 (*Ros.MS* P.410; *Arch.* 15:5, 157)	(Stephen . . . chants with joy the introit for paschal time.)
Inf. 21:112-114	Ier, più oltre cinqu' ore che quest' otta, / mille dugento con sessanta sei / anni compié che qui la via fu rotta.
	Yesterday, five hours later than now, completed one thousand two hundred and sixty-six years since the road was broken here. [Dante's journey takes place in Holy Week]

U 428:08 (*Ros.MS* P.414; *Arch.* 15:10, 162)	A dragon sandstrewer
Inf. 3:30	come la rena quando turbo spira
	like sand when a whirlwind blows

U 429:22-23 (*Ros.MS* P.415; *Arch.* 15:11, 163)	He steps forward. A sackshouldered ragman bars his path. He steps left, ragsackman left.
Inf. 10:133	Appresso mosse a man sinistra il piede
	Then he turned his steps to the left
Inf. 23:68	Noi ci volgemmo ancor pur a man manca / con loro insieme . . .
	We turned, ever to the left, along with them . . .

Inf. 29:52-53	Noi discendemmo in su l'ultima riva / del lungo scoglio, pur da man sinistra . . .
	We descended onto the last bank of the long crag, keeping ever to the left . . .
U 429:33 (*Ros.MS* P.415; *Arch*. 15:11, 163)	I who lost my way
Inf. 1:3	che la diritta via era smarrita
	for the straight way was lost
U 435:20-21 (*Ros.MS* P.421; *Arch*. 14:213)	Mr. Bloom! You down here in the haunts of sin!
Inf. 15:30	. . . "Siete voi qui, ser Brunetto?"
	"Are you here, ser Brunetto!"
U 442:09 (*Ros.MS* P.427; *Arch*. 14:215)	Followed by the whining dog he [Bloom] walks on toward hellsgates.
Inf. 8:76-82	Noi pur giugnemmo dentro a l'alte fosse / che vallan quella terra sconsolata: / le mura mi parean che ferro fosse. / . . . / Io vidi più di mille in su le porte . . .
	We came at last into the deep moats entrenching that doleful city. The walls seemed to me to be of iron. . . . Above the gates I saw more than a thousand . . .
U 445:19-21 (*Ros.MS* P.430; *Arch*. 14:217)	(With regret he lets unrolled crubeen and trotter slide. The mastiff mauls the bundle clumsily and gluts himself with growling greed crunching the bones . . .)
Inf. 6:28-30	Qual è quel cane ch'abbaiando agugna, / e si racqueta poi che 'l pasto morde, / ché solo a divorarlo intende e pugna . . .

As the dog that barking craves, and then grows quiet when he snaps up his food, straining and struggling to devour it . . . [Cerberus]

U 493:14 (*Ros.MS* P.474; *Arch*. 14:222)

caela enarrant gloriam Domini.

        Par. 27:1-2

"Al Padre, al Figlio, a lo Spirito Santo," / cominciò, "gloria!" tutto 'l paradiso . . .

"Glory be to the Father, to the Son, and to the Holy Spirit!" all Paradise began . . .

U 495:42 (*Ros.MS* P.476; *Arch*. 15:66, 216)

all at once thrusts his lipless face through the fork of his thighs.

        Inf. 25:121-123

l'un si levò, e l'altro cadde giuso, / non torcendo però le lucerne empie, / sotto le quai ciascun cambiava muso.

the one rose upright and the other fell down, but neither turned aside the baleful lamps beneath which each was changing his muzzle.

U 500:25 (*Ros.MS* P.481; *Arch*. 15:73, 223)

Lipoti Virag . . . chutes rapidly down through the chimneyflue . . .

        Par. 15:20-21

a piè di quella croce corse un astro / de la costellazion che lì risplende . . .

there darted a star of the resplendent constellation that is there, down to the foot of that cross . . .

U 503:38 (*Ros.MS* P.484; *Arch*. 14:224; 15:76, 226)

You intended to devote an entire year to the study of the religious problem and the summer months of 1882 to square the circle.

        Par. 33:133-134

Qual è 'l geomètra che tutto s' affige / per misurar lo cerchio,

As is the geometer who wholly applies himself to measure the circle

U 504:6-8 (*Ros.MS* P.484)

I wanted then to have now concluded. . . . But tomorrow is a new day will be. Past was is today. What now is will then tomorrow as now was be past yester.

Par. 17:16-18

così vedi le cose contingenti / anzi che sieno in sé, mirando il punto / a cui tutti li tempi son presenti;

so you, gazing upon the Point to which all times are present, do see contingent things before they exist in themselves.

U 504:18 (*Arch.* 15:277)

For all these knotty points see the seventeenth book

Par. 17:16-18

[Cacciaguida's explanation of contingency, in the seventeenth canto]

U 504:27 (*Ros.MS* P.484; *Arch.* 15:77, 277)

Nightbird, nightsun nighttown.

Inf. 22:96

malvagio uccello!

villainous bird!

U 505:30 (*Ros.MS* P.485-486; *Arch.* 15:79)

hunched wingshoulders

Inf. 21:34

L'omero suo, ch' era aguto e superbo . . .

His shoulder, which was sharp and high . . .

U 506:15-18 (*Ros.MS* P.486; *Arch.* 14:277)

Henry Flower comes forward . . . he carries a silver-stringed inlaid dulcimer . . .

Inf. 28:134

sappi ch' i' son Bertram dal Bornio . . .

know that I am Bertran de Born . . .

U 510:16-17 (*Ros.MS* P.490)   He sticks out a flickering phosphores-
cent scorpion tongue

                 Inf. 21:137-138   ma prima avea ciascun la lingua stretta /
coi denti verso lor duca per cenno . . .

                                           but first each pressed his tongue between
his teeth at their leader for a signal . . .

U 511:5-6 (*Ros.MS* P.490;   [Henry] (Caressing on his breast a
Arch. 14:261, 263)   severed female head . . .)

                  Inf. 28:119,121   un busto sanza capo andar sì come / . . . /
e 'l capo tronco tenea per le chiome . . .

                                           a trunk without the head going along . . .
and it was holding the severed head by
the hair . . .

U 511:12 (*Ros.MS* P.490;   He yawns, showing a coalblack throat and
Arch. 14:262)   closes his jaws by an upward push of his
parchment roll.

                     Inf. 12:77-78   Chirón prese uno strale, e con la cocca /
fece la barba in dietro a le mascelle.

                                           Chiron took an arrow and, with the notch
of it, brushed back his beard upon his
jaws . . .

U 511:24-25 (*Ros.MS* P.491;   Virag unscrews his head in a trice and
Arch. 14:263)   holds it under his arm.

                  Inf. 28:119, 121-122   un busto sanza capo andar sì come /
andavan li altri della trista greggia; / e 'l
capo tronco tenea per le chiome, / pesol
con mano a guisa di lanterna . . .

                                           a trunk without the head going along as
were the others of that dismal herd, and it
was holding the severed head by the hair,
swinging it in hand like a lantern . . .

U 539:2-3 (*Ros.MS* P.515; Arch. 14:319)

A birdchief, bluestreaked and feathered in war panoply with his assegai . . .

Par. 15:139-141

Poi seguitai lo 'mperador Currado; / ed el mi cinse de la sua milizia, / tanto per bene ovrar li venni in grado.

Afterward I followed the Emperor Conrad, who girt me with his knighthood, so much did I win his favor by good work. [Cacciaguida, the warrior captain]

U 540:23-24 (*Ros.MS* P.517; Arch. 14:322; 15:260)

The Nymph (with a cry, flees from him unveiled, her plaster cast cracking, a cloud of stench escaping from the cracks . . .)

Purg. 19:31-33

L'altra prendea, e dinanzi l'apria / fendendo i drappi, e mostravami 'l ventre; / quel mi svegliò col puzzo che n' uscia.

He [Virgil] seized the other and laid her bare in front, rending her garments and showing me her belly: this waked me with the stench that issued therefrom.

U 547:26-27 (*Ros.MS* P.523; Arch. 14:237; 15:266)

. . . the coffin of the pianola flies open, the bald little round jack-in-the-box head of Father Dolan springs up.

Inf. 10:52-55

Allor surse a la vista scoperchiata / un'ombra, lungo questa, infino al mento: / . . . / Dintorno mi guardò . . .

Then there arose to sight alongside of him a shade, visible to the chin. . . . He looked round about me . . .

U 548:1-2 (*Ros.MS* P.523; Arch. 14:332; 15:267)

(Mild, benign, rectorial, reproving, the head of Don John Conmee rises from the pianola coffin.)

Inf. 10:32

Vedi là Farinata che s'è dritto . . .

See there Farinata who has risen erect . . .

U 553:12-13 (*Ros.MS* P.528;
Arch. 14:241, 340)

(Stephen and Bloom gaze in the mirror.
The face of William Shakespeare, beard-
less, appears there . . .)

Par. 15:61-62

. . . ché i minori e' grandi / di questa vita
miran ne lo speglio / in che, prima che
pensi, il pensier pandi;

for the lesser and the great of this life
gaze into that mirror in which, before you
think, you display your thought.

U 583:28-32 (*Ros.MS* P.556;
Arch. 14:369)

Father Malachi O'Flynn, in a long pet-
ticoat and reversed chasuble, his two left
feet back to front, celebrates camp mass.
The Reverend Mr. Hugh C. Haines Love
M.A. in a plain cassock and mortar
board, his head and collar back to the
front . . .

Inf. 20:11-15

mirabilmente apparve esser travolto /
ciascun tra 'l mento e 'l principio del
casso, / ché de le reni era tornato 'l
volto, / e in dietro venir li convenia, /
perché 'l veder dinanzi era lor tolto.

each seemed to be strangely distorted between the chin and the beginning of the
chest, for the face was turned toward the
loins, and they had to come backwards
since seeing forward was denied them.

U 583:33 (*Ros. MS* P.556;
Arch. 14:369)

Introibo ad altare diaboli. ["I will go unto
the altar of the devil:" altered from "*Introibo ad altare Dei*," the opening lines of the
old Catholic Mass.]

Inf. 34:1

"*Vexilla regis prodeunt inferni* . . .

The banners of the King of Hell advance
. . .

U 592:16-17 (*Ros.MS* P.564;
Arch. 15:152, 297)

[Bloom] Stephen! (There is no answer.
He calls again.) Stephen!

Inf. 1:79	"Or se' tu quel Virgilio . . . ?"
	"Are you, then, . . . Virgil?"

U 592:24-593:1, (*Ros.MS* P.564;	. . . shadows . . . the woods.
Arch. 15:153, 298)	
Inf. 1:60, 93	là dove 'l sol tace . . . d'esto loco / selvaggio . . .
	where the sun is silent . . . this wild place . . .

U 593:1 (*Ros.MS* P.564;	A dog barks in the distance . . . the
Arch. 15:153, 298)	Hound
Inf. 1:101-102	. . . infin che 'l Veltro / verrà, che la farà morir con doglia.
	until the Hound shall come, who will deal her a painful death.

U 593:5 (*Ros.MS* P.565;	In the shady wood.
Arch. 15:153, 298)	
Inf. 1:2	per una selva oscura
	In a dark wood

U 597:27 (*Ros.MS* P.569)	they made tracks to the left
Inf. 10:133	Appresso mosse a man sinistra il piede
	Then he turned his steps to the left
Inf. 23:68	Noi ci volgemmo ancor pur a man manca / con loro insieme . . .
	We turned, ever to the left, along with them . . .
Inf. 29:52-53	Noi discendemmo in su l'ultima riva / del lungo scoglio, pur da man sinistra . . .
	We descended onto the last bank of the long crag, keeping ever to the left . . .

U 599:40 (*Ros.MS* P.571)

Stephen . . . stopped for no special reason to look at the heap of barren cobblestones

Inf. 12:28-45

Così prendemmo via giù per lo scarco / di quelle pietre . . . / . . . / Io gia pensando; e quei disse: "Tu pensi / forse a questa ruina . . .

So we took our way down over that rocky debris. . . . I was going along thinking, and he said, "Perhaps you are thinking on this ruin . . .

U 608;24-26 (*Ros.MS* P.580)

My little woman's down there. She's waiting for me, I know. . . . She's my own true wife I haven't seen for seven years now, sailing about.

Inf. 26:91-97

mi diparti' da Circe, . . . / né dolcezza di figlio, né la pieta / del vecchio padre, né 'l debito amore / lo qual dovea Penelopè far lieta, / vincer potero dentro a me l'ardore / ch' i' ebbi a divenir del mondo esperto . . .

When I departed from Circe . . . neither fondness for my son, nor reverence for my aged father, nor the due love which would have made Penelope glad, could conquer in me the longing that I had to gain experience of the world . . .

U 610:24 (*Ros.MS* P.581)

Mr. Bloom, without evincing surprise, unostentatiously turned over the card to peruse the partially obliterated address and postmark . . . *Santiago, Chile*.

Inf. 26:127-128

Tutte le stelle già de l'altro polo / vedea la notte . . .

The night now saw the other pole and all its stars . . . [Dante's Ulysses in the southern hemisphere]

U 613:42 (*Ros.MS* P.585; Arch. 15:327)

Have you seen the Rock of Gibraltar? Mr. Bloom inquired . . .

Inf. 26:107-108

. . . venimmo a quella foce stretta / dov' Ercule segnò li suoi riguardi

we came to that narrow outlet where Hercules set up his markers

U 614:26 (*Ros.MS* P.585; Arch. 15:327, 328, 329)

possibly he had tried to find out the secret for himself, floundering up and down the antipodes and all that sort of thing and over and under—well not exactly under—tempting the fates.

Inf. 26:124-132

e volta nostra poppa nel mattino, / de' remi facemmo ali al folle volo, / . . . / Tutte le stelle già de l'altro polo / vedea la notte, e 'l nostro tanto basso, / che non surgea fuor del marin suolo. / Cinque volte racceso e tanto casso / lo lume era di sotto da la luna, / poi che 'ntrati eravam ne l'alto passo . . .

And turning our stern to the morning, we made of our oars wings for the mad flight. . . . The night now saw the other pole and all its stars, and ours so low that it did not rise from the ocean floor. Five times the light beneath the moon had been rekindled and as many quenched, since we had entered on the passage of the deep . . . [Ulysses voyages to the Southern Hemisphere]

U 614:31-34 (*Ros.Ms* P.585; Arch. 15:329)

the eloquent fact remained that the sea was there in all its glory and in the natural course of things somebody or other had to sail on it and fly in the face of providence.

Inf. 26:112-117

"O frati," dissi, "che per cento milia / perigli siete giunti a l'occidente, / a questa tanto picciola vigilia / d'i nostri sensi ch'è del rimanente / non vogliate negar l'esperienza, / di retro a sol, del mondo sanza gente."

"O brothers," I said, "who through a hundred thousand dangers have reached the west, to this so brief vigil of our senses that remains to us, choose not to deny experience, following the sun, of the world that has no people."

U 615:37-38 (*Ros.MS* P.586; *Arch*. 15:329)

Fellow the name of Antonio done that. There he is himself, a Greek.

Inf. 26:73-74

Lascia parlare a me . . . / perch' e fuor greci . . .

leave speech to me . . . since they were Greeks . . .

U 616:8-9 (*Ros.MS* P.587; *Arch*. 15:331)

—Ay, ay, sighed the sailor, looking down on his manly chest. He's gone too. Ate by sharks after.

Inf. 26:139-142

"Tre volte il fé girar con tutte l'acque; / . . . / infin che 'l mar fu sovra noi richiuso."

"Three times it whirled her around with all the waters . . . till the sea closed over us." [Ulysses' last voyage ends in death]

U 618:3-4 (*Ros.MS* P.588; *Arch*. 15:333)

[Stephen said,] They tell me on the best authority it [the soul] is a simple substance and therefore incorruptible. . . . Mr. Bloom thoroughly acquiesced . . . rejoining:—Simple? I shouldn't think that is the proper word. Of course I grant you, to concede a point, you do knock across a simple soul once in a blue moon.

Purg. 16:85-86, 88

Esce di mano a lui . . . / . . . / l'anima semplicetta, che sa nulla, / salvo che, mosse da lieto fattore, / volontier torna a ciò che la trastulla.

from his hands, who fondly loves it before it exists, comes forth . . . the simple
little soul, which knows nothing, save
that, proceeding from a glad Maker, it
turns eagerly to what delights it.

U 621:31 (*Ros.MS* P.592;
Arch. 15:339, 387)

Dante and the isosceles triangle, Miss Portinari, he fell in love with . . .

VN II

She was called Beatrice . . . her image,
which remained constantly with me, was
Love's assurance of holding me.

Purg. 30:34,39

E lo spirito mio . . . / d'antico amor sentì la
gran potenza.

and my spirit . . . felt old love's great
power.

U 622:30-31 (*Ros.MS* P.593
Arch. 15:341)

He made tracks heavily, slowly . . . and
bore due left.

Inf. 26:125-126

de' remi facemmo ali al folle volo, /
sempre acquistando dal lato mancino.

we made of our oars wings for the mad
flight, always gaining on the left.

U 625:1-2 (*Ros.MS* P.595;
Arch. 15:345, 389)

he explained to them about the vulnera-
ble point of Achilles, the Greek hero—

Inf. 26:62

Deidamìa ancor si duol d' Achille . . .

the dead Deidamìa still mourns Achilles
. . .

U 644:29-30 (*Ros.MS* P.614;
Arch. 15:368, 400)

. . . he skipped around nimbly . . . to get
on his companion's right, a habit of his.

Purg. 14:140-141

e allor, per ristrignermi al poeta, / in
destro feci, e non innanzi, il passo,

and then, to draw close to the poet, I
made a step to the right, not forward.

Purg. 30:43

volsimi a la sinistra col respitto / col quale il fantolin . . .

I turned to the left with the confidence of a little child . . .

U 649:26 (*Ros.MS* P.649; *Arch.* 15:360; 403)

sirens, enemies of man's reason

Purg. 19:19-33

"Io son," cantava, "io son dolce serena, / che marinari in mezzo mar dismago"; / . . . / Ancor non era sua bocca richiusa, / quand' una donna apparve santa e presta / . . . / "O Virgilio, Virgilio, chi è questa?" / fieramente dicea; ed el venìa / con li occhi fitti pur in quella onesta.

"I am," she sang, "I am the sweet Siren who leads mariners astray in mid-sea . . ." Her mouth was not yet shut when a lady, holy and alert appeared. . . . "O Virgil, Virgil, who is this?" she said sternly; and he came on with his eyes fixed only on that honest one.

U 666:3-8 (*Ros.MS* P.634; *Arch.* 16:52)

He thought that he thought that he was a jew whereas he knew that he
knew that he knew that he was not.

Inf. 13:25

Cred'io ch'ei credette ch'io credesse . . .

I believe that he believed that I believed . . .

U 682:14-24 (*Arch.* 21:75-76)

In what order of precedence, with what attendant ceremony was the exodus from the house of bondage to the wilderness of inhabitation effected?
    Lighted Candle in Stick borne by
        Bloom
    Diaconal Hat on Ashplant borne by
        Stephen
    With what intonation *secreto* of what commemorative psalm?

The 113th, *modus peregrinus: In exitu Israel de Egypto: domus Jacob de populo barbaro*.

Purg. 1:40-45

"Chi siete voi che contro al cieco fiume / fuggita avete la pregione etterna?" / diss' el, movendo quelle oneste piume. / "Chi v'ha guidati, o che vi fu lucerna, / uscendo fuor de la profonda notte / che sempre nera fa la valle inferna?

"Who are you that, against the blind stream, have fled the eternal prison?" said he, moving those venerable plumes. "Who has guided you, or what was a lamp to you issuing forth from the deep night that ever makes the infernal valley black?"

Purg. 2:46-48

"In exitu Israel de Aegypto," / cantavan tutti insieme ad una voce / con quanto di quel salmo è poscia scripto.

"In exitu Israel de Aegypto," all of them were singing together with one voice, with the rest of that psalm as it is written.

U 682:23 (*Arch.* 21:75)   *modus peregrinus*

Purg. 2:61, 63

E Virgilio rispuose: . . . / . . . / "ma noi siam peregrin come voi siete."

And Virgil answered: ". . . we are pilgrims like yourselves."

U 682:30; 683:1-4 (*Ros.MS* P.651; *Arch.* 16:98-99)

What spectacle confronted them when they, first the host then the guest, emerged silently, doubly dark from obscurity by a passage from the rere of the house into the penumbra of the garden?
The heaventree of stars hung with humid nightblue fruit.

Inf. 34:133-139

Lo duca e io per quel cammino ascoso / intrammo a ritornar nel chiaro mondo; / e sanza cura aver d'alcun riposo, / salimmo sù, el primo e io secondo, / tanto ch'i' vidi de le cose belle / che porta 'l ciel, per un pertugio tondo. / E quindi uscimmo a riveder le stelle.

My leader and I entered on that hidden road to return into the bright world; and caring not for any rest, we climbed up, he first and I second, so far that through a round opening I saw some of the beautiful things that Heaven bears; and thence we issued forth to see again the stars.

U 683:11-13 (*Arch.* 16:101)

an observer placed at the lower end of a cylindrical vertical shaft 5000 ft deep sunk from the surface towards the centre of the earth

Inf. 34:121-126

Da questa parte cadde giù dal cielo; / e la terra, che pria di qua si sporse, / per paura di lui fé del mar velo, / e venne a l'emisperio nostro; e forse / per fuggir lui lasciò qui loco vòto / quella ch'appar di qua, e sù ricorse.

On this side he fell down from Heaven; and the earth, which before stood out here, for fear of him made a veil of the sea and came to our hemisphere; and perhaps in order to escape from him that which appears on this side left here the empty space and rushed upwards. [Dante's Hell: a great inverted cone whose apex is at the earth's center.]

U 689:14-16 (*Ros.MS* P.657; *Arch.* 16:119)

Alone, what did Bloom feel?
The cold of interstellar space . . .

Purg. 30:49-50

Ma Virgilio n'avea lasciati scemi / di sé . . .

But Virgil had left us bereft of himself.

With what meditations did Bloom accompany his demonstration to
his companion of various constellation ?

Meditations increasingly vaster : of the infinite lattiginous
scintillating uncondensed milky way, of Sirius 9 lightyoars
distant and in volume 900 times the dimension of our planet, of
Arcturus, of Orion with belt and nebula in which 100 of our
solar systems could be contained, of moribund, of nascent new
stars such as Nova in 1901, of our system plunging towards the
constellation of Hercules, of the parallax or parallactic drift
of socalled fixed stars, in reality evermoving wanderers from
emmeasurably remote eons to infinitely remote futures in
comparison with which the years, theescore and ten, of allotted
human life formed a parenthesis of infinitesimal brevity.

Were there obverse meditations increasingly less vast ?
Of the eons of geological periods recorded in the stratifications
of the earth, of the myriad minute entomological existences
concealed in cavities of the earth, beneath removable stones, in
hives and mounds, of microbes, germs, bacteria, bacilla, spermatozoa,
of the trillions of millions of molecules contained in a pinhead,
of the universe of human serum constellated with red and white
bodies, themselves universes of void space constellated with
other bodies, each its universe of divisible component bodies of
which was again divisible in divisions of redivisible component
bodies, dividends and divisors ever diminishing without actual
division till, if the progress were carried far enough, nought
was never reached.

10. In *Inferno* 34, Virgil explains to Dante that Hell, a vast inverted cone created by the fall of Lucifer, extends to the center of the earth. Joyce transformed the passage (*Inf*. 34:96-126) by suggesting that a human figure at the apex of the cone might be able to see all the way to the surface, and he placed his allusion in a starry context to give the effect of Dante's closing line, "E quindi uscimmo a riveder le stelle," "And thence we issued forth to see the stars."

U 721:21-25 (*Ros.MS* P.688)

What moved visibly above the listener's and the narrator's thoughts?

The upcast reflection of a lamp and shade, an inconstant series of concentric circles of varying gradations of light and shadow.

Par. 14:22-24

. . . a l'orazion pronta e divota, / li santi cerchi mostrar nova gioia / nel torneare e ne la mira nota.

so at that prompt and devout petition the holy circles showed new joy in their revolving and in their marvelous melody. [Dominant figure of the Tenth Heaven; circles of light]

Par. 28:22-36

Forse cotanto quanto pare appresso / alo cigner la luce che 'l dipigne / ¨. . / . . . un cerchio d'igne / si girava sì ratto, . . . / . . . / e questo era d'un altro circumcinto, / e quel dal terzo, e 'l terzo poi dal quarto, / dal quinto il quarto, e poi dal sesto il quinto. / . . . / Così l'ottavo e 'l nono; e ciascheduno / più tardi si movea, secondo ch'era / in numero distante più da l'uno;

Perhaps as near as a halo seems to girdle the light which paints it . . . a circle of fire was whirling . . . and this was girt round by another, and that by a third, and the third by a fourth, by a fifth the fourth, then by a sixth the fifth . . . So the eighth and the ninth; and each was moving more slowly according as it was in number more distant from the unit.

U 766:37; 768:12 (*Arch.* 16:348; 21:366, 374)

shall I wear a white rose . . . or shall I wear a red yes

Par. 31:1-2

In forma dunque di candida rosa / mi si mostrava la milizia santa . . .

In form then of a pure white rose the saintly host was shown to me . . .

[Molly Bloom, distinguished from the Dantean Beatrice]

U 766:41-42 (*Ros.MS* P.731;   Id love to have the whole place swimming
Arch. 16:296)   in roses

          Par. 30:124-126   Nel giallo de la rosa sempiterna / che si
     digrada e dilata e redole / odor di lode al
     sol che sempre verna, / qual è colui che
     tace e dicer vole, / mi trasse Beatrice . . .

     Into the yellow of the eternal Rose, which
     rises in ranks and expands and breathes
     forth odor of praise unto the Sun which
     makes perpetual spring, Beatrice drew
     me . . .

U 767:35-37 (*Arch*. 21:366, 368)   the Greeks and the jews and the Arabs
     and the devil knows who else from all the
     ends of Europe . . .

     [The characters in Dante's poem and
     Joyce's book]

U 768:6 (*Arch*. 21:370)   O and the sea the sea crimson sometimes
     like fire

          Par. 30:61-66   E vidi lume in forma di rivera / fulvido di
     fulgore, intra due rive / dipinte di mirabil
     primavera. / Di tal fiumana uscian faville
     vive, / e d'ogne parte si mettien ne'
     fiori, / quasi rubin che oro circunscrive.

     And I saw a light in form of a river glow-
     ing tawny between two banks painted
     with marvelous spring. From out this
     river issued living sparks and dropped on
     every side into the blossoms, like rubies
     set in gold.

Finnegans Wake

FW 4:18 (*Arch.* 44:7)	Bygmester Finnegan of the Stuttering Hand
Par. 13:77-78	a l'artista / ch'a l'abito de l'arte ha man che trema . . .
	the artist who in the practice of his art has a hand that trembles . . .
FW 18:17-19 (*Arch.* 44:84)	This claybook. Can you rede . . . its world?
Par. 23:54	del libro, che 'l preterito rassegna.
	The book that records the past.
FW 31:20	an Italian excellency named Giubilei . . . a triptychal religious family symbolising puritas of doctrina . . .
Inf. 18:29	l'anno del giubileo, su per lo ponte / hanno a passar la gente modo colto,
	in the year of the Jubilee, the Romans have taken measures for the people to pass over the bridge,
	[The first great Papal Jubilee year, 1300.]
FW 31:32 (*Arch.* 49:35)	Allegibelling
Par. 6:103	Faccian li Ghibellin
	Let the Ghibellines
FW 31:36 (*Arch.* 49:35)	We read in sybylline
Par. 33:66	si perdea la sentenza di Sibilla
	The Sibyl's oracle was lost

FW 47:19 (*Arch.* 49:59)　　　　Seudodanto

　　　　　　　　　　　　　　　[Dante]

FW 57:11 (*Arch.* 45:189; 206)　　Before he fell hill he filled heaven

　　　Par. 9:127-128　　　　La tua città, che di colui è pianta / che
　　　　　　　　　　　　　　pria volse le spalle al suo fattore

　　　　　　　　　　　　　　Your city—which was planted by him who
　　　　　　　　　　　　　　first turned his back on his maker—

FW 59:5 (*Arch.* 49:77)　　　　half in stage of whisper to her confidante
　　　　　　　　　　　　　　glass

　　　Purg. 27:103　　　　　Per piacermi a lo specchio, qui
　　　　　　　　　　　　　　m'addorno

　　　　　　　　　　　　　　To please me at the glass I adorn me here

FW 68:19 (*Arch.* 45:194; 49:91)　farfar off Bissavolo

　　　Par. 15:94　　　　　　mio figlio fu e tuo bisavol fue

　　　　　　　　　　　　　　he was my son and your grandfather's
　　　　　　　　　　　　　　father.

FW 69:05 (*Arch.* 45:215; 240)　Now by memory inspired, turn wheel
　　　　　　　　　　　　　　again to the whole of the wall.

　　　Par. 33:73　　　　　　per tornare alquanto a mia memoria / e
　　　　　　　　　　　　　　per sonare un poco in questi versi

　　　　　　　　　　　　　　by returning somewhat to my memory
　　　　　　　　　　　　　　and by sounding a little in these lines

FW 71:26, 45 (*Arch.* 4:217)　Gouty Ghibeline

　　　Par. 6:103　　　　　　Faccian li Ghibellin

　　　　　　　　　　　　　　Let the Ghibellines

FW 72:29 (*Arch.* 45:333)　　Guilphy

Par. 6:107	coi Guelfi suoi
	with his Guelphs (sole occurrence)
FW 72:34 (*Arch.* 49:97)	his groundould diablen lioundub [Dublin as Dante's *Inferno*]
FW 78:4 (*Arch.* 46:69)	lethelulled
Purg. 28:130,133	Quinci Letè . . . / . . . / a tutti altri sapori esto è di sopra
	Here is Lethe. . . . Its savor surpasses every other sweetness.
FW 78:9 (*Arch.* 49:101)	buried burrowing in Gehinnon, to proliferate through all his Unterwealth, seam by seam, sheol om sheol, and revisit our Uppercrust Sideria of Utilitarios, the divine one;
	[Dante's journey from Inferno to Earthly Paradise]
FW 80:21-22 (*Arch.* 46:71)	his nuptial eagles sharped their beaks of prey
Purg. 9:20	un'aguglia nel ciel con penne d'oro, / con l'ali aperte e a calare intesa;
	an eagle poised in the sky, with feathers of gold, its wings outspread and prepared to stoop [Ganymede]
FW 80:24 (*Arch.* 50:112-113)	araflammed
Par. 31:127	oriafiamma
	oriflamme
FW 83:08 (*Arch.* 46:183)	thorntree of sheol

Inf. 13:32	un gran pruno
	a great thorntree

FW 92:21	one among all, her deputised to defeme him by the Lunar Sisters' Celibacy Club, a lovelooking leapgirl all all alonely, Gentia Gemma . . . he, wan and pale in his unmixed admiration
	[Dante was married to Gemma Donati; he never mentions or describes her]

FW 110:9-10	this madh vaal of tares (whose verdhure's yellowed therever Phaiton parks his car
Inf. 17:107-108	quando Fetonte abbandonò li freni, / per che 'l ciel, come pare ancor, si cosse;
	When Phaethon let loose the reins, whereby the sky, as yet appears, was scorched;

FW 152:28-30 (*Arch.* 47:126; 135)	he set off from Ludstown *a spasso* to see how badness was badness in the weirdest of all pensible ways
	[Dante's pilgrimage through the After-world]

FW 152:36	at the turning of the wrong lane
Inf. 1:3, 12	che la diritta via era smarrita. / . . . / che la verace via abbandonai.
	the straight way was lost. . . . I left the true way;

FW 155:25	a lucciolys in Teresa Street
Inf. 26:28-29	come la mosca cede a la zanzara, / vede lucciole giù per la vallea,

> when the fly yields to the mosquito . . .
> [the peasant] sees down along the valley,
> the fireflies.

FW 158:29 (*Arch*. 47:199) Aquila Rapax

    Purg. 9:20 un'aguglia nel ciel con penne d'oro / con
l'ali aperte e a calare intesa;

an eagle poised in the sky with feathers of
gold, its wings outspread and prepared to
swoop.

FW 159:6-8 (*Arch*. 47:133;141) Then Nuvoletta . . . climbed over the
bannistars.

    Inf. 26:39 sì come nuvoletta, in su salire

like a little cloud ascending

FW 163:20-21 (*Arch*. 47:152;165) the more stolidly immobile *in space*
appears to me the bottom which is
presented to use in time by the top
primomobilisk &c.

    Par. 30:106 Fassi di raggio tutta sua parvenza /
reflesso al sommo del mobile primo

Its whole expanse is made by a ray reflected from the summit of the Primum
Mobile

FW 181:11-12 the bombinubble puzzo that welled out of
the pozzo

    Inf. 9:31-32 Questa palude che 'l gran puzzo spira /
cigne dintorno la città dolente

This marsh which exhales the mighty
stench

    Inf. 11:4-5 e quivi, per l'orribile soperchio / del
puzzo che 'l profondo abisso gitta

and here, because of the horrible excess of the stench which the deep abyss throws out

FW 182:21

Ser Autore, q.e.d.

Inf. 1:85

"Tu se lo mio maestro e 'l mio autore . . .

You are my master and my author . . . [Dante recognizes Virgil]

FW 182:21

a heartbreakingly handsome young paolo

Inf. 5:103-105

Amor, ch'a nullo amato amar perdona / mi prese del costui piacer sì forte, / che, come vedi, ancor non m'abbandona.

Love, which absolves no loved one from loving, seized me so strongly with delight in him, that, as you see, it does not leave me even now. [Francesca's description of Paolo]

FW 198:19 (*Arch.* 48:138)

ebro

Par. 9:89

tra Ebro e Macra

between the Ebro and the Magra

FW 207:26

Duodecimoroon? Bon a ventura?

Par. 12:127

Io son la vita di Bonaventuro / da Bagnoregio /

I am the living soul of Bonaventure of Bagnorea [Saint Bonaventure, 1221-1274, and twelfth canto]

FW 208:8 (*Arch.* 48:199)

arnoment

Purg. 14:24-26

. . . tu parli d'Arno." / E l'altro disse lui: "Perché nascose / questi il vocabol di quella riviera . . ."

... you speak of the Arno." And the other said to him, "Why did he conceal that river's name ...?"

FW 211:17-18

for revery warp in the weaver's woof

Par. 17:100-102

si mostrò spedita / l'anima santa di metter la trama / in quella tela ch'io le porsi ordita.

the holy soul showed he had finished setting the woof across the warp I had held out.

FW 212:35 *(Arch.* 48:185)

Senior ga dito: Faciasi Omo! E omo fu fò.

Inf. 1:66-67

"qual che tu sii, od ombra od omo certo!" / Rispuosemi: "Non omo, omo già fui ..." [only double occurrence in this form]

"whatever you are, shade or living man." "No, not a living man, though once I was."

FW 220:7-9 *(Arch.* 51:6; 11)

a bewitching blond who dimples delight-fully and is approached in loveliness only by her grateful sister reflection in a mirror

Purg. 27:103-105

Per piacermi a lo specchio, qui m'addorno; / ma mia suora Rachel mai non si smaga

To please me at the glass I adorn me here, but my sister Rachel never leaves her mirror and sits all day

FW 225:24 *(Arch.* 51:19)

Hellfeuersteyn

Purg. 1:129

... discoverto / quel color che l'inferno mi nascose.

... disclosed that color of mine which Hell had hidden.

FW 227:14 (*Arch*. 51:22)

Beatrice

[Beatrice third in a list of seven girls]

FW 227:21-23 (*Arch*. 51:23,
35, 218, 302)

what tornaments of complementary rages
rocked the divlun from his punch-
poll to his tummy's shentre . . .

Inf. 34:28-29

Lo 'mperador del doloroso regno / da
mezzo 'l petto uscia fuor de la ghiaccia;

the emperor of the woeful realm stood
forth from midbreast out of the ice

FW 228:22

and regain that absendee tarry easty his
città immediata, by an alley and detour

Par. 15:97

Fiorenza dentro da la cerchia antica

Florence, within her ancient circle [the
old city of Florence]

FW 229:4 (*Arch*. 51:407)

and daunt you logh if his vineshanky's
schwemmy.

[Dante]

FW 230:4 (*Arch*. 51:24)

Bill C. Babby

Inf. 34:127

Luogo è là giù da Belzebù remoto

Down there, from Beelzebub as far
removed . . .

FW 230:31

genitricksling with Avus and Avia, that
simple pair, and descendant down on
velouty pads by a vuncular process to
Nurus and Noverca . . . patriss all of them

Par. 16:58-59

Se la gente ch'al mondo più traligna / non
fosse stata a Cesare noverca . . .

If the folk who are most degenerate in
the world had not been a stepmother to

Caesar . . . [Cacciaguida tells Dante of the simple life of his old Roman ancestors, and laments the decline of the old families]

FW 232:23 (*Arch.* 51:59)

Satanly, lade!

Inf. 7:1

"Pape Satàn, pape Satàn aleppe!" [Pluto's words in the language of Hell]

FW 233:12-13 (*Arch.* 51:62)

They who will for exile say can for dog

Par. 17:71

Lo primo tuo refugio . . . / sarà la cortesia del gran Lombardo

Your first refuge . . . shall be the courtesy of the great Lombard [Can Grande]

FW 233:30 (*Arch.* 51:230)

aleguere come alaguerre

Alighieri

FW 233:33 (*Arch.* 51:27)

a skarp snakk of pure undefallen engelsk

Conv. II.vi.90-100

I say that out of all these orders of angels some certain were lost so soon as they were created, I take it to the number of a tenth part; for the restoration of which human nature was afterward created.

FW 235:9 (*Arch.* 51:465)

Xanthos! Xanthos! Xanthos!

Par. 26:69

. . . un dolcissimo canto / . . ."Santo, santo, santo!"

. . . a most sweet song . . . "Holy, Holy, Holy."

FW 238:3 (*Arch.* 51:238)

So as to be very dainty . . . verily dandy-dainty.

[Dante]

FW 239:32 (*Arch*. 51:81)	oaths and screams and bawley groans
Inf. 5:35	quivi le strida, il compianto, il lamento . . .
	the shrieks, the moans, the lamentations . . .

FW 239:33 (*Arch*. 51:81, 85-86)	With a belchybubhub and a hellabelow bedemmed and bediabbled the arimaining lucisphere.
Purg. 12:25-27	. . . che fu nobil creato / più ch'altra creatura, giù dal cielo / folgoreggiando scender, da l'un lato.
	. . . [he] who was created nobler than any other creature fell as lightning from heaven

FW 239:34-35 (*Arch*. 51:81)	Lonedom's breach lay foulend up uncouth
Inf. 34:103	ov'è la ghiaccia? e questi com' è fitto / sì sottosopra?
	Where is the ice? and he, there, how is it that he is fixed thus upside down?

FW 240:2 (*Arch*. 51:81)	and you wonna make one of our micknick party.
Inf. 4:101-102	ch'e' sì mi fecer de la loro schiera, / sì ch'io fui sesto tra cotanto senno.
	for they made me one of their company, so that I was sixth amid so much wisdom.

FW 244:2 (*Arch*. 51:248)	Daintytrees
	[Dante]

FW 247:10	Eat larto altruis with most perfect stranger

Par. 17:58-59	Tu proverai sì come sa di sale / lo pane altrui,
	You shall come to know how salt is the taste of another's bread,
FW 248:28 (*Arch.* 51:126)	When you'll next have the mind to retire to be wicked this is as dainty a way as any
	[Dante's *Inferno*]
FW 251:23-24 (*Arch.* 51:182)	dantellising peaches
	[Dante; his tropes]
FW 251:24 (*Arch.* 51:182)	the lingerous longerous book of the dark
	[Dante's *Inferno*]
FW 251:25 (*Arch.* 51:182)	Look at this passage about Galilleotto!
Inf. 5:137	Galeotto fu 'l libro e chi lo scrisse
	A Gallehault was the book and he who wrote it
FW 256:23 (*Arch.* 51:272)	and why is limbo
Inf. 4:43	Gran duol mi prese al cor quando lo 'ntesi / però che gente di molto valore / conobbi che 'n quel limbo eran sospesi.
	Great sadness seized my heart when I heard him, for I recognized that people of great worth were suspended in that Limbo.
FW 256:33 (*Arch.* 51:121)	That little cloud, a nibulissa, still hangs isky.
Inf. 26:39	sì come nuvoletta, in sù salire
	like a little cloud ascending

FW 257:4 (*Arch.* 51:387) now at rhimba rhomba, now in trippiza trappaza pleating a pattern Gran Geamatron showed them

Par. 33:133 Qual è 'l geomètra che tutto s'affige / per misurar lo cerchio . . .

As is the geometer who wholly applies himself to measure the circle . . .

FW 263:L (*Arch.* 53:309) *Mars speaking*

Par. 14:125 però ch'a me venìa "Resurgi" e "Vinci" . . .

for there came to me: "Rise" and "Conquer" . . .

FW 266:L3 (*Arch.* 52:48, 92, 167) Bet you fippence, anythesious, there's no puggatory, are yous game?

[Purgatory]

FW 269:L1 (*Arch.* 52:36, 113) undante umoroso

[Dante]

FW 269:23-24 (*Arch.* 52:43, 66) The beggar the maid the bigger the mauler.

Inf. 5:38-39 [e.g.] . . . i peccator carnali, / che la ragion sommettono al talento.

. . . the carnal sinners, who subject reason to desire.

FW 269:25 (*Arch.* 52:96, 113) And the greater the patrarc the griefer the pinch. And that's what your doctor knows.

Inf. 5:121-123 . . . Nessun maggior dolore / che ricordarsi del tempo felice / ne la miseria; e ciò sa 'l tuo dottore.

... There is no greater sorrow than to recall, in wretchedness, the happy time; and this your teacher knows.

FW 269:26 (*Arch.* 52:19)

O love it is the commonknounest thing how it pashes the plutous and the paupe.

Inf. 5:103

Amor, ch'a nullo amato amar perdona . . .

Love, which absolves no loved one from loving . . .

FW 269:note 4 (*Arch.* 52:118)

Llong and Shortts Primer of Black and White Wenchcraft.

Inf. 5:100-107

[Dante's account of Francesca]

FW 272:22-23 (*Arch.* 52:100)

sense you threehandshigh put your twofootlarge timepates in the dead wash of Lough Murph

Purg. 31:101-102

. . . la testa e mi sommerse / ove convenne ch'io l'acqua inghiottissi

. . . clasped my head and dipped me under, where it behooved me to swallow the water.

FW 272:note 3 (*Arch.* 52:100)

That's the lethemuse but it washes off

Purg. 28:127-130

da questa parte con virtù discende / che toglie altrui memoria del peccato; / . . . / Quinci Letè . . .

On this side it descends with virtue that takes from one the memory of sin; . . . Here [is] Lethe;

FW 276:26 (*Arch.* 52:174, 213)

we keep is peace who follow his law

Par. 3:85

E 'n la sua volontade è nostra pace

and in His will is our peace

FW 276:note 6 (*Arch.* 52:220)	I can almost feed their sweetness at my lisplips
Par. 33:61-63	. . . ché quasi tutta cessa / mia visione, e ancor mi distilla / nel core il dolce che nacque da essa.
	my vision almost wholly fades away, yet does the sweetness that was born of it still drop within my heart.

FW 277:17 (*Arch.* 52:214)	a little black rose a truant in a thorntree
Par. 13:133-135	ch'i' ho veduto tutto 'l verno prima / lo prun mostrarsi rigido e feroce, / poscia portar la rosa in su la cima;
	for I have seen first, all winter through, the thorn display itself hard and stiff, and then upon its summit bear the rose.

FW 278:2-3 (*Arch.* 52:215)	who wants to cheat the choker's got to learn to chew the cud.
Purg. 16:98-99	. . . 'l pastor che procede, / rugumar può, ma non ha l'unghie fesse . . .
	the shepherd that leads may chew the cud but has not the hoofs divided.

FW 280:29-31 (*Arch.* 52:241)	she shall tread them lifetrees leaves whose silence hitherto has shone as sphere of silver
Par. 33:65-66	così al vento ne le foglie levi / si perdea la sentenza di Sibilla.
	thus in the wind, on the light leaves, the Sibyl's oracle was lost.

FW 281:2-3 (*Arch.* 52:241)	a weird of wonder tenebrous as that evil thorngarth

Inf. 1:4-5

. . . qual era è cosa dura / esta selva selvaggia e aspra e forte

what that wood was, wild, rugged, harsh

FW 281:15-16 (*Arch.* 52:148, 204, 53:319)

But Bruto and Cassio are ware only of trifid tongues

Inf. 34:65-67

quel che pende dal nero ceffo è Bruto: / . . . e l'altro e Cassio . . .

the one that hangs from the black muzzle is Brutus: . . . the other is Cassius.

Inf. 34:55

Da ogni bocca dirompea co' denti / un peccatore . . .

In each mouth he champed a sinner with his teeth [Satan's three heads]

FW 281:17 (*Arch.* 53:319)

'tis demonal!

Inferno

FW 281:23 (*Arch.* 53:319)

What if she love Sieger less though she leave Ruhm moan?

Par. 10:136-138

essa è la luce etterna di Sigieri, / che, . . . silogizzò invidiosi veri.

It is the eternal light of Siger who . . . demonstrated invidious truths."

FW 281:25 (*Arch.* 53:319)

Moving about in the free of the air and mixing with the ruck.

Inf. 7:121-122

Fitti nel limo dicon: "Tristi fummo / ne l'aere dolce . . ."

Fixed in the slime they say, "We were sullen in the sweet air . . ."

FW 282:1-3 (*Arch.* 52:208, 243)

With sobs for his job, with tears for his toil, with horror for his squalor but with pep for his perdition,

Par. 25:4	. . . la crudeltà che fuor mi serra / del bello ovile . . .
	the cruelty which bars me from the fair sheepfold.
Par. 25:1-3	Se mai continga che 'l poema sacro . . . / . . . / sì che m'ha fatto per molti anni macro.
	If ever it come to pass that the sacred poem . . . that it has made me lean for many years
Inf. 14:6	. . . dove / si vede di giustizia orribil arte.
	where a horrible mode of justice is seen
FW 282:2 (*Arch.* 52:243)	with pep for his perdition
Inf. 8:44	. . ."Alma sdegnosa, / benedetta colei che 'n te s'incinse!
	"Indignant soul, blessed is she who bore you!
FW 288:3 (*Arch.* 53:19, 37)	blending tschemes for em in tropadores and doublecressing twofold truths and devising tingling tailwords
	[the poem's tropes, allegory and rhymes]
FW 289:15 (*Arch.* 53:9 21, 22, 38)	let drop as a doombody drops
Inf. 5:142	E caddi come corpo morto cade.
	and fell as a dead body falls.
FW 292:1-2 (*Arch.* 53:12, 27, 40)	lamoor that of gentle breast rathe is intaken
Inf. 5:100	Amor, ch'al cor gentil ratto s'apprende . . .
	Love, which is quickly kindled in a gentle heart . . .

FW 292:2-3 (*Arch.* 53:12)

circling toward out yondest . . . that batch of grim rushers

Inf. 5:31-33

La bufera infernal, che mai non resta, / mena li spirti con la sua rapina; / voltando e percotendo li molesta.

The hellish hurricane, never resting, sweeps along the spirits with its rapine; whirling and smiting, it torments them.

FW 293:7-8 (*Arch.* 53:249)

lost himself or himself some somnione

Par. 33:58

Qual è colui che sognando [somniando] vede . . .

As is he who dreaming, sees . . .

FW 295:27 (*Arch.* 53:136)

a daintical pair of accomplasses [Dante]

FW 296:5 (*Arch.* 53:5, 30, 41)

a capital Pee for Pride

Purg. 9:112-113

Sette P ne la fronte mi descrisse / col punton de la spada . . .

Seven P's he traced on my forehead with the point of his sword.

FW 296:11-2
(*Arch.* 53:110)

With a geing groan grunt and a croak click cluck.

Purg. 9:133-137

E quando fuor ne' cardini distorti / li spigoli di quella regge sacra, / che di metallo son sonanti e forti, / non rugghiò sì né si mostrò sì acra / Tarpea . . .

When the pivots of that sacred portal, which are of metal resounding and strong, were turned within their hinges, Tarpea roared not so loud.

FW 296:31; 297:1 (*Arch.* 53:5, 31, 41, 42)

I"ll make you to see figuratleavely in the whome of your eternal geomater.

    Par. 33:133-134

Qual è 'l geomètra che tutto s'affige / per misurar lo cerchio . . .

As is the geometer who wholly applies himself to measure the circle

---

FW 297:note 1 (*Arch.* 53:254)

Doña Speranza

    Par. 33:12-13

se' di speranza fontana vivace. / Donna . . .

the living fount of hope. Lady . . .

FW 298:L3 (*Arch.* 53:197, 256)

Ecclasiastical and Celestial Hierarchies. The Ascending. The Descending.

    Par. 28:98-129

"I cerchi primi / t'hanno mostrato Serafi e Cherubi . . . / . . . / In essa gerarcia son l'altre dee: / prima Dominazioni, e poi Virtudi . . . / . . . / Questi ordini di sù tutti s'ammirano, / e di giù vincon

The first circles have shown to you the Seraphim and the Cherubim . . . In this hierarchy are the next divinities, first Dominions, then Virtues . . . These orders all gaze upward and prevail downward.

FW 305:31 (*Arch.* 53:272, 276, 283, 299)

To book alone belongs the lobe.

    Par. 33:85-87

. . . vidi che s'interna, / legato con amore in un volume, / ciò che per l'universo si squaderna . . .

I saw ingathered, bound by love in one single volume, that which is dispersed in leaves throughout the universe . . .

FW 306:12-13 (*Arch.* 53:276, 284, 300)

We've had our day at triv and quad

    Inf. 4:110

per sette porte intrai con questi savi . . .

through seven gates I entered with those sages . . .

    Conv. II.14, 56

To the seven first correspond the seven sciences of the Trivium and the Quadrivium . . . [trans. Wicksteed, Temple ed.]

FW 307:12 (*Arch.* 53:278, 285, 301)

the Strangest Dream that was ever Halfdreamt

    Par. 33:58

Qual è colui che sognando vede . . .

As one who dreaming, sees . . .

FW 308:note 1 (*Arch.* 53:278, 281, 295)

Kish is for anticheirst, and the free of my hand to him!

    Inf. 25:1-3

Al fine de le sue parole il ladro / le mani alzò con amendu le fiche, / gridando: "Togli, Dio, ch'a te le squadro!"

At the end of his words the thief raised up his hands with both the figs, crying, "Take them, God, for I aim them at you!"

FW 320:33 (*Arch.* 54:24)

Infernal machinery having thus passed the buck to billy back from jack (finder the keeper) as the baffling yarn sailed in circles

    Inf. 17:94-117

Ma esso, ch'altra volta mi sovvenne / . . . / . . . mi sostenne; / e disse: "Gerion, moviti omai: / le rote larghe, e lo scender sia poco; / pensa la nova soma che tu hai." / Come la navicella esce di loco / in dietro in dietro, sì quindi si tolse; / . . . / Ella sen va notando lenta lenta; / rota e discende, . . .

But he who at other times had steadied
me . . . steadied me as soon as I was
mounted up, then said, "Geryon, move
on now; let your circles be wide and your
descending slow. . . . As the bark backs
out little by little from its place, so Geryon
withdrew thence . . . he goes swimming
slowly on, wheels and descends . . .

FW 334:20 (*Arch.* 54:312, 333)	O rum it is the chomicalest thing how it pickles up the punchey and the jude.
Inf. 5:103	Amor, ch'a nullo amato amar perdona . . .
	Love, which absolves no loved one from loving . . . [See also *FW* 269:26]
FW 337:30 (*Arch.* 54:340)	Donn, Teague and Hurleg
	[Dante]
FW 344:5 (*Arch.* 55:88)	Which goatheye and sheepskeer they damnty well know
	[Dante, Goethe, Shakespeare]
FW 346:05 (*Arch.* 55:94)	Hebeneros for Aromal Peace
Par. 30:124-126	Nel giallo de la rosa sempiterna, / che si digrada e dilata e redole / odor di lode al sol che sempre verna.
	Into the yellow of the eternal Rose, which rises in ranks and expands and breathes forth odor of praise unto the Sun which makes perpetual spring,
FW 360:8 (*Arch.* 55:294)	and you, Smirky Dainty
	[Dante; Joyce's first draft reads "Danty"]

FW 366:23 (*Arch*. 55:357, 402)   old ruffin sippahsedly improctor to be seducint trovatellas,

     Inf. 18:61,65-66   a dicer 'sipa' tra Sàvena e Reno; / . . . / . . . "Via, / ruffian! qui non son femmine da conio."

between Savena and Reno, to say *sipa*; "Off pander! There are no women here to coin."

FW 394:4 (*Arch*. 56:158)   when hope was there no more

     Inf. 3:9   Lasciate ogni speranza

Abandon every hope

FW 405:24 (*Arch*. 61:550; 62:5)   The Wheel of Fortune

     Inf. 15:95-96   però giri Fortuna la sua rota / come le piace . . .

therefore let Fortune whirl her wheel as pleases her . . .

FW 425:20, 24 (*Arch*. 57:174, 217, 260; 62:31)   My trifolium librotto . . .Acomedy of letters!

     Inf. 16:128   di questa comedìa, lettor, ti giuro

I swear to you by the notes of this Comedy

FW 440:5 (*Arch*. 62:49)   Through Hell with the Papes

     Inf. 7:47   . . . papi e cardinali, / in cui usa avarizia il suo soperchio.

. . . popes and cardinals in whom avarice wreaks its excess.

FW 440:6 (*Arch*. 62:49)   The divine comic Denti Alligator

[Dante]

FW 462:17-18 (*Arch.* 57:188a)	a squamous runaway and a dear old man pal of mine too
Inf. 15:122	che corrono a Verona il drappo verde
	one of those who run for the green cloth in the field at Verona . . .
FW 462:22 (*Arch.* 57:188a, 395)	Be sure and link him, me O treasauro, as often as you learn
Inf. 15:119	Sieti raccomandato il mio Tesoro
	Let my *Treasure*, in which I yet live
FW 462:34 (*Arch.* 57:385, 405)	on quinquisecular cycles after his French evolution
Inf. 15:119	il mio *Tesoro*
	[Brunetto's "*Tesoro*" was written in French: *Livre dou Tresor*]
FW 464:13-14 (*Arch.* 57:188a, 395)	me grandsourd, the old cruxader
Par. 15:94	mio figlio fu e tuo bisavol fue
	was my son and was your grandfather's father.
FW 464:36 (*Arch.* 62:188a)	You rejoice me! Faith, I'm proud of you,
Par. 15:88	"O fronda mia in che io compiacemmi . . .
	"O my branch, in whom I took delight . . .
FW 477:21 (*Arch.* 58:172)	spreading in quadriliberal their azure-spotted . . . nets
Epist. X, par. 7-9	[Dante's fourfold, quadrivial levels of meaning; Joyce originally wrote "quadribberal"]

FW 483:24 (*Arch.* 58:416; 59:9) saviour so the salt and good wee braod,

    Par. 17:58-59 Tu proverai sì come sa di sale / lo pane altrui,

        · You shall come to know how salt is the taste of another's bread,

FW 484:09 (*Arch.* 62:107) ersed irredent

        [Irish Dante]

FW 484:31 (*Arch.* 62:108) the spirit is from the upper circle

    Inf. 4:24 nel primo cercio

        [the first circle; the upper levels of hell]

FW 486:32-33 (*Arch.* 62:358) And so the triptych vision passes.

        [Dante's three realms]

FW 488:06 (*Arch.* 59:12) avicendas

    Inf. 4:143 Avicenna

FW 504:29-30 (*Arch.* 61:500; 62:135) guelfing and ghiberring

    Par. 6:103-107 Faccian li Ghibellin, faccian lor arte / sott' altro segno, . . . / . . . / e non l'abbatta esto Carlo novello / coi Guelfi suoi . . .

        Let the Ghibellines . . . practise their art under another ensign. . . . And let not this new Charles strike it down with his Guelphs . . .

FW 510:03 (*Arch.* 58:453; 62:141) the tail, so mastrodantic, as you tell it nearly takes your . . . breath away.

        [Dante and the poem]

FW 539:5 (*Arch.* 58:401, 471)   that primed favourite continental poet, Daunty, Gouty, and Shopkeeper,

[Dante, Goethe, Shakespeare]

FW 558:24-25 (*Arch.* 60:118)   for they were never happier, huhu, than when they were miserable, haha . . .

Inf. 5:121-123   . . . Nessun maggior dolore / che ricordarsi del tempo felice / ne la miseria . . .

There is no greater sorrow than to recall, in wretchedness, the happy time . . .

FW 563:9 (*Arch.* 60:259)   whose heel he sheepfolds . . . O foetal sleep!

Par. 25:5   del bello ovile ov' io dormi' agnello

the fair sheepfold where I slept as a lamb

FW 566:28 (*Arch.* 62:209, 460)   gauze off heaven. Vision. Then. O, pluxty suddly, the sight entrancing

Par. 33:55-57   Da quinci innanzi il mio veder fu maggio / che 'l parlar mostra, ch'a tal vista cede / e cede la memoria a tanto oltraggio.

Thenceforward my vision was greater than speech can show, which fails at such a sight, and at such excess memory fails.

FW 567:36 (*Arch.* 62:213)   Ghimbelling on guelflinks

Par. 6:103-107   [Ghibelline and Guelph; see *FW* 504:29-30, above]

FW 568:9 (*Arch.* 62:213)   with si so silent

Inf. 33:80   del bel paese là dove 'l sì suona

FW 593:1 (*Arch.* 63:9)

Sandhyas! Sandhyas! Sandhyas!

Par. 26:69

"Santo, santo, santo!"

"Holy, Holy, Holy!"

FW 606:3 (*Arch.* 63:38d, 38e)

ninthly enthroned, in the concentric center

Par. 28:34-42

Così l'ottavo e 'l nono; . . . /. . . / . . . Da quel punto / depende il cielo e tutta la natura. /

So the eighth and the ninth; . . . / . . . / . . . On that point the heavens and all nature are dependent.

FW 609:1-2 (*Arch.* 63:153)

touring the no placelike no timelike absolent,

Par. 1:70-72

Trasumanar significar *per verba* / non si poria; però l'essemplo basti

The passing beyond humanity may not be set forth in words; therefore let the example suffice

FW 628:06 (*Arch.* 63:259, 329)

My leaves have drifted from me. All. But one clings still. I'll bear it on me. To remind me of.

Par. 33:65-66

così al vento ne le foglie levi / si perdea la sentenza di Sibilla.

thus in the wind, on the light leaves, the Sibyl's oracle was lost.

FW 628:15 (*Arch.* 63:243, 261, 262)

The keys to. Given!

Par. 32:124-126

. . . quel padre vetusto / di Santa Chiesa a cui Cristo le chiavi / raccomandò di questo fior venusto.

That ancient father of Holy Church to whom Christ entrusted the keys of this beauteous flower.

Joyce's Letters

Vol. II:432

To Marthe Fleischmann, December 1918:

J'ai 35 ans. . . . C'est l'âge que le Dante a eu quand il est entré dans la nuit de son être.

I am 35. . . . It is the age at which Dante entered the night of his being. (trans. Christopher Middleton)

Vol. III:19

To Alessandro Francini Bruni. ?8 September 1920:

Caro Francini: Un maledetto contrattempo intralcia il mio lavoro. La cassa di libri . . . non si trova più! . . . Ma certo l'incaglio dev'essere in quel bel paese dove l'ano suona.

Dear Francini: A damned mishap is holding up my work. The case of books . . . is not to be found! . . . But certainly the hitch must be in that beautiful country where the arse is sounded. (trans. Richard Ellmann)

Inf. 33:80

del bel paese là dove 'l *sì* suona

the fair land where the *sì* is heard

Vol. I:228

To Harriet Shaw Weaver, 13 June 1925:

but as Dante saith:
1 Inferno is enough. *Basta*, he said,
un' inferno, perbacco!
And that bird—
Well!
He   oughter know!

≡ (with apologies to Mr. Ezra Pound)

Vol. I:283-284

To Valery Larbaud, 30 July 1929:

. . . Some fine morning not a hundred years from now some enterprising fellow will discover the etymological history of the orthodox word examination and begin to change his wavering mind on the subject of the book [*Finnegans Wake*] whereupon one by one others will faintly echo in the wailful choir, 'Siccome i gru van cantando lor lai.'

Inf. 5:46

E come i gru van cantando lor lai,

And as the cranes go chanting their lays,

Vol. III:318

To George Joyce, 13 August 1934:

Lasciamo da parte le gravi questioni sollevate nella tua lettera. È uno spreco di tempo discuterle. Cosa fatta capo ha.

Let us put aside the serious questions raised in your letter. It is a waste of time to discuss them. What's done is done. (trans. Richard Ellmann)

Inf. 28:107

che dissi, lasso! 'Capo ha cosa fatta,'

who said, alas! 'A thing done has an end!'

Vol. I:371

To George Joyce (in Italian), 25 June 1935:

Even if many promises are of the Kathleen Mavourneen kind, as they say in Ireland: that is, it may be for years, etc., don't give up hope. 'Seggend in piuma in fama non si vien, ne sotto coltri.' (trans. Stuart Gilbert. Italian not supplied.)

Inf. 24:47

disse 'l maestro, 'ché, seggendo in piuma, / in fama non si vien, né sotto coltre.'

said my master, "for sitting on goosedown or under coverlet, no one comes to fame."

Vol. III:364

To George Joyce, 10 July 1935:

Dopo la lettera dello zio di mamma, qualche giorno dopo, venne un'altra nella quale mi disse che mi consigliava di cambiare Lucia da Bray. Egli è molto buono ma 'vegliardo per antico pelo' . . .

After the letter of Mama's uncle, some days after another one came in which he advised me to move Lucia away from Bray. He is very good but "an old man with ancient hair" . . . (trans. Ellmann)

Inf. 3:82-83

Ed ecco verso noi venir per nave / un vecchio, bianco per antico pelo . . .

And behold, an old man, his hair white with age, coming towards us in a boat . . .

Vol. III:415

To Ezra Pound, 9 February 1938:

I don't think I ever worked so hard even at *Ulysses*. Galeotto è il libro e chi lo scrive.

Inf. 5:137

Galeotto fu 'l libro e chi lo scrisse

A Gallehault [pander] was the book and he who wrote it

Notes

INTRODUCTION

1. Richard Ellmann, *The Consciousness of Joyce* (New York: Oxford Univ. Press, 1977), pp. 71-72.

2. Northrop Frye, *Anatomy of Criticism* (New York: Atheneum, 1970), pp. 92-94.

3. T. S. Eliot, "*Ulysses*, Order and Myth," in *James Joyce: Two Decades of Criticism*, ed. Seon Givens (New York: Vanguard, 1963), pp. 198-202 at p. 201.

4. Michel Foucault, *The Order of Things* (New York: Random House, Vintage ed., 1973), p. 75. See also Robert Martin Adams, *Proteus: His Lies, His Truth* (Norton, 1973); Herman Meyer, *The Poetics of Quotation in the European Novel*, trans. Theodore and Yetta Ziolkowski (Princeton Univ. Press, 1968); Reuben Brower, *Mirror on Mirror: Translation, Imitation, Parody* (Harvard Univ. Press, 1974); W. Jackson Bate, *The Burden of the Past and the English Poet* (Harvard Univ. Press, 1970); and Harold Bloom, *The Anxiety of Influence* (Oxford Univ. Press, 1973).

5. Jackson Cope, "James Joyce, Test Case for a Theory of Style," *ELH* 21 (1954), pp. 221-236, at p. 234.

6. Hugh Kenner, *Dublin's Joyce* (London: Chatto and Windus, 1955), p. 181.

7. Francis Bacon, *The Wisdom of the Ancients* (London: Cassell, 1900), p. 283.

CHAPTER ONE: THE PRESENCE OF DANTE IN JOYCE'S FICTION

1. *Pound/Joyce*, ed. Forrest Read (New Directions, 1967), p. 197.

2. Paget Toynbee, "Benvenuto da Imola and his Commentary on the *Divina Commedia*," *Dante Studies and Researches* (1902; Kennikat Rept., 1971), pp. 204-215; Louis La Favia, *Benvenuto da Imola* (Washington, D.C.: Catholic University of America, 1978); Louis Rossi, *The Commentary of Benvenuto da Imola to the* Divine Comedy, Diss. Yale, 1954. On Pound and Eliot as translators of Dante, see William J. De Sua, *Dante Into English* (Univ. of N. Carolina Press, 1964), Chap. IV, "Craftsmen and Critics: Dante's 20th-century Translators."

3. T. S. Eliot, *Dante* (New Directions, 1966), p. 16; Irma Brandeis, *The Ladder of Vision* (Doubleday Anchor, 1962), pp. 143-145.

4. Karl Vossler, *Mediaeval Culture: An Introduction to Dante and His Times*, 2 vols., trans. William Cranstone Lawton (New York: Harcourt, Brace, 1929), Vol. 2, pp. 178-210, at p. 202.

5. *La Divina Commedia*, ed. and annotated by C. H. Grandgent (Boston: Heath, rev. ed. 1933), pp. 116-117.

6. Weldon Thornton, *Allusions in* Ulysses (Simon and Schuster, 1973), p. 305; *Inf*. 26:34-39; II Kings 2:11.

7. Richard H. Lansing, *From Image to Idea: A Study of the Simile in Dante's* Commedia (Ravenna: Longo Editore, 1977), pp. 111-123.

8. *Letters*, II, p. 248; to Nora Joyce, September 1909. Gilbert Seldes, in a review that Mary Colum said was greatly pleasing to Joyce, noted the importance in *Ulysses* of "the interests associated with 'the uncreated conscience of my race,' *i.e.*, the Catholic and Irish." Seldes commented that the book had "absolute validity and interest in the sense that all which is local and private in the *Divine Comedy* does not detract from its interest and validity." *The Nation*, 30 Aug. 1922, pp. 211-212. Quoted in Robert H. Deming, *James Joyce: The Critical Heritage* (London: Routledge, 1970, 2 vols.), vol. I, p. 238.

9. Samuel Beckett, "Dante . . . Bruno. Vico . . . Joyce," *Our Exagmination Round His Factification for Incamination of Work in Progress* (New Directions, 2d ed., 1962), p. 3. Hereafter cited as *Exag*. Since the publication of this Symposium many critics have identified parallels. Among the more extensive and circumstantial discussions are: S. Foster Damon, "The Odyssey in Dublin," (*Hound and Horn*, 1929) rpt. in *James Joyce: Two Decades of Criticism*, ed. Seon Givens (New York: Vanguard, 1963), pp. 203-242; W. Y. Tindall, "Dante and Mrs Bloom," *Accent* 11 (1951) 91; W. B. Stanford, *The Ulysses Theme* (Oxford: Blackwell, 1954), pp. 211-246; Barbara Seward, *The Symbolic Rose* (Columbia Univ. Press, 1954), pp. 187-221 and *passim*; Vernon Hall, *Explicator* 10 (June 1952); Richard Ellmann, *James Joyce* (Oxford Univ. Press, 1959), *passim*; Stanley L. Jedynak, "Epiphanies and Dantean Correspondences in Joyce's *Dubliners*," Diss. Syracuse, 1962; Robert J. Andreach, *Studies in Structure* (New York: Fordham Univ. Press, 1964), pp. 40-71; Warren Carrier, "*Dubliners*: Joyce's Dantean Vision," *Renascence* 17 (1965), pp. 211-215; Howard Helsinger, "Joyce and Dante," *ELH* 35 (1968), pp. 591-605; Mary T. Reynolds, "Joyce's Planetary Music: His Debt to Dante," *Sewanee Review* 76 (1968), pp. 450-477; Robert Boyle, S.J., "Swiftian Allegory and Dantean Parody in Joyce's 'Grace,' " *JJQ* 7/1 (1969), pp. 11-21; Sharon G. B. Mancini, "*Finnegans Wake* as Dante's *Purgatorio*," Diss. Kent State University, 1971; Francesco Gozzi, "Dante nell'Inferno di Joyce," *English Miscellany* 23 (1972), pp. 195-229; Tibor Wlassics, "Nota su Dante nell'*Ulisse*," *Revista di Letteratture Moderne e Comparate* 24 (1971), pp. 151-154; Vittoriana Villa, "Figure Paterne nel *Portrait* e nell' *Ulysses* di James Joyce," *Annali* 15 (Naples, 1972), pp. 127-144; Richard Ellmann, *Ulysses on the Liffey* (London: Faber & Faber, 1972), *passim*; Helene Cixous, *The Exile of James Joyce* (New York: David Lewis, 1972), *passim*;

Marion Montgomery, *The Reflective Journey Toward Order* (Univ. of Georgia Press, 1973), pp. 138-141 and *passim*; Carole Slade, "The Dantean Journey Through Dublin," *Modern Language Studies* 6/1 (1976), pp. 12-21; Marilyn French, *The Book as World* (Harvard Univ. Press, 1976), pp. 3-53.

10. T. S. Eliot, op. cit. (n. 3), *passim*; Benedetto Croce, *The Poetry of Dante*, trans. Douglas Ainslie (New York: Henry Holt, 1922).

11. Joyce's library included three editions (none in full) of Aquinas's *Summa*. Richard Ellmann, *The Consciousness of Joyce* (Oxford Univ. Press, 1977), Appendix: "Joyce's Library in 1920," p. 99. But see J. Mitchell Morse, *The Sympathetic Alien: Joyce and Catholicism* (New York Univ. Press, 1959), chap. VII, "Joyce and the Summa Theologia;" and William T. Noon, S.J., *Joyce and Aquinas* (Yale Univ. Press, 1957). For Joyce's Catholicism, see Robert Boyle, S.J., *James Joyce's Pauline Vision* (Carbondale: S. Illinois State Univ. Press, 1978), and Umberto Eco, *Le Poetiche di Joyce* (Milano: Bompiani, 1966), pp. 11-19.

(In 1978 a brass plaque was placed above the main entrance to University College Dublin, the Jesuit College from which Joyce was graduated in 1902, carrying three names: Cardinal Newman, Gerard Manly Hopkins, and James Augustine Joyce.)

12. See Fritz Senn, "No Trace of Hell," *JJQ* 7 (1970), pp. 255-256.

13. G. Vico, "Discovery of the True Dante," in *Discussions of the* Divine Comedy, ed. Irma Brandeis (Heath, 1966), pp. 10-11.

14. Emmet Larkin, *The Roman Catholic Church and the Creation of the Modern Irish State* (Philadelphia: American Philosophical Society, 1975).

15. Constantine Curran, *James Joyce Remembered* (Oxford Univ. Press, 1968), pp. 8-9; Kevin Sullivan, *Joyce Among the Jesuits* (Columbia Univ. Press, 1957), p. 162; Scholes and Kain, *Workshop*, p. 147.

16. Questions set for the Italian examinations in the years of Joyce's attendance at University College were kindly supplied by the National Library of Ireland, Dublin. Dr. Eileen MacCarvill generously shared with me material from her forthcoming work on Joyce's college studies. See also her "Les Années de Formation de James Joyce a Dublin," *Archives des Lettres Modernes* No. 12 (1958), pp. 1-31.

17. Noon, op. cit. (n. 11), pp. 9-17.

18. *The Complete Dublin Diary of Stanislaus Joyce*, ed. George H. Healey (Cornell Univ. Press, 1971), pp. 14, 19.

19. Jackson Cope, "An Epigraph for Dubliners," *JJQ* 7 (1970), pp. 362-364.

20. Alessandro Francini-Bruni, *Joyce Intimo Spogliato in Piazza* (Trieste: La Editoriale Libraria, 1922), trans. Harry Levin, *Inventario* II (1949). Dario de Tuoni says that Joyce had memorized several sonnets and more than one

canto of the *Divine Comedy*. *Ricordi di Joyce a Trieste* (Milan: Insegna del Pesce d'Oro, 1966), pp. 59-60.

21. *Letters*, II, p. 76; Curran, op. cit. (n. 15), "Joyce's D'Annunzian Mask," pp. 105-115.

22. Hans Walter Gabler, "Toward a Critical Text of James Joyce's *A Portrait of the Artist as a Young Man*," *Studies in Bibliography* 27 (1974), pp. 1-53; and "The Seven Lost Years of *A Portrait of the Artist as a Young Man*," in *Approaches to Joyce's* Portrait, ed. Thomas F. Staley and Bernard Benstock (Univ. of Pittsburgh Press, 1976), pp. 25-60.

23. Mary T. Reynolds, "Joyce's Editions of Dante," *JJQ* 15 (1978), pp. 380-384.

24. This copy was owned by William Edward Purser, who lived at 3 Winton Road, Leeson Park, Dublin. I am indebted to Mr. A. MacLochlainn, Director of the National Library, for assistance in identifying the book.

25. Louis Berrone, "Two James Joyce Essays Unveiled," *Journal of Modern Literature* 5 (1976), pp. 3-18, at p. 17. The essay is now available in facsimile in *James Joyce in Padua*, ed. and trans. Louis Berrone (Random House, 1977).

26. Merle E. Brown, "Respice Finem: The Literary Criticism of Giovanni Gentile," *Italica* XLVII (1970), pp. 3-27; Giovanni Gullace, "The Dante Studies of Giovanni Gentile," *Dante Studies* XC (1972), pp. 155-174; Allan Gilbert, "Benedetto Croce's Poetic," *Italica* XLI (1964), pp. 150-157; Joseph Rossi and Alfred Galpin, eds., *De Sanctis on Dante* (Univ. of Wisconsin Press, 1957); Davy Carozza, "Dante in France," *Forum Italicum* II (1968), pp. 214-233.

27. Luigi Sturzo, "Modern Aesthetics and the Poetry of the Divina Commedia," *Thought* XVII (1942), pp. 412-432.

28. G. A. Borgese, "On Dante Criticism," *52d-54th Annual Report of the Dante Society* (1936), pp. 19-70; Helmut Hatzfeld, "Modern Literary Scholarship as Reflected in Dante Criticism," *Comp. Lit.* III (1951), pp. 289-309.

29. Michelet's translation of Vico was in Joyce's library, according to Jacques Mercanton. "The Hours of James Joyce," *Kenyon Review* 24 (1962), p. 702.

30. Ellmann, op. cit. (n. 11), pp. 6-7. See also Harry Levin, "Joyce's Sentimental Journey through France and Italy," in his *Contexts of Criticism* (New York: Atheneum, 1963), pp. 131-139.

CHAPTER TWO: PATERNAL FIGURES AND PATERNITY THEMES

1. John B. Friedman, *Orpheus in the Middle Ages* (Harvard Univ. Press, 1970), pp. 87-145, 225-226. For assistance in the construction of this chapter I am specially indebted to discussions with Professor Paul H. Fry of Yale, and critical comments from Professor Rachel Jacoff, of Wellesley.

2. Helmut Bonheim, *Joyce's Benefictions* (Univ. of California Press, 1964), p. 16; Mark Schechner, *Joyce in Nighttown* (Univ. of California Press, 1974), pp. 15-19; Frederick J. Hoffman, *Freudianism and the Literary Mind* (Baton Rouge: Louisiana State Univ. Press, 1945), "Infroyce," pp. 116-149.

3. James S. Atherton, *The Books at the Wake* (Viking, 1960), pp. 11-24. For an overview of allusion in Joyce's fiction, see Weldon Thornton, *Allusions in Ulysses: A line-by-line Reference to Joyce's Complex Symbolism* (New York: Simon and Schuster, 1961, 1968); Don Gifford, *Notes for Joyce* (New York: E. P. Dutton, 1967); Don Gifford and Robert J. Seidman, *Notes for Joyce: An Annotation of Ulysses* (New York: E. P. Dutton, 1974); Ulrich Schneider, *Die Funktion der Zitate im Ulysses von James Joyce* (Bonn: Bouvier, 1970).

4. W. B. Stanford, *The Ulysses Theme* (Oxford: Blackwell, 1954), "The Wanderer," pp. 175-210; 276 n.6. Stanford's approach was challenged by Mario M. Rossi, "Dante's Conception of Ulysses," *Italica* XXX (1953), pp. 193-202.

5. Valery Larbaud, "The Ulysses of James Joyce," *Criterion* I (1922), pp. 94-103; S. Foster Damon, "The Odyssey in Dublin," *Hound and Horn*, 1929; reprinted in *James Joyce: Two Decades of Criticism*, ed. Seon Givens (Vanguard, 1963), pp. 203-242; Stuart Gilbert, *James Joyce's Ulysses* (Faber and Faber, 1930), pp. 60-66; S. L. Goldberg, *The Classical Temper* (London: Chatto and Windus, 1961), chaps. 4-5; Hugh Kenner, *Dublin's Joyce* (London: Chatto and Windus, 1955), chaps. 11-14; R. P. Blackmur, "The Jew in Search of a Son," *Virginia Quarterly Rev.* XXIV (1948), pp. 109-12; Richard M. Kain, "The Significance of Stephen's Meeting Bloom: A Survey of Interpretations," in *Ulysses: Fifty Years*, ed. Thomas F. Staley (Bloomington: Indiana Univ. Press, 1974), pp. 147-160; Francesco Gozzi, "Dante nell' Inferno di Joyce," *English Miscellany* vol. 23 (1972), pp. 195-229.

6. "When Virgil wrote of Dido, he taught Dante how to write of Virgil." Dorothy Sayers, *Further Papers on Dante* (New York: Harper, 1957), pp. 53-77, at p. 62.

7. John Freccero, quoted in Harold Bloom, *The Anxiety of Influence* (Oxford, 1973), pp. 122-123; Edward Moore, *Studies in Dante: First Series* (Oxford, 1896, 1969), p. 21. See also Harold Bloom, "Poetry, Revisionism, Repression," *Critical Inquiry* 2/2 (1975), pp. 233-251, esp. pp. 247-248.

8. Quoted in *The Workshop of Daedalus*, ed. Robert Scholes, and Richard M. Kain (Northwestern Univ. Press, 1965), p. 215

9. See *Appendix*, pp. 292-295.

10. John Freccero, "Dante's Pilgrim in a Gyre," *PMLA* LXXVI (1961), pp. 168-181. For the topography of Hell, see Singleton, *Inferno*, vol. II, pp. 44, 143.

11. Mark Musa, *Advent at the Gates* (Indiana Univ. Press, 1974), pp. 65-84, 150-153; Francis Fergusson, *Dante's Drama of the Mind* (Princeton Univ. Press, 1953), "On Interpreting Virgil," pp. 99-104.

12. Bernard Stambler, *Dante's Other World* (New York Univ. Press), "Three Poets: The Function of Fatherhood," pp. 196-242; Edward Moore, *Studies in Dante, First Series* (Oxford, 1896, 1969), pp. 32-33.

13. The Statius episode in *Purgatory* 22 (*Purg.* 22:40-41 and *Aeneid* iii:56) is Dante's demonstration of creative misreading. See Moore, op. cit. (n. 7), p. 157; Singleton, *Purgatorio* vol. II, pp. 521-524. Harold Bloom says that a strong reading is always a misreading: "The revisionist strives to *see* again so as to *esteem* and *estimate* differently, so as then to aim *correctively*." *A Map of Misreading* (Oxford Univ. Press, 1975), p. 4. (Italics Bloom's.)

14. J. A. Symonds, *An Introduction to the Study of Dante* (London, Adam & Charles Black, 4th ed. 1899), pp. 130-137.

15. Thomas M. Greene, "Dramas of Selfhood in the Comedy," in *From Time to Eternity: Essays on Dante's* Divine Comedy, ed. Thomas G. Bergin (Yale Univ. Press, 1967), pp. 103-136.

16. For Dante's censure, see Kenelm Foster, O.P., *The Two Dantes* (Univ. of California Press, 1977), chap. 6: "The Canto of the Damned Popes, Inferno XIX"; Reginald French, "Simony and Pentecost," *Dante Studies* LXXXII (1964), pp. 3-17; Robert Artinian, "Dante's Parody of Boniface VIII," *Ibid.* LXXXV (1967), pp. 71-74; A. P d'Entrèves, *Dante as a Political Thinker* (Oxford: Clarendon, 1952), "Ecclesia," pp. 60-63.

17. *Cf.* André Pézard, *Dante sous la pluie de feu* (Paris: Librairie J. Vrin, 1950), p. 20; Richard Kay, *Dante's Swift and Strong* (Lawrence: Regents' Press of Kansas, 1977), pp. 292, 297-298, 300.

18. Anne Paolucci, "Brunetto's Race," *Dante Studies* XCV (1977), pp. 153-155.

19. Cambon, *Dante's Craft* (Univ. of Minnesota Press, 1969), pp. 71-76; Singleton, *Inferno*, vol. II, pp. 255-258.

20. William Y. Tindall identified "E quando vede l'uomo attosca" as an echo of *Inferno* 6:84, but nothing in Dante's context validates this claim. *A Reader's Guide to James Joyce* (New York: Noonday Press, 1959). Corinna del Greco Lobner correctly traces the allusion to the Giamboni translation of Brunetto's *Li Livres Dou Tresor*. "The Metamorphosis of Brunetto's Basilisk in 'Scylla and Charybdis,' " *JJQ* 15/2 (1978), pp. 134-138. See also James H. Maddox Jr., *Joyce's* Ulysses *and the Assault upon Character* (Rutgers Univ. Press, 1978), pp. 152-156.

21. Robert Martin Adams, "Father Conmee and the Three Little Boys," *Surface and Symbol* (Oxford Univ. Press, 1967), pp. 13-18; Marilyn French, *The Book as World* (Harvard Univ. Press, 1976), pp. 117-120; Clive Hart, *James Joyce's* Ulysses (Sydney Univ. Press, 1968), pp. 60-62; Stanley Sultan, *The Argument of* Ulysses (Ohio State Univ. Press, 1964), pp. 206-215; C. H. Peake, *James Joyce: The Citizen and the Artist* (Stanford Univ. Press, 1977), pp. 209-212;

and Eoin O'Mahony, "Father Conmee and his Associates," *JJQ* 4 (1967), pp. 263-270.

22. William Carleton, *Traits and Stories of the Irish Peasantry* (Boston: Francis Niccolls, 1911), vol. III, "Going to Maynooth," pp. 288-482; vol. II, "The Hedge School," pp. 193-298. Joyce has memorialized this period in *Finnegans Wake* with "hedjeskool" *FW* 533:26, and "Backlane Univarsity," *FW* 287:30. For the best explanation of the latter term, see John V. Kelleher, "Irish History and Mythology in 'The Dead,'" *Review of Politics* 27 (1965), pp. 414-437.

23. Conor Cruise O'Brien, *States of Ireland* (Random House, Vintage Books, 1973), pp. 19-21, 102-127. See also J. H. Whyte, *Church and State in Modern Ireland* (Dublin: Gill & Macmillan), 1971; Desmond Fennell, *The Changing Face of Catholic Ireland* (London: G. Chapman, 1968). On the accommodation of the Irish Catholic Church to various forms of humanist thinking, see Michael Sheehy, *Is Ireland Dying: Culture and the Church in Modern Ireland* (New York: Taplinger, 1969), p. 19, *passim*. See also Conrad M. Arensberg and Solon T. Kimball, *Family and Community in Ireland* (Harvard Univ. Press, 1968).

24. Scholes and Kain, *Workshop* (cit. n. 8), p. 83.

25. Marvin B. Becker, "A Study in Political Failure: The Florentine Magnates 1280-1343," *Mediaeval Studies* 27 (1965), pp. 246-308, and "Dante and his Contemporaries as Political Men," *Speculum* XLI (1966), pp. 655-668; Stephen Miller, "Dante, Florence and the Politics of Rome," *Italian Quarterly* XII (1969), pp. 201-221; and U. Limentani, "Dante's Political Thought," *The Mind of Dante*, ed. U. Limentani (Cambridge Univ. Press, 1965), pp. 113-137.

26. Erich Auerbach, "Farinata and Cavalcante," in Mark Musa, *Essays on Dante* (Indiana University Press, 1964), pp. 110-144.

27. Scholes and Kain, op. cit. (n. 8), p. 94.

28. There is a symbolic crossing of paths produced by Father Conmee's reminiscences of Clongowes Wood College, which is southwest of Dublin. Leo Knuth, "A Bathymetric reading of Joyce's *Ulysses*, Chapter X," *JJQ* 9 (1972), pp. 405-422. See also Clive Hart and Leo Knuth, *A Topographical Guide to James Joyce's Ulysses* (Colchester: Wake Newslitter Press, 1975); Michael Seidel, *Epic Geography* (Princeton Univ. Press, 1976), pp. 182-188 and maps following p. 216, for diagrammed movements of Father Conmee.

29. Cambon, op. cit. (n. 19), pp. 80-105; on the privileged verb "muovere," pp. 59-63. Brunetto makes a final appearance in *Finnegans Wake* as "lost Dave the Dancekerl, a squamous runaway and a dear old man pal of mine too . . . just in time as if he fell out of space . . . and not on one foot either or on two feet aether but on quinquisecular cycles after his French evolution." *FW* 462:17-34.

30. See *Catholic Encyclopedia* (New York: Robert Appleton, 1907), vol. II, "Breviary," pp. 768-775; *Encyclopedia Britannica*, 11th ed., vol. IV, "Breviary," pp. 503-505; *Manual of Christian Doctrine, Authorized English Version*, 11th ed. (Philadelphia: J. J. McVey, 1909), "The Divine Office," pp. 534-536. On Joyce's fictional use of manuals of religious instruction see Wilhelm Füger, "Joyce's Use of the Maynooth Catechism," *JJQ* 13/4 (1976), pp. 407-414.

31. Herman J. Heuser, *Autobiography of an Old Breviary* (New York: Benziger Bros., 1925), pp. 120-126.

32. Robert Martin Adams, *Surface and Symbol* (Oxford, 1967), "Father Conmee and the Three Little Boys," pp. 13-17.

33. "Apprezzamenti Celesti," *Via Delle Cento Stelle* (Mondadori, 1972), p. 80; trans. in *Weeds and Transplants by T.G.B.* (Madison, Conn.: Picaflor Press, 1976), p. 11.

34. Thomas G. Bergin, *A Diversity of Dante* (New Brunswick: Rutgers Univ. Press, 1969), "Light from Mars, pp. 142-146; Edmund Gardner, *Dante's Ten Heavens* (London: Constable, 1904), pp. 129-145; Joseph Mazzeo, *Structure and Thought in the* Paradiso (Cornell Univ. Press, 1958), p. 102.

35. Raffaello Morghen, "Dante and the Florence of the Good Old Days," in *From Time to Eternity*, ed. Thomas G. Bergin (Yale Univ. Press, 1967), pp. 19-37.

36. Anne Paolucci, "Exile among Exiles: Dante's Party of One," *Mosaic* VIII (1975), pp. 117-125.

37. Singleton, *Paradiso* vol. II, pp. 299-301, notes 116, 118.

38. Hugh Kenner, "Circe," in *James Joyce's* Ulysses, ed. Clive Hart and David Hayman (Univ. of California Press, 1974), pp. 341-362, at p. 345; James H. Maddox, Jr., op. cit. (n. 20), pp. 127-128: Michael Groden, Ulysses *in Progress* (Princeton Univ. Press, 1977), p. 200.

39. Thomas G. Bergin discusses the origin of this durable image of the severed head and notes the connection with Joyce's Virag, in "Dante's Provençal Gallery," *A Diversity of Dante* (New Brunswick: Rutgers Univ. Press, 1969), p. 88. See also William D. Paden, Jr., "Bertran de Born in Italy," in *Italian Literature, Roots and Branches*, ed. Giose Rimanelli and Kenneth John Atchity (Yale Univ. Press, 1976), pp. 39-66.

40. John Henry Raleigh, *The Chronicle of Leopold and Molly Bloom* (Univ. of California Press, 1978), pp. 13-14; James H. Maddox, Jr., op. cit. (n. 20), pp. 128-131.

41. Marilyn French, *The Book as World* (Harvard Univ. Press, 1976), pp. 204-205; Mark Schechner, op. cit. (n. 2), pp. 112, 120.

42. S. L. Goldberg, op. cit. (n. 5), p. 31.

43. Vivian Mercier, *The Irish Comic Tradition* (Oxford, 1962), "Joyce and the Irish Tradition of Parody," pp. 210-236. But Virag exists at two levels, or even more. In the Virag configuration Joyce begins a complex play of verbal associations that moves eventually to the more extreme effects that engage the reader's attention below the threshold of consciousness in *Finnegans Wake*. See David Hayman, "Double-Distancing: An Attribute of the Post-Modern Avant Garde," *Novel* 12 (1978), pp. 33-47; and Ihab Hassan, "Joyce, Beckett and the Postmodern Imagination," *Triquarterly* 34 (1975), pp. 179-200.

44. Paul deMan, *Blindness and Insight: Essays in the Rhetoric of Contemporary Criticism* (Oxford Univ. Press, 1971), p. 106. But see also his essay, "The Rhetoric of Temporality," in *Interpretation: Theory and Practice*, ed. Charles S. Singleton (Johns Hopkins Univ. Press, 1969), pp. 173-209; and for a different view, M. H. Abrams, *Natural Supernaturalism: Tradition and Revolution in Romantic Literature* (New York: W. W. Norton, 1971). See also Peter Conrad, *Shandyism: The Character of Romantic Irony* (New York: Barnes & Noble, 1978).

CHAPTER THREE: THE THEME OF LOVE:
DANTE'S FRANCESCA AND JOYCE'S "SIRENS"

1. *Ulysses*, 736:5, 720:33; see John Henry Raleigh, *The Chronicle of Leopold and Molly Bloom* (Berkeley: Univ. of California Press, 1977), p. 17

2. Kenelm Foster, O.P. and Patrick Boyde, *Dante's Lyric Poetry* (Oxford: Clarendon Press, 1967), p. xvi. See also L. A. Murillo, *The Cyclical Night* (Harvard Univ. Press, 1968), pp. 68-70.

3. Jacques Mercanton, "The Hours of James Joyce," *Kenyon Review* 24 (1962) p. 724; Ettore Settanni, *James Joyce e la prima versione italiana de* Finnegans Wake (Venice: Cavallino, 1955), trans. Willard Potts.

4. Oliver St. J. Gogarty, *It Isn't This Time of Year at All* (1954), reprinted in Scholes and Kain, *The Workshop of Daedalus* (Northwestern Univ. Press, 1965), p. 215.

5. The line from the *Divine Comedy* is, "ed elli avea del cul fatto trombetta," "and he had made a trumpet of his arse," *Inf.* 21:139. Stephen silently combines it with two lines from Milton: "Orchestral Satan, weeping many a rood / Tears such as angels weep," *Paradise Lost*, Book I, 196 and 620. Milton's originals are "Satan lay floating many a rood," and "Tears such as angels weep, burst forth." William Schutte, *Joyce and Shakespeare* (Yale Univ. Press, 1957), p. 49, n. 5; also at Thornton, *Allusions in* Ulysses (New York: Simon and Schuster, 1961, 1968), p. 153. Note that the Miltonic allusion comes into Stephen's thought only when Eglinton mentions the poem. Dante's line, although it refers to a devil, does not describe Satan.

6. On Stephen's visual image of Dante's rhymes, see Tibor Wlassics, "La rima

di Dante nell'*Ulisse* di James Joyce," in *Interpretazioni di Prosodia Dantesca* (Rome: Angelo Signorelli, 1973), pp. 107-114.

7. Stephen, although he is aware of the allegorical aspect of Dante's color choices, is thinking of them here as rhetorical maneuvers. Cf. Paget Toynbee, "The color *perse* in Dante and other mediaeval writers," *Dante Studies and Researches* (Kenikat rpt., 1902, 1971), pp. 307-314.

8. In the Library chapter Stephen silently thinks, "In a rosery of Fetter Lane of Gerard, herbalist, he walks greyedauburn." This is repeated by Bloom, or by the narratorial voice, in the Sirens Chapter: "In Gerard's rosery of Fetter Lane he walks, greyedauburn. One life is all. One body. Do. But do." (*U* 199:32; 276:7). Bloom does frequently think of Shakespeare, but the sentence about Gerard is not in his diction: yet the four short expressions that follow *are* clearly in Bloom's voice, for his next words (silently) are, "Done anyhow." The intrusion of the quotation from Stephen, *the book's allusion to itself*, creates a voice for the book as it is being written. In the Eumaeus chapter one of the topics of conversation as Stephen and Bloom walk home together is, "the lutenist Dowland who lived in Fetter Lane near Gerard the herbalist" (*U* 646:2). Cf. Robert Martin Adams, *Surface and Symbol* (Oxford Univ. Press, 1962, 1967), pp. 95-97. As this book went to press I saw the magisterial essay by Ralph W. Rader, "Exodus and Return: Joyce's *Ulysses* and the Fiction of the Actual," *Univ. of Toronto Quar.* XLVIII (1978-79), pp. 149-171. See especially pp. 164-165, where the passage here quoted is linked to the red-bearded sailor of Eumaeus. The sailor's tale carries many echoes and overtones of Dante's story of the last voyage of Ulysses, in *Inferno* 26. See Appendix, pp. 292-295.

9. Some readers have been unsympathetic to Joyce's effort, others have approved it. Ernst Robert Curtius declared Joyce's "experiment" a failure, in "Technique and Thematic Development of James Joyce," *transition* no. 16-17 (June 1929), pp. 310-325. Curtius was answered in an exegesis directly inspired by Joyce: see Stuart Gilbert, *James Joyce's* Ulysses (Faber and Faber, 1930, 1969), "The Sirens," pp. 211-225. A modern composer who says that he learned much about technique from the chapter points out examples of Joyce's placement of recurring words and syllables to control cadence, thus creating progressions of sound and meaning that relate the verbal construction to the fugal pattern in music. Luigi Dallapiccolo, "On the 12-Note Road," *Music Survey* 4 (1951), pp. 318-332.

The episode is given a sensitive reading by Frederick W. Sternfeld in "Poetry and Music—Joyce's *Ulysses*," *Sound and Poetry*, ed. Northrop Frye (English Institute Essays 1956; Columbia Univ. Press, 1957), pp. 16-54. The first full technical examination of the fugal structure is made in Lawrence L. Levin, "The Sirens Episode as Music: Joyce's Experiment in Polyphony." *JJQ* 3 (1965), pp. 12-24. A complete review of the music used is made by Zack Bowen, in "The Bronzegold Sirensong: A Musical Analysis of the Sirens Episode in *Ulysses*," *Literary Monographs* I, ed. Eric Rothstein and Thomas K.

Dunseath (Univ. of Wisconsin Press, 1967), pp. 247-298, 319-320. See also Anne Hardy, "A Fugal Analysis of the Sirens Episode in Joyce's *Ulysses*," *Massachusetts Studies in English* 2 (1970), pp. 59-67; Don N. Smith, "Musical Form and Principles in the Scheme of *Ulysses*," *Twentieth Century Literature* 18 (1972), pp. 79-92; Jackson I. Cope, "Sirens," *James Joyce's* Ulysses, ed. Clive Hart and David Hayman (Univ. of California Press, 1974), pp. 217-242; and David Cole, "Fugal Structure in the Sirens Episode of *Ulysses*," *Modern Fiction Studies* 19 (1973), pp. 221-226.

10. *The Divine Comedy*, trans. Geoffrey L. Bickersteth (Harvard Univ. Press, 1965), pp. xxxi, *passim*. See also Wlassics, op. cit. (n. 6), chap. I, "Le caratteristiche strutturali della terzina;" Foster and Boyde, op. cit. (n. 2), pp. ix-xliii; Patrick Boyde, *Dante's Style in his Lyric Poetry* (Cambridge Univ. Press, 1971), pp. 1-51; Glauco Cambon, *Dante's Craft* (Univ. of Minnesota Press, 1969), chap. 3, "Francesca and the Tactics of Language," pp. 46-66; *Literary Criticism of Dante Alighieri*, trans. and ed. by Robert S. Haller (Lincoln: Univ. of Nebraska Press, 1973), bk. II, pp. 31-60; Thomas G. Bergin, *Dante* (New York: Orion Press, 1965), "The *Commedia*: Tools and Tactics," pp. 278-298.

11. Joyce's term, "fuga per canonem," simply means a composition contrapuntally written, utilizing in part canon passages. Contrapuntal writing occurs in other forms of musical composition, but in the fugue the element of circularity adds a dimension. This is because the fugal theme, or "Subject," is initially stated in two parts, as one would write a sentence with two clauses. The effect is accomplished by the second voice taking up the theme while the first goes on with a "Reply" or fugal "Answer." Subject and Answer are necessary to each other, as the sections of a circle.

Subsequent variations on the theme take their cue alternately from the one and the other. When the Subject and Answer have been announced, a second theme, the Countersubject, may be introduced. It is the combination of these three that creates the fugal counterpoint, in which three melodic lines reach the ear and register on the mind. Joyce, using significant fragments of speech, has transferred to his chapter this pattern of fugal counterpoint, creating a pattern of meaningful sound through a continuous interweaving of his Subject, Answer, and Countersubject on variations of the theme, which he announces by the title, "Sirens."

I am grateful to Professor Ed Hoover and his talented wife Mary, of the University of Pittsburgh, for sharing their knowledge of music with me in long sessions on the "scoring" of the Sirens chapter.

12. Stuart Gilbert, op. cit. (n. 9), pp. 10, 210-225.

13. Glauco Cambon, op. cit. (n. 10), p. 24; Boyde, op. cit. (n. 10), pp. 315-316. See also Tibor Wlassics, *Dante Narratore: Saggi sullo Stile della* Commedia (Firenze: Olschi, 1975), esp. chaps. I, IX, X; A. D. Scaglione, "Periodic Syntax and Flexible Metre in the *Divine Comedy*," *Romance Philology* XX (1967), pp. 1-22; von Eberhard Kreutzer, *Sprach und Spiel im* Ulysses *von James Joyce*

(Bonn: Bouvier, 1969), pp. 86-101; and Marilyn French, "The Voices of the Sirens in Joyce's *Ulysses*," *Journal of Narrative Technique* 8 (1978), pp. 1-10.

14. As Cambon has noted (op. cit., n. 10, p. 48), Hamlet also wishes to kill his uncle at a moment when his unshriven death will bring damnation. In *Ulysses*, the quotation from Dante is followed (triggered by Stephen's hearing a mention of fratricide) by a quotation from Hamlet: "And in the porches of mine ear [*sic*] did pour. By the way, how did he find that out? he died in his sleep. Or the other story, beast with two backs?" (*U* 137-138). Stephen's gloss on the line (*Hamlet* III.4) connects the quotation with the Francesca episode. See also Francis Fergusson, *Trope and Allegory: Themes Common to Dante and Shakespeare* (Athens: Univ. of Georgia Press, 1977), chap. II, "Romantic Love as Lost," esp. pp. 17-19.

15. This passage builds an emotional progression, in the fugal manner. The source of Bloom's trouble with his wife (a fact not revealed until the Ithaca chapter) is an eleven-year suspension of full sexual relations. The music that Bloom hears in the Ormond forces its way into Bloom's thoughts about Molly and finally produces a full recall of their earlier intimacy in the words: "Now! language of love . . . *ray of hope*" (*U* 270:29). The first word is Bloom's own voice; the rest of the line is in the narratorial voice. The second line, italicized, comes from the song. Immediately, Joyce makes an ironic qualification. First, he indicates that the rest of the listeners in the Ormond have been similarly affected (the irony is assisted by the low artistic level of the music—the Liebestod would have commanded too much respect for Joyce's purpose): this compositional maneuver thickens the texture of the prose in the same manner that repetition of the musical line in counterpoint produces echoes of the theme in a musical fugue. Then Joyce indicates a momentary change in direction for Bloom's thoughts; the flow of reminiscence is checked, and immediately returns to his wife, now with clear affection. It is a momentary arrest, which heightens rather than diminishes the emotional force of the passage. Through the circular pattern Joyce has unobtrusively made an important point, i.e., an association of sexual intimacy with hopefulness and love. *Cf.* Stanley Sultan, *The Argument of* Ulysses (Ohio State Univ. Press, 1964), p. 225; Cambon, op. cit. (n. 10), p. 57.

16. Francesca's language echoes the cult of courtly love. Singleton, *Inferno*, vol. 2, pp. 89-90.

17. Renato Poggioli, "Tragedy or Romance? A Reading of the Paolo and Francesca Episode in Dante's *Inferno*," *PMLA*, LXXII (1957), pp. 313-358.

18. *Letters*, II, p. 266. See Kenelm Foster, O.P., *The Two Dantes* (Univ. of California Press, 1977), "Dante and Eros," pp. 37-55; and by the same author, "Dante's Idea of Love," in *From Time to Eternity*, ed. T. G. Bergin (Yale Univ. Press, 1966), pp. 65-101.

19. Cambon, op. cit. (n. 10), p. 58.

20. Gilbert, *James Joyce's* Ulysses, p. 224; Bowen, op. cit. (n. 9), p. 260.

21. Richard Ellmann, *Ulysses on the Liffey* (Faber and Faber, 1972), p. 172.

22. A. Francini-Bruni, *Joyce Intimo Spogliato in Piazza* (1922), quoted in Ellmann, *James Joyce* (Oxford Univ. Press, 1959), p. 226; trans. in full in *Portraits of the Artist in Exile*, ed. Willard Potts (Seattle: Univ. of Washington Press, 1979), pp. 7-39, at p. 29.

CHAPTER FOUR: POETIC IMAGINATION AND LUSTRATION PATTERNS

1. For Dante's "preoccupation with technique almost for its own sake," see Patrick Boyde, "Dante's Lyric Poetry," in *The Mind of Dante*, ed. U. Limentani (Cambridge Univ. Press, 1965), p. 84. See also John Freccero, "Casella's Song: *Purg.* 2:112," *Dante Studies* XCI (1973), pp. 73-80.

2. The weaver, whose art determines every feature of the work, is implied here in Dante's word, "ordite," "to warp." Singleton, *Purgatorio* vol. II, p. 824. Joyce uses the figure at *FW* 211:18: "for revery warp in the weaver's woof for Victor Hugonot."

3. Aldo Bernardo, "Flesh, Spirit and Rebirth at the Center of Dante's *Comedy*," *Symposium* XIX (1965), pp. 335-351.

4. In the last nine pages of *Finnegans Wake* the river Liffey speaks in her own voice, with suggestions of death and rebirth. "Once it happened, so it may again. Why I'm all these years within years in soffran allbeleaved. To hide away the tear, the parted. . . . All them that's gunne. I'll begin again in a jiffey" (*FW* 625:30). The voice stops in midsentence, as the river passes into the sea, but the rest of the sentence can be found on the first page of the book, with the first word, in lower case: "rivverrun, past Eve and Adam's, from swerve of shore to bend of bay" (*FW* 3:1). Northrop Frye has found similar indications of rebirth in the opening of Dante's Purgatory: "A landscape of water, boat and reeds appears at the beginning . . . where there are many suggestions that the soul is in that stage a newborn infant." *Anatomy of Criticism* (New York: Atheneum, 1957, 1970), p. 198.

5. Jacques Mercanton, "The Hours of James Joyce" part I, Kenyon Review 24 (1962), pp. 710-711.

6. Charles S. Singleton, "In Exitu Israel de Aegypto," *Dante*, ed. John Freccero (Prentice-Hall, 1965), pp. 102-121. On the time of Dante's journey see Dorothy Sayers, *Introductory Papers on Dante* (Harper, 1954), pp. 107-108.

7. W. Y. Tindall, "Dante and Mrs Bloom," *Accent* XI (1951), pp. 84-85, and "Mosaic Bloom," *Mosaic* VI (1972), pp. 3-10; Stanley Sultan, *The Argument of* Ulysses (Ohio State Univ. Press, 1964), pp. 391-393; Mary T. Reynolds, "Joyce's Planetary Music: His Debt to Dante," *Sewanee Review* 76 (1968), pp.

450-479; A. Walton Litz, "Ithaca," in *James Joyce's* Ulysses, ed. Clive Hart and David Hayman (Univ. of California Press, 1974), pp. 399-401.

8. Ellmann, *James Joyce* (Oxford Univ. Press, 1959), pp. 383-386, 405-409. See also R. P. Blackmur, "The Jew in Search of a Son," *Eleven Essays in the European Novel* (Harcourt Brace, 1964), pp. 27-47; and Louis Hyman, "Some Aspects of the Jewish Backgrounds of *Ulysses*," in *The Jews of Ireland* (Dublin: Irish Univ. Press, 1972), pp. 167-192.

9. *Catholic Encyclopedia* (New York: Robert Appleton, 1907), vol. VI, pp. 279-283, "Orders, Holy;" *Pontificale Romanum* (1855), pp. 56-79 for the rite of ordination. Joyce's library included *Manuale ordinandorum opusculum non ordinandis solum, sed et ordinatis praesertim sacerdotibus, utilissimum* (Paris: Chernoviz, 1910), Thomas E. Connolly, *The Personal Library of James Joyce* (Buffalo: University Bookstore, 1955), p. 25.

10. The residue of Catholicism in Stephen's imagination is a configuration that Joyce renders as a counterpoint of silent thoughts, fragmentary gestures, and oblique references to remembered rituals and minor pieties. Often the context is ironically framed: the act of urinating alongside the uncircumcised Bloom (in Ithaca) makes Stephen think of the Feast of the Circumcision as it might be discussed by a mind obsessed with scholastic trivia (*U* 687:34-37; 688:1-7). When the Protestant Englishman, Haines, misunderstands Stephen's reference to an "Italian" master, a defensive reaction in Stephen calls up the "proud potent titles" of his Church with its centuries of "slow growth of rite and dogma," only to produce at the end a derisive, silent, "Hear, hear. Prolonged applause" (*U* 22:20-37). See also *U* 43:5-7, 195:13-21, 205:26-29, 383:30-31, 424:10-15, 425:10.

11. "Have you ever reflected how 'humble' is the utterance of Renan, 'Very few people have the right to abandon Catholicism.'" (To Stanislaus Joyce, 31 August 1906; *Letters* II, pp. 153-155.) Joyce was attracted to Renan as a theologian who had been afflicted by doubt; he was profoundly Christian, the mirror image of Dante, yet also like Joyce temperamentally sceptical and ironic, incapable of adhering to a faith he had ceased to believe in. There are many traces of Renan in Joyce's writings. He would have agreed with Renan's comment that, "Homer, even for his day, was a poor theologian," who knew little of the origin of his gods and was disinclined to reason out the meaning of his myths. Ernest Renan, *Etudes d'histoire religieuse: Les religions de l'antiquité*, 2d ed., Paris, 1957, p. 27; quoted in Jean Seznec, *The Survival of the Pagan Gods* (1972), p. 241 and note 82.

12. "*A Portrait of the Artist* defines with elaborate care the conditions of creativity for a particular writer, Stephen Dedalus. . . . The subtlety of the definition lies in a delicate and complex pattern of images reflecting the hero's growing conviction." Eugene M. Waith, "The Calling of Stephen Dedalus," *College English* XVIII (1957), pp. 256-261. In the "first draft" Stephen says, "My entire aptitude is for the composition of prose and verse" (*SH* 232). Geoffrey

Hartman sees Stephen as the exceptional figure, "the man who is so much greater than we are, not morally perhaps but in mode of being . . . that our familiar, democratic judgment is suspended if not disabled . . . he embodies a special fate. Stephen is the protagonist of a *modern* novel, hedged round with problematics; but Stephen is also the *hero*. It is vocation that so defines him." "The Heroics of Realism," *Beyond Formalism* (Yale Univ. Press, 1970), p. 68. See also Wayne Booth, *The Rhetoric of Fiction* (London: Univ. of Chicago Press, 1969), p. 132.

13. See "Deacons," *Catholic Encyclopedia* (1907), vol. II, pp. 647-651. The first deacon, by tradition, was St. Stephen, patron saint of Stephen Dedalus (*P* 159:35). The Easter vigil is traditionally a time for the ordination of priests. Although the date of the action of *Ulysses* is June 16, the Circe episode carries liturgical overtones of "paschal tide," suggesting that the journey of Bloom and Stephen is in some sense set in Holy Week, the established time of the journey in the *Divine Comedy*. In *Finnegans Wake* time signals suggest Holy Saturday. See Frank Budgen, "Resurrection," *Twelve and a Tilly*, ed. Jack P. Dalton and Clive Hart (Northwestern Univ. Press, 1965), pp. 11-15; Nathan Halper, "The Date of Earwicker's Dream," ibid., pp. 72-90.

Robert Adams Day, in a forthcoming essay, "Deacon Dedalus: The Text of the *Exultet* and its Implications for *Ulysses*," demonstrates brilliantly Stephen's role as a deacon in the Ithaca processional. He argues cogently that the bells of St. George's (which may represent the joyful peals with which the Easter vigil ends—and with which the last chapter of *Finnegans Wake* begins) signal the final cleansing of Stephen's sense of guilt over his mother's death, for the words in which he hears the bells, "Liliata rutilantium," are the hymn of the angels and saints welcoming his mother into heavenly glory. (*U* 704; see Thornton, *Allusions*, pp. 17-18.)

14. Five lines of conversation here produce an association of ideas involving Stephen's thoughts with the word "cardinal," which releases the hallucinatory image. The construction is Dantesque both at the surface of the text and thematically. Dante put the simoniac popes in hell (*Inf.* 19); Joyce presents the highest ranking Irish prelate with verbal indications of hell: "I'm suffering the agonies of the damned," and "the devil is in that door" (*U* 513:10, 27). Dante's rigorous standards for the clergy are matched by the implied attitudes of Stephen. It is his father in himself, drunkenly riotous, that stands condemned; but the clerical form of the image comes from Stephen's knowledge that he was attracted to the idea of a religious vocation from worldly rather than spiritual motives, hence doomed by his own unsparing inner vision. He sees himself, not as a prelate, but as a damned soul in clerical shape. See Erwin R. Steinberg, *The Stream of Consciousness and Beyond in* Ulysses (Univ. of Pittsburgh Press, 1972), pp. 47-51.

15. The Dantean exit from the dark passage to view "the heaventree of stars" is present in the Rosenbach MS, page P.651. Joyce added to the typescript the reference ("a cylindrical vertical shaft 5000 feet deep") suggesting Dante's in-

verted cone topped by the mountain of Purgatory (*U* 683:10-12; *Arch*. 16:107). The processional and the Virgilian leavetaking were added to the galleys (placards), with indications of deliberate distinction between Bloom's cosmogony and Dante's (*U* 682:14-30, 683:10-12; 684:18-20; 685:38; 686:3-4; 688-689; *Arch*. 21: 75-76, 78, 79, 83; *Arch*. 27:172-178). The connection between these Dantesque elements, gradually obscured by Joyce's additions to the text, becomes apparent when they are seen as additions to a single run of proofs.

16. Joyce added the words, "below freezing point" to the description of Bloom's sensations following Stephen's departure (*U* 689:15; *Arch*. 21:91).

17. They are preserved in the images of *A Portrait of the Artist*: e.g., ". . . the flashing gold thing into which God was put on the altar in the middle of flowers and candles at benediction while the incense went up in clouds at both sides as the fellow swung the censer" (*P* 46:19-21); " . . . vested with the tunicle of subdeacon at high mass, to stand aloof from the altar, forgotten by the people, his shoulders covered with a humeral veil, holding the paten within its folds" (*P* 158:33-36); "He would never swing the thurible before the tabernacle as priest" (*P* 162:6-7).

18. Maurice C. Bowra, *The Prophetic Element* (London: The English Association, 1959).

19. Small anachronistic elements attach the paragraph (*U* 654:7) to *A Portrait* and also to Joyce's own life. He lived at No. 14 Fitzgibbon street (in Ithaca No. 13), and he lived at No. 12 North Richmond street in 1895 (in *Ulysses*, 1898).

20. This privileged paragraph (*U* 654:7-20) takes the reader far back to "the very sources of mythological allegory." Spiritual conflict, which is the matter of *Ulysses* whenever Stephen Dedalus is in the foreground, is symbolized here as it was in the twentieth book of the *Iliad*, where "the never-ending conflict between the forces of the soul" was symbolized by the opposition of Apollo-Fire and Poseidon-Water. (Jean Seznec, op. cit. [n. 11], p. 112 n. 113.)

21. "Lustration," *Encyclopedia Britannica*, 11th ed. (1911), vol. XVII, p. 131. See John B. Vickery, *The Literary Impact of the* Golden Bough (Princeton Univ. Press, 1973), pp. 63-64, and chaps. XI-XIV. Northrop Frye remarks that only Joyce, in modern English, has carried on the "tradition of verbal exuberance," an expression that Frye applies to satirical invective but that also fits Joyce's mythological extravagances. *Anatomy of Criticism*, pp. 198-199 and 235-239.

22. "Lustrum," *Dictionary of Classical Antiquities*, comp. by Oskar Seyffert (New York: Meridian Books, 1957), pp. 365-366; Joseph Campbell, *The Hero with a Thousand Faces* (Princeton Univ. Press, 2d ed., 1968; 1973), p. 26; and "Sacrifice," *Catholic Encyclopedia*, vol. 13 (1912), pp. 309-320.

23. "The term regeneration distinguishes baptism from every other sacrament" (*Catholic Encyclopedia* [1907], vol. II, "Baptism," p. 259). But among the

doctrines anathematized by the Council of Trent, in its canons on baptism, was the idea that a metaphorical meaning only was implied in Christ's words that man must be born again *of water* and the Holy Ghost. St. Augustine found it incredible that before the rite of circumcision existed there could be no sacrament by which children might be saved. Such problematics are present in *Paradiso* 19 when Dante inquires, following Augustine, how a true justice can exclude from Heaven a man born on the Indus who has been genuinely virtuous all his life. The river Indus is present in *Finnegans Wake* in the tenth chapter, with many Dantean allusions, not (as one would expect) in the long list of river names woven into the eighth chapter (*Par.* XIX:71; *FW* 289:6).

24. Kenelm Foster, O.P., *The Two Dantes*, p. 156 and chaps. 10-12.

25. Two legendary voyages in *Purgatory* 1 must have caught Joyce's attention: the story of Ulysses, briefly recalled (*Purg.* 1:132) by Dante's allusion to his own account in *Inferno* 26, the rhyme-word "esperto" linking the two cantos; and the narrative of St. Brendan, whose legend included an elderly figure thought to be Dante's model for Cato. See *La Divina Commedia*, ed. C. H. Grandgent (Boston: D. C. Heath, 1933), pp. 327-328. Joyce's belief that St. Brendan's legend "served as a model for the poet of the *Divine Comedy*" is recorded in an essay of 1912. "The Mirage of the Fisherman of Aran," *Critical Writings*, p. 236.

26. Joseph Mazzeo, *Structure and Thought in the* Paradiso (Cornell Univ. Press, 1968), pp. 2-7, 44-49, 84-110. Edwin Honig describes the creative process in allegory as a twice-told tale in which the subject has been so completely remade that in the new version it exists for the first time. "The tale, the rhetoric and the belief work together in what might be called a metaphor of purpose." *Dark Conceit: The Making of Allegory* (Cambridge: Boars Head, 1960), pp. 12-13.

27. *Purg.* 33:113. Dante took his invention partly from Boethius, *Consolation* V.i.3-4: "The Tigris and Euphrates flow from a single source." See also Grandgent, op. cit. (n. 25), notes to *Purg.* 28:131-132, and p. 643. For the 19th century uses of the metaphor see Jerome H. Buckley, *The Victorian Temper* (Harvard Univ. Press, 1951), esp. Chap. 5: "The Pattern of Conversion."

28. Bernard Stambler, *Dante's Other World* (New York Univ. Press, 1957), pp. 113n and 341.

29. Brendan O Hehir, *A Gaelic Lexicon for* Finnegans Wake (Univ. of California Press, 1967), Appendix, pp. 355-359, 392.

30. Bernard Benstock, *Joyce-Agains Wake: An Analysis of* Finnegans Wake (Seattle: Univ. of Washington Press, 1965), pp. 258-259. See also Vivian Mercier, "James Joyce and the Macaronic Tradition," *Twelve and a Tilly*, ed. Jack P. Dalton and Clive Hart (Northwestern, 1966), p. 31.

31. Joyce saw linguistic virtuosity as a Dantesque aspect of his work, and developed his own etymology. "In the river chapter the river-names . . . are so artfully disposed that they virtually cease to bear any meaning as individual names. In this new language they are more like phonemes than like morphemes." Louis Mink, *A Gazetteer of* Finnegans Wake (Indiana Univ. Press, 1978), p. xli.

32. Singleton, *Purgatorio*, vol. II, 292-297.

33. On the mythic role of the Liffey, see L. A. Murillo, *The Cyclical Night* (Harvard Univ. Press, 1968), p. 114.

34. Most notably at the opening of *Paradiso* 25:1-9; again at *Par.* 1:22-27 and *Par.* 23:62. Dante's sense of mission is suggested again at *Purg.* 32:103 and *Purg.* 33:52-54, and also in the prophecies of Brunetto and Cacciaguida. See Erich Auerbach, "Dante's Addresses to the Reader," *Romance Philology* 7 (1954), pp. 268-278. For Joyce's sense of a prophetic element in his work, see Ellmann, *James Joyce* (cit. n. 8), p. 539.

35. Marcia L. Colish, *The Mirror of Language: Dante's Poetics* (New Haven: Yale Univ. Press, 1968), pp. 310-313, 246-256. Helmut Hatzfeld, "Modern Literary Scholarship as Reflected in Dante Criticism," *Comp. Lit.* III (1951), pp. 302-304, on Beatrice.

36. See Ellmann, *James Joyce* (cit. n. 8), p. 307.

37. Maurice Beebe, *Ivory Towers and Sacred Founts* (New York Univ. Press, 1964); Dorothy Van Ghent, *The English Novel: Form and Function* (Holt, Rinehart and Winston, 1953); Edmund L. Epstein, *The Ordeal of Stephen Dedalus* (Southern Illinois Univ. Press, 1971); Hugh Kenner, *Dublin's Joyce* (London: Chatto and Windus, 1955).

38. Hans Walter Gabler, "The Seven Lost Years of *A Portrait of the Artist as a Young Man*," in *Approaches to Joyce's Portrait*, ed. Thomas F. Staley and Bernard Benstock (Univ. of Pittsburgh Press, 1976), pp. 25-60, at p. 50.

39. Kenneth McKenzie, "The Symmetrical Structure of Dante's Vita Nuova," *PMLA* XVIII (1903), pp. 341-355; Charles S. Singleton, *An Essay on the Vita Nuova* (Harvard Univ. Press, 1958), pp. 6-7.

40. Ellmann, *James Joyce* (cit. n. 8), pp. 149-154, 306-309.

41. Barbara Seward, *The Symbolic Rose* (New York: Columbia Univ. Press, 1960), pp. 187-221.

42. Twenty-nine of the 43 items contribute to the water images identified with Stephen Dedalus, for example in the Proteus chapter of *Ulysses*. "These heavy sands are language tide and wind have silted here" becomes, in the Ithaca catalog, "Its alluvial deposits" (*U* 45:39; 656:3). See Richard E. Madtes, "Joyce and the Building of Ithaca," *ELH* XXXI (1964) 457-458; A. Walton Litz, "Ithaca," *James Joyce's* Ulysses, ed. Clive Hart and David Hayman (Univ. of California Press, 1974), pp. 388-389.

43. But see Jackson I. Cope, "The Rhythmic Gesture: Image and Aesthetic in Joyce's *Ulysses*," *ELH* 29 (1962), pp. 67-89.

44. T. G. Bergin, *Dante* (New York: Orian Press, 1965), p. 208; Edward Moore, "The Genuineness of the *Quaestio de Aqua et Terra*," *Studies in Dante, Second Series* (Oxford, 1899, 1968), pp. 303-374. In making his argument, Dr. Moore gives a detailed account of Dante's essay.

45. In Hayman and Hart, *James Joyce's* Ulysses (cit. n. 42), p. 403. On Dante's "power to see in words," see Charles S. Singleton, "Dante and Myth," *Journal of the History of Ideas* 10 (1949), pp. 482-502; Aldo S. Bernardo, op. cit. (n. 3), pp. 335-351; Morton W. Bloomfield, "Allegory as Interpretation," *New Literary History* VIII (1977), pp. 301-317.

CHAPTER FIVE: TOWARD AN ALLEGORY OF ART

1. "A writer is being allegorical whenever it is clear that he is saying, 'by this I *also* mean that.'" Northrop Frye, *Anatomy of Criticism* (New York: Atheneum, 1970), pp. 89-92. See also Edwin Honig, *Dark Conceit: The Making of Allegory* (Cambridge: Boars Head, 1960), esp. pp. 174-176; Angus Fletcher, *Allegory: The Theory of a Symbolic Mode* (Ithaca: Cornell Univ. Press, 1964); John MacQueen, *Allegory* (London: Methuen, 1970); Rene Wellek and Austin Warren, *Theory of Literature* (Harcourt Brace, 1942, 1970), chap. 15, "Image, Metaphor, Symbol, Myth"; Harry Levin, *The Gates of Horn* (Oxford Univ. Press, Galaxy ed. 1966), p. 428.

2. Charles S. Singleton, *Commedia: Elements of Structure* (Harvard Univ. Press, 1954; Dante Studies, vol. 1), p. 62. For Dante's idea of allegory, see *Literary Criticism of Dante Alighieri*, trans. and ed. Robert S. Haller (Lincoln: Univ. of Nebraska Press, 1973), esp. pp. 95-133; C. S. Singleton, Commedia, *Elements of Structure* (Harvard Univ. Press, 1954), pp. 1-17, 61-83, 84-98; Richard H. Greene, "Dante's Allegory of Poets and the Mediaeval Theory of Poetic Fiction," Comp. Lit. IX (1957) pp. 118-128, with rejoinder by Singleton, "The Irreducible Dove," *ibid.*, pp. 129-135; a summary of critical views in Marcia L. Colish, *The Mirror of Language: Dante's Poetics* (Yale Univ. Press, 1968), pp. 282-288; Robert Hollander, *Allegory in Dante's* Commedia (Princeton Univ. Press, 1969), and "Dante *Theologus-Poeta*," *Dante Studies* XCIV (1976), pp. 91-136. On mediaeval allegory see D. W. Robertson, Jr., *A Preface to Chaucer: Studies in Mediaeval Perspectives* (Princeton Univ. Press, 1962), pp. 3-137, 347-352; Rosemond Tuve, *Allegorical Imagery* (Princeton Univ. Press, 1966), pp. 3-56; Jean Pépin, *Dante et la Tradition de L'Allégorie* (Montreal: Institute d'Etudes Médiévales, 1970).

3. *Letters* II, p. 134; to Grant Richards, 5 May 1906.

4. Robert Scholes and A. Walton Litz, eds., Dubliners: *Text, Criticism and Notes* (New York, Viking, 1969), p. 297.

5. John V. Kelleher, "Irish History and Mythology in James Joyce's 'The Dead' " *Review of Politics* 27 (1965), pp. 414-433, at p. 416.

6. Robert Martin Adams, *Proteus: His Lies, His Truth* (Norton, 1973), p. 83.

7. Robert Scholes, "James Joyce, Irish Poet," *JJQ* 2 (1965), pp. 255-270. See also Chester G. Anderson, "James Joyce's 'Tilly,' " *PMLA* LXXIII (1958), pp. 285-298.

8. Richard Ellmann, *The Identity of Yeats* (Oxford, 1964), p. 229. The lines are *Aeneid* III.27-46; *Metamorphoses* II.358-363. The bush was a standard medieval ornament, and the broken branch has passed into the language.

9. Ellmann, *James Joyce* (Oxford Univ. Press, 1959), p. 414.

10. "I never broke faith with my lord" (vi giuro che già mai non ruppi fede / al mio segnor"), *Inf.* 13:73-74. See W. W. Vernon, *Inferno*, vol. I, p. 468.

11. Yeats published the revised version as, "An Old Poem Rewritten," but it appears in his *Collected Poems* (Macmillan, 1951), p. 44, with its original title.

12. La Vita Nuova *of Dante*, trans. Mark Musa (Rutgers Univ. Press, 1957), pp. 5-6.

13. Ellmann, "Portrait of the Artist as Friend," *Kenyon Review* XVIII (1956), pp. 53-67.

14. Samuel Beckett, "Dante . . . Bruno. Vico . . . Joyce," in *Our Exagmination* (New York: New Directions, 1929, 1952, 1972), p. 22.

15. Jackson I. Cope, "An Epigraph for *Dubliners*," *JJQ* 7 (1970), pp. 362-364. See also Arnold Goldman, *The Joyce Paradox* (Northwestern Univ. Press, 1966), pp. 1-21; A. Walton Litz, *James Joyce* (Twayne, 1966), pp. 47-59; and Florence Walzl, "Patterns of Paralysis in Joyce's *Dubliners*," *College English* XXII (1961), pp. 221-228.

16. Kelleher, op. cit. (n. 5), pp. 414-416.

17. T. G. Bergin, *Dante* (New York: Orion Press, 1965), p. 169.

18. Kenelm Foster, O.P., "The Theology of the *Inferno*" (Blackfriars, 1957), pp. 51-52.

19. Harry Levin, *James Joyce: A Critical Introduction* (Norfolk, Conn., New Directions, 1941), p. 30.

20. See Robert Scholes, "Further Observations on the Text of Dubliners," *Studies in Bibliography* XVII (1964), pp. 107-124; Warren Carrier, "Dubliners: Joyce's Dantean Vision," *Renascence* XVII (1965), pp. 211-215; Howard Lachtmann, "Joyce's Ecclesiastical Satire in *Dubliners*," *JJQ* 7 (1970), pp. 82-92; Clive Hart, ed., *James Joyce's* Dubliners: *Critical Essays* (Viking, 1969), esp. pp. 67-69, 91, 93, 103, 130-133, 146-149, 168; Florence M. Walzl, "Gabriel and Michael: The Conclusion of 'The Dead' " *JJQ* 4 (1964), pp. 17-31;

Donald T. Torchiana, "The Opening of Dubliners: A Reconsideration," *Irish Univ. Review* I (1971), pp. 149-160.

21. Stanislaus Joyce, "The Background to *Dubliners*," *The Listener*, March 25, 1954, pp. 526-527.

22. Marvin Magalaner, *Time of Apprenticeship: The Fiction of Young James Joyce* (London: Abelard-Schuman, 1959), pp. 99-100.

23. Robert Boyle, S.J., "Swiftian Allegory and Dantean Parody in Joyce's 'Grace,' " *JJQ* 7 (1969), pp. 11-21; Hugh Kenner, *"Dubliners,"* in *Twentieth Century Interpretations of* Dubliners (Prentice-Hall, 1968), ed. Peter Garrett, pp. 38-56; R. M. Kain, "Grace," in Clive Hart, ed., *James Joyce's* Dubliners, pp. 134-152; Brewster Ghiselin, "the Unity of Joyce's *Dubliners*," *Accent* XVI (1956), pp. 75-88, 196-213.

24. Stanislaus Joyce, op. cit. (n. 24), p. 526.

25. Ellmann, *James Joyce* (cit. n. 9), pp. 366, 391, 394.

26. *Stephen Hero* 175:16. Theodore Spencer substituted a comma for Joyce's exclamation mark.

27. John Freccero, quoted in Harold Bloom, *The Anxiety of Influence* (New York: Oxford, 1973), pp. 122-123. Freccero's interpretation of *Purgatory* 30 and 31 comes from lectures given in 1976.

28. Francesco de Sanctis, *History of Italian Literature*, trans. Joan Redfern (Barnes and Noble, 1968), vol. I, p. 237.

29. Francis Fergusson, *Dante* (New York: Collier, 1966), pp. 165-170; and "A Reading of *Exiles*," in James Joyce, *Exiles* (Norfolk, Conn., New Directions, n.d.), p. xiv.

30. Singleton, *Purgatorio*, vol. II, p. 824. The passage begins at *Purg.* 33:135.

31. Freccero, op. cit. (n. 31), Singleton, *Purgatorio* vol. II, pp. 742-745.

32. Fergusson, op. cit. (n. 33), pp. xi, xv.

33. Ellmann, *James Joyce* (cit. n. 9), pp. 366, 394, 788 n. 13; *The Consciousness of Joyce* (New York: Oxford Univ. Press, 1977), p. 32.

34. James Joyce, *Giacomo Joyce*, ed. with Introduction and Notes by Richard Ellmann (Viking, 1968), pp. 11, 13, 15, 16. For Ellmann's comments on the connections with Dante and with *Exiles*, pp. xii, xiv, xv.

35 *Exiles* (New York: Penguin Books, 1977, 1979), p. 153. See also Kenner, *Dublin's Joyce* (London: Chatto and Windus, 1955), pp. 85-86.

Joyce's decision to make Dante stand for a Catholic presence in Dublin must have included the Man in the Macintosh in *Ulysses* and also, in *A Portrait of the Artist*, (P8, 27-39) the Catholic governess nicknamed "Dante." The association of this name with an impassioned defense of the clergy, in the famous

Christmas dinner quarrel, creates an ambiguous Dantean identification with the Catholic Church which is not unlike the description of the bigoted old mother in *Exiles* (Act I; *E* 24, 25), of whom Richard Rowan says, "I fought against her spirit . . . to the bitter end"; yet he later adds, "The old mother. It is her spirit I need." A more lighthearted reference to Dante, in *Ulysses*, may be the mysterious Man in the Macintosh, "a pedestrian . . . eating dry bread who passed swiftly and unscathed across the viceroy's path" (*U* 251:6). Such a disembodied representation of the poet as exile (*Par.* 17:55-60) reminds us that several times in the *Divine Comedy* Dante, still a living man at the date of the poem, amazes the disembodied souls he meets by casting a shadow when they do not. Now the tables are turned; Dante, a shade himself on June 16, 1904, moves through the procession of horses and men invisible to all but the author. See above, Appendix, pp. 274, 279.

CHAPTER SIX: BETWEEN TIME AND ETERNITY

1. Georges Borach, "Conversations with James Joyce," trans. Joseph Prescott, *College English* XV (1954), pp. 325-327; Ellmann, *James Joyce* (Oxford Univ. Press, 1959), p. 430.

2. Irma Brandeis, *The Ladder of Vision* (Doubleday Anchor, 1962), pp. 143-144; Eleanor Cook, "T. S. Eliot and the Carthaginian Peace," *ELH* 46 (1979), pp. 341-355. Joyce's mixture of fact with fiction has received much attention; Frank Kermode suggests an association with the modernist interest in Dante of "the great men of early modernism," Pound, Eliot, Wyndham Lewis, and Joyce. [Kermode, *The Sense of an Ending* (Oxford Univ. Press, 1967), pp. 112-113.]

3. C. S. Singleton, Commedia: *Elements of Structure* (Harvard Univ. Press, 1954); *Journey to Beatrice* (Harvard, 1967); John Freccero, "The Final Image: Paradiso 30:144," *Modern Language Notes*, LXXIX (1964), pp. 14-27; T. G. Bergin, "Themes and Variations: The Design of the Comedy," *Perspectives on the* Divine Comedy (Rutgers Univ. Press, 1967), pp. 37-70; Georges Poulet, "The Metamorphoses of the Circle," trans. C. Dawson and E. Coleman, in *Dante*, ed. John Freccero (Prentice-Hall, 1965), pp. 151-169. Natalino Sapegno, "Genesis and Structure: Two Approaches to the Poetry of the *Comedy*," in *The Mind of Dante*, ed. U. Limentani (Cambridge Univ. Press, 1965), pp. 1-16.

4. Northrop Frye calls the last chapter of *Finnegans Wake*, "A vast body of metaphorical identifications. [Frye, *Anatomy of Criticism*, (New York: Atheneum, 1970), pp. 353n and 354.] On aspects of Joyce's style see Anthony Burgess, *Joysprick* (London: Andre Deutsch, 1973; Eberhard Kreutzer, *Sprache und Spiel im* Ulysses *von James Joyce* (Bonn: H. Bouvier, 1969); A. Walton Litz, *The Art of James Joyce: Method and Design in* Ulysses *and* Finnegans Wake (Oxford, 1964); Arnold Goldman, *The Joyce Paradox* (Northwestern Univ.

Press, 1966); Stephen Heath, "Ambiviolences," *Tel Quel* 50-52 (1972), pp. 22-43, 64-76; Jackson I. Cope, "James Joyce: Test Case for a Theory of Style," *English Literary History* XXI (1954), pp. 221-236; Jennifer Schiffer Levine, "Originality and Repetition in *Finnegans Wake* and *Ulysses*," *PMLA* 94 (1979), pp. 106-120; Margot Norris, *The Decentered Universe of* Finnegans Wake (Johns Hopkins Univ. Press, 1976), pp. 119-140.

5. When Joyce returned to Trieste after World War I, he sorted through the manuscripts from which, in 1915, he had produced the final version of *A Portrait of the Artist*. A discouraged letter to Miss Weaver on October 29, 1919 (*Letters* II, 455) was followed in a few days by another (unpublished), saying: "The MS of *A Portrait of the Artist as a Young Man* [this refers to the fair copy, now in the National Library, Dublin] is safe and at your disposal. . . . Though my flat has been broken into I was relieved to find that *my desk was untouched*." ALS (postcard), 1 November 1919; British Museum Add. MS 57345, Harriet Shaw Weaver Papers, vol. I. Permission to quote, gratefully acknowledged, from the Society of Authors, London, as assignees of the Joyce Estate, and also from the British Library. On the "Dublin Holograph" MS of *A Portrait*, see *Letters* I, p. 136, 6 Jan. 1920.

6. Cf. B. J. Tysdahl, *Joyce and Ibsen* (Norwegian Univ. Press, 1968), pp. 50-54, 68-86; William Schutte, *Joyce and Shakespeare* (Yale Univ. Press, 1957), pp. 79, 82, 85-86, 174, 181; Marvin Magalaner and Richard M. Kain, *Joyce: The Man, the Work, the Reputation* (New York: Collier, 1956), pp. 43, 141.

7. S. L. Goldberg, *The Classical Temper* (London: Chatto and Windus, 1961), pp. 68-69, 97. See also Howard Helsinger, "Joyce and Dante," *ELH* XXXV (1968), pp. 591-605.

8. Hans Walter Gabler, "The Seven Lost Years of *A Portrait of the Artist as a Young Man*," in Thomas F. Staley and Bernard Benstock, eds., *Approaches to Joyce's* Portrait (Univ. of Pittsburgh Press, 1976), pp. 25-60.

9. Gabler, op. cit. (n. 8), pp. 30-31, 51.

10. Gabler, op. cit. (n. 8), pp. 44-45.

11. Schutte, op. cit. (n. 6), Appendix B, pp. 178-191.

12. Schutte, op. cit. (n. 6), pp. 85-87. But see *Stephen Hero*, pp. 184-185, and the related statement at p. 79:15.

13. Schutte rightly stresses the sharpened focus of *A Portrait* in comparison with *Stephen Hero*, op. cit. (n. 6), p. 82. But see S. L. Goldberg's comment on the Hamlet theory in *Ulysses* as an "aesthetic epiphany," op. cit. (n. 7), p. 90. Schutte's view of Bloom in this book was negative, " . . . a painfully limited little man," (p. 144) but see his "Leopold Bloom: A Touch of the Artist," *JJQ* 10/1 (1972), pp. 118-131, at p. 125: "One wonders how some critics could have seen him as dull, routine, and stupid." Two recent essays illustrate the polarity of critical viewpoint that has developed around Joyce's use of Shake-

speare: Robert Storey, "The Argument of *Ulysses*, Reconsidered," *MLQ* 40 (1979), pp. 175-195, at p. 181; and Ralph W. Rader, "Exodus and Return: Joyce's *Ulysses* and the Fiction of the Actual," *Univ. of Toronto Quar.* XLVIII (1978-79), pp. 149-171, esp. pp. 154-156.

14. Ibsen is a substantial presence in *Stephen Hero*; D'Annunzio is behind the reference to "Italian novels" at *SH* 170:23 and *SH* 150:10. There is a suggestion that in the translation of the unnamed Italian novel the scandalous passages have been omitted, which happened in fact in the translation of D'Annunzio's first novel, *Il Piacere*.

15. For example, the long dialogue at *SH* 90-97, defending Stephen's interpretation of Dante and Ibsen; to this may be added the incidents remarked by Schutte, op. cit., p. 86.

16. For example, *SH* 92:5 and *SH* 158:35 for Dante; for Shakespeare, *SH* 79:15 and 184-185. See also Richard Ellmann, *The Consciousness of Joyce* (New York: Oxford Univ. Press, 1977), chap. II, "Shakespeare."

17. Goldberg, op. cit., pp. 89-92. Wayne Booth was the first to point out that Joyce has created a critical problem by placing at the center of a long work "a figure who experiences epiphanies, an epiphany-producing device." *The Rhetoric of Fiction* (London: Univ. of Chicago Press, 1969), pp. 323-398, at p. 332. For a useful approach to the question whether, and in what dimensions, an interpretation of *A Portrait* and *Ulysses* demands that Stephen's aesthetic theory be resolved, see Martin Price, "The Fictional Contract," in *Literary Theory and Structure: Essays in Honor of William K. Wimsatt*, ed. Frank Brady, John Palmer, and Martin Price (Yale Univ. Press, 1973), pp. 151-178; Lowry Nelson, Jr., "The Fictive Reader and Literary Self-Reflexiveness," *The Disciplines of Criticism*, ed. Peter Demetz, Thomas Greene, and Lowry Nelson, Jr., and "The Fictive Reader: Aesthetic and Social Aspects of Literary Performance," *Comparative Literature Studies* XV (1978), pp. 203-210; Walter J. Ong, S.J., "From Mimesis to Irony: The Distancing of Voice," *Bull. Midwest MLA* 9 (1976), pp. 1-24; Jerome Mazzaro, *Transformations in the Renaissance Lyric* (Cornell Univ. Press, 1970), pp. 73-107 and 146; and A. Walton Litz, "The Genre of *Ulysses*," in *The Theory of the Novel*, ed. John Halperin (Oxford Univ. Press, 1974), pp. 108-120, esp. pp. 118-119..

18. Bergin, *Dante* (New York: Orion Press, 1965), pp. 79-87. I am indebted to Professor Bergin for discussions on the *Vita Nuova*, and to A. B. Giamatti for suggesting the presence of a close relationship between the *Vita Nuova* and *A Portrait of the Artist*, but I do not, of course, implicate either of them in my interpretation.

19. J. E. Shaw, *Essays on the* Vita Nuova (Oxford Univ. Press, 1969), pp. 203-204. The argument for an allegorical interpretation of Beatrice focuses on Chapter XXV of the *Vita Nuova*, and on the "verace intendimento" of the poems that make up the *Convivio*. See Boyde, *Dante's Style in His Lyric Poetry*

(Cambridge Univ. Press, 1971), pp. 134-135, 293-295, 327-331. On the *Vita Nuova* see Helmut Hatzfeld, "Modern Dante Criticism," *Comp. Lit.* III (1951), pp. 289-309, at p. 302.

20. Shaw, op. cit. (n. 19), pp. 203-204.

21. Ellmann, *Consciousness* (cit. n. 16), pp. 39-44.

22. David Hayman, Ulysses: *The Mechanics of Meaning* (Prentice-Hall, 1970), pp. 37-42; Arnold Goldman, *The Joyce Paradox* (Northwestern Univ. Press, 1966), pp. 74-81.

23. W. B. Stanford, *The Ulysses Theme* (Oxford: Blackwell, 1954), p. 215.

24. Ellmann, *James Joyce* (Oxford Univ. Press, 1959), pp. 370-371; *Ulysses on the Liffey* (Faber and Faber, 1972), pp. 171-172.

25. Marilyn French, *The Book as World* (Harvard Univ. Press, 1976), pp. 85; 42-43; 166. See also Thomas F. Staley, "Ulysses," in *Anglo-Irish Literature: A Review of Research*, ed. Richard J. Finneran (New York: Modern Language Assoc., 1976), pp. 412-428; Cleanth Brooks, "Joyce's *Ulysses*: Symbolic Poem, Biography, or Novel?" in *Imagined Worlds*, ed. Maynard Mack and Ian Gregor (London: Methuen, 1968); and Robert Scholes, *Structuralism in Literature* (Yale Univ. Press, 1974), pp. 180-190.

26. Singleton, *An Essay on the* Vita Nuova (Harvard Univ. Press, 1958), p. 100.

27. Ibid., pp. 66-67.

28. Bergin, *Dante* (cit. n. 18), pp. 72-74.

29. Singleton, op. cit. (n. 26), p. 63.

30. Ibid., p. 74.

31. Barbara Seward, *The Symbolic Rose* (New York: Columbia Univ. Press, 1960), pp. 190-192. See also Edmund L. Epstein, *The Ordeal of Stephen Dedalus* (Carbondale: Southern Illinois Univ. Press, 1971), pp. 100-101, 194 n. 48.

32. " . . . the Pre-Raphaelite poets tended ultimately toward the creation of a poetic realm in which medievalism, musicality, and a vague religious feeling combined to achieve a narcotically escapist effect." *Princeton Encyclopedia of Poetics*, ed. Alex Preminger (Princeton Univ. Press, 1974), p. 662. Stephen's religious feelings are neither vague nor escapist, and are therefore far more threatening to his independence of mind.

33. Mary T. Reynolds, "Joyce's Villanelle and D'Annunzio's Sonnet Sequence," *Journal of Modern Literature* 5 (1976), pp. 19-45. For D'Annunzio as "the most monumental figure of the Decadent Movement," see Mario Praz, *The Romantic Agony*, trans. Angus Davidson (Oxford Univ. Press and Meridian, 1933, 1956), pp. 189-190, 251-269, 384-389. On the interpretation of Stephen's villanelle, a representative sample of critical views would include:

Hugh Kenner, "The Portrait in Perspective," *Dublin's Joyce*, pp. 109-133; Robert Scholes, "Stephen Dedalus: Poet or Esthete?" *PMLA* LXXXIX (1964), pp. 494-489; Geoge L. Geckle, "Stephen Dedalus and W. B. Yeats: The Making of the Villanelle," *Modern Fiction Studies* XV (1969), pp. 87-96; Richard Kell, "The Goddess Theme in *A Portrait of the Artist*," *Dublin Magazine* IX (1972), pp. 100-108; Bernard Benstock, "James Joyce and the Women of the Western World," *Litters from Aloft* (Univ. of Tulsa, Monograph No. 13, 1971), and "The Temptation of St. Stephen: A View of the Villanelle," *JJQ* 14 (1976), pp. 31-38; and Charles Rossman, "Stephen Dedalus's Villanelle," *JJQ* 12 (1974-75), pp. 281-293.

34. Joyce in 1901, as a college student, wrote an essay attacking the Irish Literary Theatre, the movement led by Yeats and Moore, whom Joyce denounced as prisoners of Aestheticism. The essay reflects with some accuracy divisions within the Irish Revival Movement. Joyce praises Yeats for "poetry of the highest order," and Moore for "wonderful mimetic ability," but he doubts their steadfastness in the face of tacit Dublin censorship (which did indeed produce riots at the Abbey Theatre in 1907, but with a vigorous defense by Yeats of the threatened play, Synge's *Playboy of the Western World*), and he suggests that the work of the Revival "has no kind of relation to the future of art." Aestheticism, Joyce says, is "the backwash of that tide which has advanced from Flaubert through Jakobsen to D'Annunzio: for two entire eras lie between *Madame Bovary* and *Il Fuoco*." (*Critical Writings*, "The Day of the Rabblement," pp. 68-72, p. 71.)

35. Bergin, *Dante* (cit. n. 18), pp. 154-157.

36. Beckett, et al., *Our Exagmination*, p. 18. See also Stephen Heath, "Ambiviolences," *Tel Quel* 50 (1972), pp. 22-43, and *Tel Quel* 51 (1972), pp. 64-67; Hugh Staples, "Growing Up Absurd in Dublin," in *A Conceptual Guide to* Finnegans Wake, ed. Michael H. Begnal and Fritz Senn (University Park: Penn State Univ. Press, 1974), pp. 173-200; Michael H. Begnal, "Who Speaks When I Dream? Who Dreams When I Speak?" *Litters from Aloft* (University of Tulsa, 1971), pp. 74-90; Donald R. Kelley, "Vico's Road: From Philology to Jurisprudence and Back," in *Giambattista Vico's Science of Humanity*, ed. G. Tagliacozzo and Donald P. Verene (Johns Hopkins Univ. Press, 1976), pp. 15-30.

37. William Carlos Williams, "A Point for American Criticism," *Our Exagmination*, p. 183.

38. Beckett, op. cit. (n. 36), p. 22.

39. G. Vico, "Discovery of the True Dante," in *Discussions of the* Divine Comedy, ed. Irma Brandeis (Heath, 1966), pp. 11-12.

40. Beckett, op. cit. (n. 36), pp. 17-18.

41. Frank Budgen, *James Joyce and the Making of* Ulysses (London: Grayson & Grayson, 1934), Chaps. I, XIV.

42. Beckett, op. cit. (n. 36), p. 18.

43. For example, Brendan O Hehir, *A Gaelic Lexicon for* Finnegans Wake (Univ. of California Press, 1967); Helmut Bonheim, *A Lexicon of the German in* Finnegans Wake (Univ. of California Press, 1967); Ian MacArthur, Verej Nersessian and Danis Rose, "Armenian in *Finnegans Wake*," *A Wake Newslitter* XIII (1976) 48-51; Rosa Maria Bosinelli, "The Relevance of Italian in *FW*," *AWN* XIII (1976) 19-32; Ioanna Ioannidou and Leo Knuth, "Greek in *Finnegans Wake*," *AWN* XII (1975) 39-54; and Danis Rose, *James Joyce's The Index Manuscript*: Finnegans Wake *Holograph Workbook* VI.B.46. (Colchester: Wake Newslitter Press, 1978).

44. Beckett, op. cit. (n. 36), p. 19.

45. Ettore Settani, *James Joyce e la prima versione italiana de* Finnegans Wake (Venice: Cavallino, 1955), p. 30, trans. Willard Potts. I am indebted to Professor Potts for calling this to my attention, and to Professor Thomas Bergin for patiently working out with me Joyce's maneuvers with the Italian language and with Dante's text, in this translation. The essay by Jacqueline Risset is "Joyce traduit par Joyce," *Tel Quel* 55 (1973) pp. 47-58, and the Italian translation, "Anna Livia Plurabelle," at pp. 59-62. Mme. Risset's sentence, perhaps too freely translated by me, is: "Joyce . . . est le seul 'disciple' de Dante, en ce sens qu'il est le seul a le reprendre reellement au niveau de l'activité scripturale," at p. 57. Nino Frank's story is now available in English in *Portraits of the Artist in Exile: Recollections of James Joyce by Europeans* (Univ. of Washington Press, 1979), pp. 74-105; and originally in Nino Frank, *Memoire brisée* (Paris: Calman-Levy, 1967), pp. 29-64. The first account of Joyce's translation was given in Ellmann, *James Joyce* (cit. n. 24), p. 713. For Louis Gillet's recollection, see his *Claybook for James Joyce*, trans. Georges Markow-Totevy (London: Abelard-Schuman, 1958), pp. 106-107. On Joyce's use of the pseudonym "Colesser," see *Selected Letters*, p. 357, and Ellmann, *James Joyce* (Oxford Univ. Press, 1959), p. 194.

46. Thomas M. Greene, "The Falling Leaf: Etiology and Literary History," *The Light in Troy: Imitative Itineraries in Renaissance Poetry*, forthcoming.

47. Ibid. On the etymological overtones of keywords, see Sean Golden, "The Kissier License: Liberty at the Wake," *A Wake Newslitter* 11 (1974), pp. 79-84; and "Bygmythster Finnegan: Etymology as Poetics in the Works of James Joyce," *Dissertation Abstracts* 38 (1977), 278A.

48. Jan Parandowski, "Meeting with Joyce," in *Portraits of the Artist in Exile*, ed. Willard Potts (Seattle: Univ. of Washington Press, 1979), p. 160. Translation by Professor Potts.

49. James S. Atherton, *The Books at the Wake* (Viking, 1960), pp. 79-82.

50. Adolph Hoffmeister, "Osobnost James Joyce" ("Portrait of Joyce"), in Potts, op. cit. (n. 48), p. 129. Translation Willard Potts.

51. Lewis Phillips, "How to Teach Geometry and Theology Simultaneously," *James Joyce Quarterly* III (1966), pp. 295-297. See also Fritz Senn, "The Aliments of Jumeantry," *AWN* III (1966), pp. 51-54; Clive Hart, "The Geometry Problem," *A Wake Digest*, ed. Clive Hart and Fritz Senn (Sydney: Sydney Univ. Press, 1968), pp. 75-77; Barbara DiBernard, "Alchemical Number Symbolism in *Finnegans Wake*," *JJQ* 16/4 (1979), 433-446; Michael J. Sidnell, "A Daintical Pair of Accomplasses: Joyce and Yeats," in *Litters from Aloft*, ed. Ronald Bates and Harry J. Pollock (Tulsa: Univ. of Tulsa, 1971), pp. 50-73; Philippe Sollers, "Joyce and Co.," *Tel Quel* 53 (1974), 64-77.

52. Singleton, *Paradiso*, vol. II, p. 582, n. 116.

53. Singleton, *Paradiso*, vol. II, p. 571. Cf. Alan Tate, "The Symbolic Imagination: A Meditation on Dante's Mirrors," *Kenyon Review (Dante Number)* XIV (1952), pp. 256-257; Hugh Kenner, "The Circle and Three Nines," *JJQ* 16/4 (1979), pp. 395-398.

54. Glasheen, *Third Census of* Finnegans Wake (Univ. of California Press, 1977), pp. li. Cf. Clive Hart, "The Irish Universe," Appendix B, *Structure and Motif in* Finnegans Wake (Northwestern Univ. Press, 1962), pp. 248-249; Ronald E. Buckalew, "Night Lessons on Language," *A Conceptual Guide to* Finnegans Wake, ed. Michael H. Begnal and Fritz Senn (University Park: Penn State Univ. Press, 1973), pp. 93-115; Roland McHugh, *The Sigla of* Finnegans Wake (London: Edward Arnold, 1976), pp. 67-76; Margaret C. Solomon, *Eternal Geomater* (Carbondale: Southern Illinois Univ. Press, 1969), pp. 103-112; W. Y. Tindall, *A Reader's Guide to* Finnegans Wake (Farrar, Straus, 1969), pp. 171-187; David Hayman, *A First-Draft Version of* Finnegans Wake (Univ. of Texas Press, 1963), pp. 142-167.

55. Philip Thomson, *The Grotesque* (London: Methuen 1972), pp. 27, 59-65.

56. To Adolph Hoffmeister, quoted in Potts, op. cit. (n. 48), p. 132.

57. J. E. Shaw, *Essays on the* Vita Nuova (cit. n. 19), p. 79; C. S. Singleton, *An Essay on the* Vita Nuova (cit. n. 26), pp. 30, 31-32, 42.

58. C. S. Singleton, "Dante in the Divine Comedy," *Italica* 18 (1941), pp. 109-116 at p. 111.

59. Ellmann, p. 551. See aso Bernard Weinberg, *A History of Literary Criticism in the Italian Renaissance* (Univ. of Chicago Press, 1961), Vol. II, Chap. 16: "The Quarrel over Dante."

60. Lowry Nelson, "Parodic Parallels of Parabolic Plants," *Yale Review* LXVII (1978), pp. 458-462.

61. Kenner, *Dublin's Joyce* (London: Chatto and Windus, 1955), p. 327.

62. Louis La Favia, "Benvenuto da Imola's Dependence on Boccaccio's Studies on Dante," *Dante Studies* XCIII (1975), pp. 161-176.

63. Bergin, *Dante* (cit. n. 18), pp. 262-263.

64. Louis Rossi, *The Commentary of Benvenuto da Imola to the* Divine Comedy, Dissertation, Yale, 1954; chap. IV, "The Myth of the Poet."

65. Louis La Favia, *Benvenuto da Imola* (Catholic Univ. Press, 1978); see also Paget Toynbee, *Dante Studies and Researches* (London: Methuen, 1901; Kennikat Rpt. 1971) "Benvenuto da Imola and his Commentary on the *Divina Commedia*, pp. 216-237; Robert Hollander, *Allegory in Dante's Commedia* (Princeton Univ. Press, 1969), pp. 266-296, "Appendix I: The Fourteenth-Century Commentators on Fourfold Allegory."

66. Scholes and Kain, *The Workshop of Daedalus* (Northwestern Univ. Press, 1965), p. 94.

67. Tibor Wlassics, *Interpretazioni di Prosodia Dantesca* (Rome: Angelo Signorelli, 1973), pp. 107-114.

68. Paget Toynbee, *Dante Alighieri*, 6th ed. (London: Methuen, 1901), p. 217.

69. Giuseppe Mazzotta, *Dante, Poet of the Desert* (Princeton Univ. Press, 1979), esp. p. 5 and Chap. 2.

Index

VITA NUOVA

General Index

LIBRARY OF CONGRESS CATALOGING IN PUBLICATION DATA

Reynolds, Mary Trackett
  Joyce and Dante.

    Includes index.
    1. Joyce, James, 1882-1941—Sources.   2. Dante
Alighieri, 1265-1321—Influence—Joyce.   I. Title.
PR6019.09Z7844   823'.912   80-7550
ISBN 0-691-06446-6